INTERNATIONAL ECONOMIC LAW SERIES

General Editor: John H. Jackson

'LIKE PRODUCTS' IN INTERNATIONAL TRADE LAW

Towards a Consistent GATT/WTO Jurisprudence

'Like Products' in International Trade Law

Towards a Consistent GATT/WTO Jurisprudence

WON-MOG CHOI

Professor of International Trade Law, Ewha Womans University
S.J.D.; Attorney-at-law; Director of The WTO Law Center
Seoul, Korea

OXFORD
UNIVERSITY PRESS

OXFORD

UNIVERSITY PRESS

Great Clarendon Street, Oxford OX2 6DP

Oxford University Press is a department of the University of Oxford.
It furthers the University's objective of excellence in research, scholarship,
and education by publishing worldwide in

Oxford New York

Auckland Bangkok Buenos Aires Cape Town Chennai
Dar es Salaam Delhi Hong Kong Istanbul Karachi Kolkata
Kuala Lumpur Madrid Melbourne Mexico City Mumbai Nairobi
São Paulo Shanghai Taipei Tokyo Toronto

Oxford is a registered trade mark of Oxford University Press
in the UK and in certain other countries

Published in the United States
by Oxford University Press Inc., New York

© W-M Choi 2003

The moral rights of the author have been asserted
Database right Oxford University Press (maker)

First published 2003

Crown copyright material is reproduced under Class Licence
Number C01P0000148 with the permission of the Controller
of HMSO and the Queen's Printer for Scotland.

British Library Cataloguing in Publication Data

Data available

Library of Congress Cataloging in Publication Data

Data available

ISBN 0-19-926078-8

1 3 5 7 9 10 8 6 4 2

Typeset by Newgen Imaging Systems (P) Ltd., Chennai, India
Printed in Great Britain
on acid-free paper by
Biddles Ltd., Guildford and King's Lynn

To Jessy,

who has always been a fiercely loyal supporter of our love
and a compassionate critic of my study

General Editor's Preface

This impressive volume is part of the Oxford University Press series of books dealing with subjects of the very broad landscape of International Economic Law. The goal of this series is to tackle the risks and dangers inherent in a 'globalized' and interdependent world such as the one in which we now live. Through this series, it is our aim to examine these risks and dangers with sufficient depth and analysis so as to contribute significantly to the urgently required understanding of the landscape of international economic law. As General Editor I am delighted to introduce the latest volume in the International Economic Law Series, a volume by Professor Won-Mog Choi, which ably fulfills the goals mentioned above.

Professor Choi's study is a particularly focused one, with enormous implications for the question of how treaties are to be interpreted. Many of the readers are familiar with the rules of the Vienna Convention on the Law of Treaties (particularly Articles 31 and 32) which suggest the modes and methodologies of treaty interpretation. Many of you are also familiar with various criticisms of these articles. One such criticism is that they are often too blunt and too ambiguous to be of very much help. Indeed, the question of treaty interpretation is not what many politicians and others seem to think. Often, there is the view among laypersons or government officials that do not have much experience with treaties, that treaty interpretation is a rather mechanical process, driven by a careful, but rather 'scientific' look at the text, even garnering the meaning of the words used from reference to such sources as dictionaries. Yet, Professor Choi demonstrates the contrary vividly, with this intriguing study. He has analysed the multiple ways that one could go about interpreting what seems like a very simple phrase, namely, 'like product.' In constructing his analysis, he remains keenly aware of the economic and political policy that can motivate interpreters to move in different directions with regard to the same language. Indeed, the Appellate Body of the WTO itself has indicated that this phrase has to be interpreted in its 'context' (which is a term mentioned in the Vienna Convention) and that in different contexts, the phrase can take on remarkably different meanings. The Appellate Body has demonstrated this point by its analysis of the interpretation of 'like product' in Article III, paragraph 2 of GATT 1994 (*Japan – Alcoholic Beverages* case[1]), compared to its similar task with regard to the same phrase in Article III, paragraph 4 (*EU – Asbestos* case[2]) of the same article.

---

[1] WTO Appellate Body Report, *Japan –Taxes on Alcoholic Beverages*, WT/DS8/AB/R (adopted 1 November 1996).

[2] WTO Appellate Body Report, *EC – Measures Affecting Asbestos and Asbestos-Containing Products*, WT/DS135/AB/R (adopted 5 April 2001).

Professor Choi demonstrates how the policy preferences lead to an interpretation of the simple phrase in different ways, but more importantly, as a
matter of an extraordinary example of analytical perception regarding treaty
law, he demonstrates that it is virtually impossible to avoid the implications of
certain policy preferences when interpreting certain phrases in treaty language.
The book thus is a lesson to all of us who have to struggle with international law
and treaties.

John H. Jackson[*]

[*] *University Professor of Law*, Georgetown University Law Center (GULC), Washington,
D.C.; Director, Institute of International Economic Law, GULC; *General Editor*, International
Economic Law Series, Oxford University Press; *Editor in Chief, Journal of International
Economic Law*, Oxford University Press.

Preface

While I have been selfishly busy completing my S.J.D. dissertation, which eventually led to this book, I have run up an enormous debt to my family. My greatest debt is to my wife, Jessy. Despite being a busy diplomat herself, she showed endless dedication and sacrifice by encouraging me and managing the household. Eventually her existence and support was all I needed for my work. It is a small recompense, but a measure of my great gratitude and love, for me to dedicate this book to her—the very first book in my life. I also dedicate it to our daughter and son, Mari and Mano.

This book is about the interpretation of the 'like products' concept in international trade law. The concept of 'like products' plays a central role in determining the coverage of various World Trade Organization (WTO) obligations prescribed in more than 50 articles of WTO agreements. Most of these obligations prohibit discriminatory treatment between products that are 'alike' to each other, whereas different treatment between 'different' products is allowed as an exercise of legitimate national regulatory autonomy. For instance, in order to determine whether a certain measure violates the National Treatment obligations in the WTO jurisprudence, one should necessarily determine beforehand whether the measure differentiates between one product category (domestic products in favour) and another 'like products' category (foreign products in disfavour).

Hence, the specific coverage of these obligations hinges upon the definition and the resulting scope of 'like products'. A broad interpretation of the like products relationship would broaden the coverage of the basic WTO obligations, whereas a narrow understanding would reduce it. In other words, the broader the concept, the broader the jurisdiction of international trade law becomes (narrowing the scope of the national regulatory autonomy). Thus, the choice among the different approaches to those definitional issues has major implications for the extent to which WTO rules will be a significant restraint on government regulatory activity. Indeed, the concept of 'like products' is located at the center field of the endless battle between the two masters of international trade law—freer trade and national regulatory autonomy.

While this subject is certainly one of the most fundamental issues in the field of international trade law, surprisingly it has not been seriously discussed by scholars or practitioners in the field. Professor John Jackson at Georgetown once told me that this subject would be one of the most important matters to be addressed in the WTO jurisprudence in the next decade.

A series of recent decisions by the WTO panels in particular, with other numerous cases that are relevant, demonstrates how important this definition is, and the broad and significant ramifications this subject would continue to have on the world trading system. These cases are, among others, *Japan Alcoholic Beverages* (1996), *Korea Alcoholic Beverages* (1999), and *Chile Alcoholic Beverages* (1999). As Christopher

Parlin at Kaye & Scholer told me four years ago when I started writing on this subject, my topic is 'ambitious and would provide an important contribution to GATT scholarship'. It is one of the few areas of which he is aware in which existing studies are 'not terribly elucidating'.

My initial interest in the 'like products' issue was formed by witnessing some serious discrepancies in the terminologies of likeness adopted in many provisions of the WTO Agreement. This was possible through my frequent participation in international negotiations concerning international trade and WTO disputes during my years as a trade official and diplomat. In an unsystematic way, terms that are slightly different are used in separate provisions, or even different sentences of a single article of the General Agreement on Tariffs and Trade (GATT). In fact, it seemed to be in quite a mess at the beginning of my research.

The judicial decisions made by GATT/WTO panels in the past have in practice worsened this seeming discrepancy. The decisions have tended to obscure the whole picture of likeness determination, not to mention the proper methodology. The only thing that was put forward by the panels through their inherent discretionary judgment in defining likeness was an emphasis on its case-by-case nature. This culminated in the Appellate Body's declaration of the 'accordion' concept.

Given the lack of guidance in the treaty itself, and by case law that has developed in an incoherent manner, many students and practitioners in the field of international trade law and policy must struggle to interpret the frequently-encountered concept of 'like products'. So far, scholarly works dealing with this subject have delivered only fragmented knowledge in the specific context of a certain GATT provision. Without exaggeration, no systemic approach has been attempted to understand the various 'like products' concepts scattered throughout the WTO agreements.

This kind of restraint in showing the whole picture and methodology might be appropriate to WTO panels as judicial bodies, whose duty is primarily to solve a particular dispute; but for me, as a scholar and practitioner, it created an enormous thirst. I really wanted to understand the subject in its entirety, and build a certain universe in which the product likeness or similarity problem was systematically solved. For a start, I felt that a demonstration of the entire framework of the likeness problem was wholly necessary, particularly in relation to the judicialization process of the WTO dispute settlement procedure.

A lot of panel decisions in the past have demonstrated two distinct schools of thought in approaching this matter. Certainly, the traditional 'Border Tax Adjustment (BTA) Report' approach makes the likeness determination simple and less time-consuming. On the other hand, the bold approach of the 'aim-and-effect' test has its own merits, of enhancing domestic regulatory autonomy in this era of rapidly changing environment for the WTO. But at the same time, each of these two approaches has its own defects. The BTA approach intentionally or incidentally has been tilted towards objective likeness factors, which creates a lot of non-flexibility in determining likeness. On the other hand, the aim-and-effect test leads to a dangerous slippery slope with regard to the relationship between GATT Article III and the Article XX exception, which is unacceptable.

With the aim of solving these problems, this book provides a conceptual and philosophical view of the like products issue based on a comprehensive analysis of past cases and textual interpretation of WTO agreements. As a methodological guideline, I believe, economic approaches should be more heavily utilized. Indeed, these economic methodologies are extremely appropriate to examine market-based subjective elements. By relying upon the market-based methodology, one could benefit from the merits of the aim-and-effect-type test while avoiding its problems: utilizing the market examination, 'aim' belongs to the Article XX exception, while we can still consider certain subjective elements under Article III for instance, which will enhance flexibility of the WTO rules. In fact, this approach allows us to return to the original letters and spirit of the BTA Report, as demonstrated in this book.

For the market examination, a framework model of likeness determination has been set up which comprises four relevant factors: objective characteristics; demand substitution; supply substitution; and potential/future competition. With regard to each factor, suggestions have been made on the substantive and methodological review points. I have also explained the interactions among those factors. With this framework, one can best handle the variations of 'likeness' or 'substitutability' in the GATT likeness provisions, especially in the upcoming age of information technology revolution.

Under the umbrella of this whole picture, the 'likeness' may be analyzed in each context of the WTO Agreement. In classifying more than 50 likeness provisions, I have worked to effect a structural and substantive adjustment of the framework of likeness so that the concept may fit into, and be analyzed within, each context of the WTO Agreement.

In carrying out this task, the likeness concept was adjusted in its scope (of broadness or narrowness) in accordance with the specific purpose of each provision and GATT drafting records or policy orientation. This adjustment was made, of course, in such a way as to maintain the ordinary meaning of the text of the provision concerned. Adjustments of methodology were also made. Supply substitutability and potential/future competition factors in particular were heavily modified according to each context of the WTO jurisprudence. Thus, the formation of a certain universe that systematically solves the product likeness or similarity problem is the main achievement of this book in the end.

Determining the likeness and substitutability of goods, which occurs throughout the various WTO/GATT provisions with different purposes, has been one of the most controversial issues in the GATT/WTO jurisprudence. So, a coherent interpretation of 'like' or 'directly competitive or substitutable' products in the WTO Agreement is pivotal with regard to the 'judicialization' process of the WTO dispute settlement system. In my belief, applying the market-oriented economic analysis in like product cases substantially solves the apparent discrepancies among the terminologies. This will allow the WTO panels to enhance consistency of rulings as well as the transparency of the decision-making process, which are the two most important aims in the process of judicialization. Furthermore, the different nuances of slightly different languages could be reflected in each of the rulings of like product cases to tailor the WTO jurisprudence to the purpose of each provision.

As the WTO system develops in the drive-to-maturity stage, international trade law is pressed to wrestle with its own normative assumptions and justification problems. This consistency, transparency, and flexibility will improve justificatory power and the acceptability of the decisions rendered by the WTO dispute settlement bodies, which is indispensable at this stage. They will enable the WTO dispute settlement procedure to come closer to its ultimate goal—to achieve a highly respected culture of peaceful resolution of international trade disputes.

As the revolution of information technology proceeds, methodological limitations in adopting the proposed analysis would gradually be overcome. Thus, this book may be called a 'work for the future'.

Most parts of this book were originally written for the purpose of a doctoral dissertation that I completed at Georgetown Law Center in February 2002. In the course of writing it, Professor Richard Diamond at Georgetown offered endless encouragement and comments, which are embedded in numerous parts of this book. Without his kind and gratefully received guidance, this book could not have been finished. Professor Jackson's vision and mastery of international economic law were always guiding lights to my study. Not only did he show me what the science of trade law was, from the basic to the top level, he also invited me to climb up to the pinnacle of the science. His teachings and discussions gave me a panoramic view of the world trading system, by which I was truly inspired. In addition, practical criticisms by Gary Horlick at O'Melveny & Myers injected helpful inputs into my research.

How fortunate I was to have these three masters as evaluators of my dissertation and this book. I want to take this opportunity once again to acknowledge my intellectual debts to them while absolving them from responsibility for my conclusions and recommendations, with which they may disagree. I also would like to thank Professor Mitsuo Matsushita of Seikei University for introducing Oxford University Press (OUP) to me. He was an important person to my study, being the presiding member of the Appellate Body that decided that very *Korean Alcoholic Beverage* case which was the most serious case I encountered with regard to the like products issue. OUP provided superb guidance to a novice author like me throughout the whole process of publication of this book. I cannot thank them enough.

Won-Mog Choi
Seoul, 2002

Contents

Tables of Cases

GATT/WTO Cases

EU and US Cases

Introduction: Purpose and Scope

The General Agreement on Tariffs and Trade (GATT) 1994[1] is a legal instrument primarily concerned with products, so it is not surprising that problems of identifying product similarities as well as problems of classifying and describing products are encountered with some frequency in that instrument.[2] There are a number of legal obligations in the Agreement that give rise to the basic difficulty of deciding when two physical items bear such a relationship to each other as to evoke legal consequences.[3] The most frequently encountered phrase that poses this interpretative problem is 'like (domestic) products',[4] but other terms, such as 'like commodity',[5] 'like merchandise',[6] 'like or directly competitive products',[7] 'like or directly substituted products',[8] 'directly competitive or substitutable products',[9] and 'identical or similar goods'[10] also occur.[11] Furthermore, the relationship problem is sometimes posed implicitly without the use of such terms.[12] Most of these terms in respective provisions of the GATT play a role in determining the scope of the provision by defining to which products the rights and obligations of the GATT apply. Far short of doing justice to the importance of the role of these concepts, the definition of 'like' or 'directly competitive or substitutable' products is yet to be settled.

The main purpose of this study rests on creating more justifiable and predictable rules through adequate interpretation of the WTO Agreement. This purpose comes to obtain much more significance when it focuses on one of the most controversial concepts of 'likeness'—a relative one that evokes the image of an *accordion*[13]—in the WTO Agreement. It seems that even if this might not be *the* most controversial concept as of now, it has enough potential to be one. In one of the GATT preparatory committees, a delegate said that the question of 'like' product presented as much ambiguity and obscurity as that of 'origin' of product, and that a sub-committee had considered the question of definitions and had proposed that the International Trade Organization (ITO) should work on that matter.[14]

Since then, various ways of determining origin of goods have been studied and sophisticated agreements have been reached.[15] By contrast, study on 'like' product issues has not progressed, partly due to the 'abortion' of the ITO.[16]

Since the establishment of the WTO system, a series of alcoholic beverages disputes have been raised to focus on the 'like' product issue: *Japan Alcoholic Beverages*, a Korean case, and a Chilean one. There are still many potentially similar disputes waiting their turn. As various new technologies are developed, and many like or competitive new products appear in the market these days, proper interpretation of the likeness/substitutability of products is an issue of crucial importance.

If one were to set proper criteria on likeness and substitutability throughout the various provisions of WTO Agreement that have different purposes respectively, this would enhance the dispute settlement procedure by providing predictability and consistency. In turn, this could be very valuable not only to those countries who are eager to find out and to punish discrimination, but also to the developing countries where sophisticated systems of classification of goods for customs or tax purposes have not yet been developed.

If the WTO,[17] faithful to the common law principle, continued to stand by and watch a substantial accumulation of case law, much confusion might ensue, to the detriment of these countries. It might bring about more new disputes than it could possibly settle. In turn, more cases would result in more unresolved disputes that could adversely affect the credibility of the WTO. It should be noted that very often predictability is more valuable in the international trading system than is the painful truth. In this light, the argument that the WTO has to provide reasonable guidelines on this matter through various channels, including the interpretation function of the Ministerial Conference and the General Council, is noteworthy.[18]

The WTO originated in response to frustration with the inadequate, highly diplomatic dispute resolution system of the GATT 1947. The Contracting Parties had come to recognize that the ambiguity of many of the GATT 1947 rules had polluted the general rule system and brought GATT 1947 rules generally, and its dispute settlement procedures in particular, into disrepute.[19] Much of the world desired a more rule-oriented system that would be transparent, consistent, and predictable.[20] This desire is explicitly stated in the Dispute Settlement Understanding (DSU).[21]

One of the most important purposes (or principles) of the General Agreement is the prohibition of discrimination and preferential treatment. Those responsible for drafting the Agreement did their best to base the new system on principles of equality, and their endeavors are reflected at many points in the text.[22] Articles I and III of GATT are key provisions that reflect the results of these endeavors. They state that in general no less favourable treatment[23] should be accorded to 'like' or 'directly competitive or substitutable' products regardless of the origin of goods in question. Hence, the need for definitions of 'likeness', 'competitiveness', and 'substitutability',[24] based on which the Agreement can root out the evils of discrimination and preferential treatment and prohibit them. On the other hand, clear definition is necessary so that the principle is not excessive or misapplied.[25]

These definitions are, at least partly, based on economics. It would be interesting to study how those concepts are accepted in the legal instrument of GATT. In this light, answers should be given to such questions as:

(1) To what extent can economics play a role in defining those terms?
(2) Is there any reason why the economic analysis[26] should be rejected, or limited in its scope of application, in GATT jurisprudence?
(3) If the economic analysis is necessary, or at least partially helpful, what kind of method should be used?
(4) Should such an economic analysis be preferred to a purpose (aim)-centered approach?

In answering these questions, *Japan Alcoholic Beverages* provides a good source with which to start. In this case, the Appellate Body formulated a new approach to determine 'like' or 'directly competitive or substitutable' product relationships that explicitly puts emphasis on the 'marketplace'.[27] As a tool for dissecting the market, the Appellate Body confirmed the utility of economic analyses. This approach has been followed subsequently by the international tribunals in *Korea Alcoholic Beverages* and *Chile Alcoholic Beverages*.[28] Although the Appellate Body noted that this approach was limited to the provision in dispute,[29] the rationale of its approach, that the WTO is concerned with markets and competitive conditions in those markets, suggests that the test it approved for Art. III:2 of the GATT is capable of broader application.[30]

The basic premises of this book are that coherent interpretation of 'like' or 'directly competitive or substitutable' products in the GATT is one of the most important issues with regard to the 'judicialization' process of the WTO dispute settlement system, and that by applying marketplace-oriented economic analysis in like product cases, WTO panels can enhance consistency among cases as well as transparency of the decision process,[31] two principal values in the process. This consistency and transparency will improve acceptability of the decisions rendered by the dispute settlement bodies, which is the ultimate goal of the WTO dispute settlement procedure. Chapter I suggests theoretical grounds for these premises.

Chapter II provides an analytical framework of the economic analysis. This framework in turn provides a useful instrument, dubbed an 'accordion' by the Appellate Body, with which one can examine the market at issue and identify product likeness or substitutability in the context of each 'like' provision of the GATT. This examination is carried out in Chapter III, by which one can confirm the practical value or future implications of adopting the market-based economic analysis in each context of the WTO Agreement.

With regard to this subject matter, there can be no definitive 'answer' for future WTO panels; the only thing that can be provided is reasonable guidelines. In the end, as the Appellate Body continues to emphasize, answers ought to be given on a case-by-case basis, relying on *the unavoidable element of individual, discretionary judgement* by the experts to whom the WTO Agreement delegated authority.

Despite the vast quantity of international trade law literature, there is little to nothing that does justice to the importance and distinctiveness of the issue of product likeness or substitutability in the WTO Agreement. Second only to actual acceptance of most of the interpretations and methodology suggested in this book, the success of this effort should be measured by its ability to provoke thought, and thereby engender a lengthy and productive debate about the issues covered.

I

Relationship between Law and Economics: Does 'Rubicon' Exist between Them?

Efforts to answer the questions and issues raised in the Introduction need to be addressed in the following, logical order.

Our main concern is to comprehend what the concepts of likeness and substitutability mean, and how they vary within the specific contexts of the GATT provisions. In other words, 'Mastering the Accordion![1] is what we aim to do.

In order to achieve this final goal, we need to have some preliminary understanding of the principle of the instrument, including how it is designed to stretch and squeeze, what the possible intermediate points are, and which aspects one should bear in mind during the performance. By having this preliminary knowledge, when playing a specific repertoire, the performer would be able to figure out more easily whether or not his or her performance is 'on the right track'.[2]

Of course, all these inquiries into common instrument, principle, and methodology of performance are possible on the precondition that every repertoire is written in a common language—'musical scales and notes'. Or at least, we should feel the necessity that the melodies be 'played' consistently from now on—according to the common language and through the common instrument—even if those repertoires were devised originally with 'birth defects'[3] and/or have been played inconsistently thereafter.[4]

What is the common language in interpreting and applying economic laws? Does not economics provide an excellent common language for international trade law? An answer to this question can be gleaned from pondering the following philosophical, and unavoidable, inquiries: What is (or should be) the relationship between law and economics in interpreting the WTO Agreement? Do the economic methodologies deployed in the field of international law make analysis of the field clearer? Do they yield valuable insights, or is there merely increased friction as authors endeavor to apply methodologies designed for other ends?[5] Does *Rubicon*[6] exist between law and economics? Only after reaching some conclusions to these preliminary questions may one return to the main concern.

1. TYPES OF LAW AND ECONOMICS

First of all, one can approach the philosophical questions by pondering the issue of the types of law and the necessity of an interdisciplinary approach. There are different kinds of laws: public and private law; economic and non-economic law; and international and domestic law. Although distinctions between these laws have become vague these days, thanks mainly to various interactions and mutual influences, in the case of international public economic law, economics has not been a familiar tool with which to analyze legal issues.

Why does such a distance exist between international trade law and economics? One powerful reason can be found in the 'two-culture syndrome' that is inherited from traditional international law jurisprudence. This syndrome provides a strong indication that international trade lawyers and negotiators have accorded priority to producing a politically acceptable solution, while economists have been mostly interested in precise fact-finding and justification.[7] All too often, in the traditional international economic environment, considerations of global efficiency[8] have been unceremoniously brushed aside.[9] Optimum, or the first-best, international economic policies are the exception rather than the rule. All governments repeatedly bend to internal political pressures and provide economic benefits to extremely focused and vociferous interest groups at the expense of the welfare of the general population.[10] In the international arena, the erection of import barriers to protect an industry from more efficient foreign producers is the most common deviation from economic theory.

Of course, different values and priorities make up the core of the contents of international economic policy of each state. In particular, national security and domestic well-being are so important to every government that each has generated a large bureaucracy operating in two different worlds.[11] International economic policy thereupon becomes a target of both national security and economic policy camps; the natural consequence is that international economic policy must serve these two masters.[12] In a sense, international economic policy becomes a means to the end of both domestic economic/political and foreign political success.[13] In this traditional environment, international trade lawyers and negotiators have considered the peaceful resolution of disputes as possible where they could garner consensus between dominant interest groups of both countries in dispute, thus putting the acceptability of certain solutions at the centre of the dispute settlement process.[14] Justice was not a priority for them.[15]

Indeed, this emphasis on the political dimension might have been no more than the choice of international trade law struggling to survive in a power-oriented environment, and this trend seems to have brought disregard for, or detachment from, economic analysis.

It is interesting to witness a clear contrast between international trade law and other legal fields in this regard. Such relative paucity of economic analysis of international trade law issues is especially striking when compared to the proliferation of law-and-economics analysis in various fields of competition law.[16] Antitrust law, which requires inquiries related to those of international trade law, has been explored in great detail through economic analysis for several academic generations.[17] The dominant modes of discourse in antitrust and international trade law—even on issues that are nearly identical—remain far apart.[18]

The Panel in *Korea Alcoholic Beverages* emphasized differences between competition law and international trade law:

The general objective of competition law is to preserve a certain degree of competition against action by the market participants. If the competition authorities of a certain country aim at maintaining a high degree of effective competition, they will apply the relevant criteria strictly, thereby arriving at a narrow definition of the relevant market. On the other hand, the purpose of GATT Article III:2 second sentence is to prevent Members from applying internal taxation so as to afford protection to domestic production. Unlike the objective of competition law, the objective of Article III:2 second sentence, is furthered by a broad interpretation of the relevant criteria, rather than a strict one.[19]

Although this view did not elaborate the specific implications of the difference between the two laws, clearly it emphasizes that the objective of competition law is to 'maintain competition', while that of the GATT national treatment obligation is to 'prevent protectionist intervention'[20]—the purpose of most GATT likeness provisions. Hence, the general conclusion is that the concept of likeness in the General Agreement should have a broader coverage than that of competition law.[21]

The GATT primarily aims to protect comparative advantage, which will lead to economic efficiency, and ultimately to the *optimal* use of the world's resources.[22] As an 'action agenda' to achieve this ultimate goal, the General Agreement adopts the non-discrimination principle.[23] In other words, the authors of the GATT seem to have presumed that once members reached a path of non-discrimination, they would be able finally to arrive at their destination of economic efficiency and the optimal use of resources. It goes without saying that this path would offer a much 'quicker' journey, in that it would substantially reduce international or domestic conflicts in political economy of the world trading system.[24]

Most 'like' provisions in the GATT are geared up to preserve this relationship between economic efficiency and the non-discrimination principle. In this regard, it is no wonder that most of these provisions are equipped with a common standard form of non-discrimination obligation, i.e. that members are prohibited from applying discriminatory treatment to a foreign product so as to afford protection to other 'like' or 'directly competitive or substitutable' products.

This objective and the path of the GATT become clear by comparison with those of competition law. It can generally be said that competition law adopts a straighter path: it 'directly' attacks economic efficiency[25] by preserving a certain calculated degree of competition against anti-competitive actions by the market participants.[26] In other words, competition law does not much rely upon the virtuous cycle that the GATT presupposes: whereas the premise of the GATT is (i) non-discrimination → (ii) competition → (iii) economic efficiency, the premiss of competition law is (i) competition → (ii) economic efficiency.[27]

Given the different jurisdictions of the two laws, this subtle difference in 'action agenda' might seem natural: while competition law regulates private behavior,[28] the GATT regulates governmental intervention. It is this difference that has generated the methodological difference in approaching problems. Indeed, GATT's non-discrimination policy was a 'rule of game among sovereignties' that was taken on in order to 'encourage the contracting states to afford equal commercial opportunities' and to 'establish their trade on a footing that would make it impossible to dig pitfalls for other countries' in a post-World War situation of progressing rampant protectionism and insecurity in the international trade regime.[29]

One might also argue that this difference brings with it a different 'primary' focus: the primary focus of GATT's non-discrimination policy tends to be on a competitive relationship between *products* (thus *producers*);[30] while that of competition policy is directly aimed at *consumer* welfare.[31] In other words, trade law has come to focus upon the protection of *competitors* rather than on the protection of *competition* (or *competitive process*) which is the goal of competition law.[32]

This difference should not be overly emphasized, however. It should be noted that, despite this difference in 'action agenda', the ultimate aims of the two laws are not different. The reason why competition law makes an effort to 'maintain competition' in the market is to enhance consumer welfare by preserving competitive relationships; the reason for the GATT to 'prevent protectionist intervention' is to preserve a competitive relationship between products, which is needed to enhance world welfare in the global market. In this era of globalization and interdependency, the consumer welfare of each jurisdiction of competition law cannot be regarded separately from the world's welfare, which is left in GATT's jurisdiction.[33] Both legal instruments aim at raising the standards of living through the removal of obstacles that hinder the proper functioning of the comparative advantage—whether they are governmental interventions (GATT) or private anti-competitive practices (competition law).

In this light, the Havana Charter for the ITO,[34] announcing that trade liberalization and competition policy share a common aim to achieve an open market and to enhance undistorted competition, prescribed the principle that governmental trade liberalization should not be impeded by barriers to market access for the private sector.[35] The Charter shows this fundamental commonality between the two areas by emphasizing a cooperative relationship between trade and competition policy.[36]

In this seeming discrepancy between these common goals and different approaches, one can raise a few fundamental questions with regard to GATT jurisprudence. What is the 'discrimination' that is built into the non-discrimination approach of the GATT? Is there any complete way of determining it? How far does the GATT's jurisprudence have to reach in order to discipline 'discrimination'? Is it a bad idea to use competition law standards (or at least some of its methodology) for the purpose of drawing a distinction between discrimination and non-discrimination?

The concept of 'like products' is at the center of these questions. In a tapestry woven from three intermediate pieces of *de jure* (or *facial*) discrimination, *de facto* discrimination, and legitimate regulatory autonomy, definitions of 'likeness' create a boundary between the discrimination that the GATT aims to punish, and the domestic regulatory autonomy that is legitimate under the General Agreement. With this said, two questions arise: Where should the line be drawn? What standards and criteria are relevant to do the work?

Answers to these questions can be sought by noting that, given the common goal, there can be no absolute dichotomy between the non-discrimination agenda of the GATT and the competition agenda of antitrust law. The standard of 'likeness' of the GATT is ultimately appraised by the extent to which it contributes to the achievement of the goal of the Agreement. This is similar to the success of the relevant market standard of competition law that is judged by the improvement of the competition law objective.[37] Thus, there is no reason why the criteria, or at least the methodology, used for the purpose of defining the relevant market in competition law should not be referred to for the purpose of determining 'likeness' in the GATT jurisprudence.

With this assertion the Panel in *Chile Alcoholic Beverages* seems to agree. Referring to the substitutability of pisco and imported spirits, as defined by the Chilean competition agency (Commission) for antitrust purposes, the Panel reasoned that:

We note that the Commission was dealing with the question of competition from an anti-trust perspective, which generally utilizes narrower market definitions than used when analyzing markets pursuant to Article III:2, second sentence . . . Consequently, it seems logical that competitive conditions sufficient for defining an appropriate market with respect to antitrust analysis would *a fortiori* suffice for an Article III analysis. We would, therefore, regard the findings of the Commission as tending to confirm the finding that in the Chilean market, pisco and imported distilled spirits are directly competitive or substitutable products.[38]

Some people might have tried, or still try, to find the ground of inherent ambivalence between the two laws. Their rationale might have relied on the GATT's birth defect, and/or still relies on the incurable difference between international and domestic 'soils' as they are applied respectively. But, with a completely cured 'birth defect', and in a world where fast globalization connects every economy, this rationale is losing ground, not to mention the rationale for different *methodological approaches* between the two laws.

Still, they might point out the general trend that whereas the scope of the relevant market tends to have been reduced in the competition law context,[39] the scope of the likeness concept of the GATT has been broadened in general.[40] However, this apparent ambivalence between the two laws is in fact based on similar objectives and is directed toward a common destination. A narrow definition of 'relevant market' is needed to increase competition through the strict application of the competition law. Similarly, a broad scope of 'like product' reflects the general trend toward strict application of the General Agreement: through thorough protection of comparative advantages against *de facto* or disguised discrimination, it increases competition, which is beneficial to the world economy.

Having departed from different starting points, the GATT and competition law are heading toward a common destination. As this convergence proceeds, the GATT non-discrimination agenda will come close to the path of the competition agenda. The more frequently and closely the one refers to the other, the faster the convergence will occur. This process, as it accelerates, will bring about an increase in the amount of accumulated wisdom of competition law influencing the jurisprudence of the GATT.

Even if one accepts the inherent ambivalence, if any, between the two laws, it might only be used as an excuse for applying 'different standards' between competition law and the General Agreement. This difference (or ambivalence), if any, is not enough to justify a lack of economic analysis in the international trade law field. Since variety in legal doctrines (reflected in governmental measures) or practices usually evolves from different socioeconomic contexts, each of them tends to be under the cloak of unique justification. Accordingly, the need for examining those doctrines or practices using a uniform standard becomes greater.

Having said this, it is worth noting that the WTO Agreement is being implemented in various cultural environments throughout the world. As may be expected, with these varying cultures come various preferences, customs, and structural conditions that will affect markets to which the Agreement is applied. A series of economic analyses can uncover common denominators (and differences) that underlie superficial differences (or common denominators) across these markets and national legal systems. Rather than having to make a judgement on the legal culture and market of one nation, while dwelling in those of others, the economic analysis of trade law offers to *translate* all those factors into a common language of economics—the universal language.[41]

Putting forward the metaphor of the accordion, the WTO Panel and Appellate Body in *Japan Alcoholic Beverages* proclaimed that they had a universal language called '*the Unavoidable Element of Individual Discretionary Judgement*'.[42] But one should note that this instruction provides little guidance—in fact, what it provides is only the first few bars of the score. When one plays the accordion, one must know how far the accordion should stretch and squeeze at particular points of playing. Playing without music and/or training would produce discord. The same melody would sound differently every time one played, and sometimes different melodies would begin to sound similar. As a result, an ordinary audience would feel confused, dissatisfied, and even angry that they did not get what they paid for. Some might not ever return to the concert hall again. It is thus doubtful that, with the deficient score, the tribunal will be able to produce a series of harmonious symphonies throughout its various performances in the future.

2. CONSTRAINTS OF DISCRETION, JUSTIFICATION, AND ACCEPTABILITY

Analyzing the necessity of the economic approach in international trade law, one should pay attention to such issues as the discretion of the international tribunal, the constraints on that discretion, and the desire of the different parties to accept the decision rendered by the tribunal.

Critics of the use of economic analysis in WTO decision-making (dispute settlement procedure) might put emphasis on the channelling of discretion that inevitably accompanies more determinate decision frameworks.[43] At bottom, they might raise a broader objection to the use of strict economic analysis because it would inevitably limit the discretion of the decision-makers in Geneva, whether they are panels or Contracting Parties.

This way of thinking might further intensify the argument that limiting administrative discretion violates the intent of the GATT drafters. The argument is based on the proposition that by leaving the terms 'like' and 'directly competitive or substitutable' vague, drafters intended to give some amount of discretion to panels, or they wanted to leave some room for negotiation for Contracting Parties when attempting to solve disputes.[44] According to this opinion, thorough application of economic analysis would destroy the intention by depriving tribunals or parties of such discretion.

However, the above criticism overestimates the constraint that the economic analysis places on decision-makers, and underestimates the benefit that the analysis can bring to negotiators. According to the general understanding, when a result of more accurate and predictable economic analysis is presented, the room for discretion to be exercised by the international tribunal is reduced. But even 'perfect' economic analysis cannot nullify that discretion. What economics does basically is to show what the fact is and what it will be, using the transparent universal language.[45] Most contributions or revelations that economics can make are confined to this descriptive and predictive field of function.[46] In other words, value judgements are left outside economics. In the seamless tapestry of product relationship, the decision of *how much* 'likeness' is necessary to be 'like' will be determined by a value judgement based on the purpose of each provision of the GATT and policy orientation. The 'likeness' concept in the GATT cannot be free from the inherent involvement of matters of degree, approximation, and judgement. Determining the ultimate value of a dispute settlement procedure must be judged by some normative standard—whether the activity at issue has made the world better or worse. Then, one can say that this function will be left forever to the dispute settlement bodies of the WTO.[47]

Most importantly, what the criticisms attack is the most valuable contribution economic analysis can offer to the international trade law: the resolution of disputes in a predictable and consistent manner through the use of transparent tools. Application of economic analysis may import some constraint, but that constraint is not so much a determinant of the amount or frequency of trade relief as it is a limiting factor on a panel's ability to be inconsistent across cases. This benefit will make the loss of discretion, if any, so much more, or even more, valuable. This tailored discretion, backed up by accurate and predictable economic analysis, can finally be deserving of the title, '*the Unavoidable Element of Individual Discretionary Judgement*'.

Even in cases in which economic analysis fails to be perfect, it offers a way of reducing the range of expected results, which will set limits to the unbridled discretion of international tribunals.[48] At the very least, once one knows the basic inputs to positive economic analysis, one is able to understand a great deal about the range of possible outcomes and about the determinations that will drive those outcomes.[49] This sort of predictability reduces significantly any possibility of arbitrary judgement or injustice caused by the intervention of the decision-makers' interests or incentives with regard to the outcome of the dispute.

In his dialogue, *Protagoras*, Plato writes that a sense of justice is a prerequisite to living a civic life, and to living in Community.[50] The non-violent resolution of disputes, the *sine qua non* of civic life, requires that losing parties understand outcomes as being 'right'.[51] When people speak of decisions as being 'right' or 'just', they speak of the outcomes not in a descriptive sense but in an evaluative or justificatory sense. In other words, they are talking about the acceptability of outcomes.[52] If individuals consider an outcome to be 'just', they consider it acceptable, and its acceptability involves reference to particular criteria. Thus their notion of justice is quite closely linked conceptually and etymologically to justification.

The acceptability of the decision of the international tribunal becomes directly related to its enforceability. In other words, the more justifiable the decision, the more acceptable—and thereby the more enforceable—it is.[53] International trade law needs this justification process more than any other field because, different from domestic law, international trade law has inherent weaknesses with regard to enforcing decisions.

Economic analysis provides the best criteria for such justification. The more accurate and predictable the process of economic analysis, the more sophisticated the justification that will be provided. As a result, decisions become more acceptable. Since the losing party will be satisfied by objective evidence, it can return home and easily persuade domestic interest groups.[54]

The first stage of the world trading revolution—*take-off* stage—launched the WTO successfully. From there, the second stage of development—*the drive to maturity*—is now occurring. One of the most important challenges confronted in this stage is that of governance. The necessity for a decision-enforcement practice is pressing international trade law to wrestle with its own normative assumptions and justification problems. As shown by the exposition of the economic approach phenomenon in the *Japan Alcoholic Beverages* case, the bell marking the beginning of this struggle is ringing.[55]

In a sense, the Panel and the Appellate Body in the Japanese case, by approving the use of cross-price elasticity of demand and by referring to a series of other econometric analyses, have crossed the Rubicon.[56] The tribunals have now entered into a hostile territory, where economics (or empirical studies) governs and where no traditional guidance has been given since the 1970 Working Party Report on *Border Tax Adjustments*.[57]

This observation gains more ground when one considers that the economic approach phenomenon has been continuing through the subsequent 'likeness' cases of *Korea* and *Chile Alcoholic Beverages*, as will be discussed in detail in Chapter II. Even though these panels shied away from admitting an 'indispensable role' for, or even the 'necessity' of, economic analyses,[58] their decisions heavily relied on the implications of such analyses.

At this stage in the struggle, predictability, consistency, and transparency are premium values. The more accurately, predictably, and transparently economic analyses back up decisions, the better and more sophisticated the justification that is provided, thereby increasing the acceptability of tribunals' decisions. The more enforceable the revolutionary system of the WTO becomes, the further the tribunals' march toward Rome would progress. The Universal Empire of world citizens, where justice, fairness, and enforceability are guaranteed, finally could be achieved through this march for justification and consistency. Setting standards and criteria through adequate interpretation of 'like' or 'directly competitive or sub-stitutable' products of the WTO Agreement, using appropriate tools of economic analysis, would help this march by providing predictability and consistency, and thus enforceability. Adding necessary bars to the score, these efforts will ensure that the accordion players are in harmony.

The role of the international tribunal in the *drive-to-maturity* is to provide legal security and predictability with regard to the meaning of WTO law. In a sense, the tribunal, through its case law, has to lend a hand in its own demise: it must make the meaning of WTO law so predictable that litigation will not be needed.[59] This is comparable with the incentive structure of an independent judiciary that applies the same law to the same facts—independent of the parties to the dispute.[60] It is particularly important for international adjudicators, who, unlike their municipal counterparts, lack a monopoly of enforcement power and have only the power to persuade the addressees of their decisions that those decisions are correct.[61] The international judiciary acquires its legitimacy through the consistent and coherent application of law.

For the march of the 'mature demise', the concepts of likeness and substitution, and the methodology employed to examine those, in the context of competition law could provide an excellent basis with which to begin. Notwithstanding the *Korea Alcoholic Beverages* Panel's hesitation,[62] it seems that the concept or methodo-logical tool of substitution analysis developed in competition law can be referred to and applied, after appropriate methodological adjustment or modification, to 'likeness' and 'substitutability' analysis in the field of international trade law. It should be noted that in the application process, even though the guideline of competition law could be followed, there still remains a question of whether the anti-competition standard should be the same as the international trade law standard. This issue of setting standards is inherently the value judgement procedure reserved for the dispute settlement panels of the WTO.

In conclusion, the necessity for the economic approach in international trade law is germane to the 'likeness' or 'substitutability' issue where, due to the vagueness of the concepts, controversy is inherent and acceptability of the panels' decisions is always in peril. Justifications based on economic analysis can greatly contribute to dealing with these problems by providing objective criteria of judgement, by enhancing the consistency, predictability and transparency of the dispute settlement system, which thereby increases the acceptability of decisions made by the WTO tribunal.

Continuous application of economic analysis will help to develop certain standards, or criteria, with regard to product likeness in the GATT jurisprudence. Such standards will be useful, particularly for many developing countries, where sophisticated tax and/or customs systems have not yet been put in place. According to these standards, such countries could adjust their domestic tax or duty regime, which is an extremely difficult task, without an authorized paradigm.

Order cannot exist without an understanding of what constitutes permissible behavior. This seemingly commonsensical statement becomes even truer in this interrelated world economy, where no more absolute hegemony governs. In this environment, the most fundamental as well as prevalent standard of behavior is unavoidably legal in character.[63] Therefore, the significance of the consistent and transparent definition of product likeness or substitutability is enduring and vital. It provides an indispensable framework for the process of political economy. *Ubi societas, ibi ius.*

II

Applying the Relationship to GATT Law: Across the Rubicon!

Accepting the conclusion that the role of economic analysis is necessary in the GATT/WTO, one can proceed to deal with the main concerns of this book:

(1) deciding which *elements* should be examined in order to determine 'likeness' or 'substitutability';
(2) determining which *economic methods* should be used to examine those elements; and
(3) setting up a *common analytical framework* that includes those elements and with which one can best handle the variations of 'likeness' or 'substitutability' in various GATT provisions.[1]

This inquiry can start with the establishment of an analytical flow chart for the 'likeness' or 'substitutability' analysis, which will guide the inquiry by providing a conceptual order and appropriate scope to it.

First of all, one needs to understand the *general* meaning of terms, such as 'like', 'competitive', and 'substitutable', and to distinguish one from another, which will be done in a way detached from the context of each provision of GATT. In spite of the necessity that the specific scope of the likeness or substitutability, employed in each provision, should be adjusted by subsequent considerations, including the purpose of each provision, this 'generalization' is important in the first place. The adoption of specific language in treaties indicates that there exists a general meaning to the language, and that this meaning was employed to deal with certain specific situations or contexts of the treaty in question. This is especially true when there is repeated use of the same term in a single treaty that shows that there was a common situation or context to be represented by the term—even if diversity of negotiators and/or different times of negotiation, which actually occurred during the GATT negotiations, are taken into account. For instance, it is reasonable to understand that when GATT drafters employed the common terms 'like', 'directly', 'competitive', or 'substitutable' in many provisions of the Agreement, they paid attention to certain common denominators that could be drawn from the general meaning of such terms.

Thus, to find out what were the common denominators or the general meanings of the terms used is necessary to provide a firm basis for interpreting those terms in the context of each provision or specific market condition. Starting from the basic understanding, one can adjust the specific scope of 'likeness' or 'substitutability', taking account of the purpose of each provision or condition of each marketplace. Indeed, without such a general understanding in advance, one could have difficulty in defining each instance of 'likeness' or 'substitutability' in the maze of numerous GATT provisions that confuses even the cleverest inquirer. Through this process of generalization, one may produce certain conceptual gradations of product relationship that allow the various terms used in each provision of the WTO Agreement to be reflected. This task—'Conceptual Classification of Relationship between Goods'—will be carried out in section 1 below.

Secondly, based on the common denominators or the general meanings identified, one may attempt to pinpoint *elements* to define 'likeness' or 'substitutability'. This will be a demanding process in which one has to glean those elements in a systematic manner from a complicated cluster of 'like' product cases formed by traditional as well as recent GATT/WTO panels. Section 2 below is assigned for this purpose.

Lastly, by analyzing and grouping these elements, one can produce certain *factors*, as discussed in section 3, which will constitute the Framework Model of 'Likeness' or 'Substitutability'. This Model is the master instrument with which one can proceed to examine each 'like' product provision of the GATT.[2]

1. CONCEPTUAL CLASSIFICATION OF RELATIONSHIP BETWEEN GOODS

If one were to draw a line of product relationship, one would put the concept of 'identical' at one end, and the concept of 'different' at the other end. The concept of 'identical goods' represents the closest relationship between products, whereas the concept of 'different goods' reflects no relationship whatsoever. In between these extremes, one would be able to locate such concepts as 'similar', 'directly competitive or substitutable', and 'indirectly competitive or substitutable'.[3]

For the definitive interpretations of those basic categories of product relationship, the texts of the GATT and several multilateral agreements annexed to the WTO Agreement provide a good basis.

1.1. Identical

Article 15 of the Customs Valuation Agreement provides a definitive interpretation of the concept of 'identical':

Identical goods means goods which are the same in all respects including physical characteristics, quality and reputation. Minor differences in appearance would not preclude goods otherwise conforming to the definition from being regarded as identical.

Considering that this interpretation is shared in Art. 2.6 of the Antidumping Agreement and Art. 15.1, fn 46 of the SCM Agreement, one can borrow it to understand the concept of 'identical product' for the purpose of approaching the narrowest meaning of 'like' product relationship throughout the General Agreement.[4]

Therefore, an 'identical product' means *alike (or the same) in all respects, including physical as well as functional characteristics,* to the product under consideration, which represents the closest relationship between products in the GATT product 'likeness' problem.

1.2. Similar

Article 15 of the Customs Valuation Agreement provides a definitive interpretation for the concept of 'similar goods':

Similar goods means goods which, although not alike in all respects, have like characteristics and like component materials which enable them to perform the same functions and to be commercially interchangeable. The quality of the goods, their reputation and the existence of a trademark are among the factors to be considered in determining whether goods are similar.

This understanding seems to be shared by the Antidumping Agreement as well as by the SCM Agreement:

In the absence of such [an identical] product, another product which, although not alike in all respects, has characteristics closely resembling those of the product under consideration.[5]

Since there is no requirement of 'alike in *all* respects' here, one may question how far the concept of 'similar' can reach. If products in comparison share *most* of the significant characteristics, they can be safely designated as being 'similar' products. But what if those products share fewer than most characteristics; or only *one* characteristic?[6] What if they have like component materials but do not share like functions?

It should be noted that the concept 'similar' could be quite inclusive depending on the context of the cases with which it is involved: in particular, when a product has multiple functions, it could attract different similar products according to each function. Thus, this concept can be conceptually divided into two parts: *closely similar* goods and *remotely similar* goods.[7] The former applies to the relationship of products that share as many significant physical as well as functional characteristics as possible. With regard to the latter product relationship, there are as few characteristics shared as possible.

It should be emphasized that the latter concept of 'remotely similar' covers the question of physical similarity: the products in comparison should share *physical* characteristics (or physical component materials), if only to a minimal extent, to qualify as being 'remotely similar'. If a product loses the *physical* similarity at all through processing or commercial manipulations, it should be considered outside the scope of the 'similar product' coverage, no matter how close the *functional* relationship it shares with the product in comparison. In such a case, the next stage, of a 'competitive or substitutable' relationship, may be utilized to cover the situation.[8]

1.3. Directly Competitive or Substitutable

The *Addendum* (*Ad*) to Art. III: 2 of the GATT reads as follows:

A tax conforming to requirements of the first sentence of paragraph 2 would be considered to be inconsistent with the provisions of the second sentence only in cases where *competition was involved* between, on the one hand, the taxed product and, on the other hand, a *directly competitive or substitutable* product which was not similarly taxed.[9]

With respect to the meaning of the term 'directly competitive or substitutable', a series of questions and problems need to be addressed. The first question involves the meaning of 'directly'. Are there any 'indirectly' competitive or substitutable products? One can try to answer this question by examining the following four examples:

(1) To start with the basic understanding of the relationship between consumption and income, since purchasing a certain product removes a certain amount of money from the buyer's budgetary pool, at some level all products or services are at least indirectly competitive. Because consumers have limited amounts of disposable income, they may have to arbitrate between various needs, such as giving up going on vacation in order to buy a car, or abstaining from eating in restaurants in order to save to buy new shoes or a television set.[10] This point extends to the concept of cross-price elasticity. If the price of an exercise machine goes up, potential purchasers of the machine might decide not to buy it and purchase more foods with fewer calories instead, e.g. skimmed milk. Or daily necessaries, such as kitchen paper, will be purchased more as a result of random choice. This emphasizes the point that virtually all products have at least a minimum cross-price elasticity with one other. Indeed, products that could conceivably be substituted for each other yield a very broad field of choice.[11] From the illustrations given above, one should not come to the conclusion that the relationship between a vacation and a car, a meal in a restaurant and a TV set, and an exercise machine and skimmed milk (or kitchen paper) is that of 'directly competitive or substitutable' products. An assessment of whether there is a direct competitive relationship between two products requires evidence that consumers consider the two products as *alternative ways of satisfying a particular need or taste*.[12]

(2) The second example might be the situation of chains of substitution. A product can have many functions. In regard to each function, it can have competitive or substitutable products.[13] Hence, in general, the more functions a product has, the more competitive or substitutable it will be.[14] Suppose that a product P has two different functions;[15] it could have two substitutable products, X and Y, one for each function. The relationship between X and Y can be called *indirect* competition or substitution because those two products are related to each other indirectly through P. Even if product P is a demand substitute for both X and Y, X and Y themselves should not be treated as

'directly competitive or substitutable' products (unless there happens to be a separate, direct competitive relationship between them). With regard to the 'direct' relationship between P and X or P and Y above, it should be noted that sometimes P's (X's or Y's) having many functions could lead to an indirect relationship of substitution. For instance, electricity and petroleum may not be determined as being 'directly competitive or substitutable products' because respectively they possess *numerous* functions other than heating houses.[16]

(3) Further elucidation is given by the relationship between substitute goods and complementary goods.[17] One could strongly argue that coffee and tea are 'directly competitive or substitutable' goods. A good example of goods complementary to *coffee* is sugar. From the above substitutive-complementary relationship, one should not conclude that *tea* and sugar are 'directly competitive or substitutable' products, even though the demand of sugar will be increased as a result of a rising price of tea.[18] Indeed, sugar is related to tea 'indirectly' through coffee.

(4) Should this 'directly substitutable' relationship be reciprocal, or would a mere unilateral relationship be enough? This question arises in regard to the 'inferior–superior goods' relationship. Some might argue that the directly substitutive relationship between the goods should be reciprocal, not unilateral: consumers should consider the two products as 'alternative' ways of consumption. According to this view, a black and white TV (inferior good) and a color TV (superior good)[19] should not be defined as being 'directly substitutable' because the former is often replaced by the latter, while the opposite is seldom true.[20] However, demanding reciprocity in substitutability regardless of the situation seems to narrow too far the scope of the 'directly substitutable' concept. Thus, taking account of the circumstances in which cases are brought, the following solution may be suggested:

(a) If the complainant is a country producing the superior goods (and the defendant is a producer of the inferior goods), the relationship in most cases should be defined as being 'directly substitutable'.

(b) In contrast, if the defendant is producing the superior goods, it should not be defined a 'directly substitutable' relationship.

Indeed, black and white TV producers have enough protectionist reasons to harm color TV imports while the opposite is seldom correct.

To summarize, GATT 'like' product provisions (and Art. III in particular) should be concerned, in the broadest sense, with 'directly' competitive or substitutable relationships. Otherwise, the coverage of GATT obligations would be too broad.[21] Commonsensical as it is, it should be emphasized that the drafters, using the word 'directly' immediately before 'competitive or substitutable' in all relevant provisions without exception,[22] had the intention of excluding any 'indirectly' competitive or substitutable relationship.[23]

Therefore, in example (2) above, X and Y will not be subject to a national treatment obligation, although both of them will be constrained by P's pricing. Also, in example (3), tea and sugar will not be subject to the obligation even though there might exist a substantial cross-price elasticity of demand.[24]

This insight leads us to the second question: does the word 'directly' define only 'competitive' or both 'competitive' and 'substitutable'? In fact, this question is easily answered by referring to the French text of the Interpretative Note, which employs the phrase: '... un produit *directement* concurrent ou un produit qui peut lui être *directement* substitué...'.[25] Still, out of intellectual curiosity one might ponder this issue further. Both of those interpretations being possible grammatically, the better interpretation should be '*directly* competitive or *directly* substitutable'. Aside from the concern about over-broad coverage of GATT obligations,[26] the reasons are as follows:

(1) 'Competitive' is a term used more from a producer's than a consumer's view-point; whereas 'substitutable' describes the situation from the perspective of the end-user/consumer.[27] This point becomes clear when the phrase 'directly competitive or substitutable' is compared with the phrase 'directly competitive' in GATT Art. XIX:[28] Art. XIX uses only the term 'competitive' because the provision, on the whole, is written from the *producer's* point of view.[29]

(2) The scope of 'directly competitive' product (from the producers' perspective) is most often the same as that of the 'directly substitutable' product (from the consumers' viewpoint). If two products are not regarded as being 'directly substitutable' for consumers, there is little reason for producers to view those products as being 'directly competitive'. If the producers feel that those products are 'directly competitive', it is mainly because they are 'directly substitutable'—direct substitution is, in most cases, a necessary and sufficient condition for direct competition.[30]

(3) Article XI:2(c) of GATT uses the term 'directly substituted'.[31]

Therefore, it can be concluded that the word 'directly' defines not only 'competitive' but also 'substitutable'. If two products are either 'directly competitive' products or 'directly substitutable' products then they are 'directly competitive or substitutable' products within the meaning of GATT Art. III.

It is now possible to address the third question: what is the *definition* of 'directly substitutable' or 'directly competitive'? *Webster's Dictionary* defines 'substitutable' as 'capable of being put in place of something else or available for use instead of something else <honey is an excellent substitute for sugar in many recipes>'. A contextual elaboration on this definition was provided in *Chile Alcoholic Beverages*. Ruling that, despite physical differences,[32] pisco and whisky were 'directly competitive or substitutable products' in Art. III:2, the Chilean Panel explained that:

In evaluating substitutability in end-use, it may be useful in this regard, to refer to an approach in consumer theory which has been gaining ground.[33] According to the theory, goods are, in the eyes of consumers, never really perceived as commodities that are in themselves direct objects of utility; rather, it is the properties or characteristics of the goods from which utility is derived that are the relevant considerations. It is these characteristics or attributes that yield satisfaction and not the goods as such. Goods may share a common characteristic but may have other characteristics that are qualitatively different, or they may have the same characteristics but in quantitatively different combinations. Substitution possibilities arise because of these shared characteristics. The oft-cited hypothetical textbook example of butter and margarine may be instructive. Butter and milk are both dairy products that share important characteristics that margarine does not have. However, butter and margarine each have combinations of characteristics that make them good substitutes as complements for bread, which is not the case with milk. The characteristics of butter and margarine can be expressed as physical properties such as spreadability, taste, colour and consistency. These physical characteristics combine to render both products good substitutes as bread complements. The latter represents the end-use of the commodities as determined by their combination of characteristics derived from certain physical characteristics.[34]

What was decisive for the Panel in this case was the 'shared common characteristic of satisfying a similar need' between the two products in question.

One should note that a similar definition was adopted earlier by the Appellate Body in *Korea Alcoholic Beverages*: '... according to the ordinary meaning of the term, products are competitive or substitutable when they are interchangeable or if they offer, as the Panel noted, "alternative ways of satisfying a particular need or taste".'[35]

Thus, it might be said that the definition of 'directly competitive or substitutable' products includes three conditions: one should be able to use one product (1) in place of the other; (2) for the similar purpose of satisfying a particular need or taste; and (3) (from the angle of consumer utility) without significant reduction of consumption utility.[36]

Of course, 'indirectly' competitive or substitutable products cannot satisfy these conditions. Going back to previous examples, one finds that such pairs of products as P and X, P and Y, or coffee and tea satisfy the above conditions, whereas X and Y, tea and sugar, or exercise machines and kitchen papers do not, because of lack of common purpose of consumption and because there will be a substantial difference in their utility.[37] The pair consisting of an exercise machine and a skimmed milk product might be said to satisfy conditions (1) and (2) above, but cannot satisfy condition (3).[38]

Although the GATT/WTO tribunals, including those listed above, did not distinguish the concept 'directly competitive' from 'directly substitutable', one can propose a possible distinction. In this regard, it is interesting to see that *Webster's Dictionary* defines the term 'competitive' in a different manner from the term 'substitutable'. According to the dictionary, the word 'competitive' means 'characterized by, arising from, or designated to exhibit rivalry among two or more equally matched individuals or forces esp. for a particular goal, position, or reward', or 'produced by ... rivalry of economic endeavor and without presence of monopoly or collusion'. This shows that the term 'competitive' is a producer-oriented concept. As already pointed out, since producers' main attention is directed towards the viewpoint of consumers, 'directly competitive' products are mainly determined by what are viewed as 'directly substitutable' products. But producers tend to take account of such additional factors as relationships with competitors, production and marketing constraints, long-term consumption trends, business risks, sunk costs, etc.[39] In general, it can be said that producers consider more long-term strategic aspects than do consumers.

Thus, overall, both supply-side considerations *and* demand-side substitutability will determine whether the products in question are 'directly competitive'. Rare as it is, sometimes even though two particular products are considered to be 'directly substitutable' by consumers, they would not be viewed as being 'directly competitive' by producers because of the existence of strong production or marketing constraints.[40] For example, even if soft drink producers currently had excess capacity, the legal requirement to bottle spring and mineral water at source could make it impossible for them to switch any possible spare capacity to bottle such water.

In such a case, the complete interpretation of 'directly competitive or substitutable' may require the focus to be not only on the demand side (as shown by *demand substitutability*), but also on the supply-side review of the specific market structure (as shown by *supply substitutability*). This understanding will be further pursued in sections 2 and 3 below.

With the above definition of 'directly competitive or substitutable' product, one can approach the concept of 'like' product. First of all, looking at the Articles concerned—Arts III:2, XI:2(c),[41] and XIX:1(a), (b)[42] in particular—'like products' should be viewed as being a subset of 'directly competitive or substitutable products'.[43] In this light, all 'like' products are, by definition, 'directly competitive or substitutable' products, whereas the opposite does not always hold true.[44] Therefore, it can be said that if two products in question are physically identical or nearly identical (similar) but not substitutable, those are not 'like' products. One would not encounter this type of situation often. But if most consumers of a product have very strong and persistent national preferences because of certain religious or spiritual reasons (and one proves this strong and persistent nature), those physically identical products could be not substitutable, and thus not 'like'. Korean ginseng and Chinese ginseng might serve as an example of this.[45]

How, then, can one distinguish the 'likeness subset' from the 'substitutability whole'? What makes the 'like' product relationship different from a mere 'substitutable' relationship? Although the GATT/WTO tribunals have shied away from clearly defining what a 'like product' is, one could start to posit a definition from the *Japan Alcoholic Beverages* case, in which 'like' products were implied, in the context of Art. III:2, as being 'products having no substantial noticeable differences in physical characteristics'.[46]

To rephrase, what is essential in the 'like' product concept is whether the two products in question share physical characteristics close enough to be considered virtually identical or substantially similar (so as not to be considered noticeably different). For instance, organically grown beef and hormone-treated beef are 'like' products, but pork (or even tofu) is not a 'like' product to beef (aside from being a 'directly substitutable' product to beef).[47] A caveat here is that differences in variety (organoleptic difference), price, quality, and freshness do not make a difference when considering 'likeness', as many GATT/WTO panels emphasized.[48] But this generalization is valid only as far as 'general' market conditions are concerned; it is not impossible that ordinary beef and hormone-treated beef would fail to qualify as being 'like' products in certain circumstances. This point will be discussed further in the following chapters.

Moreover, it is very difficult in a substantial number of cases to determine whether the products in question share such characteristics. The concept of virtual identity or substantial similarity might not be clear-cut at all, and it needs to be understood in the light of the context or purpose of the specific provision, marketplace, etc.

This vagueness in demarcation between 'like' and 'substitutable' becomes more serious in a case in which the relationship between fresh and processed products, or between processed products having different stages of processing, is at issue.[49] Are tomatoes and tomato concentrates like products? What about oranges and orange juice; orange juice and orange concentrates; or orange and canned orange (not juice-or-concentrate type)—are they 'like' products? It seems that these pairs are substitutable products for each other. It is not clear, however, whether they are 'like' or 'directly substitutable' products. Hence, it is necessary in the end to undertake the detailed 'adjustment' procedure on a case-by-case basis, relying on the context and purpose of each provision and possible differences in market conditions, in which the 'likeness' of products is examined.

Therefore, depending upon context and purpose of each provision of the WTO Agreements, the 'like' product concept would be endowed with a different range of likeness, from the narrowest to the broadest meaning of the term, stretching from the concept of 'identical' to the concept of 'remotely similar' as defined above. In other words, the *narrowest* interpretation of the 'like' product concept would lead to an understanding of 'identical', and a *narrow* interpretation would allow the concept to include 'closely similar' as well. A *broad* understanding of the 'like' product concept would include 'identical', 'closely similar', and 'remotely similar'.[50]

One might suggest an additional understanding of the *broadest* form that would encompass the 'directly competitive or substitutable' concept. But this 'excessive' interpretation could not be justified unless there was clearly a supporting indication in the GATT preparatory work and there existed a compelling reason such as to avoid a manifestly absurd or unreasonable result.[51]

Hence, in general, the 'like' product relationship stretches or squeezes within the boundary of physical similarity. Physical similarity is an attribute of products, whereas substitutability or competitiveness is an attribute of consumers or producers. In other words, even though in reality a substantial portion of the two will overlap, there exist two different 'conceptual' dimensions: (1) physical characteristics, as attributes of products; and (2) functional interchangeability, from the perspective of use by consumers and producers. It should be noted that the 'like' concept is based on both of those dimensions, whereas the 'competitive' or 'substitutable' concepts are linked only with the latter dimension. Thus, in order to be 'like', the two products being compared should have both physical similarity and 'non physical' competitiveness or substitutability. By contrast, in the substitutability test, the former dimension is disregarded (except for such a case as when the former is referred to as a proof of existence for the latter dimension).

Despite this conceptual differentiation, it is not easy to draw a line in a specific case between physical similarity and mere functional interchangeability. Do coffee beans and ground coffee share physical similarity so that they may be defined as being at least 'remotely similar' products? What about sugar cubes, loose sugar, powdered sugar, and sugar supplements? After all, all goods are composed of common chemical elements (C, H, O, N, etc.). These are borderline cases in which traditional approaches based on objective characteristics fail to be persuasive. This failure enforces the reason why one needs an economic analysis as a complementary tool to determine 'likeness', as discussed later.

To summarize, in general, the concept of 'like product' remains within the boundary of physical similarity: the products in comparison should share at least one physical characteristic (e.g., common component materials) to be considered 'like' products in the broadest sense. Losing the similarity at all through processing or through commercial manipulations should be considered as taking them outside the scope of the 'like product' coverage. In such a case, the next stage of 'directly competitive or substitutable' relationships might be utilized to cover the situation.

Based on this general insight, the specific scope of likeness or substitutability can be determined in individual cases. In the context of GATT Art. III:2, however, distinguishing 'like' from 'directly competitive or substitutable' is not especially rewarding, because, according to the Appellate Body, there is no substantial difference in result between 'like' in the first sentence and 'directly competitive or substitutable' in the second sentence.[52] Determining whether there is 'direct competition or substitutability' or not has practical importance in the provision.[53]

In other provisions, drawing a distinction between the terms 'like' and 'directly competitive or substitutable' has substantial importance. Such provisions include Arts I, III:4, VI, IX, XIII, and XVI (in which only the 'like' product concept is employed), and Art. XI:2 (in which the concepts of 'like' and 'directly substituted' are utilized in a 'mutually-exclusive' manner).[54] This contextualization of the definitions of 'likeness' will proceed in Chapter III.

Figure II.1 summarizes this conceptual classification of the product relationship.[55] The division and comparison made in the figure will provide a basic conceptual tool, based upon which one can approach, in a unified manner, the likeness or substitutability provisions scattered throughout the GATT. After all, returning to the image with which we began this book, it is handy to have a preliminary fundamental knowledge of how far the accordion can stretch and squeeze, and

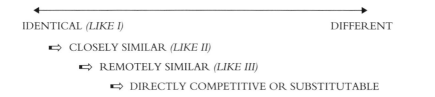

IDENTICAL *(LIKE I)*   DIFFERENT

⇨ CLOSELY SIMILAR *(LIKE II)*

⇨ REMOTELY SIMILAR *(LIKE III)*

⇨ DIRECTLY COMPETITIVE OR SUBSTITUTABLE

⇨ INDIRECTLY COMPETITIVE OR SUBSTITUTABLE

Figure II.1: Conceptual Classification of Relationship between Goods

which intermediate points the player should particularly bear in mind during the performance.

2. EVIDENTIAL ELEMENTS TO DEFINE LIKENESS OR SUBSTITUTABILITY: 'GENERAL', 'MARKET-BASED', 'POTENTIAL' END-USE

Which evidential elements can be referred to in identifying such physical similarities or functional interchangeability between products under consideration? In contrast to the previous matter of the conceptual classification of likeness or substitutability, on which the GATT/WTO panels have (except for announcing the existence of the 'accordion') shied away from putting forth guidelines, the panels have established quite a solid jurisprudence on the present subject matter.

One of the common denominators confirmed by the GATT/WTO panels is that there exist common elements to be taken into account when determining the likeness or substitutability of products. In other words, despite the lack of textual guidance in the GATT, the panels have developed some rules of general application in regard to the definition of 'likeness'. The Report of the Working Party on *Border Tax Adjustments* (BTA) set out the basic elements of consideration for the interpretation of 'like or similar products' generally scattered through the various provisions of the GATT: the product's end-uses in a given market; consumers' tastes and habits, which change from country to country; and the product's properties, nature, and quality.[56] The Appellate Body announced that this approach was followed in almost all adopted panel reports after the *Border Tax Adjustments* Report.[57]

A close look at the above Report leads to the conclusion that the GATT likeness elements are (1) the properties of the product itself—its properties, nature, quality, and *end-use in general* (or general end-use)[58]—and tariff classification; and (2) the ways that products with such properties are treated by users and others—product *end-use in a given market* and consumers' tastes and habits.[59] In other words, the definition of 'like' products encompasses both more objective (apparent) elements, i.e. (1) above, and more invisible (market-based) elements, (2) above.[60]

2.1. From 'General' End-Use to 'Market-Based' End-Use Approach

In contrast to the fact that the above classification of elements has often been referred to, most panels have tended to narrow the scope of their consideration to more visible and objective elements such as product properties, general end-use, and tariff classification:

(1) In *EEC—Measures on Animal Feed Proteins*, the Panel, dealing with the issue of whether vegetable proteins and denatured skimmed milk powder were 'like' or 'directly competitive or substitutable' within the meaning of Arts I and III, considered such elements as the number of products and tariff items carrying different duty rates and tariff bindings, contents of protein, origin of the protein products, and end-uses.[61]

(2) In *Spain—Tariff Treatment of Unroasted Coffee*, the Panel noted, in the context of Art. I, 'organoleptic differences' resulting from geographical differences, cultivation methods, processing of beans, the genetic factor, the uniqueness of Spain's tariff regime, and end-uses.[62]

(3) In *United States—Taxes on Petroleum and Certain Imported Substances*, the Panel mainly focused on general end-uses in the Art. III:2 context.[63]

(4) In *United States Gasoline*, the Panel and the Appellate Body referred to 'the same physical characteristics, end-uses, tariff classification, and perfect substitutability' of conventional and reformulated gasoline as relevant elements in the context of Art. III:4.[64]

(5) In *Japan Wine and Liquor*,[65] the Panel focused mainly on general end-uses in an Art. III:2 context.[66]

(6) In *Japan Alcoholic Beverages*, the Panel and the Appellate Body referred to physical characteristics, general end-uses, and tariff classifications with regard to the interpretation of 'like' products in the first sentence of Art. III:2.[67]

Thus, one can say that in the 'like product' test of GATT, a preoccupation with objective elements, to the exclusion of any careful consideration of market-based elements, such as consumer preference, habit and tradition, is evident.[68] Notwithstanding this preoccupation, however, this objective-element approach itself is not contrary to the rules set in the *Border Tax Adjustments* Report. It would seem that the statement, '. . . *a fair assessment in each case of the different elements* that constitute a "similar" product' sets a ceiling on the number of elements to be considered without making reference to a minimum requirement, so that subsequent panels could choose any combinations of elements from the pool. Due to this carefully designed language, subsequent panels that did not carefully consider invisible elements seem not to be inconsistent with the Report.

It should be noted, however, that this rule—reinforced by subsequent panels' adoption—has engendered a substantial flexibility in choosing likeness elements.[69] One might argue that allowing for this flexibility excuses any lack of analytical methodology in carrying out a 'likeness' test. Furthermore, it might be a tacit

expression of panels' willingness to react to, according to circumstances, the resulting pressures, if any, coming from outside; or, at least, an announcement of willingness to entertain a time benefit until the point of accumulation of a substantial
number of cases.[70]

The panels' preoccupation with objective criteria is particularly borne out with
respect to understanding 'end-use'. Interpreting the concept, GATT panels have
heavily relied upon examination of 'end-use *in general*' rather than 'end-use *in the
given market*':[71]

(1) In *EEC Animal Feed Proteins*, the Panel focused on the 'technically substitutable
    nature' of vegetable proteins and denatured skimmed milk powder in terms of
    their 'protein source for use in feeding stuffs for animals'.[72]
(2) In *Spain Unroasted Coffee*, the Panel's attention was mostly aimed at the fact that
    coffee was 'universally regarded as a well-defined and single product intended
    for drinking'.[73]
(3) In *Canada Periodicals*, the Panel and the Appellate Body rejected Canada's argu-
    ment that whereas the end-use of US magazines was as vehicles for informa-
    tion, that of Canadian magazines was as vehicles for entertainment and
    communication.[74]
(4) In *Japan Wine and Liquor*, the Panel prescribed that the various alcoholic bever-
    ages in question had a common end-use, i.e. they were a 'well defined and
    single product intended for drinking'.[75]

Among these, one might nominate the Japanese Panel as the leader of the universal
end-use approach or, more broadly, the 'objective-element approach'. Justifying its
reliance on this approach, the Panel explicitly described its philosophy:

. . . even though the Panel was of the view that the 'likeness' of products must be examined
taking into account not only objective criteria (such as composition and manufacturing
processes of products) but also the more subjective consumers' viewpoint (such as consumption and use by consumers), the Panel agreed with the arguments . . . that Japanese
shochu (Group A) and vodka could be considered as 'like' products in terms of Article III:2
because they were both white/clean spirits, made of similar raw materials, and their
end-uses were virtually identical (either as straight 'schnaps' type of drinks or in various
mixtures). Since consumer habits are variable in time and space and the aim of Article III:2
of ensuring neutrality of internal taxation as regards competition between imported and
domestic like products could not be achieved if *differential taxes could be used to crystallize consumer preferences* for traditional domestic products, the Panel found that the traditional
Japanese consumer habits with regard to shochu provided no reason for not considering
vodka to be a 'like' product.[76]

The original form of this philosophy—that 'differential treatment should not be
used to crystallize consumer preferences'—can be found in one of the decisions of
the European Court of Justice concerning the interpretation of EC Treaty Art. 95
(now Art. 90).[77] In *UK Taxes on Wine and Beer*,[78] the Court ruled that 'the tax
policy of a Member State must not crystallize given consumer habits, essentially

variable in time and space, so as to consolidate an advantage acquired by national industries concerned to respond to them'.[79]

Looking at this decision, one should not disregard the fact that Art. 90 (ex Art. 95) of the EC Treaty is 'planted' in a different 'soil' from Art. III of the GATT. Although the two treaties are directed at a common goal of 'improvement of standards of living through expansion of trade',[80] the EC Treaty and the GATT both possess different characters (regional arrangement as opposed to multilateral treaty) and, thus, adopt fairly different paths. Whereas the GATT is an instrument to 'eliminate discriminatory treatment',[81] the EC Treaty is geared towards the 'harmonization' and 'unification of the people of Europe'.[82]

This difference is clearly expressed in the language used in Art. III of the GATT and Art. 90 (ex Art. 95) of the EC Treaty. The language of the EC Treaty is straightforward and starts with a sweeping prohibition, whereas that of the GATT is *cautious*.[83] The national treatment of GATT, based on the premiss of full tax autonomy preserved for each member state, prescribes a boundary beyond which such autonomy ceases to exist. That is, Art. III (and the GATT generally) is relevant only in the area of discrimination, *de jure* or *de facto*.[84]

Having made a distinction between the European law and the GATT, one is able to ask a well-informed question: If certain traditional consumer preferences or habits result in substantial differences in usage in the market between the two products in question that have similar end-uses in general, should the country be obliged to impose the same tax on both products? Certainly, the answer would be 'Yes' for the European Court of Justice; different traditional preferences do not help, and indeed do harm to, the *'harmonization* and *unification* of the *people* of Europe'. Is the same answer guaranteed under the General Agreement?

Approaching this difficult question, one needs to understand that it is possible that two products that brag of a perfect substitutable relationship in market A may *not* be 'competitive', or at least 'not directly competitive', in market B. This is because substitutability is decided in the market in question, and the condition of each market, reflecting the accumulated consumers' tastes and habits, could be substantially different. A specific example in this regard may be sought by scrutinizing an analogy raised at a preparation committee for the GATT. Providing an explanation of the language of the second sentence of Art. III:2, the Geneva Session of the Preparatory Committee noted that *apples* and *oranges* could be directly competitive or substitutable.[85]

No general classification should be permitted, however. If the market concerned is a *desert area*, all kinds of juicy fruit may be directly substitutable for one another; even water could be considered a directly substitutable product for oranges. On the other hand, if oranges and apples are sold in a *humid area*, and the people in the region are very sensitive about taste, those people might think that the two products are not directly substitutable and, accordingly, the end-use of the two products in the market would be different. In this situation, if the country located in a *desert area* imposes a tax on various fruit that is 'proportional' to their respective water content, is this tax measure 'crystallizing' consumer habits?[86]

Not only traditional habits rooted in geographical conditions, but also social or cultural environments affect market condition. One should not disregard the fact (or possibility) that there are (or could be) certain traditional preferences or perceptions that are too entrenched to be changed, or at least to be changed in the near future.[87] Can the General Agreement obligate Hindus to impose the same tax on both *beef* and pork? Can any tribunal obligate Americans to levy the same tax on *dog meat* as on pork? Is America 'crystallizing' its traditional consumer preferences by not imposing the same tax on both dog meat and pork? What about taxes on dog meat and live dogs?[88]

Here arises a fundamental dilemma of GATT law: while reduction of differences in preferences among countries might be able to facilitate a freer flow of trade,[89] should we allow the international tribunal to order preference changes, even in cases in which such preferences are deeply rooted (or at least not changeable in the near future)? Is it not possible that such judicial activism will end up generating political trouble for the government concerned and fail to facilitate free trade?[90] Indeed, it is difficult to give full support to the Japanese Panel's reasoning after all of these questions.

The point is that the Panel is missing one link in the chain of its reasoning (without prejudice to its conclusion). To simplify, the Panel's reasoning is: 'Different tax treatment of a product that is purchased by people possessing different habits should be condemned because it makes the habits permanent (crystallization); this is why we do not consider consumer habits in determining likeness.' The missing point is that not all tax based on different consumer habits crystallizes consumer habits: higher tax on beef has not crystallized Hindus' preference for pork. Hence, the Panel should have examined whether the different tax imposed on shochu and vodka *would be likely to crystallize* consumer habits in Japan, just as any panel examining likeness between dog meat and pork should do. In other words, if the force of condemnation comes from the possibility of crystallizing consumer habits (thereby depriving imports of competitive opportunities), one should at least pay due attention to the 'possibility'.

No consideration was given to this point by the Japanese Panel: the tribunal simply assumed that all taxes imposed differently according to different consumer habits would result in such crystallization because *all consumer habits are variable*.[91] What the Panel in *Japan Wine and Liquor* ultimately succeeded in proving was little more than the truth, that nothing is permanent under the sun, including the sun itself.

This is not to argue that all consumer tastes or habits are relevant in determining 'likeness'. The argument is that certain consumer habits are *intertwined with market conditions so strongly and steadily* that the former cannot be conveniently separated from the latter. Indeed, such habits survive as long as the market goes on. Taking account of these 'obvious' elements does not make the GATT likeness test unstable. Sometimes, controversial cases might be raised concerning the strength and stability of the consumer habits in question. Thus, 'evidence' from a market-based economic analysis will be needed in order to invite the panel to take account of such market-based elements.

Recently, with respect to the interpretation of 'directly competitive or substitutable' in the second sentence of Art. III:2, the Appellate Body in *Japan Alcoholic Beverages* put forward a new approach, which explicitly endorsed the need to look not only at such elements as physical characteristics, common end-uses, and tariff classifications, but also at the 'marketplace'.[92] This is an endorsement for the Panel's unusual announcement in the same case that 'two products could be considered to be directly competitive or substitutable in *market A*, but the same two products would not necessarily be considered to be directly competitive or substitutable in *market B*'.[93]

One could say that this emphasis on the marketplace reflects a 'new trend' in likeness or substitutability tests, but it should be noted that this is not a 'new invention' of the Appellate Body. What it means, or at least what it results in, is a revival of the market-based factors already indicated in the *Border Tax Adjustments* Report.

As a result of this trend, mere references to similar physical characteristics, 'general' end-uses, and/or the same tariff classification are not enough; a balanced consideration should be given to the marketplace. In other words, whether consumers in the relevant market consider the two products in question to be sufficiently competitive or substitutable has become an important element to be taken into account. In order to examine the marketplace, the body acknowledged that the existence of the common end-use between products in comparison should play a decisive role.[94]

Hence, the essence of the change (or new trend) of the Appellate Body's position lies in a shift of focus of analysis from end-uses *in general*[95] to end-uses *in the given market*, in addition to such traditional analyses as physical characteristics and tariff classifications. This new trend can be called the '*market-based end-use* approach' in comparison to the old '*general end-use* approach'.[96]

This Appellate Body's endorsement of the market-based end-use approach applies to the 'like product' test as well as to the 'directly competitive or substitutable product' test. This point was recently confirmed by the Appellate Body in *EC Asbestos*, in which the Panel's ruling on 'likeness' in the context of GATT Art. III:4 was reversed by the reason of lack of the market-based approach.[97] According to the *EC Asbestos* Appellate Body, an examination of the market-based evidence relating to consumers' tastes and habits is an 'indispensable (although not, on its own, sufficient) aspect' of any determination that products are like under Art. III:4. In other words, each and every criterion stated in the *Border Tax Adjustments* Report must be 'examined and weighed in making an overall determination'.[98] In any event, as indicated by the Panel in *Japan Alcoholic Beverages*, 'like products' should be viewed as being a subset of 'directly competitive or substitutable products', and all 'like products' are, by definition, 'directly competitive or substitutable products'.[99]

Specific application of the market-based approach necessitates the following delicate distinction between the 'likeness' and 'substitutability' tests, as the

Japanese Panel indicates:

In the Panel's view, the decisive criterion in order to determine whether two products are directly competitive or substitutable is whether they have *common end-uses, inter alia, as shown by elasticity of substitution*. The wording of the term 'like products' however, suggests that commonality of end-uses is a necessary but not a sufficient criterion to define likeness. In the view of the Panel, the term 'like products' suggests that for two products to fall under this category they must share, *apart from commonality of end-uses, essentially the same physical characteristics*. In the Panel's view its suggested approach has the merit of being functional, although the definition of likeness might appear somewhat 'inflexible'. Flexibility is required in order to conclude whether two products are directly competitive or substitutable. In the Panel's view, the suggested approach can *guarantee the flexibility required*, since it permits one to take into account specific characteristics in any single market; consequently, two products could be considered to be directly competitive or substitutable in market A, but the same two products would not necessarily be considered to be directly competitive or substitutable in market B.[100]

Accordingly, whether the products in question are 'like' or 'directly competitive or substitutable' hinges on the commonality of end-uses *in the given market*; and, in the case of a 'like' product test, an additional requirement of commonality in essential physical characteristics is needed. Furthermore, as a methodology of examining the market-based end-use, the Panel and the Appellate Body suggest an economic analysis (elasticity of substitution), with a caveat that this is not the only method.[101]

With regard to the methodology to be employed, the *Japan Alcoholic Beverages* Panel has given some indications. In this case, the Panel noted a time-series analysis showing that as a result of the 1989 Japanese tax reform, the market share of domestic whisky fell;[102] and that this, according to the European Communities' evidence, led to a rise of both shochu's and foreign produced whisky's market shares in Japan.[103] Evaluating this analysis, the Panel held that 'the fact that foreign produced whisky and shochu were competing for the same market' might be used as evidence that there is an elasticity of substitution between them.[104]

In fact, the Japanese Panel's attention was more heavily focused on the result of a study by ASI Market Research (ASI Study) and a survey submitted by Japan, which were static demand elasticity analyses, than on the results of time-series and historical studies.[105] Against the survey that showed that between 4 and 10 per cent of consumers would switch from shochu to whisky or vice versa respectively if one was not available any more (Non-Availability Analysis), the Panel ruled that: '. . . in case of non-availability of shochu, 10 per cent of the consumers would switch to spirits and whisky. This, in the Panel's view, was proof of significant elasticity of substitution between shochu, on the one hand, and whisky and spirits, on the other.'[106] According to the Panel and the Appellate Body, a 10 per cent switch is a 'significant' substitution.[107]

Indeed, this preference for the static cross-price elasticity method by the Japanese Panel is well shown from the following statement:

In the Panel's view, the decisive criterion in order to determine whether two products are directly competitive or substitutable is whether they have common end-uses, *inter alia*, as

shown by elasticity of substitution...its suggested approach has the merit of being functional...In considering the study, the Panel took account of the views of the parties and of
general econometric principles. The Panel noted that the extent to which two products are
competitive in economics is measured by the responsiveness of the demand for one product to the change in the demand for the other product (cross-price elasticity of demand).
The more sensitive demand for one product is to changes in the price of the other product, all other things being equal, the more directly competitive they are.... In the case of
product demand and product substitutability (i.e., the direct competitiveness of products),
the relevant information includes prices, quantities, and incomes. Ideally, one would like to
test for the relationship between the price of one product and the demand for another, all
other things being equal.[108]

From the above, it is interesting to see that even though in *Japan Alcoholic
Beverages* the 'universal' end-use philosophy of the Panel in *Japan Wine and Liquor*
(ten years earlier) was substantially amended to a new position of the 'market-
based' end-use approach, that restored the balance between the 'objective' and
'market-based' criteria,[109] the final determinations of the tribunals were virtually
the same: Japanese shochu and other imported liquors should be subject to the
same tax. The technique was in fact simple: lowering the threshold to be 'directly
substitutable' under the new market-based approach, as seen above.

Given the similarity of the subject matter, it is no wonder that this market-based
approach was followed by the WTO tribunals in *Korea Alcoholic Beverages* and *Chile
Alcoholic Beverages*.[110] The decision by the Korean tribunals relied heavily upon the
'merit' of the Dodwell Study,[111] which was a cross-price elasticity of demand
analysis similar to the ASI Study of the Japanese case. It is interesting to see that,
based on such a market-based approach, the Korean Panel paid attention to such
elements (in addition to traditional elements) as channels of distribution and points
of sale, price difference, other comparable markets, and, most importantly, potential competition.[112]

Similarly, the Chilean tribunals relied upon the results from the Search Marketing
Survey,[113] which was a combination survey of both non-availability analysis—
similar to the non-availability survey shown in *Japan Alcoholic Beverages*—and
the cross-price elasticity of demand analysis—similar to the ASI Study and the
Dodwell Study. In addition, against the Gemines Study,[114] in which a cross-price
elasticity of demand for pisco with respect to whisky turned out to be 0.26, the
Chilean Panel held that such a 'low' level of elasticity is 'not necessarily fatal to a
claim of direct competitiveness or substitutability', although a high coefficient of
cross-price elasticity would be 'important evidence to demonstrate that products
are directly competitive or substitutable, provided that the quality of the statistical
analysis is high'.[115]

In *Canada Periodicals*, Canada submitted the results of an economic study as
a means of showing the Panel the existence of only 'imperfect substitutability'
between Canadian and American magazines.[116] According to the study, Canadian
magazines had many functions, such as being an advertising medium and a medium

of communication; and although US magazines might be substitutable with Canadian magazines for the former function, they were not substitutable at all for the latter function because of differences in editorial content.[117] Against this argument, the Appellate Body stressed that perfect substitutability is not necessary for the substitutability put forth in the second sentence of Art. III:2.[118]

Looking at these decisions with regard to the methodology of examining market-based end-uses, what kinds of conclusions can one draw? First, although *Japan Alcoholic Beverages* provided a 'numerical' decision, the 10 per cent standard gives little assistance because:

(1) the non-availability analysis,[119] upon which the 10 per cent switch was based, does not reflect a real world situation: the absolute absence (non-availability) of one product as opposed to the full existence of the other competitive product is not likely to happen in the real market;

(2) even in the least likely of situations, in which the analysis acquires relevance, the non-availability analysis tends to exaggerate the switching rate: if a product is 'not available' any more, even the most faithful of consumers of the product in question would be forced to switch to other products;[120] thus

(3) one should use a cross-price-elasticity (or at least own-price-elasticity) analysis[121] to examine the end-use in the market, which will reflect a real world situation and internalize the price element that has the greatest effect on consumers' choice.

Secondly, dealing with the real world situation of cross-price elasticity, the Chilean Panel put forward a cautious statement that the elasticity of 0.26 (i.e. a 10 per cent rise in the price of whisky leads to an increase of 2.6 per cent in the demand for pisco) was 'low'.

Thirdly, in *Canada Periodicals* the Appellate Body did not elucidate further than to say that perfect substitutability is not needed in the Art. III:2 second sentence test.

Consequently, since the tribunals in all the cases listed above did not express a requirement in the test for a specific degree of 'minimum' substitution, the question of what degree of substitutability is necessary remains.

2.2. Up To 'Potential/Future' End-Use Approach

Korea Alcoholic Beverages deepened the concept of market-based end-use. The Korean Panel held that:

End-uses constitute one factor which is particularly relevant to the issue of *potential* competition or substitutability. If there are common end-uses, then two products may very well be competitive, either immediately or in the near and reasonably predictable future. In this regard, we do find it relevant, albeit of less relative evidentiary weight, to consider the nature of the competitive relationship in other markets. If two products compete in a market that is relatively less affected by government tax policies, it might shed light on whether those same two products are potentially competitive in the market in question. Such a comparison is not dispositive by any means; neither should it be ignored. Its relevance consists primarily in whether it tends to corroborate the trends seen in the market in question or whether it reveals inconsistencies with complainants' case that deserve further consideration. In this regard, we note that in Japan there was *increasing end-use substitutability* between western-style beverages and Japanese shochu as consumers became increasingly familiar with the new product. Both soju and shochu are traditional drinks in their respective countries. Both markets involved small but growing import penetration following partial liberalization. The trends that the panel and Appellate Body observed in Japan appear to be beginning in Korea.[122]

This is an announcement that the concept of end-use is determined under the additional dimension of 'potentiality'. Not only current end-use (in general or in the given market), but also 'potential' or 'future' end-use is relevant: according to the Panel, whether there is '*increasing* end-use substitutability' is important.[123]

Looking at the statement above, one might utilize the following metaphor: The Korean Panel, building a 'strong fence of potential competition' around the 'wild horse dubbed as Market-Based End-Use', is now enjoying its freedom or ability to look over the 'neighbor's ranch' and/or of speculating on future development of 'its own pasture'.

In fact, these concepts of potential and anticipatory substitutability have sufficient scope to be used as tools for excessive regulation of domestic policies: with such handy tools, virtually all products in question could be determined as 'directly competitive or substitutable' products. They might be used as fallback tools, being brought out whenever tribunals or complaining parties are incapable of finding empirical evidence. One can easily over-ride the horse in one's hands.

Moreover, these concepts enable panels to refer to other markets whenever they want, just as the Korean Panel referred to the Japanese market. No justification or evidence was given about why the Japanese market was comparable with the Korean market, except for a line of factual description that 'both soju and shochu are traditional drinks in their respective countries'. No careful consideration was given to whether trends in the Japanese market, where shochu and imported western-style beverages became increasingly used for the same purposes, would become a dominant trend in the Korean market in the near future. No timescale was suggested in regard to the interpretation of the word 'near'.[124] No empirical evidence was provided to show that there was enough 'potentiality' of substitution between soju and whisky. To all these problems, the Korean Panel could give only its standard answer—*unavoidable element of individual, discretionary judgement*.[125] In the end, the WTO tribunal seems to be equipped with an accordion in each hand—one being the traditional 'accordion of provision-by-provision'[126] and the other the brand-new 'accordion of potentiality'.[127] The tribunal could stretch and squeeze those powerful instruments, concurrently or *alternatively*, as much as it wants, as far as it wants, and case by case.

Hence, GATT tribunals' inquiry into evidential elements to define 'likeness' draws a long line from the 'universal' end-use concept, through 'market-based' end-use, up to 'potential' end-use. Conceptually, this is a desirable direction, for the GATT is, after all, an instrument used to protect the expectation of competitive opportunities in the market. The instrument should be capable of extending to the potential market as well as to the current one, as long as it aids global market governance. This does not mean, however, that the fundamental authority of the GATT justifies any sacrifice. As discussed above, there is a clear danger that the *market-based* end-use might become no different a concept from end-use *in general*, with the effective assistance (via the accordion) of *potential* end-use. At any rate, this trend does not, and should not, justify a return to the traditional approach, under which the 'end-use in general' played a decisive role, while market-based elements were largely disregarded. Rather, this should mean an improvement of likeness analysis and an attempt to keep pace with a changing environment, in which sophisticated justification rather than intuitive judgement is becoming indispensable. As more discretion is provided to the tribunal, so much responsibility should follow upon it. The concepts of future and potential end-use (or competition) should be evaluated with great care.

The 'end-use in general' provides a good preliminary clue as to whether products are 'like' or 'directly competitive or substitutable'. What transforms this clue into evidence, especially in difficult cases, is the 'market-based end-use' analysis. Examination of 'potential end-uses' completes the picture. How much evidential weight should be given to the three concepts depends upon the purpose of each provision at issue.

In this light, the Panel's approach in *Indonesia National Car*[128] provides a good example of the new market-based end-use analysis:

Turning first to the argument of the European Communities that all passenger cars should be considered 'like products' to the Timor, we consider that such a broad approach is not appropriate in this case. While it is true that all passenger cars 'share the same basic physical characteristics and share an identical end-use', we agree with Indonesia that passenger cars are highly differentiated products. Although the European Communities have not provided the Panel with information regarding the range of physical characteristics of passenger cars, all drivers know that passenger cars may differ greatly in terms of size, weight, engine power, technology, and features. The significance of these extensive physical differences, both in terms of the cost of producing the cars and in consumer perceptions regarding them, is manifested in huge differences in price between brands and models. It is evident that the differences, both physical and non-physical, between a Rolls Royce and a Timor are enormous, and that the degree of substitutability between them is very low. Viewed from the perspective of the SCM Agreement, it is almost inconceivable that a subsidy for Timors could displace or impede imports of Rolls Royces, or that any meaningful analysis of price undercutting could be performed between these two models. In short, we do not consider that a Rolls Royce can reasonably be considered to have 'characteristics closely resembling' those of the Timor.[129]

Special attention should be paid to the announcement by the Indonesian Panel that this market-based approach is equally relevant to the interpretation of 'like' products under the SCM Agreement, the first sentence of Art. III:2, and Art. I of the GATT.[130]

In short, although the market-based approach suggested by the WTO panels and the Appellate Body improved likeness or substitutability tests by restoring the balance between the objective and the market-based elements and by providing subsequent panels or member states with some methodological guidance, the tribunals' emphasis on discretionary judgement and the limited effect of economic analysis should be reviewed with a critical eye. Presently, it is a problem that such terms as 'like', 'directly', 'competitive', 'or', 'substitutable' and 'competition was involved'[131] are still vague. A more serious problem is that questions of how and why the definitions of these terms should vary from clause to clause and how much different interpretation of identical terms may be possible within a clause are left wholly unanswered.[132]

In particular, it should be noted that the Appellate Body in *Japan Alcoholic Beverages*, by stressing that an economic (elasticity of substitution) analysis should not be the decisive criterion, made these problems worse, because it actually relied heavily on the study of elasticity of substitution.[133] It can be argued that this dependence on studies of elasticity of substitution, combined with the Appellate Body's denial of the utility of the studies as *the* decisive criterion without giving any other decisive criteria, created confusion and hindered the predictability mandated by the DSU.[134] The same problem extends to *Korea Alcoholic Beverages*, in which no other decisive criteria were suggested by the Panel or the Appellate Body, except for an emphasis upon potential competition factors—yet another no less vague criterion.[135]

One might argue that this hesitancy reflects an effort to preserve a discretionary power for the international tribunal, or to highlight the necessity of its existence—'For further clarification, please return to our forum!'

As a result, evidentiary-type questions are left open, such as:

(1) What is the 'marketplace' mentioned by the Appellate Body, and how can it be considered when analyzing competitiveness or substitutability? In this regard, can consumer habits and preferences, which have been put aside in analyzing 'likeness' tests,[136] join 'competitiveness or substitutability' tests?

(2) In determining 'like' or 'directly competitive or substitutable' products, to what extent can economics play a role? To what extent should panels rely upon the *unavoidable element of individual, discretionary judgement*?

(3) If economic analysis is necessary, should static analysis carry more weight than dynamic and historical studies?[137] Or will well-established historical studies, which in contrast to the Japanese study are supported by a substantial amount of data and well-recognized techniques, prevail? Undergoing static analysis, should panels undertake a more economically rigorous approach, such as the cross-price elasticity analysis?[138]

(4) Where econometric and/or statistical analyses are performed, what degree of substitutability is legally required for products to be 'like' or 'directly competitive

or substitutable' products? Should panels turn to outside experts to proceed with the economic analysis, as provided for under Art. 13 of the DSU?[139]

(5) Should any supply-side impediments or elasticity be ignored?

(6) Lastly, what is potential end-use or competition, and how do we find it out? In the face of an apparent danger of vagueness or abuse, how can we take potentiality into consideration in the likeness determination?

Answers to these all questions ought to be duly provided.

3. ANALYTICAL FRAMEWORK FOR LIKENESS OR SUBSTITUTABILITY ANALYSIS

3.1. Relevant Market and Likeness or Substitutability

In order to proceed with a successful economic analysis by which comprehensive evidence can be taken to determine likeness or substitutability, the starting point should be a 'Relevant Market',[140] where all of these factors have been interacting and various useful clues to product relationship are latent. The GATT is a commercial agreement, and the WTO is concerned, after all, with markets.[141] Since markets are composed of many goods and actors, it is necessary to define and analyze a 'relevant market' that is directly related to the 'like' or 'directly competitive or substitutable' products in question. The European Commission provides an excellent definition of the 'relevant market' for the purposes of competition law:

A relevant product market comprises all those products and/or services which are regarded as interchangeable or substitutable by the consumer, by reason of the products' characteristics, their prices and their intended use ... The relevant geographic market comprises the area in which the undertakings concerned are involved in the supply and demand of products or services in which the conditions of competition are sufficiently homogeneous and which can be distinguished from neighbouring areas because the conditions of competition are appreciably different in those areas ... The relevant market within which to assess a given competition issue is therefore established by the combination of the product and geographic markets.[142]

Even though this definition was rendered for competition law purposes, the basic concepts and criteria used to define the relevant *product* market could be referred to in establishing whether products are 'like' or 'directly competitive or substitutable' for the purposes of GATT.[143] Bearing this point in mind, one can then proceed to examine relevant elements with which to define likeness or substitutability in the GATT.

There is a range of evidence that facilitates the assessment of the extent to which substitution would take place.[144] In individual cases, certain types of evidence will be determinant, depending very much on the characteristics and specificity of the products that are being examined.[145] In most cases, a decision will have to be based on consideration of a number of criteria, different pieces of evidence,[146] and factors comprising the relevant market.

One such factor, an analysis of the *product characteristics* and its *general use* (or end-use in general), allows, in the first step, limitation of the field of investigation of likeness or substitutability tests.[147] In many cases, indeed, examination of such objective characteristics can provide a reasonable conclusion with regard to product likeness or substitutability. In a substantial number of cases, however, product characteristics and general use are insufficient to determine whether two products are 'like' or 'directly substitutable'. Physical similarity or general functional interchangeability may not provide, in themselves, sufficient criteria, because the responsiveness of customers to relative price changes may be affected by other considerations as well.[148] For example, there may be different product substitutability or competitive constraints between the original equipment market for car components and the market for spare parts, thereby leading to a distinction of two relevant markets.[149] That is, even though there are strong similarities and functional interchangeability between original car components and spare parts, the two products can be not substitutable if, in reality, they appeal sufficiently to separate consumer groups.[150] As mentioned previously, Korean ginseng and Chinese ginseng cannot be considered to be directly substitutable on the Korean market despite their close similarity. Likewise, it might be argued that Korean people have a strong preference for their national alcoholic beverage, soju,[151] and that this preference has been reflected in the country's consumption pattern so persistently that it has resulted in a significant reduction in substitutability between soju and whisky.

Conversely, differences in objective characteristics are not in and of themselves sufficient to exclude product substitutability, because substitutability depends, to a large extent, on how customers value different characteristics.[152] This is the matter of *demand substitutability*, the second factor to be considered in likeness or substitutability analysis. The traditional preferences or consumer perceptions underlying demand substitutability can be changed unless they are persistent ones.[153] In addition, current discriminatory impediments in the market may have helped to create or freeze these preferences or perceptions. One needs in those circumstances to take into account the future or the distortion effect in order to allow for a possible transitional change to occur. The WTO tribunals, notably in *Korea Alcoholic Beverages*, tried this by intentionally paying less attention to preferences and perceptions in determining likeness and, thereby, broadly interpreting the scope of GATT obligations.

Even though the tribunals have rendered their decisions in reliance on poor evidence resulting from a lack of methodology, this effort by the tribunals may be supported by the basic objective of the GATT/WTO. The Agreement adopts as its principal goal the enhancement of economic efficiency by facilitating free trade. In particular, 'full employment and a large and steadily growing volume of real income and effective demand' are what the Agreement seeks to achieve through the '*optimal* use of the world's resources'.[154] For the 'effective demand' leading to economic efficiency, differentiation based on 'transitional' (not permanent) consumer preferences or perceptions could be undesirable, because it increases transaction costs and sometimes is used as an excuse for discriminatory treatment. Accordingly, our analysis needs to include *potential or future competition* as a valid factor with which to examine any possible developments of the market and potential substitution of products in it.[155]

The next factor to be included in the likeness or substitutability analysis involves supply-side considerations. The general practice of panels since the *Border Tax Adjustments* Report does not give due attention to *supply-side factors* such as supply substitutability,[156] supply-side impediments, and their possible development. Why should these supply-side considerations be disregarded in the likeness test?[157] Returning to the basic objective of the GATT will help to solve this conundrum.

One may recall the virtuous cycle of the GATT:

(1) The GATT primarily seeks to protect comparative advantage, which will lead to economic efficiency and ultimately *optimal* use of the world's resources.

(2) As an 'action agenda' to reach the path of economic efficiency and to achieve the ultimate goal, the General Agreement adopts the non-discrimination principle.

(3) Following this agenda, most 'like' provisions in the GATT are equipped with a common standard form of non-discrimination obligation, that members are prohibited from applying discriminatory treatment to foreign products so as to afford protection to other 'like' or 'directly competitive or substitutable' products.[158]

Therefore, the 'practical' objective of these provisions is principally directed towards prohibiting governments from intervening in the flow of comparative advantage between *products* and, thus, of competitive relationships between the *producers* of the products.[159] Indeed, in order to realize free trade through market openness, the protection of competitive relationships between product sectors obtained through GATT negotiations is indispensable.

It may be recalled that this methodological emphasis in approaching problems has brought about different 'primary' focuses between the GATT and competition law: the primary focus of the former's non-discrimination provisions is on the competitive relationship between *producers*; while that of the latter is on *consumer* welfare in each jurisdiction.[160] Of course, in the end, this producer orientation of the GATT is not in conflict with the consumer orientation of competition law. Realization of free trade through the producer-oriented approach will finally lead to an enhancement of *consumer* welfare[161] and to an optimal use of world *resources*,[162] which is the final goal of the General Agreement and world trade liberalization.

Having this aim of GATT in mind, one could ponder on whether or not the inclusion of a supply substitutability test in the likeness or substitutability determinations of the Agreement might enhance the goal. This is the 'general' examination, and its implications for each provision of GATT will be discussed in Chapter III.

The starting point is with pure *welfare economics*; we then move on to the *legal and policy considerations* under the GATT. This is designed to show that, if there are no meaningful problems under the latter considerations, the supply substitutability test should be included in the GATT likeness test under the former point of view that encourages its inclusion.

It will be helpful to take a hypothetical case involving the national treatment obligation, the most frequently invoked obligation concerning the product likeness or substitutability problem. Suppose country X imposes a higher tax on product B, *imported* from country Y, than on domestic product A. The domestic production of B in country X, the importation of B from any third country into country X, and the production of A in country Y are assumed to be negligible.[163] The 'short-run' and 'long-run' effects[164] of the tax measure could be examined respectively, based on the two-sector equilibrium model of economics under the competitive market structure[165] in each of the following *situations*.

First, suppose that, in country X, *demand substitutability* between A and B is *high* in actuality, and *supply substitutability* between the two products is *high* as well (SITUATION I):

(1) *Short-run effect*—Producers of B will try to transfer the tax burden to consumers by raising price of B (from S to S/tax in sector B: *see* Appendix II).[166] But since consumers soon change their consumption to the highly substitutable product A, the price of B will not rise much.[167] In sector B, a new equilibrium will be formed at much lower numbers of transactions without much of a price increase (*see* Q_B^* in Appendix II), to the substantial detriment of the foreign producer of B. By contrast, the increasing demand in sector A (because of demand substitution) will increase the price of A and result in a new equilibrium (Q_A^*) that will be formed with the increased number of transactions under the competitive market structure.[168] This additional number of transactions, supplied by the increase in domestic production of A, will create a larger producer surplus for the domestic producer of A[169] as opposed to a decreased producer surplus for the foreign producer in sector B. With this said, what is the effect on consumers of country X? Consumers of B are forced to switch their consumption from B to A and have to pay more to buy A. But assuming that the tax revenue taken by government X is efficiently distributed to consumers through various welfare policies, the overall loss to consumers would not be large if the benefits from those welfare policies could compensate a substantial portion of the loss. After all, consumers in country X will avoid the worst situation because they will be able to switch their consumption to another highly substitutable product. To summarize, in the short run, the discriminatory tax measure will change the competitive relationship between *producers*, while loss of *consumer* welfare will not be substantial under the appropriate governmental policy.

(2) *Long-run effect*—Because there is high supply substitutability between sectors A and B, the foreign company will switch its production from sector B to sector

A and export product A to country X,[170] thereby sharing the increased producer surplus in sector A with the domestic producer of country X (at Q_A^{**}). Or, if any third producer enters the profitable A market, the domestic producer of A, the foreign producer switching away from B, and the third producer will divide the surplus in sector A. Either way, this supply substitution will more or less mitigate the short-run disadvantage for the foreign producer, which can be called the *mitigation effect*. In other words, in the long run, the tax discrimination will not largely change the overall competitive relationship between domestic and foreign *producers*. In the product B market in country X, decreased supply (due to a production switch) will meet demand at a higher price (at Q_B^{**}). By contrast, in market A, increasing supply (due to the switch) will form a new equilibrium at a lower price level (Q_A^{**}). On the other hand, the additional price rise of product B will induce additional demand substitution (pushing D/sub up to D/sub+ in sector A), which will generate more mitigation effect in sector A for the benefit of the foreign producer (at Q_{A+}^{**}). Overall price difference between sectors A and B would not be great (*compare the price level at Q_B^{**} with that at Q_{A+}^{**}*) in comparison with other situations below, indicating that the *product* relationship is not greatly worsened.[171] Consumers would not be greatly affected because increased unhappiness of consumers due to the price rise in both products would be more or less offset by their increased happiness under the appropriate governmental welfare policy. In the world market, a substantial portion of the product B sector will be replaced by an increased sector of product A, which will result in an altered distribution of resources between the two sectors. But considering that differences in productivity between the two sectors would not be large (which can be largely inferred from 'high supply substitutability'), one could not say that the new equilibrium (Q_B^{**},Q_{A+}^{**}) deviates far from the point for the *optimal* use of world resources (Q_B,Q_A). In other words, the 'deadweight loss'[172] in sector B, caused by the restriction of consumption and production below the efficient level that is achieved in the market prior to the tax imposition, would be more or less fixed by the increased producer and consumer surpluses in sector A ('deadweight gain') generated by additional consumption and production.

To summarize, in the short run, tax discrimination between products having both high demand and high supply substitutability would bring about a substantial change in the competitive relationship between *producers*, but the long-run effect of supply substitution will mitigate this detrimental impact on *producers*. Also, the overall impact on consumers and on distribution of world *resources* would not be substantial.[173] Appendix II, SITUATION I graphically demonstrates this whole process.

Secondly, suppose in market X there exist *high demand substitutability* and *low supply substitutability* between products A and B (SITUATION II). Similar to SITUATION I, the short-run effect of the measure would be great on the *producer* relationship (*compare Q_B^* with Q_A^**). Moreover, this short-run disadvantage against the foreign producer will not be mitigated in the long run in that, since the foreign producer of product B cannot easily switch his or her production resources from B to A, the only choice for the producer is to reduce production of B according to shrinking demand (up to Q_B^{**}) without much increase of overall price. Accordingly, the foreign industry would experience, *ceteris paribus*, unemployment and excessive production facility,[174] unless it could effectively find other markets for product B.[175] Free from the concern about market entry by the foreign industry (i.e. a switch from B to A by the foreign producer), the domestic producers of A would enjoy benefits from the additional production and price increase, or, at least, share the benefits with a third party in the case of new entry. But this increased transaction in sector A will not be large enough to generate consumer and producer surpluses to the extent of compensating the deadweight loss created in sector B.[176] Consumers would not be greatly affected: their increased unhappiness due to a rise in price of both products could be more or less offset by their increased happiness under the appropriate governmental welfare policy. To summarize, the discriminatory measure between products having high demand and low supply substitutability would result in a distortion in the competitive relationship between *producers* as well as in the distribution of world *resources* (*see* Appendix II, SITUATION II).[177]

Thirdly, suppose the situation of *low demand substitutability* and *high supply substitutability* (SITUATION III):

(1) *Short-run effect*—As a result of the price increase in sector B caused by the imposition of the discriminatory tax, most consumers of product B would reduce their amount of consumption without switching from their favourite item (low demand substitutability). A new equilibrium will be formed in the product B market via the higher price and fewer numbers of transactions (Q_B^*), which would cut both consumer and supplier surpluses: consumers of B would suffer because they have to pay a higher price,[178] and the producers of B would suffer because they have to pay a portion of the tax burden from their surplus and, in addition, reduction of production deprives them of the potential profits that could be obtained by further production (deadweight loss on the production side).[179] Although, through the effective return of the tax revenue collected by the measure, consumer loss could be minimized, the 'deadweight loss' of efficiency, generated by the reduction of transaction level, remains; it should be noted that, different from SITUATIONS I and II, there are little increased surpluses in sector A.[180]

(2) *Long-run effect*—Taking account of the long-run supply-side effect could bring mixed results to the losses of producer and consumer surpluses. Since there is high supply substitutability between sectors A and B, the foreign producers of B might want to switch some of their resources to the production of A, if it is more profitable.[181] If this switch were to occur, a new equilibrium would be formed in sector A with a lower price (Q_A^{**}), and in sector B with a higher

price (Q_B^{**}). As a result, B's consumers in country X would suffer more—they would increasingly compete against one another to obtain the smaller quantity that is available[182]—while consumers of A would enjoy lower prices. Therefore, the long-run effect on total *consumer* welfare is not certain.[183] With regard to the effect on *producer* surplus, it can be said that the profit obtained by supply substitution will make the foreign producer better off by allowing him or her to recover more or less from short-run losses. By contrast, the decrease in the price of A would reduce the producer surplus of domestic producers of A.[184] Thus, the short-run surplus gap between domestic and foreign *producers* will be reduced (*mitigation effect*). By contrast, the long-run effect on *product* relationships could be larger than the effect in the short run if supply substitution occurs: the price gap between A and B becomes larger in the long run.

To summarize, one can conclude that price distortion created by tax discrimination between products having low demand and high supply substitutability would certainly change the competitive relationship between domestic and foreign producers in the short run, but this distortion could be reduced in the long run according to the mitigation effect of the supply substitution. If supply substitution occurred, it would make a secondary impact on product relationship through price change, but the overall impact on consumers is not likely to worsen (*see* Appendix II, SITUATION III).[185]

Fourthly, suppose the situation of *low demand substitutability* and *low supply substitutability* (SITUATION IV). Product B market will have a new equilibrium on higher price. But this makes little impact upon product A or producers of A. There will be no significant movement of consumers or resources between the two sectors. They are effectively sealed off from interaction. Absence of the mitigation effect by supply substitution would make the foreign producer suffer more than in SITUATION III (*see* Appendix II, SITUATION IV).

What about the situation in which *demand substitutability* is '*slightly*' *lower or higher* than the threshold level and *supply substitutability* is *high* (SITUATION V)? An important point is that high supply substitutability between sectors A and B gives a flexibility of production switch to the producers of the foreign product at a short-run disadvantage. Such flexibility would provide a useful opportunity to mitigate the foreign producer's loss caused by the discrimination. This increased opportunity would be greater if there were a substantial amount of switch in consumption: the higher the demand substitutability, the more transactions of product A will occur. Thus, in the present situation, this 'mitigation effect' would not be as large as in SITUATION I, but it would not be as small as in SITUATION III because the demand substitution in the present situation would be in between SITUATIONS I and III. Furthermore, it is most likely that the impact on consumer welfare in the present situation would also be in between SITUATIONS I and III, because the demand substitution would be in between those situations while there exists the same degree of supply substitutability.

By contrast, one cannot expect this mitigation effect by way of high supply sub-stitutability in the situation of *medium demand substitutability–low supply substitutabil-ity* (SITUATION VI). Thus, the overall impact on the relationship between producers would be more benign in SITUATION V than in SITUATION VI.

Having examined the basic situations, then, what kinds of conclusions can one draw? Among many possible ones, the following deals with a matter of focus: *High supply substitutability mitigates distortion in competitive relationships between foreign and domestic producers generated by discriminatory measures.*[186] As seen from the above examples, the distortion effect is greater in SITUATIONS II, IV, and VI (low supply substitutability cases) than in SITUATIONS I, III, and V (high supply substitutability cases) respectively. The logical corollary is that the necessity to provide certain pro-tection under the GATT by determining products as 'like or directly competitive or substitutable' is greater in the former type of situations, in which more distor-tion occurs due to low supply substitutability.

Can this conclusion be generalized throughout the GATT likeness provisions? By restructuring the hypothetical problem in the context of national treatment to that of the most-favoured-nation (MFN) context, one can confirm that the con-clusion holds in other provisions of the GATT, at least in those in which the com-mon standard form of the non-discrimination formula is used. Suppose another country, Z, exports product C to country X; in country X's market, product B of country Y and product C of country Z are imported. Country X then imposes a higher tax on B than on C. Replacing A with C in the original national treatment hypothetical, a similar conclusion can be sustained here in the context of MFN: price distortion created by tax discrimination between B and C would certainly affect the competitive relationship between producers of B and C in the short run, and this effect could be mitigated in the long run according to the supply substitution. This mitigation effect becomes greater in cases in which demand substitutability is higher, that is, the effect is great in SITUATION III, greater still in SITUATION V, and greatest in SITUATION I.

It can be easily understood that this conclusion holds when types of discrim-inatory measures other than taxes are utilized. Tariffs or quantitative restrictions play a similar role in raising the price of imports, or of providing protection for domestic industry. Foreign producers who are at a short-run disadvantage can mit-igate their losses by switching away from high tariff or restricted product sectors to the favoured sectors.

According to the specific context of the provision at issue, the degree or extent to which the mitigation effect is considered in the likeness or substitutability determination may vary. It should be noted that some provisions might not allow such a complementary role for the supply substitutability factor because of their purposes and/or structural problems. This contextual analysis of the factor will be treated further in Chapter III.

So, can the above conclusion based on origin-neutral (*de facto*) discrimination cases hold in cases of origin-based (facial) discrimination?[187] It should be noted that, in the case of origin-based discrimination, high supply substitutability does not function well. In other words, since foreign producers cannot switch production to the favoured sector of 'domestic-origin' goods, high supply substitutability between the two products in comparison can play only a limited role, if any. To mitigate the disadvantage caused by origin-based discrimination, the foreign producers must find other markets that are free from such discrimination, or establish production facilities in the territory of the regulating state through, for example, foreign direct investment. This task is in many cases impossible, or at least will involve huge additional expense: the mitigation effect virtually will be inert. As a result, the foreign producers in SITUATIONS I, III, and V above (high supply-substitution situation) would suffer more losses under origin-based discrimination than in the origin-neutral discrimination cases. In contrast, domestic producers of favoured goods could now have more flexibility; they could switch to the other sector as necessary (since under origin-based discriminations, they are free from paying the higher burden, including higher tax rates) to completely absorb, or share with other domestic new entrants, the domestic demand for both goods.[188]

In short, since origin-based discrimination will suppress the mitigation effect, one loses ground with regard to the inclusion of the supply substitutability factor in the GATT likeness test. Thus, in origin-based discrimination cases, demand substitutability should play a decisive role in the market-based economic analysis.

Having concluded the examination from the point of view of welfare economics, it is possible to derive the logical corollary that the likeness determination based on demand substitutability alone would sometimes (in origin-neutral discrimination cases) result in digression from the efficiency rule. According to the demand-side-only approach, products A and B will be determined as 'like or directly competitive or substitutable' not only in SITUATION II above, but also in SITUATION I. This result, of *total* inclusion of SITUATION I in the likeness definition (without considering the mitigation effect), might cause an 'over-inclusiveness' in the likeness or substitutability protection of the GATT in origin-neutral discrimination cases. Moreover, because the demand-side-only approach does not make distinctions between SITUATIONS V and VI, it is not difficult to predict that not only over-inclusiveness would occur (in SITUATION V), but also 'under-inclusiveness' (in SITUATION VI).

One should bear in mind, however, that this evaluation is from the point of view of welfare economics and efficiency, and has yet to be filtered through the perspectives of law and diplomacy. Other than pure economic considerations, these perspectives require textual, contextual, teleological, and policy-oriented analyses.

The first step is the textual analysis. The GATT, as a treaty, should be interpreted in good faith in accordance with the ordinary meaning to be given to the terms in their context and in the light of the treaty's object and purpose.[189] Adopting treaty terms such as 'like product', 'like merchandise', 'like commodity', 'directly competitive or substitutable product', 'directly competitive product', and 'directly substituted product',[190] the General Agreement does not give any explicit clues as to their meaning. Hence, questions are left open as to whether these terms are based on (1) the consumer's perspective on demand substitution; (2) the producer's perspective on demand substitution;[191] (3) the producer's view on supply substitution; or (4) all or some combination of these perspectives.

According to the 'ordinary meaning' of these terms, it is not 'legally' deficient to define the product relationship in SITUATION I (high demand and supply substitutability) as being, *without exception*, 'like or directly competitive or substitutable'. Indeed, if *both* consumers and producers view certain *products* as highly substitutable, it is not possible to find any legal (textual) reason why those products should be determined as *not* being 'like or directly competitive or substitutable products'.[192] Hence, in SITUATION I, aspects of welfare economics, in general, and considerations of the mitigation effect, in particular, should give way to *the clear textual understanding of the General Agreement*. In other words, one need not consider the point that even if the like or substitutable relationship were denied in the situation,[193] it would not result in a substantial change in the competitive relationship between the domestic and foreign *producers* (due to the mitigation effect); neither would it affect *consumer* welfare in the long run (under the proper governmental welfare policy).[194]

The same rationale applies to SITUATION IV (low demand and supply substitutability) to yield the opposite result. When both consumers and producers view the products at issue as being rarely substitutable, those products should not be defined as 'like or directly competitive or substitutable products'. There will be little reason to condemn the tax measure imposing different rates on two products that are viewed as not being substitutable by both consumers and producers. The only rationale for such condemnation might be the global harmonization of the tax system, which is not acceptable at the current stage of world trading system.

In contrast to the above situations, in which the 'ordinary meaning' of the treaty text solves the problem, SITUATIONS II, III, V, and VI necessitate more complicated interpretations. Given a situation in which demand substitution is high and supply substitution low (SITUATION II), or vice versa (SITUATION III), or in which only some degree of demand substitutability exists (SITUATIONS V and VI), the examiner's dilemma is to determine which factor, as between demand and supply substitution, has to be predominant in defining likeness or substitutability.

Critics opposing the inclusion of the supply substitutability factor in a likeness test might propose that, because product similarity is after all determined in the market, the perspective of consumers, *as main actors*, should be decisive,[195] thereby suggesting the 'demand-substitutability-only' approach. It should be noted, however, that the plain meaning of the treaty terms of likeness or substitutability is flexible enough to accommodate all three perspectives mentioned above—the producer's views on supply substitution in addition to the consumer's and producer's views on demand substitution—particularly in regard to the interpretation of the term 'competitive'.[196] Therefore, the matter needs to go through the further stage of 'contextual and teleological' interpretation.

Opponents to the supply-substitutability approach might argue that the General Agreement, by articulating various obligations into 'product' relationships, reveals its short-run orientation. According to them, relying upon the aftermath of a long-run supply-side substitution would make the GATT obligations uncertain, and this uncertainty would put the foremost value of predictability in peril; the concept of likeness in GATT provisions should be defined only by demand substitutability—the most immediate and conspicuous factor concerning product relationships. Indeed, they might argue that, by relying exclusively upon the demand substitutability factor in the likeness test, GATT drafters wanted to provide effective armour for the competitive relationship between products.

It is true that demand substitutability deserves a predominant position in the determination of likeness or substitutability, because it provides the most immediate and conspicuous factor concerning the competitive relationship between products. This does not mean, however, that other factors cannot play a complementary role in the process. As long as the ordinary meaning of the treaty language allows for other factors, and the purpose of the General Agreement is thus enhanced, such a complement should be encouraged.

The supply substitutability analysis plays this complementary role in the GATT likeness test. This function is best exercised in SITUATIONS V and VI, in which the tribunals, faced with difficult cases of *de facto* discrimination, are presented with controversial results from a demand substitutability test. In these situations, without considering supply substitutability, many tribunals would not be able to render decisions tailored to the GATT objective, as discussed in the hypothetical situations. Moreover, in a situation in which demand substitutability tests *fail to produce* sufficient clues as to product likeness or substitutability, a credible result of supply substitutability between the products can provide the examiner with a good chance to reflect policy orientation on the likeness test.

This orientation may be stated as follows: High supply substitutability (SITUATION V) would produce high mitigation effects through supply substitution, which will recover, to a certain degree, the competitive opportunities between producers of the products in question, whereas low supply substitutability (SITUATION VI) does not generate this effect. Hence, the foreign producer who is at a disadvantage needs more protection in SITUATION VI than in SITUATION V, which can be achieved by tying the foreign product to the 'like or directly competitive or substitutable' relationship with the domestic product.[197]

The ultimate role of the 'likeness tool' built into most of the GATT likeness provisions should extend beyond catching only immediate and conspicuous threats of discrimination. As the aim of these provisions is to protect the expectation of competitive relationships, there is little reason why the long-run repercussions of the threats, which can be internalized by the supply substitutability analysis, should not be considered. Such long-run consideration does not make the GATT system uncertain or unpredictable. Not only demand substitutability, but also supply substitutability are 'irresistible' forces for reasonable producers; supply substitutability is a legitimate factor constituting competitive *opportunity* between producers. Analyzing supply substitutability together with demand substitutability would make likeness or substitutability analysis more complete, to be in line with the GATT's objectives.

Nonetheless, one can expect that the most analytical criticism of the inclusion of the supply substitutability factor might be founded on the 'division of labour' between the elements that one has to establish in many of the cases of violation of GATT non-discrimination provisions. Such elements are: (1) products in comparison are like products; (2) less favourable treatment is given to the foreign product of the complaining party; and (3) there is no justification for such discrimination.

In this three-prong test, the opponents to the supply substitutability analysis might argue that the supply substitutability factor should be considered, if it has to be considered at all, in the second prong, instead of the first. In other words, there should be a kind of division of labour between demand substitutability, which is employed exclusively to examine the first prong, and supply substitutability, which belongs to the second.

It is true that the supply substitutability factor could be examined in the second stage. Since one aim of the GATT non-discrimination provisions is to protect 'competitive opportunities' between the two product sectors in question, if a producer of a less-favourably-treated product can easily switch production out of the disadvantaged sector, one might be able to say that such discrimination does not inflict much harm to the competitive *opportunities*, thereby not constituting the 'less favourable treatment'. Logically and practically, however, this point does not totally discount the utility of the supply substitutability factor in the first prong test. One should note that the second prong examination of the 'less favourable treatment' does not exist in many likeness provisions of the GATT, e.g., Art. III:2, first sentence, and most likeness provisions other than the non-discrimination clauses. In these provisions, the only way in which the supply substitutability factor (thus, policy consideration) could be considered is through a likeness test (the first stage) itself.

Moreover, even in the non-discrimination clauses that have the second prong test for determining violation, it is not illogical or undesirable to consider supply substitutability in the second prong as well as in the first. Such a 'two-fold' consideration would enhance the objective of the GATT by eliminating the over-protection problem in determining 'like product' as well as in examining 'less favourable treatment'.

All the above insights lead one to conclude that supply substitutability should be included in the GATT likeness or substitutability test as a valid factor to be considered. But it should also be noted that the specific role of the factor is quite a limited one, being a complementary factor mostly in SITUATIONS V or VI, as already shown.

In real world situations, supply substitutability is not high in general.[198] Hence, in practice, the determination of likeness or substitutability will mostly be dependent upon the results of demand-substitutability analysis.[199] In other words, if two goods share high demand substitutability, they are likely to be determined as 'like or directly competitive or substitutable' products protected by the GATT jurisprudence. Thus, the practical role of the supply substitutability test can be played out in situations where *high* supply substitutability, combined with a *controversial* degree of demand substitutability, exists. Even if demand substitutability between the two products under consideration turned out to be a bit higher (or lower) than a certain threshold established in the context of each likeness provision, high supply substitutability could be invoked to determine the overall relationship between the products as being *not* 'like or directly competitive or substitutable'. Sometimes, if a demand substitutability test does not produce a definitive result, credible results from the supply substitutability test could be referred to with more weight in overall determinations.[200]

Throughout the long history of GATT/WTO likeness cases, only one case seems to demonstrate the complementary role of the supply substitutability test—*United States Automobiles*.[201] Dealing with the US luxury tax that imposed a higher rate on cars costing more than $30,000, the US Panel emphasized that a high selling price did not appear to be 'inherent' to EC or other foreign automobiles, and that EC, US, and Japanese manufacturers *could* produce cars on both sides of the threshold.[202] The Panel extended the 'inherency test' to analyze the other subject matter, the US gas-guzzler tax, which imposed different tax rates on cars above and below a 22.5 mpg threshold. Again finding that the nature of the distinction created by the threshold 'did not appear to create categories of inherently foreign or domestic origin', the Panel concluded that foreign automobiles below the 22.5 mpg threshold were 'unlike' domestic automobiles above the threshold. The Panel did not regard as being 'inherent' the fact that some producers concentrated on exporting luxury autos to the US market, since many had 'the design, production, and marketing capabilities to sell automobiles below the $30,000 threshold'.[203] Similarly non-inherent were the sale of high fuel consumption autos[204] and the choice not to export light trucks.[205]

From this inherency test, it is not difficult for reasonable people to identify a supply-substitutability-type analysis, although it is not explicit. In determining whether foreign luxury cars (costing over $30,000) were 'like' domestic small cars, and whether foreign cars polluting more (above the 22.5 mpg threshold) were 'like' products to the domestic cars that polluted less, the Panel took account of the fact, among others, that foreign car manufacturers could easily switch their production from the disadvantaged category to the favoured category. Even though there might be a substantial degree of demand substitutability, this relatively high degree of supply substitutability between the two categories was referred to as one of factors that led to the determination of 'unlikeness'.

In fact, under the inherency test, WTO members will have considerable discretion to adopt otherwise prohibited regulatory measures. So long as the measure seems rationally related to its purported purpose, the only major restriction under the measure would be provided by the need to avoid singling out 'inherently foreign' traits of goods.[206] The Panel's definition of 'inherently foreign' is very narrow; it seems to distinguish between characteristics of the foreign goods that are merely due to market specialization and characteristics that are inherent in the sense of being a necessary and unavoidable part of the foreign industry's position.[207] The decision suggests that in a substantial number of cases, a government will not be charged with a protective purpose, or effect, if its regulations target the existing market characteristics of a foreign producer.[208]

Despite the fact that this decision was based on the 'aim-and-effect' test,[209] which has been rejected by subsequent panels, and that the decision was not adopted by the Contracting Parties, the basic insight remains as 'useful guidance'[210] for future panels, waiting for the chance to be adopted by those panels as a valid element constituting the supply substitutability factor of the market-based approach, which is far more circumvention-proof than the aim-and-effect test.[211]

Current strict time limits for WTO panel deliberation, and the limited resources available to the tribunals, compel most panels to rely upon a formalistic approach in which the likeness concept is defined mostly by objective factors and by the discretionary judgement of the panel. Moreover, the seemingly bifurcated approach of the GATT non-discrimination provisions and Art. XX raises the dilemma that only a small amount of domestic policy autonomy is permitted under the latter provision.[212] Given that all regulatory measures impose some burdens on regulated businesses, and that such burdens are often distributed according to fortuitous market circumstances that are not even known (or at least not investigated) at the time the regulation is promulgated, the fact that in some cases a measure causes a disproportionate burden on foreign interests could be sometimes nothing more than a matter of random distribution of unintended effects.[213] In these circumstances, the complementary role of the supply substitutability factor could provide a likeness test with some range of flexibility within which the examiner could exercise policy considerations. Although it is not as great as that of the aim-and-effect theory, this flexibility would reflect a practical balance between the danger of the under-inclusiveness of violation that could result from the application of the aim-and-effect test, and that of the over-inclusiveness of violation that would most likely result from the application of the traditional *de facto* discrimination analysis, which sometimes sacrifices innocent, run-of-the-mill regulations along with devious, bad faith discriminations.[214] Hence, despite the superficial rigidity of Art. XX, the GATT could begin to evolve more flexible but tailored legal doctrines regarding facially neutral regulations. In this regard, the following remarks made by US Trade Representative Mickey Kantor right after the *United States Automobiles* decision, shed light: 'I would expect the panel's report to help steer the debate when GATT countries take up trade and environment issues under the new World Trade Organization'.[215]

Regardless of the depth or true meaning of these remarks, taking account of supply substitutability indeed can make a significant contribution to legitimate environmental regulations.[216] To explain, from the position of environmental regulators, at least two conditions should be satisfied for successful environmental regulations: (1) they should be allowed to differentiate between environmentally-friendly products and products that cause adverse environmental effects; and (2) it should be easy for the supplier of the latter products to switch production to the former product sector.

Since the first condition is an obvious one, one should examine the reasons behind the second condition more closely. The ultimate goal of environmental policies should not be sheer prohibition or punishment. Rather, it must be to reward producers with incentives to switch from harmful sectors to green, or at least less harmful, sectors. Accordingly, a legitimate environmental strategy would most likely succeed in two sectors in which a high degree of supply substitutability exists. Thus, by taking account of the high supply substitutability of these 'promising' sectors, and thus rendering determination of the two products as being *not* 'like or directly substitutable' in spite of a slightly high (or ambiguous) degree of demand substitutability, one could 'open the door' for the incentive system of legitimate environmental policies.[217]

For a full examination of supply substitutability, some regard should be had to the factor of '*potential* or *future competition*'. If current impediments in the market are removed, some producers might want to switch their production from sector A to sector B *now*. Or, even though some producers may not want to switch their production right away, they may want to do so *in the near future*. Considering that the concept of 'potential or future competition' is mostly based on the producers' position according to a hypothetical change of price or other market conditions, one might argue that it is basically the same concept as supply substitutability. But it should be noted that, despite their seemingly similar nature, these concepts can be conceptually separated and have different functions, as will be discussed later.[218]

To summarize, products are subject to three main sources of competitive constraints in the relevant market: demand substitutability, supply substitutability, and potential or future substitution and competition. Among these factors, the most immediate and effective way to define product likeness or substitutability comes from demand substitutability, because *the very product likeness or substitutability is the dominant reason for the consumers' choice*. The further reason is that demand substitutability is one of the significant factors determining supply substitutability: the existence or degree of demand substitutability is directly related to the amount of sales and profit between related products, which is determinant in pricing or supply substitution decisions by producers or suppliers.[219]

An examination of supply substitution complements the demand-side analysis by enabling the examiner to proceed with a comprehensive analysis that internalizes considerations about producer relationships, distribution of resources, and domestic welfare policies.

Future or potential substitution or competition analysis completes the likeness or substitutability test by transforming it into a dynamic cross-temporal examination; it empowers the GATT instrument to catch imminent or hidden threats that are also detrimental to the free trading system.

The above conclusion is illustrated by Figure II.2.

This is the instrument we are looking for—the *accordion*! For the sake of clarity, the general function of this instrument may be shown as illustrated in Figure II.3. Assuming that the four-dimensional shape of the 'LIKE SPHERE' has been

FACTORS OF LIKENESS OR SUBSTITUTABILITY MODEL:

(1) A reasonable person's view of the objective characteristics of products, evidenced by similarity in PHYSICAL CHARACTERISTICS, TARIFF CLASSIFICATION, GENERAL END-USE (height).
(2) The consumer (producer)'s view of end-use in the market, shown by DEMAND SUBSTITUTABILITY (length); plus, a reasonable person's view of the potential/future change of the end-use, evidenced by POTENTIAL OR FUTURE SUBSTI-TUTABILITY (time).
(3) A producer's view of market condition and profitability, shown by SUPPLY SUBSTITUTABILITY (breadth); plus, a reasonable person's view of the potential/future development in market conditions and profitability, evidenced by POTENTIAL OR FUTURE COMPETITION (time).

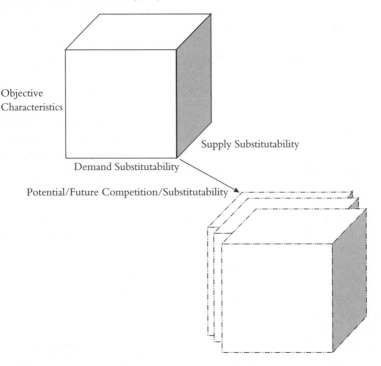

Figure II.2: GATT Likeness or Substitutability Analysis

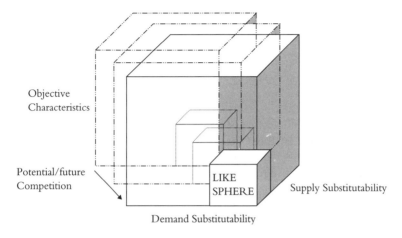

Figure II.3: GATT Likeness or Substitutability Analysis

obtained as a result of an ongoing examination of all four factors, products A and B can be concluded as being like (or directly competitive or substitutable) products only if the relationship between the two is located within the coverage of the shape. But it should be noted that the size of the four-dimensional shape could be different in each of the GATT provisions, since each of them could have a different purpose and policy consideration. This task, of modification of the sphere, will proceed in Chapter III.

3.2. Relevant Factors

Given the complexity of the subject matter, each of likeness or substitutability factors identified above requires elaboration. One needs to inspect what components build up each factor, how those components and factors of the instrument are designed to work, and what guidance, if any, in this regard has been given by previous GATT/WTO tribunals.

3.2.1. *The First Factor: Objective Characteristics*

The first factor, objective characteristics, consists of such elements as physical properties, tariff classification, and general end-use of the products in question.

With regard to the *physical properties* of products, the practice or general tendency, formed by the international tribunals, has been to pay little attention to organoleptic differences between the products in question. Taste, aroma, texture, genetic factors, alcoholic strength, and general aesthetic appearance have not played an important role in determining 'likeness'. *Spain Unroasted Coffee* delivered a message that these differences become even more unimportant when conjoined with such practices as product-blending, which mix several products together to produce a final commodity to meet the variety of consumer tastes.[220] By the same token, *Japan Alcoholic Beverages* ruled that a difference in the physical characteristics of products with varying alcoholic contents did not preclude a finding of 'likeness', especially since alcoholic beverages are often drunk in diluted form.[221]

In *Korea Alcoholic Beverages*, the Panel pointed out that organoleptic differences in raw materials, additives, percentages of alcohol, flavour, smell, and colour have to give way to the consideration of potential or future competitive relationships. According to the Korean Panel, despite these differences, the alcoholic beverages in question shared 'nearly' identical characteristics because 'there is a great potential for a direct competitive relationship'.[222]

This general position of the WTO tribunals is interesting enough to raise a question: how much organoleptic difference is necessary for products to be considered not 'like' or 'directly substitutable'? Is a rare vintage Bordeaux a directly substitutable product to a cheap table wine or shochu (should both products be subject to the same tax or duty rate under the *specific* tax or tariff regime)? Is there great potential for a directly competitive relationship between them, despite such 'minor' differences in raw material, flavour, smell, color, proof, age, reputation, and price? Should there be no limitations on the ideas that 'alcoholic beverages are alcoholic beverages' and 'coffee is coffee'?

Sometimes, small technical changes in product properties could lead to products that are very different for consumers. It often happens that the addition to a food or drink product of small amounts of an unpleasant substance, or a substance perceived to be unpleasant, may cause demand for the product to fall to nearly zero.[223] As time goes by, organoleptic differences could come to be more important for consumers, especially with regard to environmental and health protection issues. Sooner than expected, a new generation of environmentally oriented consumers might appear. To them, it would be hardly persuasive to determine that Indian tap water and Alpine natural mineral water are like or directly substitutable.

An examination of physical properties should not be a decisive criterion. This is true not only in 'directly competitive or substitutable product' determinations but also in 'like product' tests.[224] More evidentiary weight may be given to the physical properties element in the latter test, sometimes leading to a *presumption* of likeness,[225] but, without appropriate market-based substitution analysis to evidence likeness, the results of the objective characteristic examination cannot complete the determination. The market-based analysis will reduce the 'stiffness' of the test and help it to adapt to changing environments, in which not only high 'organoleptic differences' but also 'non-physical characteristics', such as brand loyalty, brand image and reputation, after-sales service and resale value, are becoming more and more important.[226]

The second component of the objective characteristic factor is the *tariff classification*. As many GATT panels have noted,[227] one of the main objectives of the GATT is to protect the effect of tariff concessions granted under Art. II. In order to support this objective, one has to take account of the tariff classification when determining likeness.

In referring to the tariff classification element in interpreting likeness, important aspects to be examined are whether the responding party reserved a distinct category of classification only for the product in question, and whether this distinction can be qualified as a general practice followed by other countries. So far, GATT panels seem to have given more weight to the latter factor in that, even though the tariff classification concerned showed an artificial sophistication, the existence of common practice of the classification justified the classification.[228] This tendency suggests that an agreement, explicit or tacit (such as practices), or a common perception among GATT members play a significant role in determining the 'like' product concept.[229] This can be said to reflect efforts to be faithful to the meaning or contractual perception that the parties originally agreed to when they signed the tariff concession agreement.

A series of MFN cases confirms this tendency of paying deference to existing practices of tariff classification and member countries' agreement to it. Concluding that the two types of fertilizers, ammonium sulphate and sodium nitrate, were not like products, the Working Party in *Australian Subsidy on Ammonium Sulphate* paid great attention to the fact that the importing country, Australia, as well as other countries, classified them as being separate items in their tariff schedules.[230] In *Germany Imports of Sardines*, Norway submitted that sprats, herrings, and sardines were like products because all of them belong to the same family. The Panel rejected the submission because, in previous negotiations between the two countries, there was an express or tacit agreement on understanding of the 'unlikeness' of the products.[231] The strongest ground in support of this decision, based on an estoppel-type[232] reasoning, is that if the parties concerned previously agreed to a certain understanding, it would be difficult to conclude that the expectation of competitive relationships was harmed by measures consistent with the understanding. In fact, such a reasoning seems to be based on the Panel's practical consideration that if there had existed common practices in international society, the international tribunal would be cautious, or even unwilling, to intervene in parties' agreements and the international consensus building process.

One additional point to consider is that the *Japan SPF Lumber* Panel,[233] ruling that the Canadian case was not established, required a 'universal' product category in order to proceed to the likeness test. According to the Panel, since the tariffs referred to by the General Agreement were those of the individual member country, a claim of likeness raised by a member in relation to the tariff treatment of its goods on importation by some other member should be based on the classification of the importing country's tariff. Since the dimension lumber (the product category at issue), as defined by Canada, was a concept extraneous to the Japanese tariff and to any internationally accepted customs classifications, it was not an appropriate basis for establishing the 'likeness' of products under Art. I:1 of the General Agreement. The natural corollary of this reasoning would be that any state challenging the tariff scheme of another country would have to establish the product in issue as a product category well accepted by the other country; or at least, it would have to establish a classification scheme that has some measure of internationally accepted standards of product presentation.[234] For example, a country exporting cow tongues to another country cannot successfully argue that the product should not be treated less favourably than beef in terms of tariff measure unless the exporting country establishes that 'tongue' is a distinct product category in the tariff scheme, well accepted in the importing country and/or in the international community. This requirement would prevent tariff-related claims, based on overly detailed product categories, from being successfully raised in GATT tribunals. One can say that the Panel's decision is in line with the previous Panel's cautiousness in attacking tariff systems of member countries.

By the same token, if the importing country's tariff schedules were aberrant in comparison with other countries' schedules, deviated from a scheme that focused on the physical characteristics of the goods, or were based on distinctions that were not commercial in nature,[235] no deference has been shown to these kinds of schedules. In such cases, there was no presumption that the tariff schedule was a legitimate basis for distinguishing between imported products. It seems that for the most part the burden fell on the importing member to show that the tariff differentiation was not a disguised form of discrimination. For example, in *Spain Unroasted Coffee*, the GATT Panel concluded that all types of unroasted coffee are like products, notwithstanding admitted differences among the types of coffee involved, based largely on the fact that no other country applied different duty rates to different types of coffee.[236]

It is interesting to consider whether this close relationship between tariff classification and the 'like product' concept can be maintained in a new world trade environment, and whether the close relationship in the MFN context may be equally relevant in other contexts. Since the Harmonized System (HS)[237] of tariff classification has been adopted and implemented throughout the world, the uniformity and objectivity of the tariff classifications of each state have been much increased. The HS classification nomenclature focuses on the physical characteristics of imported goods, particularly the way in which the product is assembled and its material composition.[238] Interpretation is to be objective, rejecting extrinsic circumstances, such as industrial origin and specific use, which may not be apparent on observation at the border.[239] In this environment, certainly, the tariff classification is one of the objective factors to be considered in likeness test, as the *Border Tax Adjustments* Report indicated.

But it should be noted that there are still many products that are not covered by the tariff schedules of WTO members,[240] and that the tariff classifications of many developing countries are not sufficiently detailed. As a substantial number of WTO members have not yet succeeded in applying the HS to its full extent, and even if the HS is fully applied it allows for a certain amount of variation between national classification systems, the individual classification systems of the member states still vary considerably.[241]

Furthermore, as the general level of tariffs has been substantially lowered through several rounds of trade negotiations, and since other various non-tariff barriers have emerged as principal matters to be dealt with, the GATT's objective of protection of tariff concessions has lost much of its attraction in relative terms. Obviously, this new threat of non-tariff barriers compels one to find ways to interpret the likeness concept beyond the context of protecting *competitive* benefits obtained by signing tariff-binding agreements. What carries great weight now is to preserve the *comparative* advantage—a more fundamental value of the GATT—which WTO members acquired by signing the entire package of the WTO Agreement.

Therefore, one can conclude that the tariff classification of products should not be an exclusive criterion for a determination of likeness, although it provides a useful element, especially when it is sufficiently detailed.[242] The degree of such reliance on the tariff classification criterion would ultimately be determined according to the purpose of each provision, and to whether or not the specific classification at issue could be justified by international practice or other legitimate reasons.

The third element in the objective characteristic factor is *end-use in general*.[243] As discussed already in section 2 above, the end-use element in the GATT likeness test has stretched from general end-use, to end-use in the market, up to potential end-use. Among these, 'end-use in the market' and its 'potentiality' are extensively examined by a market-based economic analysis as core elements of the product substitutability and potential competition factors. After all, what the market-based economic analysis seeks to establish is whether a sufficient degree of substitutability exists between the two products in question; this is closely related to the problem of whether or not the two products at issue share a common end-use in the relevant market. Thus, these two concepts will be discussed in 3.2.2 to 3.2.4 below.

The present discussion focuses on the concept of 'end-use in general' as an element of the objective characteristic factor. It is natural that this inquiry begins by looking at *physical characteristics*. In many cases, similar physical properties are needed to serve similar end-uses. Indeed, Korean ginseng and Chinese ginseng are no different in shape, weight, color, or taste. Likewise, the Timor and Corolla cars share common physical characteristics in terms of size, weight, engine power, technology, and features. These similar features will often be enough to endow them with a common end-use in general.

In other cases, a common *purpose* of consumption or general *function* of products may need to be referred to. Despite the lack of shared close physical properties, similar purposes of consumption would allow apples and oranges, or beef and pork, to have similar end-uses in general. It is also true that what makes a Timor and a Rolls Royce, or shochu and whisky, share similar end-uses in general is their purpose of consumption or their general function.

In addition, such additional check points as end-uses in other markets[244] and channels of distribution[245] would be helpful to identify the general end-use for the product in question.

Since it focuses on intended utility or universal consumer needs in the abstract—not looking at whether the two products in question actually share a substantial degree of substitution in the given market—the concept of end-use in general is therefore quite a broad one. Virtually all alcoholic beverages would share the same end-use in general, except those used for medical purposes, mainly because of the common purposes of consumption, 'relaxation',[246] and 'socializa-tion'.[247] The only hurdle that stops this broad category of alcoholic beverages—as a 'well defined and single product intended for drinking'[248]—from reaching soft drinks is the strong purpose of 'thirst quenching' shared by consumers of the latter. The general end-use of magazines does not recognize the distinction between 'information media' and 'entertainment/communication media' as long as the products serve the same group of readers.[249]

In fact, the element of end-use in general can be a good starting point for any likeness test. Furthermore, when it is combined with physical properties and/or tariff classifications, its examination can create a presumption of likeness in certain GATT provisions in which the narrowest definition of likeness is adopted.[250] Moreover, the element of end-use in general can constitute 'one factor which is particularly relevant to the issue of *potential* competition or substitutability'.[251] If there are common end-uses then two products may very well be competitive, either immediately or in the near and reasonably predictable future.[252]

Nonetheless, the broadness and abstract nature of the element, as discussed above, does not allow for a complete analysis, particularly in close cases. Whether two products are actually sharing common end-uses in the market in question, and whether there is a potential common end-use in that market, should be analyzed before declaring that all ginsengs, all passenger cars, or all similar-looking meats are 'like' or 'directly competitive or substitutable' regardless of place or time.

3.2.2. *The Second Factor: Demand Substitutability*

Aside from the potentiality factor that will be examined at 3.2.4 in order to complete this analysis, demand substitutability is a central tool used to examine market-based end uses. So, using which methodology is it possible to determine the demand substitutability of products?

As indicated at section 2 above, their merits of paying attention to the market-place notwithstanding, the methodological guidelines formed through the GATT tribunals in *Japan Alcoholic Beverages, Canada Periodicals, Korea Alcoholic Beverages,* and *Chile Alcoholic Beverages* have many defects. But bearing such defects and merits in mind, one could suggest the following demand substitutability analysis.

In general, one of the most reliable approaches for competitiveness or substi-tutability analysis is to analyze existing data or information. *Direct views of end users* about substitute products or marketing studies, commissioned by companies in the past and which are used by companies in their own decisions on pricing of their products and/or marketing actions, may provide useful information.[253]

The 'market segmentation approach' taken by the *Indonesia National Car* Panel provides an excellent example of this direct view analysis. According to the Panel, one reasonable way to approach the 'like product' issue is to look at 'the manner in which the automotive industry itself has analyzed market segmentation'.[254] Relying on a marketing analysis carried out by a group of automobile producers,[255] which set five different market segmentations of consumer demand on passenger cars,[256] the Indonesian Panel made 'like products' determinations under the SCM Agreement and Art. I and III of the GATT.[257]

Undertaking this 'direct view analysis', one should note that the producers' view, not to mention the consumers' perception, of the *demand* substitutability of the products in question can be taken into account in the circumstances. Sometimes, common channels of distribution and points of sale give an indirect indication of demand substitutability between products, viewed from the producer's perspective.[258] Even if, on most occasions, there would be little difference between the consumer's and producer's perceptions, rarely one may find a difference.[259] This difference of perception might be treated less seriously in 'like' product cases than in 'directly substitutable' product cases, because the former are determined according to more 'objective' criteria focusing on physical characteristics. In any event, if there exist differences between the two perceptions, and they cannot be bridged by objective observation, the difficult problem of allocating weight to the two perceptions remains. A solution may be found in a purpose-based approach: since each provision at issue may have a different purpose, weight should be allocated according to the difference in purposes. For instance, in interpreting 'like products' in Art. XIX, more evidentiary weight should be given to the producer's perception, because the primary purpose of the provision is to protect domestic industry rather than general consumers.[260]

In the absence of existing direct view data, *consumer surveys*, carried out on an *ad hoc* basis by the parties to the dispute[261] or other expert groups, may be referred to. In general, surveys carried out by independent expert organizations should be preferred. Such surveys collect data that provide a detailed description of the resource, its current condition, and hypothetical changes to its condition. Competition law has developed this *ad hoc* survey method in order to define the scope of 'relevant market', using cross-price elasticity of demand analysis. The Commission Notice of the European Community gives the following guideline:

The assessment of demand substitution entails a determination of the range of products which are viewed as substitutes by the consumer. One way of making this determination can be viewed, as a thought experiment, postulating a hypothetical small, non-transitory change in relative prices and evaluating the likely reactions of customers to that increase. . . . The question to be answered is whether the parties' customers would switch to readily available substitutes or to suppliers located elsewhere in response to an hypothetical small (in the range 5%–10%), permanent relative price increase in the products and areas being considered. If substitution would be enough to make the price increase unprofitable because of the resulting loss of sales, additional substitutes and areas are included in the relevant market. This would be done until the set of products and geographic areas is such that small, permanent increases in relative prices would be profitable. ... A practical example of this test can be provided by its application to a merger of, for instance, soft drink bottlers. An issue to examine in such a case would be to decide whether different flavours of soft drinks belong to the same market. In practice, the question to address would be if consumers of flavour A would switch to other flavours when confronted with a permanent price increase of 5% to 10% for flavour A. If a sufficient number of consumers would switch to, say, flavour B, to such an extent that the price increase for flavour A would not be profitable due to the resulting loss of sales, then the market would comprise at least flavours A and B. The process would have to be extended in addition to other available flavours until a set of products is identified for which a price rise would not induce a sufficient substitution in demand.[262]

United States antitrust law has applied similar techniques in the context of mergers.[263]

One could say that this technique provides a good basis for approaching product competitiveness or substitutability because it not only shows the 'existence' of a substitutive relationship between the products in question, but it also reveals the specific 'extent' of the relationship. Given this merit, one can borrow it to analyze demand substitution in the GATT likeness context. The following hypothetical example demonstrates this analysis:

Two products, X and Y, are alleged to be 'directly competitive or substitutable' products. Hundreds, or even thousands, of consumers[264] of product X would be asked a hypothetical question: if the price of product X rose by a certain percentage, would you stay loyal to product X or switch your consumption to product Y? In judging the response to this query, it is possible to conclude that only if more than a certain threshold percentage of respondents switch to product Y will products X and Y have a sufficient substitution in demand.

This technique is called 'contingent valuation', because the respondents' willingness to switch is contingent on the hypothetical change to the resource (price of X). Product price is known as the most important consideration for consumers. It is reasonable to assume that if the price of X were to double, twice as many consumers would switch their consumption to directly substitutable products (if such products exist), provided that the price rise was not too large or small and the original market price had been set at not too high or low a level (concerning this condition, *see* Appendix III). In other words, a 2.2 per cent switching rate under a 3.3 per cent price change would involve the same degree of substitution as a 4.4 per cent switching rate under a 6.6 per cent price change. Hence, one can add to the contingent valuation model an additional condition that the *threshold* switching rate should be proportional to the hypothetical price change rate.[265] With this added condition, this model could be named the 'Contingent Valuation Analysis on *Proportional* Cross-Price-Demand Substitutability' (CVA-PCPDS).

What, then, is the most appropriate minimum substitution rate (threshold) in the analysis for the two products in question to be determined as being 'directly competitive or substitutable'?[266] The 'Price-Substitution Equivalence Standard' (PSE Standard) might be suggested. This standard defines the threshold as a point at which price change rates equalize with substitution rates. For instance, if the questionnaire presumes an 8 per cent price rise in product X, the threshold rate is established at the same 8 per cent under this standard. In other words, in order for X and Y to be determined as being 'directly competitive or substitutable products', *at least* 8 per cent of respondents, facing an 8 per cent price increase, need to switch their consumption from X to Y. One can combine this standard with the above analysis and call it the 'CVA-PCPDS with PSE Standard'.

What is the rationale for the PSE Standard (e.g. 8 per cent price increase–8 per cent threshold switching rate; 12 per cent price increase–12 per cent threshold)? In theory, the switching rate from one product to the other in the case of an 8 per cent price change of one product could turn out to be from 0 to 100 per cent. A 0 per cent switching rate indicates that two products are not substitutable at all, whereas 100 per cent shows perfect substitutability between the two products. Hence, the reasonable threshold of a 'directly competitive or substitutable' relationship could be located between the two extremes.

Among the numerous intermediate points, what the 8 per cent switching rate from X to Y represents in the case of an 8 per cent price increase of X is a benefit–loss turning point for X producers. In other words, if the switching rate is more than 8 per cent when the price rises 8 per cent, the seller of X will suffer losses as a result. Indeed, the turning point would be greatly referred to when the producer or the supplier makes market decisions. Hence, based on the implications of the turning point, one can infer a competitive relationship between products.

To support this inference, one can say, in general, that evidence for the existence of competition in the market can be taken from the question of whether a company producing X can benefit by the increase of X price. If the company loses as a result of a price increase, it means that the company has competitors in the market, and that the market price of X is largely free from producer manipulation. In contrast, if the company can successfully increase the price without suffering a loss, it means that there are no substantial competitors in the market. Thus, from this competitive relationship between producers, one can reasonably infer the existence of a directly substitutable relationship between their products.

Against this inference, critics might argue that the PSE Standard would work as an appropriate criterion in the competition law context rather than in the GATT context because the basis of the standard is the competitive relationship between 'competitors'. Indeed, the following statement made by a prominent antitrust law scholar shows the suitability of the standard for purposes of competition law:

If we ask why a slight increase in the price of a product might result in a substantial drop in the quantity demanded from the sellers—why, in other words, demand is elastic at the current price—two possibilities come to mind. The first is that the *product has good substitutes* at that price, so that even a slight increase in price would deflect many consumers to them. The second possibility is that the *makers of some other product* (which need not be a good substitute in consumption) *can readily switch* to producing this product and would do so if its price rose any further, because at the new price they could earn a higher return by making this product instead of whatever they are making now. In short, the ability of a group of sellers to collude is limited by the existence of sellers of products that are *good substitutes either in consumption or in production*, and we have to include these additional sellers to delimit a group of sellers that can be assumed to be facing a relatively inelastic demand. The expanded group is a market in the sense, which is the only one relevant to an economic analysis of competition and monopoly, of a group of sellers who have the power to increase their profits by merging or colluding. A merger that slightly reduced the costs of collusion to such a group would be a cause for concern.[267]

However, it should be noted that, in general, the reason why the two producers compete against each other in the same market is because their products are directly competitive or substitutable. Indeed, since the ability of consumers to turn to other suppliers keeps a company from raising prices above the competitive level, the *definition of the 'relevant market' rests on a determination of available substitutes.*[268] What the relevant market test of competition law aims to do is to enclose all those *available substitutes* within the boundary of a relevant market. Hence, products that are 'reasonably interchangeable by consumers for the same purposes'[269] are nothing more than 'directly competitive or substitutable' products.

The very statement quoted above—that *own*-price-elastic demand substitution arises because 'the product has *good substitutes* at that price' (the first possibility)—confirms this point. If applied to cross-price elasticity (not own-price elasticity), the logical corollary of this statement is indeed the admission that cross-price-elastic substitution (switch more than the PSE level) between X and Y arises because the two products are *good substitutes*, which are directly competitive with or substitutable for each other. Therefore, one can use the PSE Standard (benefit–loss turning point) as a threshold level for 'directly competitive or substitutable' product relationships: the threshold is set at the same rate as the price change rate. For instance, if the price change of X is hypothesized at 8 per cent, (1) more than an 8 per cent switching rate from X to Y provides evidence that products X and Y are directly competing against each other in the same market; and (2) less than an 8 per cent switching rate from X to Y means a lack, or at least insufficient evidence, of direct substitution between the two products. This switch, which is less than 8 per cent, would indeed be an insufficient degree of substitution to qualify as being 'direct' competition or substitution: rather, what it does represent is a random switch by way of income effect,[270] or a switch by a small group of consumers who are overly sensitive to price.

Of course, there remains the second possibility, quoted by the antitrust scholar, that 'the *makers of some other product* (which need not be a good substitute in consumption) *can readily switch* to producing this product'. This possibility points to supply substitutability and/or 'future competition' factors. Since these aspects are covered in the proposed model of GATT likeness or substitutability analysis as discussed already and to be elaborated later, covering the second possibility in the relevant market analysis cannot be exclusive to antitrust jurisprudence. It does not provide the rationale that the PSE Standard would work as an appropriate criterion in the competition law context rather than in the GATT context.

Still, relying on consideration of the 'potential competition or substitution' factor (in a narrow sense),[271] the critics might argue that the competition law standard of PSE could not be applied as a standard of trade law. According to them, the main difference between the two standards would lie in the 'potential competition or substitution' factor. When applying GATT likeness provisions, panels need to take account of the 'potential competition or substitution' (beyond the actual competition existing under current measures) that might materialize between the products concerned in the absence of the discriminatory measure in dispute.[272] In contrast, competition authorities tend to consider current barriers (e.g., different tax rates) in the market as being permanent barriers to competition, and hence disregard any additional competition that may arise from the removal of those barriers.[273] As a result, the scope of 'relevant product' markets defined for competition purposes would generally be narrower than the scope of 'directly competitive or substitutable products' defined for the purposes of the GATT, when such barriers exist. Thus, the PSE Standard, designed to examine substitutability based on *current* substitution rates, would not be appropriate to be applied to the GATT.

This possible position of the critics is well expressed in the report of the Panel in *Korea Alcoholic Beverages*. In this case, relying on the role of 'potential substitution' in the context of the GATT, the Panel tried to discount the necessity for any numeric threshold in the demand substitution analysis:

> While a high degree of cross-price elasticity of demand would tend to support the argument that there is a direct competitive relationship, it is only one evidentiary factor. If there is a high quantitative level of competition between products, it is likely that the qualitative nature of the competition is direct. However, the lack of such evidence may be due to the governmental measures in question.... This is particularly a problem if the products involved are consumer items that are so-called *experience goods* which means that consumers tend to purchase what is familiar to them and experiment only reluctantly.... Thus the question is not of the degree of competitive overlap, but its *nature*. Is there a competitive relationship and is it *direct*? It is for this reason, among others, that quantitative studies of cross-price elasticity are relevant, but not exclusive or even decisive in nature.[274]

Responding to this view, one has to admit that the *premiss* of the above criticism is true: the potentiality factor necessary for the likeness definition of the GATT is not internalized in the CVA-PCPDS with PSE Standard. But one should also admit that this point is not enough to deny the utility of the PSE Standard with regard to the GATT likeness test. Logically and practically, any consideration of potentiality should come after a standard-setting process. What a demand substitution standard provides is not a final determination; it sets a good *base* figure of product substitutability, starting from which one can subtract or add appropriate figures under the 'potential competition or substitution' consideration[275] as well as the supply substitutability consideration that follows. Thus, the 'qualitative' nature of potential competition and uniqueness of 'experienced goods' does not justify the absence of a certain threshold rate of substitutability in the first place in GATT demand substitution analysis.

In sum, just as the PSE Standard fits well within the purpose of identifying the 'relevant market' in the competition law context in general, and in merger or abuse of dominant position cases in particular, the standard is also a useful tool for determining whether 'demand is elastic at the current price' and, thus, whether 'the product has good substitutes at that price' in the likeness or substitutability test of the General Agreement. The final determination of product likeness or substitutability in the GATT is made after taking account of the comprehensive factors, including the differences between the GATT and competition law and between the natures of the products in question, as will be discussed later. In this determination process, the CVA-PCPDS with PSE Standard provides an excellent base criterion.

In fact, the real weakness of the CVA-PCPDS with PSE might lie in a structural defect of the questionnaire. The question given to respondents in the analysis is with regard to the choice between X and Y only, in the event of hypothetical changes in the price of X. Considering that, in reality, consumers make choices among many available products, one might say that the limited 'pairwise' choice in the analysis could not reflect a real substitutive relationship in the market. Therefore, critics of the analysis might argue that if the survey method is used, it is crucial to keep track of the relationships among interrelated products as a whole, as looking at the relationship between two products in isolation can be misleading. According to this view, what is needed is not a partial equilibrium analysis but, rather, a general equilibrium analysis, which takes account of the true linkage among all related product sectors.

Indeed, pairwise choices and three-way choices can make for different results. In particular, a choice between only two products could bring about problems of overvaluation or undervaluation, as the following illustration shows:

(1) The 8 per cent switching rate obtained through the hypothetical assumption of an 8 per cent price increase (by using the CVA-PCPDS method) may have been 'overvalued': some respondents might have switched reluctantly because there were no other alternatives. For example, in *Japan Alcoholic Beverages*, Japan questioned the relevance of the ASI study by noting that 'consumers were not allowed to choose other than the mentioned eight products'[276] (i.e., they were not allowed to choose beer, sake, or wine). According to Japan, if choices are too limited, 'even such disparate products as hamburger and ice cream could be argued to be directly competitive or substitutable products'.[277]

(2) The partial equilibrium analysis could bring an 'undervaluation' problem. One could think of the situation of multiple substitutes in which 50 products are actually directly substitutable for each other. The cross-price elasticity between any *two* of them would be very small. One should not use this small figure to deny direct substitutability between any two products without comparing with other figures.

It should be noted that the above problems arise mainly because the hypothetical questionnaire is constructed to examine the effects of change in demand for

Y responsive to the price change of *only* X. To solve this problem, one might amend the questionnaire to include as many choices as possible. This amended questionnaire might be called the 'Expanded Questionnaire Approach' (EQA), as opposed to the 'Pairwise Questionnaire Approach' (PQA) which was suggested in previous paragraphs in relation to the PSE Standard.

With the EQA, one is able to examine (1) what will happen to the demand for Y, if *all* other prices change, or (2) given the price change of *one* product, how many consumers would switch away from that product and towards which other product(s). The latter approach would be more practical because it is easier to construct such a questionnaire. But the problem of the EQA is that it is hardly workable with the PSE Standard: when the EQA is used, it is difficult to determine the point of the price-substitution equivalence. To illustrate this, one needs to change the original hypothetical slightly so as to include another product, Z, as an available choice:

Now, two products, X and Y, are alleged to be 'directly competitive or substitutable' products. Hundreds of consumers of product X are asked a hypothetical question, that if the price of product X rises by 8 per cent, what will they consume among products X, Y, *and* Z. Only if more than certain threshold percentage of consumers of product X switch to product Y can it be concluded that X and Y have a sufficient substitution in demand. The additional condition, that the threshold switching rate should be proportional to the hypothetical price change rate, is added here.[278] Assume that the result of the survey turned out to be that 6 per cent of respondents switched to product Y and 4 per cent of them to product Z.

In this new hypothetical based on the EQA, how can one calculate the PSE threshold point? Since the price change of product X is 8 per cent, according to the definition of the PSE, the PSE threshold substitution rate should be established at 8 per cent (benefit–loss turning point for X producer). (Note that the 10 per cent (i.e. 6 per cent + 4 per cent) loss in demand of X represents an own-price elasticity of demand of X, and the 6 per cent switching rate represents a cross-price elasticity of demand between X and Y. Here, one sees that the own-price elasticity satisfies the PSE threshold of 8 per cent, whereas the cross-price elasticity falls short of the threshold point.) But it is possible that the 6 per cent switching rate to Y in the hypothetical above might have reached 8 per cent if the PQA (between X and Y) instead of EQA had been adopted in the first place. Thus, the same product relationship (between X and Y) could be determined differently depending on which method (PQA or EQA) is employed. One should note that the different percentage rate between 'own-price elasticity' and 'cross-price elasticity' signals that problem.

From the above example, one might say that the 8 per cent PSE threshold is inappropriate for the EQA because it might be too high in some circumstances. Slight variation of the hypothetical would confirm this point. If, in reality, Y and Z are just (marginally) directly substitutable products to X *to the same degree*, then the 8 per cent demand loss of X would be equally divided into 4 per cent of the switching rate for Y and Z, respectively. According to the PSE Standard, both Y and

Z would fail to meet the 'directly substitutable products to X' qualification, which goes against reality. Hence, using the EQA, one would experience substantial difficulty in setting an appropriate threshold rate of substitution.

In short, the PQA method is simpler and easier to administer, but more likely to fail in multiple substitutes situations. Thus, if the first step analysis of objective characteristics shows that such a multiple substitutes situation does not exist, the PQA could be employed to examine market-based substitutability. In such cases, the PSE Standard would prove its utility. But if the first step signals a multiple substitutes situation, the EQA would be the better choice because it reveals over- and under-valuation problems, even when it fails to produce an appropriate threshold point.

With regard to the proper threshold standard for the EQA approach, one possible solution could be to set it after a comparison of own- and cross-price elasticity of demand has been made. If there is no substantial difference between them, the threshold could be set at the PSE level. By contrast, if there turned out to be substantial differences (i.e., if the switching rate is distributed quite evenly over multiple substitutable products), a certain percentage could be subtracted from the PSE base rate to produce the final threshold rate. How much of a discount rate should be taken depends primarily upon the size of the difference combined with a comparison of other cross-substitution rates.

In this process, one could use the Combined Questionnaire Approach (CQA, combining the pairwise-choice questionnaire with the extended-choice questionnaire). This method will be helpful in the multiple substitutes situation, in that it provides the examiner with consumer responses to both pairwise and multiple-choice questions with regard to the same products. Of course, the ultimate determination of demand substitutability will be made through the *unavoidable element of individual discretionary judgement* of the examiner, based on information obtained through this methodology.

Despite the possible methodological problems, or necessity of adjustment in relation to the PSE, the CVA-PCPDS provides two important benefits. The first is that two key factors, not only quantity but also price, are taken into account when deciding the minimum degree of substitution. In other words, the greater the hypothetical price change is, the larger the required switching rate becomes ('proportional' substitutability). It must be recalled that the 10 per cent switching rate that the *Japanese Alcoholic Beverages* Panel referred to reflects no such price factor: it is not the result of cross-price demand substitutability but of non-availability analysis. That is, what this method shows is that 10 per cent of all whisky consumers would switch to shochu if whisky were not available. This methodology does not reflect the real world situation and tends to exaggerate the switching rate, as already discussed.[279]

The second benefit, which is most important, is that, relying upon this suggested analysis, WTO tribunals can increase consistency and transparency in their decisions. Continuous use of this method by subsequent panels would build up, in the specific context of GATT provisions, certain practices or consensus concerning the threshold level of substitution that is necessary for products in question to be determined as being 'directly competitive or substitutable'. Some trial and error may occur; but once the practices are established, these standards will play an important role in cases with similar facts, which will increase the transparency and consistency of the WTO dispute settlement procedure, the two primary values in the *drive-to-maturity* stage of the GATT.

In this light, the Appellate Body's standard-setting effort made in another area deserves credit: facing discrepancy between the phrase 'in excess of' in the first sentence of GATT Art. III:2 and the phrase 'not similarly taxed' in the second sentence, the Appellate Body in *Japan Alcoholic Beverages* set the '*de minimis* level' as the standard of distinction.[280] Although this distinction was made according to quite an arbitrary judgement, there can be no doubt that the *de minimis* standard would increase the consistency and transparency of subsequent panel decisions.

In contrast, it should be recalled that the *Japanese Alcoholic Beverages* Panel decided, without providing any explanation, that 10 per cent substitution in non-availability analysis was a 'significant' degree of substitution,[281] and that the *Chile Alcoholic Beverages* Panel held a cross-price elasticity of 0.26 to be 'low'.[282] These tribunals did not say anything about the minimum degree of substitution required for the substitution test, even though one must anyway have a certain 'numeric' threshold point (or range) in order to make a determination from the numeric data at hand.

Sometimes, authoritative standards provide WTO members with a good excuse to proceed with reform. Due to the *de minimis* standard set by the Appellate Body, the Japanese Government may feel that it can reduce the liquor tax differential between vodka (Art. III: 2, first sentence matter) and whisky (the second sentence matter) within the *de minimis* level, as it will suffer less pressure from domestic industries. In the absence of such a standard, any such reform might be 'lukewarm', resulting in *Japanese Alcoholic Beverages III*.

To summarize, the PSE Standard as employed in the CVA-PCPDS analysis may be used as a basic standard to determine demand substitutability in various GATT provisions, with specific adjustments on a case-by-case basis in multiple substitution situations. It should be noted that the PSE Standard indicates the 'lowest' (for the use of 'directly competitive or substitutable') among the possible thresholds to be employed for various concepts of like or substitutable product relationships. This means that specific thresholds, other than the PSE threshold, could be set in each provision of the GATT, in which a degree of likeness or substitutability higher than 'directly competitive or substitutable' is required. For instance, the determination of 'like' product in Art. III:2, first sentence would need a different standard from that of the PSE: surely, a higher threshold would be required here because the 'like' concept is stricter (narrower) than the 'directly competitive or substitutable' concept employed in the second sentence. Indeed, the PSE threshold would fit best with the test for a 'directly competitive or substitutable' product relationship under Art. III:2, second sentence, because the relationship represents the broadest scope of likeness among all likeness provisions in the GATT, as will be discussed later.[283]

This lack of general applicability notwithstanding, the PSE standard shows how a specific threshold rate of substitution can be combined with the CVA-PCPDS that tends toward general application. In actuality, the standard would be helpful in many likeness or substitutability tests because, after all, it sets a sweeping 'bottom line', starting from which the tribunal can determine an individual threshold appropriate for each likeness or substitutability in question.

Complemented by supply substitution and potential competition analysis, as will be discussed later, and combined with the previous step of consideration of objective characteristics, the methodology suggested above could play an essential role in determining 'like' or 'directly competitive or substitutable' products in the General Agreement.

Having concluded this, one needs to examine procedural matters concerning the application of the CVA-PCPDS. In general, the following recommendations may be made in this regard:

(1) First of all, this survey analysis should be scrutinized with the utmost care because, unlike pre-existing studies, it has not been prepared in the normal course of business for the adoption of business decisions; it could contain a mistake or an intentional distortion. For example, in *Japan Alcoholic Beverages*, a survey conducted among consumers and an econometric study submitted by Japan were pointed out as having several significant defects.[284] Aside from any possible intentional distortion by the survey, one should rightly fear that there could be a problem with individuals misrepresenting their true preferences for strategic reasons. For example, facing lower prices for whisky, advocates of cheaper whisky might give responses that indicate an enormous willingness to switch from shochu to whisky, hoping that a high response will tilt the result in their favour.

(2) This strategic issue might not be a major problem because most people who are surveyed are ignorant of the purpose of the survey, or of the implications of the questions involved.[285] A more fundamental difficulty is that some individuals often may not give thoughtful or *meaningful* responses to the question, inasmuch as it does not involve a decision that they actually will make.[286] Researchers have long known that people's answers to survey questions about their behavior often bear little resemblance to what they actually do.[287] Because there is no cost to being wrong, survey respondents have little incentive to undertake the mental effort needed to be accurate: talk is cheap.

(3) As discussed above, this methodology may have greater problems with respect to reliability, but it does have the advantage that one can obtain trade-off information regarding a wide range of product choices. The underlying issue is how we can best frame the survey questions to elicit the true underlying economic preferences of individuals. In this light, it should be noted that in proceeding with the CVA-PCPDS, several important preconditions should be met:

(a) A sufficient number of consumers should be selected from regular consumers of the product in question, who represent various age groups, both sexes, and regions.[288]

(b) The survey itself must provide respondents with all relevant information. Since that information may be the sole basis for each respondent's choice, it should be noted that slight variations in how it is presented could have a huge impact on the preference a person reports. For example, simply asking 'As you can see, there are five types of spirits and photos of typical brands of these types. Which spirit would you choose at these prices?' may result in less than accurate responses. After all, as it stands, the question could be understood by some respondents as being a one-time offer such as, 'Would you try a bottle of cognac if it was offered at so-and-so price?' These respondents are more likely to answer affirmatively than those interpreting the question as asking 'Would these prices cause you to change your drinking habits?' In this respect, it should be made clear that the hypothetical price change is suggested as a permanent, not transitory, change for the respondents.[289]

In addition to the CVA-PCPDS, i.e., cross-price demand substitutability analysis, proposed above, the *dynamic (non-static) economic analysis* will be helpful in supplementing the static analysis. Good examples of this come in the guise of time-series analyses,[290] such as market share analysis and price comparison studies. Unlike the static study, the results of these analyses confirm dynamic evidence of 'changes' in market share and price, thereby reflecting relative price differentials between the products in question. Furthermore, if successful enough, these analyses can show the transition of consumer tastes and preferences.

Such dynamic studies can be used to verify the correctness of the results of static surveys. Sometimes very reliable results from dynamic studies can substitute for those of static analyses proven to have serious methodological defects. In addition, trends or dynamic evidence obtained through these studies can be used to prove the existence of potential or future competition, as discussed later. Efforts to introduce the dynamic economic analysis into GATT jurisprudence can be found in the decisions of several panels.

In *Canada Periodicals*, Canada submitted a report which showed that the market share of imported and domestic magazines in Canada had remained constant over 30-plus years.[291] But the report was rejected by the Appellate Body on the ground Canadian protection measures could have affected its result.[292] In the analysis, it should be noted that any protection effect must be taken into account. This point leads to the concept of future or potential competition or substitutability, which will be discussed at 3.2.4 below.

In *Japan Alcoholic Beverages*, the Community submitted a market share study showing that, as a result of the 1989 Japanese tax reform, the market share of Japanese domestic whisky fell, which led to a rise in both shochu's and foreign produced whisky's market shares.[293] This analysis showed that shochu and foreign whisky were in fact capturing the market share lost by domestically produced whisky. The fact that the two products in question were competing for the same market was effective evidence that there was elasticity of substitution between them.[294] Against this study, Japan submitted the results of a time-series statistical analysis, which showed no meaningful elasticity of substitution between shochu and whisky.[295] But the results were attacked and not accepted by the Panel because of several significant defects in methodology, such as trends effect,[296] autocorrelation,[297] multicollinearity,[298] and inflation and income effect.[299]

This trend of referring to time-series econometric evidence continued in *Chile Alcoholic Beverages*. The EC, the complaining party, submitted the Gemines Study, which estimated the cross-price elasticity rate between pisco and whisky on the basis of historical sales and price data covering the period 1985–1992.[300] In rebuttal, Chile submitted another regression study over the longer period of 1983–1997, conducted by the Chilean industry, that showed a much lower elasticity than the counterpart study had.[301] But the problem of multicollinearity in this study was strongly indicated by the EC to discount its validity.[302]

In statistical studies involving time-series data, one could normally expect to encounter all of these problems. Therefore, by using relatively standard methods and by taking account of the range of possible errors, one might enhance their credibility.

Furthermore, a 'price comparison study' can be used as a method complementary to time-series statistical analyses. Since the price transition between substitutable goods tends to be similar,[303] this study tests the similarity of price movements over time.[304] Thus, 'indifferent' movements of price over long periods between the two products in question could be used to attack the validity of the time-series analysis.[305]

In addition, studies on 'substitute–complementary' or 'inferior–superior' relationships between goods will be helpful, as reasoned in section 1 of this chapter, in identifying and sorting out *directly* competitive or substitutable relationships in a cluster of interrelated goods.[306]

Figure II.4 summarizes the above discussions.

3.2.3. The Third Factor: Supply Substitutability

Having concluded in 3.1 above that an examination of supply substitutability is necessary to complement demand substitution analysis in certain situations, one must answer the next question: how do we determine supply substitutability?

No guidance has been given in the GATT jurisprudence because no case, until now, has paid due attention to the supply substitution factor in likeness tests (except for limited consideration in *United States Automobiles*, as discussed in 3.1 above). Hence, the only choice is to create a methodology based on the definition of supply substitutability and in reference to demand substitution analysis.[307]

In the first place, an intuitive judgement on the 'ability or willingness of producers to switch their production factors from one product sector to the other'[308] can be made by examining the degree to which the two product sectors have common manufacturing facilities and production employees, and distribute

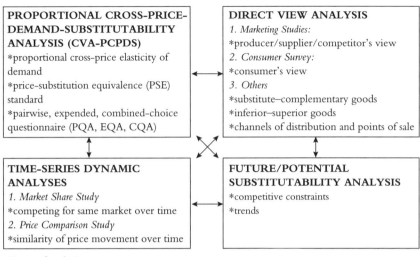

| PROPORTIONAL CROSS-PRICE-DEMAND-SUBSTITUTABILITY ANALYSIS (CVA-PCPDS)
*proportional cross-price elasticity of demand
*price-substitution equivalence (PSE) standard
*pairwise, expended, combined-choice questionnaire (PQA, EQA, CQA) | DIRECT VIEW ANALYSIS
1. *Marketing Studies:*
*producer/supplier/competitor's view
2. *Consumer Survey:*
*consumer's view
3. *Others*
*substitute–complementary goods
*inferior–superior goods
*channels of distribution and points of sale |
| TIME-SERIES DYNAMIC ANALYSES
1. *Market Share Study*
*competing for same market over time
2. *Price Comparison Study*
*similarity of price movement over time | FUTURE/POTENTIAL SUBSTITUTABILITY ANALYSIS
*competitive constraints
*trends |

*Focus of analysis

Figure II.4: Demand Substitutability Analysis

through common or similar distribution channels. Aside from this examination of the 'objective characteristics', one can proceed to market-based supply-substitutability analysis, such as direct view analysis, static cross-price supply-substitution analysis, and dynamic time-series analysis.

Studies about producers' (suppliers') *direct view* of supply substitutability on an *ex ante* or *ex post* basis[309] may provide useful information. These may be based on views expressed by suppliers, including producers, importers and exporters, wholesalers, and retailers. The key question, in this regard, would be whether producers are capable of switching their installed capacity from production of one product to production of the other without a substantial loss of investment. Thus, sometimes, even though the two products in question are considered as being directly substitutable by consumers, they cannot be viewed as being directly competitive by producers because of the existence of certain production or marketing constraints.[310] Demand substitutability is only one of the aspects to be considered by producers in making supply substitution decisions. Any marketing studies or production factor analyses that companies have commissioned in the past, and that are used by companies in their own decision making with regard to production switches, may provide useful information.

In addition to this direct view analysis, or as a more sophisticated variation of it, one can examine the *cross-price elasticity of supply* between the two products in question. This examination proceeds with *surveys* that provide a detailed description of the resource, its current condition, and hypothetical changes in its condition.

Similar to the demand substitution analysis, this kind of study postulates a hypothetical small and non-transitory change in relative prices and evaluates the likely reactions of producers to that change. The question to be answered is whether the respondents would switch their production to the sector in which the relative price has increased in response to a hypothetical small[311] and permanent relative price change between the products in comparison.[312]

As in demand substitutability analysis, the 'proportionality' condition may be continued with this contingent valuation method because product price is directly related to benefits by production switches, and it is reasonable to assume that a two-fold increase in product price would induce, *ceteris paribus*, twice as much supply substitution in the range of not too high or low a price increase.[313] Application of this 'Contingent Valuation Analysis on *Proportional* Cross-Price Supply Substitutability' (CVA-PCPSS) is shown in the following example:

Suppose that two products, X and Y, are alleged to be 'directly competitive or substitutable' products. A certain number of producers of product X could be asked the hypothetical question: if the price of product Y rose by a certain percentage, what would they do?[314] If more than a certain threshold percentage of producers were to switch their production to Y, it would be possible to conclude that X and Y have sufficient supply substitutability. According to the proportionality condition, the threshold switching rate should be proportional to the hypothetical price change rate.[315]

So, what should the threshold switching rate be? If the hypothetical price increase is assumed to be 8 per cent, it is possible to set the threshold rate at a certain point or range between 0 per cent and 100 per cent. Certainly if nobody wanted to switch their production, the two sectors could be said to have low supply substitutability. In contrast, if every respondent answered that they would switch, it would mean that the two sectors have high supply substitutability. But, what rate of switch can reflect the turning point between high and low substitution rates?

There can be no single 'right' answer. Different from the case of cross-price substitutability of demand, here there is no rationale to adopt the PSE Standard because the same 8 per cent threshold of 'supply' substitution in the case of an 8 per cent price rise has nothing to do with a benefit–loss turning point between competitors.[316] In other words, in supply substitution analysis, the price-substitution equivalence (PSE) rate (i.e., the same 8 per cent threshold rate, above) is nothing more than a randomly selected rate.

Having considered that, one might calculate, if available, the average cross-price supply substitutability rate of the 'industry' concerned as a whole and refer to that rate. This approach may be called the 'Industry Average Substitution Rate' (IASR) Standard (see below for its rationale). Here, the word 'industry' means a group of producers producing a similar category of products in a broad sense, such as the 'alcoholic beverage' industry, the 'automobile manufacturing' industry, the 'textile and clothing manufacturing' industry, the 'toy' industry, etc.

To take an example, suppose that shochu and *vodka* were alleged to be directly competitive or substitutable products. The hypothetical questionnaire was constructed to ask whether shochu (vodka) producers would switch to producing vodka (shochu) if there was an 8 per cent price increase for vodka (shochu). Suppose that the result of the CVA-PCPSS turned out to be a 20 per cent switch from one to the other. As noted, one can set as a threshold rate the average supply-substitution rate (cross-price elasticity of supply in case of an 8 per cent price increase) of the 'alcoholic beverage industry'.[317] Hence, shochu and vodka can be said to have high supply substitutability if the IASR of the 'alcoholic beverage industry' is known to be less than 20 per cent.

To change the products in question, suppose that shochu and *whisky* were alleged to be directly competitive or substitutable. Suppose that the CVA-PCPSS rate between shochu and whisky turned out to be 6 per cent.[318] In the above example, suppose that the IASR of the alcoholic beverage industry proved to be 10 per cent. It is possible to conclude that shochu and *vodka* share high supply substitutability and that shochu and *whisky* have low supply substitutability. Suppose that demand substitutability between shochu and *vodka* turned out to be high enough, whereas demand substitutability between shochu and *whisky* proved to be barely higher than the threshold.[319] What should be the outcome of these cases? One can exclude any considerations of potential or future competition for the moment. A high demand substitutability between shochu and *vodka* would lead to a determination of 'directly competitive or substitutable' despite the high supply substitutability (SITUATION I). With regard to shochu and *whisky*, because the low supply substitutability cannot generate the mitigation effect, shochu and whisky will be determined to be 'directly competitive or substitutable' according to the satisfied result of demand substitutability (SITUATION VI). (See further, 3.1 above.)

For the sake of full coverage of possible cases, one can create another category of alcoholic beverage, 'V', that shares with shochu a demand substitutability slightly lower or higher than the PSE threshold level and a supply substitutability that is substantially higher than the IASR threshold (SITUATION V). In this case, excluding any considerations of potential or future competition, one should determine that shochu and V are not directly competitive or substitutable products with regard to origin-neutral discrimination cases involving 'supply-substitutability-test-friendly' provisions.[320] The high supply substitutability between shochu and V and the resulting mitigation effect should be considered in defining the overall relationship between them.

The rationale for the IASR Standard mainly lies in the fact that each industry has its own technology and initial fixed costs, which varies the average supply substitutability across industries. Capital-intensive industries tend to require large investment from the start. For example, one needs to put a lot of money into R & D and production facilities in order to launch semiconductor, automobile, and heavy industries. This will reduce the average supply substitutability—i.e., the 'ability or willingness of producers to switch their production factors from one

product sector to the other'—to a relatively low level in capital-intensive industries. On the other hand, it is known that labour-intensive industries do not require
large amounts of initial investment. Neither do industries based on electronic
commerce. This relatively low fixed cost will lead to a relatively high level of supply substitutability. Of course, both capital- and labour-intensive industries are
composed of numerous separate industries, and each one will possess a different
average supply substitutability.

Hence, different from *demand* substitutability analysis, in which the PSE threshold
provides good guidance, it makes little sense to establish a common threshold of substitutability across all industries for *supply* substitutability analysis. Judgement criteria
of high or low supply substitutability should be based on the given situation and on
the character of each industry, not on the overall market. Indeed, considering that the
reason for taking account of the supply substitutability factor is to accommodate
the mitigation effect, such an across-the-industries threshold does not assist: given the
question whether shochu producers can easily switch to whisky production, why calculate the degree of the switching rate between Timor and Rolls Royce cars? Of
course, in some rare cases in which 'inter'-industry substitutability is at issue, one
needs to define the term 'industry' broadly enough to include both industries
concerned and work out the IASR according to the definition.

The CVA-PCPSS model based on the IASR Standard provides at least two benefits, as does the CVA-PCPDS (see 3.2.2 above). The first benefit is that two key
factors, quantity and price, can be taken into account when deciding the threshold
degree of substitution. In other words, the greater the price change is, the higher
the required switching rate becomes for the two products to qualify as being
supply-substitutable.[321] This benefit cannot be furnished by any non-availability-type
analysis,[322] which tends to exaggerate actual substitution rates.

The second benefit is, most importantly, that, relying upon the standard, WTO
tribunals can increase consistency and transparency in their decisions. Continuous
use of certain criteria by subsequent panels would build up certain practices or
consensus concerning threshold levels of supply substitution that is necessary to
complement demand-side analyses.

Other than these basic merits, one should note that the IASR Standard,
compared to the PSE Standard, has less of a structural problem in designing the
questionnaire. Whereas the question presented to respondents in the CVA-PCPDS
with PSE Standard should basically involve a pairwise choice (see 3.2.2 above), the
IASR Standard does not impose this limitation on the CVA-PCPSS because there
is no need to calculate a benefit–loss turning point. Thus, the CVA-PCPSS
questionnaire can be designed to ask multiple-choice questions; suppliers can
respond to hypothetical situations much closer to the real business world. As a
result, problems of overvaluation or undervaluation would be substantially eliminated. Indeed, if the shochu price were to rise, not only might vodka producers
switch in, but some whisky producers might do so as well (vodka producers would
take into account this effect). On the other hand, if the shochu price were to fall,

some shochu producers would switch not only to vodka, but also to whisky, sake, beer, or even wine. Of course, this merit presupposes that the multiple-choice-type IASR is obtainable.

To summarize, the IASR Standard as employed in the CVA-PCPSS could be used as a standard to determine supply substitutability in various GATT provisions. Combined with potential or future competition analysis, as discussed at 3.2.4 below, and considerations of objective characteristics as described at 3.2.1 above, this analysis and standard could be used to complement demand substitutability analysis. This combination could cure many of the possible problems of demand-side-only approaches, and make the likeness provisions more consistent with the purposes of the GATT.[323] Several methodological recommendations made in the context of the application of the CVA-PCPDS analysis can be similarly suggested here, such as caution against possible intentional distortion or misrepresentation by respondents, and guidelines for constructing neutral questionnaires and maintaining representative samples.[324]

In addition to the CVA-PCPSS, *dynamic economic analyses* can be helpful in supplementing a static analysis. Certain time-series data, or analyses of supply substitution practices of enterprises, or market entry information can be referred to. Using the dynamic evidence of the 'changes' reflected in these information and data, one could verify the correctness or representativeness of results from the CVA-PCPSS. Sometimes, very reliable results from dynamic studies can substitute for results from static analyses proven to have serious methodological defects. Moreover, the trends or dynamic evidence obtained through these studies can be used to prove the existence of 'potential competition', as discussed at 3.2.4.

In appraising the value of dynamic data, one should pay attention to frequently encountered statistical errors, such as trends effect, autocorrelation, multicollinearity, and inflation and income effect.[325]

This discussion is summarized in Figure II.5.

3.2.4. *The Fourth Factor: Potential or Future Competition or Substitutability*

The last factor in the analytical framework to which regard should be had is that of potential or future competition. It is not clear how much consideration, if any, the GATT drafters gave to the 'potentiality' factor in defining likeness or substitutability, when they worked on various like product provisions. It seems, though, that it caught at least one delegate's attention at the Havana Conference. According to that delegate, a tax on coal in a particular case might be designed to protect the fuel oil industry.[326] Most power generation systems are set up to utilize either coal or fuel oil, but not both, thereby making the two products not directly competitive;[327] but some larger power generators may be convertible from coal to fuel oil or a series of power stations in a particular market could be due for replacement and alternative fuel sources might become viable alternatives. In such instances, according to the delegate, one might be able to say that there is 'potential' direct competition.[328]

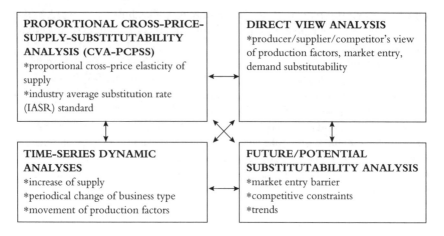

Figure II.5: Supply Substitutability Analysis

Many GATT likeness provisions are designed to protect the expectation that a competitive relationship will exist between like products. These provisions are designed not only to protect current trade, but also to create the predictability needed to plan future trade. Thus, in the case of these predictability-oriented provisions, one can argue that even if a given regulation in its application does not currently discriminate between products, it violates the obligation if it poses the risk of discrimination in the future.[329]

The best example for the purpose of this argument would be the national treatment obligation in Art. III of the GATT.[330] Under this provision, consideration of potential or future competition has been reflected in such rulings as:

(1) the Art. III prohibition on discriminatory taxes and regulations is not conditioned on a 'trade effects test',[331]
(2) the obligation is not qualified by a *de minimis* exception[332], and
(3) it is not subject to an offsets rule in which less favourable treatment of some imported products can be balanced against more favourable treatment for other imported products.[333]

It should be noted that the common focus of these rulings is on the interpretation of the phrase, 'no less favourable treatment'.[334] For the present purpose, however, our concern is whether consideration of potential or future competition should be reflected in the interpretation of the terms 'like', or 'competitive or substitutable'. In other words, what the aforementioned rulings have generally considered is whether *potentially less favourable treatment* is given to the foreign product sharing a 'current' likeness relationship with the favoured product. On the other hand, our focus here is on whether a *potential likeness* relationship should be included in the likeness test in addition to a current likeness relationship; and if so, how these relationships may be brought together.

Aside from *Canada Periodicals*, in which the potentiality factor was taken into consideration to discount the validity of a market share analysis showing 'unlikeness' between domestic and foreign magazines,[335] the strongest support for the role of potentiality in defining 'likeness' was given in *Korea Alcoholic Beverages* in the context of Art. III of the General Agreement. First, with regard to the definition of potential competition, the Panel in this case prescribed that:

Panels should look at evidence of trends and changes in consumption patterns and make an assessment as to whether such trends and patterns lead to the conclusion that products in question are either directly competitive now or can reasonably be expected to become directly competitive *in the near future*. . . . such an analysis also requires making an assessment about *what would happen* in the theoretical case of the tax differentials being removed.[336]

Then the Panel turned to the subject matter:

We do not agree with Korea's narrow interpretation. The Panel is examining the nature of the competitive relationship and determining whether there is an actual or potential relationship sufficiently direct to come within the strictures of Article III:2, second sentence. The physical characteristics themselves must be reviewed for if two products are physically identical or nearly so, then it obviously means that there is a greater potential for a direct competitive relationship.[337]

This Panel's heavy reliance on the potentiality factor was fully supported by the Appellate Body in *Korea Alcoholic Beverages*, which held that:

The term 'directly competitive or substitutable' describes a particular type of relationship between two products, one imported and the other domestic. It is evident from the wording of the term that the essence of that relationship is that the products are in competition. This much is clear both from the word 'competitive', which means 'characterized by competition', and from the word 'substitutable', which means 'able to be substituted'. The context of the competitive relationship is necessarily the marketplace since this is the forum where consumers choose between different products. Competition in the marketplace is a dynamic, evolving process. Accordingly, the wording of the term 'directly competitive or substitutable' implies that the competitive relationship between products is *not* to be analyzed *exclusively* by reference to *current* consumer preferences. In our view, the word 'substitutable' indicates that the requisite relationship *may* exist between products that are not, at a given moment, considered by consumers to be substitutes but which are, nonetheless, *capable* of being substituted for one another. Thus, according to the ordinary meaning of the term, products are competitive or substitutable when they are interchangeable.[338]

It is no wonder that this emphasis on potential competition reappeared soon in the similar case of *Chile Alcoholic Beverages*, in which the Panel relied upon the potential competition factor to discount results of low cross-price elasticity between pisco and imported spirits, shown by several economic analyses.[339]

Table II.1: Potential Competition Factor

Point of examination	Consumer's viewpoint	Supplier's viewpoint
But for illegal competitive restraints	'Potential substitution'	'Potential competition'
Clear and stable future development	'Future substitution'	'Future competition'

In general, the concept of *potential competition, as a generic term,* can be quite a broad one that includes the following four categories. If current impediments in the market are removed, some consumers might want to switch their consumption from A to B *now,* which can be called 'potential *substitution'*. Or even though others do not want to switch now, they might want to do so *in the near future,* which represents 'future *substitution'*. The same can be said of producers; their supply substitution decisions depend not only on current impediments ('potential *competition'* in a narrow sense), but also on future prospects ('future *competition'*) (see Table II.1).[340]

It seems impossible to draw absolutely clear lines among these concepts. In fact, there could exist substantial overlap between such concepts and analysis of demand or supply substitutability, on the one hand, and 'potential or future substitution or competition', on the other. Behind every transaction, many *potential* buyers exist. Some of them would switch immediately to substitutable products, others would watch for future price developments. The scope of potential sellers is extensive too. If a certain product is selling very well in a certain market, earning extreme profits for the producer of that product, producers of other 'not-substitutable-at-all' products might want to switch their production activity to this golden business; this possibility becomes greater in the long run.

In fact, it may be argued that most production factors are not fixed. For example, the vats used to brew beer and the stamping presses used to build auto bodies could be said to be not substitutable for each other, and so these different kinds of equipment are industry-specific. Given time, however, it is possible to redirect investment from auto factories to breweries, or vice versa, and so, in a long-term sense, both vats and stamping presses can be considered to be two manifestations of a single, mobile factor called capital.[341] Workers too could be said to be quite mobile.[342] Thus, it can be said that in certain circumstances, most products have the potential to be substituted, no matter how small the potentiality is.

For the purpose of the GATT likeness test, this 'ordinary' understanding of potentiality is not what 'potential competition or substitution' means. The concept of '*potential* competition or substitution' presupposes a situation in which any protective effect created by the discriminatory measure is removed. It gives rise to the question of what would happen in the theoretical case of the allegedly discriminatory measures being removed. Does it make a difference for likeness or substitutability? 'Demand or supply substitutability', discussed at 3.2.2 and 3.2.3 above, does not have this presupposition.

Accordingly, the '*potential* competition or substitution' examination proceeds throughout a certain time frame: one examines possible change in demand or supply substitution over a period under the above-mentioned presupposition. Usually, this examination covers the period during which the protective effect has been in place. By contrast, demand or supply substitution in the CVA-PCPDS or CVA-PCPSS is an on-the-spot concept focused on current status. What is the 'current' rate of demand or supply substitutability between the products under consideration?

'*Future* substitution or competition' is a flow concept as well. During an extended time-period, the 'future substitution or competition' test examines possible developments of *current* demand or supply substitutability as well as the development of '*potential* substitution or competition'. In other words, the test asks what would happen, in a designated future time frame, to current demand or supply substitution; and what would happen in the same period if the allegedly discriminatory measures were removed.[343]

The Panel and the Appellate Body in *Korea Alcoholic Beverages* recognized that 'potential substitution' and 'future substitution' were relevant factors in the likeness determination of Art. III of the GATT. In fact, the Korean Panel's decision relied heavily upon the concept of 'future and potential substitution'.[344] Justifying this reliance, the Panel reasoned that trade law generally focuses on the promotion of economic opportunities for importers, and that Art. III of the GATT, in particular, protects 'expectations' not of any particular trade volume, but rather of the 'equal competitive relationship' between imported and domestic products.[345]

Proponents of this view would emphasize that this reasoning given by the Korean tribunal is relevant not only to Art. III of the GATT, but also to international trade law in general. The main goal of international trade law is to facilitate free trade by prohibiting various discriminatory endeavours; thus, the law generally extends its focus to the protection of economic opportunities for importers, beyond the mere correction of current distortions in the market. These economic opportunities could not be fully protected unless such factors as potential or future competition were taken into account as well. Therefore, according to such proponents of the view, 'time' and 'opportunity (potentiality)' factors should be added to the basic aspects to be considered in likeness or substitutability analysis, and complete analysis of likeness or substitutability cannot be obtained through a 'static' understanding but requires a 'dynamic' one.

On the other hand, opponents of this view might put forward a textual argument that relying heavily upon the concepts of future and potential competition does not fit with the language of the GATT in that: (1) Art. III:1 and Art. III:2, first sentence, speak of products 'imported into the territory' of a contracting party; (2) according to *Ad* Art. III:2, a complaint must show that competition was 'involved', requiring the 'existence' of substitution between directly competitive products; and (3) not mere competition but a 'direct' competitive relationship should be shown. The practical concerns of such opponents would mostly revolve around the implications that the potential or future competition criteria could bring into the likeness or substitutability determination. Indeed, these criteria have enough 'potential' to be used as a tool for an overly broad strike-down of legitimate governmental policies, as discussed in 2.2 above. It should be restated that these concepts of potential and anticipatory substitutability, enabling panels to refer to other markets whenever they want,[346] might be used as a fallback tool, being invoked whenever panels cannot find empirical evidence.

What, then, might be the most appropriate position about the admissibility of the potential or future competition factor in the GATT likeness test?

With regard to '*potential* competition or substitutability', the answer could be easily sought by striking a balance between the two opposing views mentioned above. As far as protecting the expectation of competitive opportunities is concerned, which is the basic purpose of the GATT non-discrimination provisions, the GATT likeness determination should pay due regard to the concept of 'potential substitution or competition' as necessary. As indicated by the Korean Appellate Body, the very language of 'substitut*able*' in relevant provisions contains such flexibility.[347] At the same time, working on the potentiality factor, one should pay due attention to the legitimate concern over possible abuses. The application of the potentiality factor in a specific determination of likeness or substitutability should not be justified unless no less favourable regard is given to the possible misuse of the powerful tool. In other words, the international tribunals must not be allowed simply to 'speculate' that, absent discrimination, there might be now, or at some stage in the future, a directly competitive or substitutable relationship between the products in question. Differences between speculation and qualified discretion do not lie in the declaration but in the evidence. Information on trends and change of consumer or producer choice, obtained through proper economic analyses, will provide a helpful source of such evidence.

The inclusion of 'potential substitutability' or 'potential competition' into the likeness test is less controversial than the inclusion of 'future substitutability' or 'future competition'. In the potentiality analysis, there could be relatively ample information from which tribunals could draw justifiable conclusions. Indeed, if the potentiality factor were not taken into account, those nations maintaining the highest trade barriers would effectively be protected, because there would be no 'actual' competition in the market between domestic products and imported like or substitutable products that are already excluded from the market.[348] Where 'future substitution or competition' is concerned, however, controversy is inherent. One could question whether it is desirable for international tribunals to intervene and issue orders about future relationships between products, about which it is only possible to speculate.[349] Whereas the 'potentiality' factor deserves to be included in the likeness test because the defending party in a certain dispute would be responsible for the barriers that have prevented that potentiality from being realized, speculation about the 'future realization' of the competitive relationship does not create such a responsibility for the party—at least not now. Accordingly, opponents of the future competition analysis might have some grounds for arguing that it would not be too late to bring the case before the international tribunals after the *future* competition or substitution is *realized* into at least *potential* competition or substitutability. At that point the door of the WTO is open.

This should not be to argue, however, that *any* future competitiveness or substitution aspect should be excluded from the consideration of likeness. What it should lead to is the idea that the future aspect must not be an 'independent' or an 'important' basis on which to render a determination of likeness. Examination of future substitution or competition should proceed only in order to confirm the validity of the contemporary or potentiality analysis, or to complement it. For example,

(1) when a potential competition test returns a result slightly below a certain threshold, a strong prospect of future competition may be referred to in making the opposite determination; or

(2) despite present or potential substitution tests giving a result a little above a certain threshold, a strong prospect of diminishing future substitutability may be taken into account, with the consequence that the determination may favour the other side.

In particular, this complementary role of the future competition factor becomes important in high-tech, short shelf-life product sectors, such as semiconductors, in which current competitive relationships between products may predictably be transitory. In these sectors, competitors strive to sell high volumes of the product quickly before it becomes obsolete following the development of a new, more powerful, more commercially appealing product. Governments may have strong but short-lasting incentives to afford protection to such products against similar foreign products or future superior products. In these circumstances, if the GATT likeness test does not internalize considerations of future substitution or competition, the likeness provisions might be of limited use, because by the time a ruling by the tribunal is handed down, the technology involved is likely to have moved on to the next generation of products. In an extreme case, one might be able to envisage circumstances in which the competitive relationship that may have existed between two products when the complaint was filed will have dissipated by the time the dispute settlement procedure is over. On the other hand, a superior product may be in the early stages of eliminating all rivals at the time of a ruling, so that present competitive relationships between other products are of no consequence to a reasonably predictable future relationship.[350]

As a result, implementing a panel decision that does not reflect the future dimension could bring no practical meaning for the complaining industry. Furthermore, such GATT rulings would hardly have disciplinary force on future GATT violators. The law might never quite catch up to technological advancement. This problem can be effectively dealt with by relying on the complementary role of the future substitution or competition test. The test enables the examiner to focus not just on one particular type of semiconductor—e.g., the 32 M DRAM—but on likely future generations of such chips as well—the 32 M DRAM *and above*. If the tribunal were to find discriminatory a measure with respect to this broadly defined like product, new generations of dynamic random access memory semiconductors having memory capacities larger than 32 megabites would presumably be subject to the GATT discipline.[351] This would save energy and resources for a new fact-finding mission and a new determination by the tribunal, to be commenced as soon as the current procedure is completed. On the other hand, the examination of future substitution or competition enables the tribunal to 'graduate' from the likeness or substitutability coverage of the 16 M DRAM, which will surely disappear from the market by the time the panel decision is rendered.

It should be noted that this expansive definition of likeness based on the future factor makes international trade law more flexible and responsive to the needs of high-technology industries. Such responsiveness could result in a greater reliance upon the law, as well as in less legislative effort to amend the law sweepingly so as to accomplish the same objective.[352]

Having included potential/future substitution or competition into the likeness test as the fourth factor, one's attention turns to the methodology for assessing the evidence of potential or future relationships. The following was suggested by the Korean Panel:

We will not attempt to speculate on what could happen in the distant future, but we will consider evidence pertaining to what could reasonably be expected to occur in the near term based on the evidence presented. How much weight to be accorded such evidence must be decided on a case-by-case basis in light of the market structure and other factors including the quality of the evidence and the extent of the inference required. To try to limit the inquiry as to what might happen this instant were the tax laws changed would involve us in making arbitrary distinctions between expectations now and those in the near future. Obviously, evidence as to what would happen now is more probative in nature than what would happen in the future, but most evidence cannot be so conveniently parsed. If one is dealing with products that are experience based consumer items, then trends are particularly important and it would be unrealistic and, indeed, analytically unhelpful to attempt to separate every piece of evidence and disregard that which discusses implications for market structure in the near future.[353]

Furthermore, as an economic analysis submitted by Korea presented a low co-relationship between Korean soju and foreign whisky, and as the validity of the Dodwell Study[354] submitted by the complainants was effectively attacked by Korea, the Panel turned its attention to the Japanese market, which was, according to the Panel's view, a 'comparable' foreign market to the Korean market:

We continue to disagree that the only relevant market for collecting data is the Korean domestic market. Rather the Korean market is the one that is the subject of our decision. In assessing the potential for products to be directly competitive with or substitutable for the domestic products it is relevant to look at how the domestic Korean companies produce, advertise and distribute their products in other markets as well as in Korea. Such evidence may be valuable for confirming or challenging trends and identifying important characteristics of the market that is the subject of the determination. In this case, the trends in the Japanese market where shochu and imported western-style beverages became increasingly used for the same purposes and the behaviour of Korean firms that met the challenge of imports with versions of soju increasingly similar to such imported beverages are relevant confirmation of what exists, albeit in a somewhat nascent form, in the Korean market.[355]

Even though the Korean Panel, confronting the difficult issue of potential or future competition, put forward the workable methodology of the 'Comparable Market Approach', the Panel's heavy reliance on the approach should be reviewed from a critical point of view. One should be cautious about the negative implications that this approach might bring. It should be noted that the decision on which foreign market is a comparable market to the market at issue is one for the WTO tribunals alone, and they are usually strangers to the markets concerned.

In the worst case scenario, this approach might return the nascent market-based end-use analysis to the 'old cabinet' that contains mostly objective characteristics, as indicated at 2.2 above. In other words, it is possible that, being forced to be compared with the competitive relationship in a foreign market selectively chosen by the tribunals, the likeness or substitutability concept in the *market at issue* might lose its market-based elements altogether. Starting from the abstract (separated from the marketplace) in 1970, the GATT likeness test might return to the abstract again, with the 'effective' assistance rendered by the potential or future competition factor.

Having this potential danger in mind, one might suggest the following methodology to parse the potentiality and time factor in the likeness or substitutability analysis. First, how can the examiner obtain reliable information on a 'potential *substitution*' between products A and B? One of the best answers lies nowhere else than in the CVA-PCPDS (see 3.2.2). Because 'potential substitutability' means a substitution rate that would exist 'but for' an allegedly discriminatory measure, one can calculate the specific degree of potential substitutability by referring to consumer responses to survey questions, in which small hypothetical price changes are given starting from a certain *base price level that would have existed now but for the discriminatory measure* ('pre-measure price' (PMP); see Appendix III). In other words, by using the PMP, not the actual price, in the questionnaire of the CVA-PCPDS, one could remove the protective effect, created by the discrimination, from the outcome of the analysis. The same can be said of 'potential *competition*'. By using the PMP in the questionnaire ('PMP Questionnaire') of the CVA-PCPSS (see 3.2.3), the examiner could obtain the 'genuine' supply substitutability.

In proceeding with this PMP Questionnaire approach, one noteworthy problem is that this methodology might not remove all possible distortions created by the protection—the 'undervaluation' problem. The Panel in *Korea Alcoholic Beverages*, as can be seen in the following extract, raised this point:

The use of cross-price elasticity of demand was approved but it was specifically noted that it is not the decisive criterion. While a high degree of cross-price elasticity of demand would tend to support the argument that there is a direct competitive relationship, it is only one evidentiary factor. If there is a high quantitative level of competition between products, it is likely that the qualitative nature of the competition is direct. However, the lack of such evidence may be due to the governmental measures in question. As noted, both panels in *Japan—Taxes on Alcoholic Beverages I and II* made the observation that government policies can influence consumer preferences to the benefit of the domestic industry. It was stated that:

> a tax system that discriminates against imports has the consequence of creating and even *freezing preferences* for consumer goods. In the Panel's view, this meant that the consumer surveys in a country with such a tax system would likely *understate the degree of potential competitiveness* between substitutable products.[356]

This is particularly a problem if the products involved are consumer items that are so-called *experience goods* which means that consumers tend to purchase what is familiar to them and experiment only reluctantly... Thus the question is not of the degree of competitive overlap, but its nature.[357]

The point is that the 'pre-measure-price methodology' is not effective enough to melt down, at the time of the survey, the *already-frozen preferences* of consumers who are subject to the questionnaire, and that this is all the more true in cases involving so-called 'experience goods'. The same can be said of the 'potential competition' factor. Since the producers were not sufficiently 'experienced' for supply substitution because of the protectionist measure, the producers responding to the PMP Questionnaire of CVA-PCPSS might express their preferences for *potential* supply substitution at a level lower than the 'genuine' rate of substitution.

It is true that this problem of undervaluation could be more relevant for experience goods, such as alcoholic beverages, tobacco, and some kinds of pharmaceutical products, because consumer preference for those products tends to be frozen more solidly. How can this problem be avoided? One solution is the following. To reduce the effect of the 'frozen preferences' in the potential competition or substitution analysis, the examiner should pay special attention to the composition of the respondents. By choosing respondents for the PMP Questionnaire who are 'neutral' consumers (or suppliers), undervaluation might be prevented or reduced. For example, if the subject is whether shochu and whisky are 'directly competitive or substitutable' products, respondents to the PMP Questionnaire could be drawn from consumers (or suppliers) who have substantial experience of buying (or producing) *both* shochu and whisky. Or more weight could be given to young respondents who have not 'frozen' their preferences for any alcoholic beverages yet.[358] To achieve this 'neutrality', additional questions would need to be included in the questionnaire—for instance, 'How often do you consume shochu and/or whisky?'. Answers to this type of question would help to distinguish experienced consumers from the inexperienced, and thus to identify neutral respondents.[359]

Lastly, our inquiry into the framework for the GATT likeness or substitutability analysis requires a further question to be addressed: how can one parse the controversial factor of 'future substitutability or competition' for use in certain limited situations?[360] Only one answer is possible: reasonable speculation based on evidence. The future does not exist, neither has it been blocked by discriminatory measures. A practical methodology might be to insert additional questions in this regard into the PMP Questionnaire. One might call this the 'Future Competition Questionnaire' approach. Examples of such questions are:

(1) For each hypothetical change of price, to which product will you switch consumption (or production) in the near future, if not now?
(2) Do you expect a persistent price increase (or decrease) in sectors A or B? If so, what effect would the price change have on your general consumption (or production) pattern?
(3) What are the bases for the answers given to the questions listed above?

A specific time frame could be suggested to the respondents. Given that the average duration of the WTO dispute settlement procedure is one to two years, the 'near future' in question (1) above could be defined as meaning within the next two years.[361]

Answers to these questions should be examined with the utmost care. These speculations by consumers or producers should be supported by evidential factors in the market concerned, such as a strong and persistent trend concerning the transition of consumer preferences, price increases within a certain sector, technological development, and age group distribution.[362] Sometimes, a trend of change in other countries' markets provides such evidence: for example, a trend of change in one country may indicate what will happen to future demand in another country. In this regard, a well-designed Comparable Market Approach (as suggested by the Korean Panel, above) may be used to confirm the result of the Future Competition Questionnaire approach.

Of course, because each provision of the GATT has a different purpose, the specific extent or degree of potentiality or future effect to be considered in those provisions could be different too. This is discussed further in Chapter III.

3.2.5. Any Other Factor?: Aim and Effect

From time to time, mostly in the context of GATT Art. III, factors other than those mentioned in the *Border Tax Adjustments* Report have been suggested as elements to be taken into account, or as further conditions that have to be satisfied in order for products to be 'like'.[363]

In *United States Malt Beverages* and *United States Automobiles*, account was taken of both the 'purpose or aim' and the 'effect' of the measures in question.[364] Since these decisions seem to be the only ones in which non-BTA factors were actually reflected in the Panels' like product determinations,[365] the 'aim-and-effect'-based interpretation of the likeness or substitutability should be thoroughly reviewed.

In *United States Malt Beverages* and *United States Automobiles*, attention was paid to both the purposes and the effects of the measure in question to determine likeness.[366] In fact, the idea of considering 'purpose and effect' goes back to the earlier case of *EEC Animal Feed Proteins*, in which the 'objective and effect' of the regulation in question were taken into account as valid factors to determine direct substitutability.[367] This debate, as to whether the 'aim and effect' of legislation restricting imports should modify the scope of 'like' or 'directly competitive or substitutable' products, has played a significant role in the interpretation of likeness and substitutability. Given its heavy reliance on the subjective factor of 'aim', the 'aim-and-effect'[368] theory may be dubbed an 'anti-economic approach' to the interpretation of likeness or substitutability.

The proponents of the aim-and-effect test say that whether two products are like or substitutable depends on the 'perspective' from which they are viewed, and suggest an example: '*A fox and an eagle are like animals to a hare but not to a furrier . . .*'.[369] According to them, since the 'perspective' cannot be examined without looking at both the aim and effect of the measure in question, the aim and effect must be considered as being central factors in determining likeness. Therefore, based on the language of Art. III:1,[370] this view leads to the understanding that if the tax distinction in question is not being 'applied so as to afford protection to domestic production', the products between which the distinction is drawn are not to be deemed 'like or directly substitutable products' for the purpose of Art. III.

Most of what is attractive about the aim-and-effect approach lies in its function of enhancing the regulatory autonomy of member states. Proponents of the aim-and-effect theory argue that since GATT Art. XX, imposing the harsh burden of proof on the regulating party,[371] lists limited policy goals that justify measures deviating from the other provisions,[372] the aim-and-effect test can justify more legitimate policies by distinguishing between different product categories.[373]

Despite this attractive aspect, the aim-and-effect theory cannot overcome its critical weaknesses—namely, the lack of textual basis and the ample risk of circumvention. First, although the United States indicated in *Japan Alcoholic Beverages* that (1) 'legitimate objectives' are not exhaustively defined in the TBT Agreement Art. 2.2;[374] (2) the European Court of Justice (ECJ) had taken a similar aim-and-effect type approach in interpreting Art. 95 (now Art. 90) of the EC Treaty;[375] and (3) the General Agreement on Trade in Services (GATS) has a narrower exceptions list than the GATT does,[376] Art. III:2, first sentence, and Art. III:4 do not make reference to the first paragraph of Art. III:1,[377] in which the phrase 'so as to afford protection' appears and which plays a critical role as the textual basis of the aim-and-effect approach. There is no other specific language in the GATT itself that supports an aim-and-effect-based interpretation.

Secondly, although the aim-and-effect test has its merits in relation to Art. XX, in far more cases it can be used to justify circumvention of the carefully designed requirements defined in the chapeau (i.e. introductory part) of Art. XX. Since the conditions for Art. XX exceptions are more restrictive than those for the aim-and-effect approach in the context of Art. III,[378] no member would bother to invoke

Art. XX. As a consequence, the burden of proof, which in GATT Art. XX lies with the respondent, is subtly, but effectively, shifted to the complainant.[379]

The 'independent' approach to interpreting likeness or substitutability, rejecting the aim-and-effect test and, further, excluding any extraneous factors from the scope of the consideration, has its merits. It can play a significant role in enhancing predictability by allowing panels to concentrate on the likeness or substitutability test itself and by requiring them to make the utmost efforts to find out the truth of the matter.

Since the *Border Tax Adjustments* Report, many panels have heavily relied upon visible and objective elements in determining like products, to the detriment of invisible, market-based elements. It seems that this preoccupation is, more or less, due to the 'implicit' effect of an aim-and-effect approach. In other words, when the legitimacy of the aim of the measure is in doubt in a panel's mind, that itself gives panels 'courage' to *limit* their investigations to examination of objective characteristics. Preoccupied with objective elements, they do not bother to reject the results of abstract likeness tests that lack balance or sufficient evidence. Whether the regulation in question was imposed 'so as to afford protection' has played a *de facto* supplementary role in determining likeness or substitutability.

Indeed, because of that danger, it seems that the Appellate Body was at pains to emphasize that 'likeness' and the 'affording protection' factor were 'entirely separate'.[380] Rejecting the aim-and-effect test and requiring more thorough and transparent analyses will cure the preoccupation syndrome.[381] The notion of the 'like' or 'directly competitive or substitutable' product should be, in all cases, an independent one, free from any extraneous considerations. The purpose (or aims) and the effect of a regulatory measure should be totally alien to that notion. An apple does not cease to be an apple only because the legislator does not pursue evil intentions when decreeing that it is an orange.[382] Similarly, *a fox and an eagle can be seen as like animals to a hare, but they are different animals when the hare happens to be put on top of a tree: what makes a difference is not the aim of the hare but the tree.* That is why the fox and eagle should look at the tree, i.e., the market.

Although the Appellate Body in *United States Gasoline, EC Bananas, and Japan/Korea/Chile Alcoholic Beverages,* followed the above principle, hinting that aim and effect is not the proper test,[383] extraneous considerations are always a latent issue in theory and practice. Indeed, despite its serious problems of not squaring with the text of the GATT and the great risk of circumvention, the attraction of the aim-and-effect theory might indicate that there is a loophole in the GATT, and this possibility is strong enough to make one ponder a solution. This might be sought by taking note of, and giving full meaning to, the phrases 'not in a manner contrary to the principle' (Art. III:2), 'no less favourable' (Art. III:4), and 'similarly taxed' (*Ad* Art. III:2), so that these phrases would have the flexibility to accommodate certain tax differences based on legitimacy and transparency (i.e., by paying attention to the differences between 'discrimination' and 'differentiation' while putting aim–and–effect factors outside the remit of likeness or substitutability tests). Any detailed discussion of this matter is beyond the scope of this book.

3.3. 'Likeness or Substitutability Model' and its Application Methodology

Beginning with the conceptual classification of the relationship between goods, our inquiry has brought us a long way, up to the relevant factors for the GATT likeness or substitutability analysis. It has attempted to produce consistent interpretations of such terms as 'like', 'competitive', 'substitutable', 'directly', 'demand substitutability', 'supply substitutability', 'potential competition/substitutability', 'future competition/substitutability', and 'market-based end-use'. Based upon these interpretations, it has established four factors to constitute the likeness or substitutability analysis of the GATT/WTO: objective characteristics; demand substitutability; supply substitutability; and potential/future competition. To examine demand and supply substitutability, two economic models and two economic standards were suggested: for demand substitution, the CVA-PCPDS with PSE Standard; and for supply substitution, the CVA-PCPSS with IASR Standard. These models were extended to examine 'potential competition or substitutability' and 'future competition or substitutability'. In the process, the PMP Approach was taken and questions were added to the Questionnaire to identify 'neutral' respondents as well as to examine future consumption or supply. To confirm the validity of the results of these models, dynamic analysis and direct view analysis were suggested. Possible methodological defects and procedural guidelines in applying these models and standards were also discussed.

These discussions and suggestions are based on the rationale or theoretical ground, as discussed in Chapter I, that economic approaches can improve transparency and consistency in the dispute settlement procedure of the WTO, which will enhance the enforceability of the General Agreement in the forthcoming *drive-to-maturity* era.

Of course, the reality of the situation is not always so pleasant. Unfortunately, most of the time, the methodological luxuries suggested above are not entirely available to the GATT/WTO examiner who is determining likeness or substitutability. It is more likely that the kind of information necessary to construct the full analytical framework will almost never be available, to say nothing of its being amenable to the WTO dispute settlement procedure. Parties and enterprises tend to resist disclosure efforts and, even when outsiders can obtain access, the accuracy of the information is always in peril.[384] Information about how consumers will react at a given time to a price increase is not easily obtainable, and estimates are unlikely to be very reliable. For example, if the price of shochu were to rise from $2.00 per bottle to $2.20, what would vodka consumers, whisky consumers, wine consumers, and producers of these products do? Some would switch immediately to substitutes, others would regard shochu as a bargain at an even higher price, and a third group might hedge its bets while awaiting future price developments.[385] Since a comparable price increase usually will not occur, estimates will necessarily be speculative. In any event, the amount and complexity of information necessary to measure product substitutability with a high degree of accuracy would swamp any tribunal.[386]

This may be the most important reason why each and every tribunal involved with the likeness issue has gone to great lengths to emphasize the *unavoidable element of individual, discretionary judgement*. A tribunal cannot explore the world economy in order to reach a decision in one, particular case and, therefore, is compelled to simplify.[387] As a result, most tribunals start out with the 'physical properties–tariff classification–general end-use' test, despite its recognized shortcomings.[388]

The test is workable enough in simple cases not only because it enables the examiner to simplify, but also because in many cases the four factors are correlated with each other. There may be a strong correlation, for example, between objective characteristics and demand substitutability;[389] demand substitutability and supply substitutability;[390] or objective characteristics and potential/future competition.[391] Sometimes, albeit very rarely, all four factors might be perfectly correlated with each other. In this case, examination of the objective characteristic factor alone would be enough to render an appropriate likeness determination. However, when the examiner insists on the simplified test even though the degree of correlation is unknown, controversy is latent. A more serious problem could arise when the examiner continues to rely on the test, resisting a widely-known low correlation among the four factors with regard to the subject matter and/or in the relevant market at issue. Hence, this test, which is otherwise workable, breaks down when tough questions are raised.

The WTO tribunals often do face extremely close like product questions. For example, does domestic sherry compete with imported sauternes? Are shochu and cognac directly competitive or substitutable products? What about beer? Are buses and subway trains directly competitive products? What about canned orange and apple juice? Tomato sauce for pasta, tomato juice, and concentrated tomato? Among Lincoln Continentals, Mercedes-Benz, Mercury Mystiques, and Hyundai Elantras, which cars are like products? Which of these cars are directly competitive or substitutable products? What about used Honda Civics? Does it make a difference whether it is a 1970s Civic or a 1990s Civic? Among liquid sugar, syrup, granulated sugar, and industrially produced sugar substitutes (such as saccharine, cyclamates, or aspartame), which one is a like product to sugar and which one is a directly competitive product to sugar? Are such products as wine, sangria, cider, perry, and mead[392] directly substitutable products? What about magazines dedicated to news, gardening, chess, sports, music, and cuisine? Lastly, what are the answers to these questions in each like product provision of the GATT?

In these examples, it is important, in the first place, for tribunals to remember that likeness or substitutability tests are tools for the authoritative determination of product similarity or substitutability, rather than scientific tests that produce a single, objective answer. It should also be kept in mind, however, that science could provide excellent research tools with which the tribunals could render consistent and transparent rulings. Playing the accordion is, in essence, an art, rather than a science, but the performance will be appreciated by the audience all the more if it is a scientific art.

Problems could arise in many ways. First, a panel, facing a difficult case, may permit or require the parties to exhaust enormous resources and efforts in a most probably fruitless search for some ideal of likeness or substitutability. The economic reasoning might go on almost endlessly, if permitted, or the party with the fewest experts, market research techniques, and other resources might eventually collapse.[393]

Secondly, having invested heavily, often with less than satisfying results, in this unusual fact-finding venture, the tribunal might feel impelled to make use of the results in its findings and opinion, perhaps making them appear more cogent and relevant to the decision than they really are.[394] The worst outcome is when the substitution rate thus produced is treated as being dispositive and all the reasoning is constructed to support the outcome; indeed, there are many tools available for this purpose, notably 'the accordion of potential or future competition'.

Furthermore, given the difficulties of proof, the panel in close cases might try to set a tentative conclusion based on its intuition, and then turn to data and information only to sort out those in favour of the tentative conclusion.

An important consideration in taking any line of evidence into account is the practical one of assessing the quality of the data available and the nature of problems that will be encountered in introducing such evidence into a legal proceeding.[395] The most desirable approach would be to allow the tribunals to proceed without committing themselves to final judgements about the market before them, in which all the relevant evidence is latent. In fact, in most cases, the tribunals would touch upon only a part of the whole. Their dilemma is that, no matter what, they have to render decisions based on perceptions gleaned from the part. Throughout the long history of the GATT, many pragmatic tribunals have worried about the impact rather than the righteousness of their decisions. Other normative tribunals have simply presumed that the rest of the whole is identical in nature to the part; or some of them might have been brave enough to deny the existence of the whole for the perfection of their partial impressions.

Given the current speed of innovation in information technology that makes many things possible, it will be possible to examine a more substantial portion of the whole, given the willingness and proper methodology. For instance, the system of bar-coding products enables one to obtain valuable information on the relationship between price change and purchasers. Using this information, one can calculate the cross-price-elasticity of demand (or supply) more easily and more correctly. What about e-commerce sales data, or consumer survey methods through the Internet? It is certain that these sources of information and methodology will greatly expand the amount of time and resources available to tribunals by increasing direct accessibility to the market participants.

As the information technology revolution proceeds, any excuse based on methodological barriers would continue to lose its credibility. Accordingly, the persuasive range of the '*unavoidable* element of individual discretionary judgement' would necessarily dwindle. In this regard, Art. 13.2 of the Dispute Settlement Understanding (DSU) deserves attention. The provision authorizes panels to seek information from any relevant source, and particularly to consult experts to obtain their opinions on certain aspects of the subject matter.[396] Appendix 4 to the DSU sets forth rules for establishing expert review groups, and the procedures that such groups should follow. Recently, this procedure has been utilized by several WTO panels, most of which were dealing with certain difficult and controversial judgements.[397]

Indeed, referring to the independent experts, at least on factual issues, would be a good way for the international tribunal to enhance the credibility of its decisions, and thus to avoid political controversy. It seems that this trend will increasingly prevail in the future as more factually difficult and politically sensitive cases are brought before the tribunal and as the *drive to maturity* is pressed forward.

This political demand may encourage the tribunals to turn to the independent experts, who will proceed with the likeness or substitutability test based on market-based economic analyses, with the support of future technologies. Individual experts, or expert research groups, could be chosen by panels on an *ad hoc* basis,[398] sometimes from names submitted by the parties. Or such expert research groups could be established as a permanent facility under one of the WTO committees.[399]

The parties may be given opportunity to comment on the qualifications or credibility of the potential experts. Reports of the experts may be submitted for comment to the parties.[400] Considering those reports and comments, the tribunal could make the final determination based on the *unavoidable discretionary judgement*. In rendering the final determination of likeness or substitutability, the expert opinion may not bind the panel at all;[401] or the panel may be required to take the opinion into consideration,[402] or to accept the opinion without modification.[403]

The larger the portion of the experts' opinion or conclusion that is accepted into the final determination, the greater the assistance that will be provided to the panel struggling with the legitimacy and enforceability of its decisions. This independent opinion founded on the market-based likeness test will provide the tribunal's otherwise controversial decisions with credibility and transparency.

It is true that, for the full benefit of this mechanism to take hold, better technology, more resources, and urgent political necessity are required. In the meantime, while waiting for the advent of technological innovations and political solidification that would lead to the environment of a full-fledged methodological luxury, one could suggest, in general, the following three-step approach for the GATT likeness or substitutability analysis.

First, the tribunal examines the objective characteristics of the products under consideration (after the complaining party establishes a *prima facie* case of likeness). If this examination led to clear conclusion with regard to likeness or substitutability ('easy case'), the tribunal would make determinations according to its conclusion.[404] Of course, the party opposing this conclusion may put forward any convincing results of market-based economic analyses that show otherwise to invite the tribunal to go forward.[405]

Secondly, if the examination of the objective characteristics does not reach a clear conclusion ('tough case'), or if the opposing party submits its own convincing results, the examiner proceeds to the test of demand substitutability between the products concerned. The focus of this step is end-use in the relevant market, shown by the cross-price elasticity of demand of the products. In order to examine the elasticity, the CVA-PCPDS with PSE Standard may be employed to determine whether there is a large enough degree of elasticity of substitution to conclude that the products are 'like' or 'directly competitive or substitutable'. In this process, the PQA, EQA or CQA (see 3.2.2) can be used, as necessary; and by using the PMP Questionnaire that includes questions to identify 'neutral' respondents, the examiner could reflect the 'potential substitution' consideration in the results of the analysis.

In verifying the result of the analysis, the end-use in the market shown by the direct view approach and/or the time-series analysis (see 3.2.3) can be referred to. Sometimes, highly reliable results of these methods can be substituted for the questionable results of the CVA approach.

If the result of these analyses shows a substantially higher degree of demand substitutability than the threshold level, the examiner determines the products to be 'like' or 'directly competitive or substitutable'. If there turned out to be a substantially lower degree of demand substitutability, the opposite determination follows.

As for the third step, if the margin of high or low demand substitutability (as a result of the above analyses) proves to be small, the examiner could consider supply substitutability between the products. The CVA-PCPSS combined with the IASR Standard can be applied to examine this factor. To internalize the 'potential competition' factor into the outcome of the analysis, the examiner can employ the PMP Questionnaire.

On the other hand (separate from supply substitutability analysis), if the margin is small and the parties in dispute submit clear and convincing evidence concerning future competition or substitutability, the examiner can proceed to the future competition or substitutability test. To do this, relevant questions regarding future aspects can be added to the PMP Questionnaire of the CVA-PCPDS or CVA-PCPSS.

In verifying the reliability of these analyses of supply substitution or future substitution or competition, the results (and their implications) of the direct view approach, time-series analysis and/or comparable market approach can be referred to.

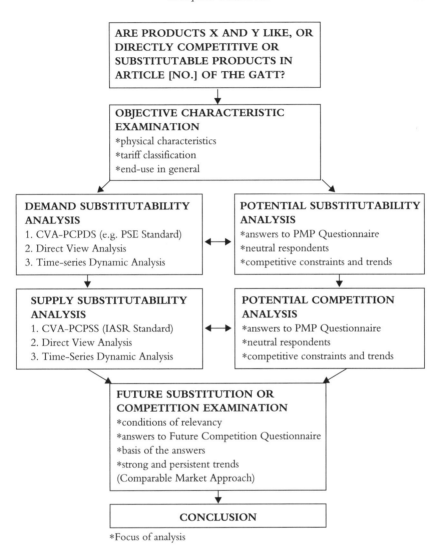

Figure II.6: Framework Analysis of GATT Likeness or Substitutability

The overall determination will vary depending upon the combination of supply substitutability and the degree of future competition:

(1) If the supply substitutability combined with 'future competition' (supply-side factors) turns out to be sufficiently low (*low mitigation effect*) *and* the persistent trend of high 'future substitutability' is proven by clear and convincing evidence (*high future demand effect*), the products under consideration are determined to be 'like' or 'directly competitive or substitutable' products.

(2) If the supply-side factors turn out to be high (*high mitigation effect*) and the 'future substitutability' is proven to be low (*low future demand effect*), the products are determined to be *not* 'like' or 'directly competitive or substitutable'.

(3) If both supply-side factors and 'future substitutability' turn out to be high or low together, the difficult problem of striking a balance between the 'mitigation effect' and the 'future demand effect' arises. In this instance, the ultimate decision would be made by the unavoidable discretionary judgement of the tribunal. One guideline: if the purpose of the provision in question is to protect the *expectation* of competitive opportunities (non-discrimination provisions; see Chapter III, section 1), the 'future demand effect' should be accorded more weight; whereas if the purpose is to provide producers with relief from import surges (fair-trade provisions; see Chapter III, section 2), the balance should tilt in favour of the 'mitigation effect'.

This three-step approach is well suited to the non-discrimination provisions of the GATT. In other GATT provisions that do not have anti-discrimination as their primary purpose, this approach is still workable as a basic framework. Each and every provision of the General Agreement has subtle differences in the usage and scope of 'likeness', or in its context in which the likeness concept functions. Thus, it should be remembered that, in each provision, the weight of each element in each factor, or even the specific threshold of required substitution, could be different.

In any event, in order to measure the difference and reflect it into specific contexts of the GATT, we need, in advance, a framework instrument written in a common language. Figure II.6 illustrates the instrument (the accordion) and the language (law and economics), with which one can perform the scientific art throughout various notes prescribed in the old music entitled the GATT.

III

Progressive Interpretation of 'Like' and 'Directly Competitive or Substitutable' Products in the Provisions of the GATT/WTO Agreement: Playing the Accordion!

Complete understanding of such terms as 'like' or 'directly competitive or substitutable' in a specific provision of the GATT needs combined consideration of two aspects. One is how broad or narrow the likeness or substitutability concept is in the provision concerned; the other is how to find such likeness or substitutability as defined in the specific provision of the GATT.

First, the general comprehension of 'like' or 'substitutable' established in Chapter II should be adjusted for the *narrowness or broadness* of its scope according to each provision of GATT at issue. As an early GATT preparatory work indicates, 'the expression had different meaning in different contexts' of the Agreement.[1] One could argue, in the first place, that since both Arts I and III are basic anti-discrimination provisions at the heart of the General Agreement, the terms should be construed broadly in those articles so as to strike down discriminatory measures wherever possible.[2] On the other hand, one might argue that the terms should be interpreted most narrowly in the case of Arts VI, XI, and XIX, since those provisions establish exceptions to general GATT rules.[3] Among those 'basic' provisions of Arts I and III, however, the likeness concept is not the same. Although several early GATT panels took the view that the term 'like product' had the same meaning in Arts I and III,[4] the Appellate Body in *Japan Alcoholic Beverages* made it clear that there was a difference.[5] It indicated that even among the various paragraphs of Art. III, the accordion of 'likeness' was meant to be squeezed differently.[6] Moreover, it is doubtful whether one could designate Arts VI, XI, and XIX as being 'exceptions' to the extent of endowing a narrow interpretation on the key concept of likeness employed in those provisions.[7] In the case of Art. VI, this problem of interpretation of the scope of likeness seems to be less serious, because Art. 2.6 of the Antidumping Agreement provides a definitive interpretation of the concept (see Chapter II, at 1.1 and 1.2). But still there remains a problem of analyzing the definitive interpretation.

In the midst of this ambiguity and confusion, the above position of the Appellate Body in the Japanese case leaves open the questions of how the definition of the term should vary from clause to clause, and of how different it is possible for interpretations of the same clause to be on a case-by-case basis.

Undertaking the provision-by-provision analysis, one should principally focus on the ordinary meaning of each provision, which should be understood in the

context and in the light of the objects and purpose of the provision[8] (thereby allowing policy considerations to be taken into account). In addition, the relationship
with other provisions or agreements and any subsequent practice of interpretation
should be taken into consideration.[9] One can also refer to the preparatory work in
order to confirm obscure or ambiguous meanings.[10] This 'text-based teleological
approach'[11] will form the basis of the interpretation suggested in this chapter.

In this process, a certain method of classification of the various provisions is
helpful, given their complexity and diversity. The likeness or substitutability concept is based on a comparison between two categories of products: one is a
product category against which alleged discrimination has been performed; and
the other is another product category with which the former product is compared.
Accordingly, it is natural to find that each likeness provision of the GATT is based
on one of the following four types of comparison:[12]

1. a category of imported goods and a category of goods imported from any third
   country;[13]
2. a category of imported goods and a category of domestic goods of the importing country;[14]
3. a category of imported goods and a category of goods sold in the exporting
   country;[15] or
4. a category of imported goods and a category of goods *imported* from the same
   exporting country.[16]

What are the implications of this classification? Except for category (2), in which
foreign and domestic goods are compared, all comparisons are made between foreign-origin (categories of) goods. More importantly, the first two categories are
concerned mostly with MFN and national treatment obligations geared up to
eliminating discrimination in international trade, and thus should be classified as
'non-discrimination provisions'.[17]

Article XI:2 in the second type is prescribed as an exception to the prohibition
of quantitative restrictions, and thus the principle of prohibition of quantitative
restrictions in Art. XI governs the interpretation of the provision. This provision is
not directly related to the non-discrimination principle. But, it must be noted that
the sweeping prohibition of quantitative restrictions under this provision assists the
non-discrimination principle because it disciplines any discriminatory distribution
of quota which was a common practice in the past. Given this relationship, one
may discuss the likeness concept of Art. XI:2 along with the 'non-discrimination
provisions'.

Category (3) above is related to antidumping or subsidy provisions ('fair trade
provisions'), and category (4) encourages procedural fairness and transparency in
custom valuation contexts ('other provisions').

This categorization and characterization of likeness provisions provides a good
base from which to proceed to the provision-by-provision interpretation of

likeness or substitutability. From this starting point, one can apply a conceptual classification of relationships between goods and the basic understanding of the concepts 'like' or 'directly competitive or substitutable product', discussed in Chapter II. This application will lead to the final goal of this book—the progressive interpretation of the likeness or substitutability concept in each provision of the GATT.

The second question is about the *methodology* to be employed to find out the likeness or substitutability tailored to each provision of the GATT. The answer will be given by examining how the likeness factors or elements constituting the Framework Model should be weighed to fit the specific context of the General Agreement. Also, the *general* threshold level used in the model has to be modified to produce a *specific* threshold tailored to the context of each provision. This examination will be carried out in the context of each category of the likeness provisions as classified above.

1. NON-DISCRIMINATION PROVISIONS

The GATT achieves its goal of promoting free trade primarily through four legal commitments:

1. the unconditional most-favoured-nation (MFN) obligation that prohibits WTO members from discriminating against or giving preferences to the like product of any other country, regardless of whether the latter has made any trade concessions to the former;
2. the national treatment obligation, which requires that imports be treated no less favourably than the domestic like product insofar as taxes and internal domestic regulations are concerned;
3. binding commitments to reduce tariffs on imports; and
4. the elimination of quotas on imports.

These pillars of the GATT are based on the non-discrimination principle as a prevailing proposition. The likeness concepts in these provisions are primary geared to supporting this principle.

1.1. Most-Favoured-Nation

Article I:1 obligates GATT members to accord no less favourable treatment to all like products from or destined for other members. Article XIII:1 mandates the same approach for the prohibition or restriction of imports and exports. This MFN obligation extends to the equality of treatment in marks of origin of imports in Art. IX:1 and in dealing with traffic in transit in Art. V:5. The 'likeness' determination in all of these provisions requires a comparison between a category of imported goods and a category of goods imported from any third country.

At first sight, the like product concept in all these MFN provisions seems to have the same meaning and scope. The primary purpose of the four provisions is to prohibit discrimination between products originating from different countries. The *economic* rationale for the MFN commitment is the basic, but compelling, idea that discrimination can lead to wasteful trade diversion: in the absence of the MFN obligation, the most efficient producers might not have equal access to foreign markets because of discriminatory trade preferences in favour of less efficient producers from other countries.[18] The unconditional MFN principle fosters economic efficiency by promoting the most efficient allocation of resources, thereby lowering transaction costs, increasing consumer choices, and promoting world economic growth.[19] The obligation also serves the important *political* functions of lessening tensions among nations, inhibiting government temptation to rely on short-term, *ad hoc* policies, and facilitating trade negotiations that would otherwise become extremely knotty if reciprocity were demanded as a condition for receiving the benefits of a trade concession.[20]

1.1.1. Article I:1

GATT *drafting records*[21] give some clues to the interpretation of 'likeness' in Art. I:1. Two in particular deserve analysis. First, at one of the London Conference meetings, a French delegate inquired whether the MFN obligation applied when one state was involved with shipments of 'wheat cereal' and another with shipments of 'different cereals'. The question was whether all cereals can be considered 'like' products within the meaning of Art. I:1. In response, the Rapporteur from the United States indicated that only wheat cereals would be viewed as being 'like' products.[22]

If one can draw an implication from this record, it will be that the drafters, by excluding from the concept of the like product any cereals other than wheat cereals, did not want to extend the 'like' product coverage to its broadest level so as to include the 'competitive or substitutable' product concept. Clearly, the Rapporteur's response reflects no necessity whatsoever for paying attention to a possible competitive or substitutable relationship between wheat and other cereals.

This drafter's intention was followed by subsequent GATT tribunals. In *Australian Subsidy on Ammonium Sulphate*, one of the earliest decisions, the Working Party stated that the 'like' concept was different from the 'competitive or substitutable' concept, determining that ammonium sulphate and sodium nitrate were not 'like' products in the MFN context.[23] *German Sardines* also drew exactly the same distinction between the two concepts.[24]

If another inference is to be drawn, it is that since the response was not confined to covering only wheat cereals having identical or very similar tastes, colors, etc., any organoleptic differences or product-process or region-based differences should not be taken into account in the MFN context. However, this inference is not guaranteed, in that the Rapporteur's response could be a simple result of a lack of adequate sensitivity to the distinctions between, on the one hand, identical or closely similar products and, on the other hand, products which are remotely similar while not losing their physical similarity. For example, admitting that white wheat and gray wheat are 'like' products, one can still raise the question of whether wheat 'grain' and wheat 'powder' may be considered 'like' products.[25] Given this lack of sensitivity, the exact scope of the concept is yet to be determined under other considerations.

The second record emanates from the Havana Conference. At one of the committee sessions, responding to a Turkish delegate's inquiry into the meaning of 'likeness' in Art. I, the chair of the committee, Mr Wilgress, used the example of a nation state with a tariff schedule distinguishing between 'automobiles of under and over 1,500 kilograms' in weight. According to his understanding, these two categories were not 'like' products as contemplated in Art. I.[26] A safe inference from this hypothetical example might be that mere competitive or substitutable relationships do not satisfy the likeness concept of the provision. Although other inferences do not seem to be guaranteed, one might argue, though, that exact identity or very close similarity is not required for products to be considered 'like' one another because the response focuses on only one criterion, i.e. weight, despite the fact that there could still be many differences in shape, capacity, function, etc. within the same weight category of automobiles.[27] This inference might indicate an awareness on the drafters' part that, so long as the vehicles can be characterized as similar, they need not be identical or closely similar in many respects.[28]

Although the above preparatory materials of Art. 1:1 provide for no crystal-clear conclusion, the professed *purpose* of the provision suggests quite clearly a flexible reading of the term 'like'. A historical observation of this MFN provision will offer a helpful starting point in this regard. It became clear, at least, from the announcement of Woodrow Wilson's 'Fourteen Points' in 1918 that equal treatment among countries was regarded as an essential obligation for a free trade system.[29] At the London Conference in 1946 it was apparent that any final text of an international trade agreement would include the MFN obligation; the seminal proposal for an ITO Charter, submitted at the conference by the United States, included MFN as one of five basic principles.[30] The Geneva Conference confirmed that the obligation would be an essential part of any trade negotiations.[31] Throughout the process, the principal question was not whether MFN itself should be included in the final agreement, but the scope of the MFN obligation.[32]

The scope of the obligation largely depends upon the scope of the 'like' product concept. With respect to the latter, first, it should be noted that fine product distinctions have *traditionally* been accepted as an appropriate means of protecting the competitive benefits accruing from reciprocal tariff bindings.[33] This point signals a narrow understanding of the concept. An overly broad interpretation of it might compel GATT members to extend the benefits of tariff concessions, obtained through lengthy negotiations, to a large variety of products, without any corresponding *quid pro quo*. This free-rider problem might result in an impediment to trade liberalization efforts, because member countries would become reluctant, or reduce their offer level, when negotiating tariff concessions at multilateral rounds. Clearly, this consideration led the *SPF Lumber* Panel to suggest that negotiators should be able to agree on narrow classifications.[34]

It should also be noted, however, that after this free-rider problem was substantially reduced,[35] the like product concept in the MFN context functioned mainly as a tool for prohibiting 'tariff specialization' aimed at discriminating between 'like' products. While the GATT gives each member the freedom of tariff classifications, the member's discretion is limited by the MFN obligation of Art. I. Claims of likeness have been effectively raised as a defense against such arbitrary tariff classifications that accord *de facto* favourable treatments to products from certain countries.[36] The practical effect is that if an imported product is 'like' another imported product, the importing state is prohibited from imposing different charges by invoking the fact that one is classified differently from the other.[37] This function requires a broad interpretation of the likeness concept for its effectiveness.

In the end, this *sine qua non* obligation for the free trade system allows each state to take full advantage of its negotiated or indigenous economic strengths. Without the obligation, any competitive benefits obtained through tariff negotiations would be eroded or eliminated by more favourable trade concessions to a third country competing for the same export markets.

Beyond this purpose of securing the benefit of the bargain, the MFN obligation concerns efficiency. By preventing discriminatory trade patterns from developing, MFN trade concessions ensure that the most efficient producers will have equal access to export markets regardless of the country of origin.[38] Without the obligation, comparative advantages from individual diligence would always be at the mercy of discriminatory self-interest and protectionism.[39] By pursuing international trade on a non-discriminatory basis, the MFN principle helps suppress aggression in international relations.[40] Trade conducted on an MFN basis promotes the development of multilateralism and acts as a prophylactic against discriminatory trade barriers, which together reduce trade frictions among trading nations.[41]

The 'like product' concept employed in Art. I works as a standard for identifying these vices and virtues so as to protect the benefits and advantages that are the valuable source of free trade. In this regard, any suggestion of a narrow scope for likeness in the provision seems to have less merit: any simple and superficial change of a few of the product characteristics might provide a justification for unequal treatment that could alter the normal competitive conditions between the products in question.

This anti-narrowness sentiment leads to an understanding that products can be considered 'like' one another even though they are not identical or closely similar, as long as the products can be characterized within the boundary of 'remotely similar'. If one GATT member can justify less favourable treatment for another on the grounds that the products in comparison are not sufficiently identical or closely similar, even though those products are still sharing common *physical* characteristics no matter how small the commonality is, then the benefits of negotiations or comparative advantages can be more easily rendered nugatory. The resultant higher duty or requirement would increase the price of the product subject to the discrimination, which will affect competitive conditions between the products that are seen as being 'physically' interchangeable by consumers.

In summary, in order to support the fundamental function of the provision as a *sine qua non* of the GATT, and to provide an effective check against the possibility of abuse of discretion in tariff classification,[42] the 'like' product concept in Art. I:2 should be understood broadly enough to cover products that are even 'remotely similar'. However, it should be interpreted more narrowly than the concept of the 'directly competitive or substitutable' product because there is no clear indication to support the broadest understanding in the preparatory work, neither does there exist any compelling reason such as to avoid a manifestly absurd or unreasonable result.[43] In fact, as stated above, records of negotiating history show clear warnings against such overly broad understandings. Moreover, one should note that there exists a strong practical reason against the broadest scope of likeness, as discussed in 1.1.2 below.

Therefore, the concept of 'like product' in the context of Art. I ceases to stretch beyond the boundaries of physical similarity. In other words, the product in comparison should not lose its physical similarity altogether through processing or commercial manipulations in order to qualify as being 'like' in the provision.

1.1.2. *Articles XIII, IX, V:5*

With respect to 'like product' concepts in the other MFN provisions of Arts XIII and IX, it is hard to find drafting records. One might argue that this absence itself suggests that the scope of likeness in these provisions should be understood as being the same as in Art. I, i.e. the drafters paid little attention to the concepts in these provisions because they believed that they would be interpreted in the same way as in Art. I. Certainly, GATT MFN provisions share the same *purpose* of protecting the competitive benefits accruing from reciprocal tariff bindings or from natural comparative advantages. If one country were to deviate from, or circumvent, Art. I obligations using the discriminatory rules of marks of origin or quantitative restriction, the world trading system would also deviate from the benefits. The three Articles—I, XIII, and IX—buttress the MFN obligation in different contexts.

Article XI:1 sets out one of the four pillars of the GATT,[44] the prohibition of quantitative restrictions in international trade. Article XIII supports this commitment by imposing an obligation of non-discriminatory administration on any possible quantitative restrictions permitted under the exceptions to Art. XI:1.[45] This MFN obligation acts as a check on arbitrary distribution of quotas, thereby minimizing the detrimental effect generated by the exceptional deviation from the prohibition.

Article IX:1 further prescribes MFN obligations in the rules regarding the marking of country of origin, one of the non-preferential rules of origin.[46] GATT Art. IX:1 and the Agreement on Rules of Origin[47] are aimed at ensuring that the marking rules themselves do not create unnecessary obstacles to trade[48] beyond their original purpose of providing consumers with information regarding country of origin.[49]

In the same context, the WTO 'work programme' has been initiated to harmonize non-preferential rules of origin.[50] While the harmonization process continues, the WTO concentrates its effort to ensure that the individual rules of origin do not create unnecessary obstacles to trade. In order to achieve this goal, the Agreement on Rules of Origin has adopted more discipline in the administration of the rules by providing a framework for notification, review, consultation, and dispute settlement.[51] These efforts are enhanced by the MFN obligation regarding marks of origin in GATT Art. IX:1.

In addition, one should note that the benefits of the MFN obligation extend not only to *imported* products, but also, *traffic in transit*. GATT Art. V:5 buttresses the obligation in that context.[52] The SPS and TBT Agreements also have provisions including the MFN obligation, which will be discussed in 1.2.6 below.[53]

The nature of the MFN provisions as fundamental obligations and their common purpose lead to the conclusion that the like product concept in Arts I:1, XIII:1, IX:1, and V:5 includes products that are 'identical', 'closely similar', or 'remotely similar'.[54] One caveat regarding the concept 'remotely similar' is that in practice, the scope of likeness within those provisions may not be as broad as 'remotely similar' when each provision is applied. Indeed, one sees this practical consideration incorporated in *Ad* Art. V:5, in that the provision, with regard to transportation charges, limits Art. V:5's application to 'like products *being transported on the same route under like conditions*'.[55] Similarly, the applicable scope of likeness in Art. IX:1 could often be narrower than 'remote similarity', because there might be certain reasonable restrictions necessary to provide consumers with adequate information. For example, the MFN clause of the provision can apply only among like products *having similar surfaces or types of container (package)*, if a costlier marking methodology is technically or economically required due to the different surface materials of products or types of containers. Also, in Art. I, 'remote similarity' indicates the 'general' (or maximum) scope of the likeness. A specific scope can be determined case by case by referring to the agreement reached in specific tariff negotiations. If two countries negotiated tariff classifications on the basis of merely 'identical' products, or if certain narrow tariff classifications are supported by common international practice, the likeness in the actual application may be narrower than remote similarity, in accordance with the agreement or practice.

Either way, it should be noted that this argument in favour of a broad interpretation of the likeness concept in general in MFN provisions is not strong enough to encompass the concept of 'directly competitive or substitutable'. Since a single product may have several functions, the introduction of the competitiveness or substitutability criterion tends to reduce the number of permissible distinctions between products. The effect is well illustrated by Professor McGovern:

Suppose the test (substitutability test) is applied to an internal tax, and that products A, B and C have initial tax rates of 10, 20 and 30 per cent. Suppose also that B has several functions, one of which it shares with A, and another with C. If an MFN rule were applied on the basis of economic or commercial significance, importers could insist on the 10 per cent rate being extended to B because of its common function with A, and then to C because of its common function with B. Probably for this reason GATT applies this criterion only in the context of internal measures, especially internal taxation of goods. Most countries have no more than a few internal tax rates in contrast to the hundreds if not thousands of duty rates in customs tariffs.[56]

As indicated at 1.1.1 above, the two GATT drafting records support this interpretation. In *EEC Animal Feed Proteins*, the argument that the term 'like product' is synonymous with the concept of 'directly competitive or substitutable product' was rejected.[57] The Panel feared that if this view were adopted, it would lead to a broad 'like product' definition encompassing far more items than would be the case using tariff classifications.[58]

Nonetheless, an interesting argument was raised recently, that the above is true only to the extent that 'tariff classification problems' are concerned. Emphasizing that Art. I is related not only to *border measures* but also to *internal measures*, this view suggests that the meaning of likeness varies according to the context in which it is used.[59] In other words, departing from the scope of likeness applied to border measures, the interpretation of 'like products' when applied to an *internal measure* should be parallel to the interpretation of likeness in each corresponding paragraph of Art. III.[60] According to this view, scope of likeness in Art. I would vary, ranging from 'remotely similar' when applied to internal regulations (in parallel with the scope of likeness in Art. III:4), to 'directly competitive or substitutable' when applied to tax measures (in parallel with the scope of likeness in Art. III:2), as will be discussed at 1.2.4 and 1.2.3 respectively. The essence of this view seems to lie in the parallelism between the two principal obligations of MFN and national treatment, which is arguably needed in order to support the fundamental function as the *sine qua non* of the GATT.

In any event, since Art. I's interpretation of likeness encompasses 'remotely similar', *as in Art. III:4* (as discussed at 1.2.4), the only practical difference that this view results in is that likeness in the MFN clause comes to include even the broadest concept of 'directly competitive or substitutable' when applied, concurrently with Art. III:2, to *internal tax* measures. That is, in such a case, the scope of the MFN obligation needs to extend to the background of a 'directly competitive or substitutable' product relationship.

Appreciating this view, one should note in the first place that as opposed to such provisions as Art. III (in which such flexibility is built into each paragraph or sentence as a textual difference, i.e. III:2 as against III:4) and Arts XI and XIX (in which such flexibility explicitly resides in the terms 'like or directly substituted' and 'like or directly competitive'), the language of Art. I contains no vestige of the concept of 'competitive' or 'substitutable'. Moreover, there is no clear indication in the preparatory work to support the broadest understanding, neither does there exist any compelling reason, such as to avoid a manifestly absurd or unreasonable result, to have the same scope between the MFN and national treatment obligations when applied together to internal tax matters.[61] Dealing with the same subject matter of internal taxation, the MFN can play a role within the 'remotely similar' product relationship, while the national treatment obligation has its own role with regard to 'directly competitive or substitutable' products. Again, there is no compelling reason for the two players to share the same sphere of activity. The reference from Art. I to Art. III:2 is not meant to extend the MFN obligation to 'directly competitive or substitutable' product relationships.[62]

In short, the likeness concept in MFN clauses should be understood as broad enough to cover products that are 'remotely similar', regardless of the context of the application. This will provide an effective check against the possibility of abuse of discretion in tariff classifications,[63] or discriminatory internal measures that violate MFN obligations.

1.1.3. *Performance*

What is required now is to produce a specific methodology with which to determine whether there exists a like product relationship in the MFN context. The first step toward establishing the methodology would be to make proper modifications to the Framework Analysis of Likeness or Substitutability (suggested in Chapter II) for use in the MFN context. Also worth pondering is how, in specific determinations of 'likeness', the likeness factors of the Analysis should be weighed?

As discussed in Chapter II, the first step of the likeness or substitutability analysis focuses on objective characteristics. At this stage, an important point is that *high regard should be paid to the tariff classification* element in the Art. I likeness test. In favour of this point are (1) the fact that tariff classifications are generally drafted on the basis of objective characteristics of the goods themselves, and (2) more importantly, the cooperative function between the tariff concession of Art. II and the MFN obligation of Art. I. Indeed, the MFN clause works hand in glove with tariff bindings. Through the operation of the unconditional MFN commitment, negotiated tariff concessions are generalized and multilateralized; benefits accruing from tariff negotiations are secured by the effective function of the MFN obligation. Indeed, without a close reference from the like product concept (that is determinate of coverage of the MFN obligation) to the tariff classification criteria, the *integrity* of tariff classification nomenclature might be harmed from time to time.[64]

As an entity embodying such concessions, the tariff classification can provide a useful criterion for the likeness determination under GATT Art. I, especially in cases where it is sufficiently detailed and supported by international practice.[65] Due to the Harmonized System (HS) of tariff classification, adopted and implemented throughout the world, the uniformity and objectivity of tariff classifications of each state have been greatly increased.[66] Hence, the close relationship between the tariff classification criteria and the Art. I likeness determination has been further promoted. In this regard, it is noteworthy that an early suggestion was made in the GATT preparatory work to accept national tariff classifications and tariff structures as being 'presumptively conclusive' in answering the question of whether two products are 'like' each other for MFN purposes.[67] The degree of reliance on the national tariff classification nomenclature would be ultimately determined by whether the specific classification under consideration could be justified by international practice or legitimate reasons, such as an agreement, explicit or tacit, or a common perception among GATT members. This point has been confirmed, as already discussed in Chapter II, by a series of MFN cases, including *Australia Ammonium Sulphate, Germany Imports of Sardines, Japan SPF Lumber*, and *Spain Unroasted Coffee*.[68]

Therefore, the use of tariff classification nomenclature should be the starting point in 'like product' analysis in the context of Art. I. However, an excellent starting point does not always guarantee a successful completion. As explained in Chapter II, there could be many areas or problems in which tariff classification nomenclature might not provide effective guidance for the likeness concept. Examples are products not covered by the tariff schedule of WTO members; tariff classifications of many developing countries, which are not sufficiently detailed; and areas relating to non-tariff barriers in which the objective of protecting benefits from tariff concessions is less dominant, and the rationale for tariff classification as a criterion of likeness therefore weak.[69]

In these problem areas, there exists a compelling necessity for the examiner to find 'non-tariff criteria' to interpret the likeness concept. With these criteria, the examiner may be less constrained by the need to secure the *competitive* benefits obtained by signing tariff binding agreements, and may proceed to the further examination focusing on the more fundamental value of the entire package of the WTO Agreement, i.e. preserving the *comparative* advantage.

When the MFN obligation involves non-tariff issues, it is natural that non-tariff criteria become important to the likeness test. Such cases arise in the MFN clauses of GATT Arts V, IX, and XIII, and in the TBT and SPS Agreements.[70] It can also occur within Art. I, when an importing country imposes an MFN 'tax' rate on imported products from every foreign country except country A. In such a case, country A can allege an Art. I violation with regard to the non-tariff issue.

Thus, for a likeness test in those provisions or cases, the tariff classification element should not play a decisive or presumptive role in determining likeness, because those provisions are not directly related to the process of generalization of tariff concessions and because the like product determination under those provisions does not affect the integrity of tariff classification nomenclature. In these provisions, three elements of the objective characteristic factor (physical characteristics, tariff classification, end-use in general: see Chapter II, at 3.2.1) should be considered with equal evidentiary weight.

When the tariff classification criteria combined with other objective characteristics do not yield clear conclusions, or when a party puts forward convincing results of market-based economic analyses that contradict a clear conclusion of the first step examination ('tough cases'), the examiner needs to proceed to examine consumer and supplier views in the relevant market by using market-based substitution analysis. Of course, this necessity becomes more pressing when using MFN to ensure that irrational discriminatory treatment does not occur than when using it to protect the deal in the tariff bindings.

In order to obtain information on demand substitutability between two products in comparison, the CVA-PCPDS may be employed (see Chapter II, at 3.2.2). By using the PMP Questionnaire including questions to identify 'neutral' respondents (see Chapter II, at 3.2.4), the examiner can internalize the 'potential substitution' factor and superimpose it onto the result of the analysis. A problematic question that arises is what the threshold substitution rate should be for the products to be considered as 'like' in the MFN context. Given that the spectrum of MFN 'likeness' stretches from 'identical' to 'remotely similar', one could state, in the first place, that the threshold should be higher than that of the PSE Standard (see Chapter II, at 3.2.2). To take an example, in the case of an 8 per cent change in the hypothetical price of product X, how much of the demand for X must switch to product Y for the two products to be defined as being 'remotely similar'? The price-substitution equalization (PSE) point used for the determination of '*directly competitive or substitutable*' products requires at least the same 8 per cent, as justified in Chapter II at 3.2.2, but this rate is not high enough to be used as a standard for products to be labelled '*remotely similar*'. What then, is the appropriate threshold level for the 'remotely similar' product relationship in MFN clauses?

No single 'right' answer is possible. The higher the threshold is, the narrower the scope of likeness becomes in MFN clauses. As a consequence, national governments would be able to interrupt, more easily, the flow of the competitive benefit or the comparative advantage. On the other hand, too low a threshold point, close to the 8 per cent in the above example, would invalidate any distinction between 'remotely similar' and 'directly competitive or substitutable'. This would often result in the impairment of the integrity of the customs tariff system of the regulating state, which is constructed with hundreds of duty rates.[71] Hence, the possible answer should lie somewhere in between. So, what rate?

Considering that there should be, by definition, a gradual increase of the degree of substitutability within the concepts 'directly competitive or substitutable', 'remotely similar', 'closely similar', and 'identical', one might set the threshold in question at *twice* the rate of the hypothetical price change rate—the 'Double-Price Standard' (DPS). In other words, going back to the example, a 16 per cent substitution rate may be used as the threshold for a 'remotely similar' relationship, while a substitution rate of more than 8 per cent would lead to the conclusion that there is a 'directly competitive or substitutable' relationship.

Interestingly enough, one could extend this idea to define other concepts. For the 'closely similar' relationship, one may set the 'Triple-Price Standard' (TPS); and for the 'identical' concept, the 'Quadruple-Price Standard' (QPS) could be used. Hence, according to this idea, in order for the products X and Y to become 'identical' products, a 32 per cent substitution rate, at least, is needed in response to a price change of 8 per cent. In other words, if the hypothetical price change is given as 25 per cent, the entire demand for one product should switch to the other to qualify them as having an 'identical' product relationship.[72] These standards will be used later in determining 'identical' or 'closely similar' product relationships under the relevant provisions of the GATT.

This series of standards is based not so much on theoretical grounds, if any, as on practical simplicity. Indeed, those various stages of product likeness or substitutability ('identical', 'closely', 'remotely', 'directly') are hardly matters of empirical verification. Rather, their scope is an issue of definitive judgement by the law in the standard-setting process.

Of course, empirical resources should be injected, as greatly as possible, into this process. Our effort has utilized those resources to good effect. But in the end we have come to the conclusive issue of interpretation of the terms 'close', 'remote', and 'direct'. These terms are amenable only to pure legal judgement that is controlled by norms of predictability and enforceability. Indeed, as discussed already, the WTO Appellate Body once exercised this type of pure legal judgement in the context of interpretation of differences between the phrases 'taxed in excess' and 'not similarly taxed'.[73] Here, the term 'similarly' was not a matter of economics but of law.

The DPS for the determination of likeness in the MFN clauses provides a predictable and enforceable standard for future tribunals, who are otherwise destined to wander a 'land of mazes' in which no standards are given except for the *unavoidable elements of individual discretionary judgement*.

To assist the judgement on demand substitutability, the direct view approach and/or the time-series analysis could be referred to, as reasoned in Chapter II.

In a tough situation in which the judgement regarding demand-side factors is difficult, supply substitutability could be considered to complement it. As discussed in Chapter II, section 3, there is no textual or economic reason to exclude the supply-side consideration from determining likeness under the MFN clauses. Moreover, the inclusion of supply substitutability can take into consideration the mitigation effect, which will help render decisions tailored to the GATT objectives. The CVA-PCPSS combined with the IASR Standard provides a useful tool for examining cross-price supply substitutability, as explained. Here, different from the demand side in which the CVA-PCPDS *with PSE* was modified to the CVA-PCPDS *with DPS*, one need not modify the Industry Average Substitution Rate Standard. Because the main purpose of considering supply substitutability is to take into account the impact of the discriminatory measure upon the *producers* at disadvantage, there is little necessity to change the standard according to the different degree of likeness or substitutability concepts. In other words, regardless of whether the matter at issue is the 'directly competitive or substitutable', 'similar', or 'identical' relationship, the examiner needs to focus only on whether the producers are capable of switching from one sector (e.g. shochu) to another (e.g. whisky) more easily than the average industry (alcoholic beverage industry).

The direct view and time-series analyses on supply substitution could complement the CVA-PCPSS. In addition, the examiner could take account of clear and convincing evidence concerning the persistent trend of 'future competition or substitutability' (see Chapter II, section 3).

1.2. National Treatment

The likeness concept employed in the national treatment provisions calls for a product comparison to determine whether there is different or discriminatory treatment of the imported product *compared with that of the domestic 'like' or 'directly competitive or substitutable product'* in the importing state. GATT Arts II:2, III:2, and III:4 deal with this situation, which extends to the national treatment clauses of the TBT and SPS Agreements. Also, Art. III:1 presupposes this comparison between like products implicitly without use of such a term.

Compared to the concept of MFN likeness (see 1.1 above), one should be aware that likeness in the national treatment provisions is particularly vulnerable to domestic protectionist pressures. This inherent vulnerability comes from the fact that the scope of the likeness here bears directly upon the interests of the domestic like product producers in the importing state. Thus, proceeding with the likeness analysis, one should be cautious about the possibility of abuse of the likeness concept in the national treatment clause.

GATT Art. II generally proscribes the imposition of customs duties in excess of those referenced in the appropriate tariff bindings. Paragraph 2 of the provision, however, allows for the imposition of certain charges in excess of the bindings. Specifically, sub-para (a) of the second paragraph confirms the member state's right to impose a charge equivalent to an internal tax, which is imposed consistently with Art. III:2 in respect of the 'like domestic product'.[74] Thus, the issue of likeness interpretation in Art. II:2 yields to that of Art. III.

Article III of the GATT prohibits internal charges and laws, regulations and requirements from being imposed for protectionist purposes. Despite this common objective of the provision, each of its paragraphs employs a slightly different language, which generates many possibilities for different interpretations. As the likeness concept is at the core of the provision, it is no wonder that one encounters the concept at the center of disputes. This is why, to interpret the like product concept and understand its proper scope, it is necessary to understand the purpose and basic structure of Art. III.

1.2.1. Article III in General

Article III is the central provision regulating the application of domestic policies to imported products, which requires WTO members to accord national treatment to imported products.[75] The broad and fundamental purpose of Art. III is to avoid protectionism in the application of internal tax and regulatory measures.[76] More specifically, the purpose of Art. III is to ensure that internal measures are not applied to imported or domestic products so as to afford protection to domestic production,[77] which is reflected in Art. III:1.[78]

To this end, Article III obliges WTO members to accord no less favourable competitive conditions for imported products than for domestic products.[79] The intention of the drafters of the General Agreement was clearly to treat the imported products at least as favourably as the like domestic products once they had been cleared through customs.[80]

Article III:4 of the GATT reads in part:

The products of the territory of any contracting party imported into the territory of any other contracting party shall be accorded treatment no less favourable than that accorded to like products of national origin in respect of all laws, regulations and requirements affecting their internal sale, offering for sale, purchase, transportation, distribution or use . . .

This provision applies to all internal measures except those of a fiscal nature.[81] Fiscal measures are regulated in Art. III:2, first sentence, which states that imported products 'shall not be subject, directly or indirectly, to internal taxes or other internal charges of any kind in excess of those applied, directly or indirectly, to like domestic products'. The second sentence of Art. III:2 broadens this rule by declaring that 'moreover, no contracting party shall otherwise apply internal taxes or other internal charges to imported or domestic products in a manner contrary to the principles set forth in paragraph 1'.[82]

In interpreting these provisions, it should be noted that Art. III protects expectations not of any particular trade volume but rather of the equal competitive relationship between imported and domestic products.[83] It is irrelevant that the 'trade effects' of the tax differential between imported and domestic products, as reflected in the volumes of imports, are insignificant or even non-existent. So long as this equal competitive relationship is preserved, WTO members are free to pursue their own domestic goals through internal taxation or regulation.[84]

When considering the relationship between Art. III and other provisions of the WTO Agreement, one should remember that one of the general themes of GATT Art. III is to prohibit members from circumventing tariff concessions through non-tariff barriers to import trade that might undermine the benefit of a tariff reduction.[85] Specifically, Art. III acts to reinforce the tariff bindings made pursuant to Art. II by limiting the circumstances in which it is permissible for a nation to accord treatment for domestic goods in its national legislation and programs which is more favourable than that for imported goods.[86] A GATT binding to limit a tariff on a particular product would be valueless if there were not some limitations on the types of internal taxation or regulation that a country could impose to afford protection against such imports.[87]

Although the protection of negotiated tariff concessions is certainly one important purpose of Art. III, this function should not be over-emphasized.[88] The sheltering scope of Art. III is not limited to products subject to tariff concessions under Art. II.[89] This obligation clearly extends also to products not bound under Art. II,[90] as confirmed by the negotiating history of Art. III.[91] The broad purpose of Art. III is to avoid protectionism in the application of internal tax and regulatory measures. Article III ensures that internal measures are not applied to imported or domestic products in a way that affords protection to domestic products. To that end, WTO members are obliged to accord at least equality of competitive conditions for imported goods *vis-à-vis* domestic like products.[92]

While the principle underlying these provisions is clear, its application in specific situations gives rise to a series of interpretative issues.[93] General interpretation is that the first sentence of Art. III:2 is concerned with the treatment of 'like' products, whereas the second sentence is concerned with the treatment of 'directly competitive or substitutable' products, which is a broader category of products than like products.[94] The Interpretative Note *Ad* Art. III:2 clarifies this distinction by providing an example in which the first sentence of Art. III:2 is not violated whereas the second is, thus confirming the existence of two distinct obligations in Art. III:2.[95]

With regard to the relationship between Art. III:2 and Art. III:1, it is generally accepted that the latter contains general *principles* concerning the imposition of internal taxes, internal charges, and laws, regulations and requirements affecting the treatment of imported and domestic products, while the former provides for specific *obligations* regarding internal taxes and internal charges. The words 'recognize' and 'should' in Art. III:1, as well as the wording of Art. III:2, second sentence—'the *principles* set forth in paragraph 1'—make it clear that Art. III:1 does not contain a legally binding obligation, but rather states general principles.[96] In contrast, the use of the word 'shall' in Art. III:2, both sentences, makes it clear that that Article contains two legally binding obligations.[97]

Consequently, the starting point for an interpretation of Art. III:2 is Art. III:2 itself and not Art. III:1.[98] Recourse to Art. III:1, which constitutes part of the context of Art. III:2, may be made to the extent that it is relevant and necessary.[99]

It should be noted that while Art. III:2, second sentence contains a reference 'to the principles set forth in paragraph 1', no such reference is contained in Art. III:2, first sentence.[100] The significance of this distinction lies in the fact that whereas Art. III:1 acts implicitly, as a principle, in addressing the following two issues that must be considered when applying the first sentence, it acts explicitly as an entirely separate issue that must be addressed along with the following two other issues that are raised when applying the second sentence.[101]

Therefore, for an internal fiscal measure to be in conformity with the first sentence of Art. III:2, it is necessary to determine (1) whether the taxed imported and domestic products are 'like', and (2) whether the taxes applied to the imported products are 'in excess of' those applied to the like domestic products.[102] By comparison, for the measure to be in conformity with the second sentence of the Article, three elements must be examined: (1) whether the imported and domestic products are 'directly competitive or substitutable' and 'competition was involved'[103]; (2) whether the directly competitive or substitutable imported and domestic products are not 'similarly taxed'; and (3) whether different taxes are levied on imported and domestic directly competitive or substitutable products 'so as to afford protection to domestic production'.[104]

In any case, these elements that must be addressed in determining whether there is such a violation must be addressed clearly and separately on a case-by-case basis.[105] Furthermore, in every case, a careful and objective analysis must be made of each and every relevant fact and of all relevant circumstances in order to determine 'the existence of protective taxation'.[106] In addressing this issue, it should be taken into account that the drafting history confirms that Art. III:2 was designed with 'the intention that internal taxes on goods should not be used as a means of protection'[107] and that this accords with the broader objective of Art. III 'to provide equal conditions of competition and to protect thereby the benefits accruing from tariff concessions'.[108]

1.2.2. *Article III:2, First Sentence*

At the London Conference, a subcommittee draft considered by delegates referenced 'identical or similar products' in conjunction with the national treatment obligation.[109] It should be noted that GATT Art. III, as it emerged later, failed to refer to the 'similar' product concept. One might say that this indicates a narrow scope of likeness (thus, a narrow coverage of the national treatment obligation) in the provision: the concept 'identical' seems to inform the scope of the likeness concept. Subsequent records of the Geneva Conference, however, show that there was a lot of criticism against the narrow understanding. In the debates regarding Art. III, both the United States and British delegates indicated that an importing state was not free to levy internal charges on an imported item by reason of the fact that the same kind of item was not produced by the importing state.[110] The obvious reason for insisting that imports not be subject to internal burdens in such a situation is to avoid creating adverse effects on competitive conditions between imports and domestic goods. They expressed their objection to internal taxes on the imported product when the effect is to protect a 'similar' domestic product that is untaxed.[111]

These records suggest that many drafters wanted to read the concept of likeness more flexibly. In fact, it seems that they did not put much emphasis on, or pay much attention to, the 'non-binding' nature of Art. III:1. They understood that the obligation of the second paragraph of Art. III could not be separated from the first paragraph obligation, and that the combination of these two paragraphs demanded a broader interpretation of likeness. Furthermore, comments by the delegates from the United States and United Kingdom clearly support this point: '. . . importing states are not permitted to impose internal taxes on imports (when those states do not even produce items, the same as what is imported) in order to favor domestic production of similar, competitive, or substitutable items.'[112]

These efforts to broaden the national treatment obligation resulted in the inclusion of the phrase 'directly competitive or substitutable' in the original version of

Art. III of the GATT at the Geneva Conference in 1947. The Geneva version reads, in relevant part, as follows:

[I]n cases in which there is no substantial domestic production of like products of national origin, no contracting party shall apply new or increased internal taxes on the products of the territories of other contracting parties for the purpose of affording protection to the production of *directly competitive or substitutable products* which are not similarly taxed; and existing internal taxes of this kind shall be subject to negotiation for their reduction or elimination.[113]

This strong support for the broad obligation seems to have continued up to the time of the subsequent attachment of an *Addendum* to Art. III by a 1948 amendment.[114] This amendment was designed to revise the text of the Geneva version, thereby bringing it more in line with the corresponding provision of the Havana Conference's ITO Charter.[115]

The net result of the modification of the provision is that, due to the *Addendum*, the coverage of Art. III:2, second sentence extends well beyond the 'like' concept. It should be particularly noted that the coverage of the Art. III:2 obligation became broader than that of the previous text of the Geneva version: the Geneva version catches the 'directly competitive or substitutable product' only when 'there is no substantial domestic production of like products of national origin',[116] whereas the modified version (current version) does not have this limitation.[117] As a result, we have the national treatment obligation on the 'directly competitive or substitutable' products as a 'regular player' on the team instead of a mere 'substitution player' or a 'pinch-hitter'.[118]

The practicality of this difference is that now one could safely say that, since the second sentence of Art. III:2 provides for a separate and distinctive obligation for the different categories of product relationships (not 'like' but 'directly competitive or substitutable') from the category of the first sentence, the first sentence of Art. III:2 must be construed strictly so as not to condemn measures that its rigid terms are not meant to condemn.[119] This can be done by construing the term 'like product' in the sentence as such a narrow concept as 'identical product'. At least two additional points support this narrowest understanding of likeness:

1. because the first sentence does not incorporate Art. III:1 into its legal obligation, no consideration is given, when analyzing the sentence, as to whether the measure in question was applied with a 'protectionist design, architecture and revealing structure';[120] and
2. the first sentence employs the phrase 'imposed in excess of' as an identification standard of discrimination. Compared with other standards such as 'not similarly taxed' in the second sentence and 'treated less favourably' in the fourth paragraph of Art. III, the 'in excess of' standard is extremely strict. A small amount of tax differential would be enough to be considered 'in excess of'. No exceptions, including a *de minimis* exception, would be allowed.

The combined effect of this pair of straitjackets would be enough to stifle any room reserved for national autonomy once a product is determined as the 'like' product in the first sentence. A very small difference in taxes between like products would conclusively be deemed to be a violation of the national treatment obligation, with no need to examine protectionist applications.

Hence, by having the narrowest understanding of likeness, i.e. 'identical', in the sentence, one could limit the instances in which this stiff stricture of the sentence would apply. This interpretation would make the *actual application* of the national treatment obligation more in line with the principle of the obligation prescribed in the first paragraph of Art. III. Indeed, this interpretation seems to be what the Appellate Body meant by the statement that 'Article III:1 *acts implicitly in addressing the two issues that must be considered in applying the first sentence*'.[121]

Notwithstanding this interpretation, it seems that this reduced scope of 'like' in the first sentence brings about only a limited difference in a practical sense. Due to the concurrent application of the second sentence,[122] which is invigorated by the Appellate Body's ruling that there is *little* difference between the standards 'in excess of' and 'not similarly taxed',[123] the debate over the scope of 'like' products in the first sentence lost most of its practical value.[124] What is more important is the scope of the concept 'directly competitive or substitutable' in the next sentence.

1.2.3. Article III:2, Second Sentence

By establishing a concurrent application between the first and the second sentences, as prescribed in the *Addendum*, the national treatment obligation finally reaches even those product relationships in which the two products in question share absolutely no physical similarity with each other, as long as they appeal to the consumers as 'directly competitive or substitutable'.

The developmental history of Art. III:2 analyzed at 1.2.2 above suggests that the concept of 'directly competitive or substitutable' must be broader than any possible reading of the term 'like'. This difference in scope might have been clearer if the reference to the phrase 'directly competitive or substitutable' was made through juxtaposition with the term 'like product' in the main text of Art. III:2, as seen in the Geneva version, rather than in the *Addendum*.[125] But the fact that the reference appears in *Addendum* does not change the relationship between the two terms. Nothing in the records of the Havana Conference suggests that the relocation was designed to change the relationship, or to broaden the concept of likeness as stipulated in the precursor Geneva version.[126]

In the Geneva Conference, it was indicated that the concept of 'directly competitive or substitutable' should be broad enough to encompass even distinctly different kinds of goods. According to an exemplary explanation in the Conference, a country that imposes an internal tax on imported 'oranges', which it does not produce but on which it has given a tariff binding, should be resoundingly condemned when the country affords a consequent protection to domestic 'apples' by tax exemption.[127]

More direct evidence of the meaning of 'directly competitive or substitutable' can be taken from the Havana Conference records. According to statements made by the delegates who had been involved in the drafting process of Art. III:2, 'tung oil'[128] would be considered competitive with or substitutable for 'linseed oil',[129] and 'coal' in certain cases would be considered competitive with or substitutable for 'fuel oil'.[130] Other examples taken were domestic 'synthetic rubber' and imported 'natural rubber'.[131] These records show that there was some agreement at the Havana Conference that the obvious dissimilarities between the two products in comparison did not hinder them from being 'directly competitive or substitutable' products.

Accordingly, going back to the comparison between wheat cereal and non-wheat cereal in the MFN context,[132] one can say that many non-wheat cereals could be 'directly competitive or substitutable' products to wheat cereal, thereby being subject to the national treatment obligation. This result clearly indicates a broader scope of the concept of 'directly competitive or substitutable' products than the most flexible scope of the 'like' product concept in the MFN context.

Still, since other provisions, such as Art. XI:2 and Art. XIX:1, employ the slightly different terms 'directly substituted' and 'directly competitive' respectively, one's inquiry into the possible differences in meaning or scope among those concepts should continue.

1.2.4. Article III:4

It is noteworthy that the national treatment obligation was broadened to cover 'directly competitive or substitutable' products only in regard to fiscal measures contemplated in the second paragraph of Art. III of the GATT and the accompanying *Addendum*. Measures other than fiscal measures are still governed by the term 'like products' in Art. III:4. This seeming imbalance brings up one of the most difficult interpretative problems in the GATT.

Considering the basic purpose of the national treatment obligation, one can say that the results of this imbalance could be quite painful. The following example illustrates the 'pain'. Suppose that a member state imports whisky. The state imposes a higher rate of tax or certain internal charges on imported whisky so as to afford protection to the domestic production of soju. Presuming that soju and whisky are determined as being 'directly competitive or substitutable' products, most likely the tax or charge discrimination would be struck down as a violation of Art. III:2, second sentence. Suppose, however, that the same state imposes a maximum selling price requirement for alcoholic beverages. As a result, since whisky is usually more expensive than soju, the sale or importation of foreign whisky would be restricted.[133] Even in cases in which the restrictive effect due to the requirement would be greater than that of tax discrimination, the maximum selling price requirement would not violate Art. III:4, unless soju and whisky are determined as being 'like' products within the meaning of that provision. The result would be that a measure generating more adverse effects on the competitive relationship between imported and domestic products would survive, whereas the other measure creating a less onerous effect on the same relationship would be struck down. Of course, this situation is difficult to accept, especially in the context of Art. III.

Facing this apparent 'unfairness', an 'equal-scope argument' might be put forward.[134] Interpreting the 'like product' concept in Art. III:4 as broadly as possible, this argument understands that the total elimination of the unfair situation necessarily requires the term 'like' in the fourth paragraph to be read with the same scope as that of the term 'directly competitive or substitutable' in the second paragraph, as the Appellate Body in *EC Asbestos* has recently intimated.[135] According to this view, such 'excessive' interpretation is necessary in order to give a full meaning to the purpose of the national treatment provision expressed in Art. III:1. Addressing equally both internal taxes and charges, on the one hand, and laws, regulations and requirements, on the other, the paragraph demands the broadest scope of likeness: any law, regulation, or requirement imposed so as to protect domestic products could be harmful to the comparative advantage of foreign products that are in a *directly competitive or substitutable* relationship with the domestic products. Moreover, since Art. III is concerned with internal measures, there is no need to be concerned about the possibility that this broadest interpretation might affect the integrity of tariff classification nomenclature.[136] Indeed, there is no evidence that drafters of *Ad* Art. III intended to make a distinction between the fiscal measures of para 2 and the general regulations of para 4. The main concern that the drafters had in mind when they attached the *Ad* Article was to clarify the meaning of Art. III so that it would be easier for members to ascertain the precise scope of their obligations under the Article.[137]

As a textual basis, this argument relies on the language of the chapeau of *Ad* Art. III, which employs the common term 'like domestic product' for *both* fiscal measures and other regulatory measures.[138] However, this 'equal-scope argument' should not be accepted for the following reasons. First of all, the argument cannot give answers to the series of following questions based on the *text* of the provision:

1. Why should the same term 'like products' (in para 2, first sentence, and para 4) be interpreted to have such a vastly different scope ('identical' *v* 'directly competitive or substitutable', respectively) under the same Article—especially when para 2 itself explicitly distinguishes 'like' from 'directly competitive or substitutable'?
2. Does the argument not ignore the fact that the GATT, whenever necessary, employs such *full* terms as 'like or directly competitive products',[139] or 'like . . . or product . . . directly substituted'?[140]
3. Is it not disregarding the fact that the original text of Art. III, agreed before attaching the *Ad* Article, already employed different terms in the second and the fourth paragraphs,[141] indicating that drafters had in mind different meanings for the two paragraphs?

Secondly, consideration for the *purpose* of the provision (fairness) on which the validity of the argument mainly relies does not hold true in many cases. It should be noted that permitting different interpretations between 'like' in para 4 and 'directly competitive or substitutable' in para 2 will *not result* in much different coverage of obligation between the two paragraphs. To elaborate, suppose the likeness of the two paragraphs has different interpretations: i.e., 'like products' in para 4 means '*remotely similar*' products; whereas 'directly competitive or substitutable products' in para 2 means '*directly competitive or substitutable*' products. Taking a modified version of the previous example, if the country imposed different tax rates or a maximum selling price requirement on *domestic whisky* and *imported whisky*, both measures would be struck down by reason of violation of Art. III:2, first sentence, and Art. III:4 respectively. Thus, as far as regulation of 'like' products is concerned, the results are the same.[142] Even if 'directly competitive or substitutable' products are concerned, as in the case of the original example, so long as the different tax was imposed so as 'not' to afford protection, the results are the same: both measures will be saved. That is, in the case of the tax measure, the 'so as to afford protection' factor (one of the elements for the measure to violate the national treatment obligation) is absent; in the case of the maximum price requirement measure, the 'likeness' factor would not be established.

Different outcomes between tax measures and regulatory measures will arise only when *directly substitutable products* are involved *and* the tax measure in question is imposed *so as to afford protection*: the tax measure will be struck down, whereas the price requirement will still be saved. One could call this situation the 'Problematic Area'. In actuality, however, one will not often encounter the Problematic Area because situations satisfying the delicate conditions above will not often arise. Therefore, one can say that the 'artificial' interpretation, providing the same scope for 'like' in para 4 as the scope for 'directly competitive or substitutable' in para 2, does not have 'great' practical meaning.

In fact, bestowing the *same scope* on the two terms ironically could result in 'unfairness', depending on the circumstances of the situation. If one granted equal scope to the two terms, since Art. III:4 does not refer to Art. III:1 whereas Art. III:2, second sentence does, the different *tax* between domestic soju and imported whisky, imposed so as 'not' to afford protection, would not be struck down, whereas the maximum selling price *requirement* of alcoholic beverages imposed 'so as not to' as well as 'so as to' afford protection would be struck down if the requirement created less favourable treatment for imported products.[143] In other words, a broad understanding of the term 'like' in Art. III:4 does not necessarily guarantee fairness.

Even accepting the practical significance of the Problematic Area, the third reason why the term 'like' in para 4 need not have the same scope as 'directly competitive or substitutable' in para 2, lies in the *relationship with other provisions or agreements*. The point is that, different from the latter paragraph, the former may be able to be protected against its violation concurrently by other provisions. In other words, with regard to para 4 issues, one can usually expect the additional application of a different agreement, the General Agreement on Trade in Services (GATS), instead of the missing '*Ad* Article III:4'. Indeed, Art. III:4 is closely related to the GATS. Even though certain measures involving substitutable products might escape from the narrow scope of 'likeness' in Art. III:4, they will often be caught by the well-updated national treatment obligation of the Services Agreement.

This concurrent application may be elaborated as follows. Article XVII of the GATS restates the national treatment concept in a more detailed manner than does GATT Art. III. The GATS provision prescribes that foreign and domestic 'like services' and 'like service suppliers' shall not be accorded less favourable treatment.[144] A standard of identification and comparison set by GATT Art. III:4 is 'all laws, regulations and requirements affecting the like product's internal sale, offering for sale, purchase, transportation, distribution or use'. The comparable standard for GATS Art. XVII is 'all measures affecting supply of like services and like service suppliers'.

A possible solution to the dilemma of the two paragraphs in Art. III may lie in the *different scope* of these two standards. Especially if coverage of 'likeness' in the 'like service or supplier' context of GATS is broader than 'likeness' in the 'like product' context of GATT Art. III:4, the Problematic Area dwindles. For instance, if certain services or service suppliers selling not only 'like' products but also 'directly competitive or substitutable' products might be defined as being 'like services' or 'like service suppliers', then even the deep inside of the Problematic Area, for which the GATT national treatment clause is not available, could be dealt with by the WTO disciplinary force, by way of the GATS national treatment obligation. In other words, as long as the subject matter is involved with the GATS as well as the GATT, one could say that the Problematic Area exists only in theory and in the area of GATT, and that the actual coverage of WTO obligations with regard to *regulatory* discrimination (i.e. GATT Art. III:4 + GATS Art. XVII) is almost the same as the coverage regarding *tax* discrimination (i.e. GATT Art. III:2). Thus, the objective of the national treatment obligation of the 'WTO Agreement System' would be fully achieved.

It should be noted, however, that this 'back-up' function of concurrent application has a limitation: the GATS national treatment obligation applies to the extent (and provided) that member states have made concession to it. Nonetheless, one can still find additional back-ups from other agreements. Additional requirements including 'necessity', 'transparency', and 'conformity to international standard', incorporated into the TBT Agreement and the SPS Agreement, help in identifying dishonest *regulatory* measures and/or in preventing them from circumventing the narrow stricture of Art. III:4 'likeness'.[145] Given that these requirements are imposed on regulatory measures rather than on tax measures, one can say that the regulatory force of para 4 is fortified to that extent.

The fourth reason for rejecting the 'equal-scope argument' concerns policy consideration. One has to be concerned about the possibility that giving too broad a scope to Art. III:4 'likeness' could result in an excessive intrusion on domestic regulatory autonomy. Indeed, the provision has already marched deep into the autonomous area. By utilizing such terms as 'sale or offering for sale', 'purchase', 'transportation', 'distribution', and 'use', and by connecting these terms with other flexible terms such as 'affecting' and 'treatment no less favourable', the national treatment obligation has extended its coverage throughout all stages of transaction of a good.[146] If it obtained more power through very broad interpretations of likeness (i.e. 'directly competitive or substitutable'), the Art. III:4 obligation might become overly intrusive in the regulatory autonomy of the national government.[147]

It is most likely that this policy consideration led the drafters of the GATT, facing the seamless continuum between the evil of discrimination and the necessity of regulatory autonomy, to draw two sets of boundary lines for 'likeness' between fiscal measures and other regulations: for the former, all the way from 'identical' up to 'directly competitive or substitutable'; and for the latter, only up to 'remotely similar' (abstaining from going beyond the limitation of physical similarity). It seems that the drafters regarded the use of internal taxes and charges as the most obvious and probable means of circumventing tariff concessions, thereby attaching *Ad* Art. III:2 to catch fiscal measures protecting 'directly competitive or substitutable' domestic products. On the other hand, the GATT preparatory works show that several members raised objections to extending the national treatment obligation beyond fiscal measures to government regulations.[148] This political atmosphere might have also led to the adoption of different standards of discrimination between the two paragraphs: 'not in excess of' in para 2 and 'no less favourable treatment' in para 4 (of course, the latter is more flexible). The point is that in this circumstance it must have been inconceivable to include such broad language as 'directly competitive or substitutable' in para 4 by attaching an '*Ad* Article III:4'.

Presently, despite a 50-year evolution of the world trading system, this political reality and the resulting policy considerations are still valid. In fact, they will continue to survive, if only in weakened form, until a single customs union of the 'United Economic Community of Nations' replaces the current WTO system.

In conclusion, the term 'like' in Art. III:4 should be understood as meaning 'remotely similar', which is the same scope as in MFN clauses. Of course, this understanding is a result of a compromise between the basic purpose of the national treatment obligation, which encourages as broad a scope as possible,[149] and the problems and points indicated above, which reject the broadest scope of 'directly competitive or substitutable'.

Therefore, in order to examine whether laws, regulations, and requirements are in conformity with Art. III:4, the following should be determined:

(1) whether the domestic product and imported product are 'like' (*identical, closely similar, or remotely similar*) products;
(2) whether the laws, regulations, and requirements affect the imported product's internal sale, offering for sale, purchase, transportation, distribution, or use; and
(3) as a result of the effect, whether less favourable treatment is given to the imported product.[150]

1.2.5. Article III:1

As already indicated, the broad and fundamental purpose of Art. III is to avoid protectionism in the application of internal tax and regulatory measures, which is largely expressed by the first paragraph prescribing that internal measures 'should not be applied to imported or domestic products so as to afford protection to domestic production'.[151] In order to examine whether certain internal measures are imposed so as to afford protection to domestic production or not, one needs to identify, in the first place, the 'likeness' relationship between imports and domestic products to which the measures allegedly afford protection. Thus, despite the absence of any explicit use of the term 'like' product in Art. III:1, it is necessary to define the likeness relationship implicitly as long as the paragraph is involved with an issue of *legal obligation*.

Such an issue may arise in relation to the interpretation of Art. III:2, second sentence, and of Art. III:5,[152] which have incorporated the first paragraph as a legal obligation.[153] As far as the second sentence of Art. III:2 is concerned, the likeness issue of the first paragraph is merged into the issue of interpretation of 'directly competitive or substitutable product' in that sentence. This is the logical and practical result of the 'incorporation' as prescribed by the Interpretative Note to the paragraph. Since the interpretation of 'directly competitive or substitutable product' has already been discussed at 1.2.3 above, we now turn to the question of implicit likeness in Art. III:5.

Paragraph 5 basically has the same language of 'incorporation' as found in the second sentence of para 2: 'Moreover, no contracting party shall otherwise apply internal quantitative regulations (or internal taxes or other internal charges to imported or domestic products) in a manner contrary to the principles set forth in paragraph 1.' Thus, the first inquiry is directed to the possibility of whether, for symmetry with the second sentence, the likeness in para 5 may stretch even to 'directly competitive or substitutable product' relationships.

One should note that unlike the second sentence of Art. III.2, the fifth paragraph has no explicit endorsement (e.g., through '*Ad* Article III:5') of such a stretch to include 'directly competitive or substitutable' relationships. Indeed, it is noteworthy that, contrary to *Ad* Art. III:2 (which broadens the coverage of the paragraph beyond a mere likeness relationship by adding the substitutability relationship), *Ad* Art. III:5 tries to limit the scope of the paragraph by excluding 'any case in which all of the products subject to the regulations are produced domestically in substantial quantities'.[154] In addition, it would go against the 'ordinary meaning' of the paragraph to extend the likeness to include 'directly competitive or substitutable' relationships without explicit endorsement, particularly when the chapeau of *Ad* Art. III mentions only 'like domestic product' as a sort of 'fallback' relationship of likeness.[155]

Moreover, this difference in the scope of likeness between para 5 and the second sentence of para 2 becomes clear when one pays attention to the 'context or purpose' of para 5. The fifth paragraph is a specific subset of the fourth paragraph.[156] Hence, the symmetry should be drawn not between Art. III:2 and III:5, but between Arts III:4 and III:5. Therefore, considering that Art. III:4 'likeness' has a scope of 'remotely similar' as discussed at 1.2.4 above, one can conclude that the 'likeness' implicit in Art. III:5 should have the same scope.

1.2.6. TBT Agreement, Arts 2:1, 5:1, 5:2, Annex III:D; SPS Agreement, Annex C:1

Does the understanding of likeness in GATT Art. III:4 (see 1.2.4 above) extend to the interpretation of 'like product' in the national treatment clauses of the TBT and SPS Agreements?

The TBT Agreement contains several provisions involving national treatment obligations[157] prescribing that members shall ensure that:

(1) 'in respect of technical regulations, products imported from the territory of any Member shall be accorded treatment no less favourable than that accorded to *like products* of national origin and to like products originating in any other country' (Art. 2.1);

(2) 'conformity assessment procedures are prepared, adopted and applied so as to grant access for suppliers of *like products* originating in the territories of other Members under conditions no less favourable than those accorded to suppliers of *like products* of national origin or originating in any other country, in a comparable situation . . .' (Art. 5.1.1);

(3) when implementing the provisions of Art. 5:1, 'conformity assessment procedures are undertaken and completed as expeditiously as possible and in a no less favourable order for products originating in the territories of other Members than for *like domestic products* [Art. 5.2.1] . . . any fees imposed for assessing the conformity of products originating in the territories of other Members are equitable in relation to any fees chargeable for assessing the conformity of *like products* of national origin or originating in any other country . . .' (Art. 5.2.5);

(4) 'In respect of standards, the standardizing body shall accord treatment to products originating in the territory of any other Member of the WTO no less favourable than that accorded to *like products* of national origin and to like products originating in any other country' (Annex III.D).

In addition, the SPS Agreement prescribes:

Members shall ensure, with respect to any procedure to check and ensure the fulfilment of sanitary or phytosanitary measures, that:

(a) such procedures are undertaken and completed without undue delay and in no less favourable manner for imported products than for *like domestic products*;

. . .

(f) any fees imposed for the procedures on imported products are equitable in relation to any fees charged on *like domestic products* or products originating in any other Member and should be no higher than the actual cost of the service . . . (Annex C:1)[158]

Attention should be focused on the point that the TBT provisions support Art. III:4 of the GATT, particularly in regard to *de facto* discrimination contexts,[159] and that the SPS Agreement contains obligations concerning technical standards-type barriers in the area of agriculture and food products.[160] Thus, one could argue in the first place that the scope of likeness here should be 'remotely similar' in order to be in line with the scope of 'likeness' in Art. III:4.

It is true that the TBT and SPS Agreements go substantially beyond the mere requirement of non-discrimination put forth in the GATT, and address the question of the scientific justification necessary for standards that might inhibit imports.[161] Furthermore, even as between the SPS and TBT Agreements, there exists a subtle difference in the means used to determine whether a measure is protective in nature. The TBT Agreement relies primarily on a test of whether a measure discriminates against imported products; whereas the SPS Agreement focuses on whether a measure is based on scientific principles and on a risk assessment.[162] These new 'spirits', or approaches, were reflected in relevant provisions of the TBT and SPS Agreements, calling for a basis of scientific evidence,[163] harmonization/equivalence,[164] risk assessment/conformity assessment,[165] and transparency.[166]

It should be noted that not only these provisions codifying 'new spirits' are found in the TBT and SPS Agreements. The 'old spirit' of non-discrimination coexists with them as well. The quoted clauses in the present subject matter are nothing more than provisions codifying old non-discrimination obligations rooted in GATT Art. III:4. The principle of non-discrimination is set out in Art. 2.1 of the TBT Agreement and applied in each specific context of the technical barriers to trade through Arts 5.1.1, 5.2.5, and Annex III:D. Similarly, items (a) and (f) of Annex C:1 to the SPS Agreement are specific applications of the Art. 2.3 non-discrimination principle, announcing that 'Members shall ensure that their sanitary and phytosanitary measures do not arbitrary or unjustifiably *discriminate* between Members where *identical or similar conditions* prevail, including between their own territory and that of other Members.'[167]

These two new Agreements do not include any provisions that provide a definitive interpretation of the term 'like products'. This contrasts with other new agreements such as the Customs Valuation Agreement, the Antidumping Agreement, and the SCM Agreement.[168] One could argue that this omission expresses a silent acceptance of the old rule of interpretation of 'like product', laid down in GATT Art. III:4. Therefore, a parallel should be drawn between the 'like product' concept of GATT Art. III:4 and that concept as expressed in the SPS and TBT Agreements. As a consequence, the 'remotely similar' product relationship has become the common understanding of 'likeness' in the MFN, GATT Art. III:4 national treatment, and the TBT/SPS national treatment clauses.

One interesting point is that the present subject matter provisions juxtapose not only *national treatment*, but also the *MFN* obligation in the same sentence: '. . . no less favourable treatment than that accorded to like products *of national origin* and/or to like products *originating in any other country* . . .'.[169] This juxtaposition *in the same sentence* may provide strong 'textual' evidence indicating the same scope between likeness in Art. III:4 national treatment clauses and the MFN clauses, which proves the correctness of our conclusions up to this point in the present chapter.

1.2.7. Performance

How can the Framework Analysis of GATT likeness or substitutability apply to the various scopes of the likeness concept in the national treatment provisions, which stretch from 'identical' in the first sentence of Art. III:2, through 'remotely similar' in Art. III:4 (Art. III:1 as incorporated in Art. III:5 and the SPS/TBT national treatment clauses), to 'directly competitive or substitutable' in the second sentence of Art. III:2?

The initial focus of the Analysis is upon no other factor than objective characteristics. Physical properties, tariff classifications, and end-uses in general should be taken into consideration with equal evidentiary weight, as shown by relevant GATT/WTO decisions, including *Japan Wine and Liquor, United States Malt Beverages, United States Automobiles, United States Gasoline, Japan Alcoholic Beverages, Canada Periodicals, Korea Alcoholic Beverages*, and *Chile Alcoholic Beverages*. This means that, different from the MFN context, here the element of tariff classification does not provide a 'special evidentiary point' of the likeness or substitutability analysis, let alone a 'presumptive conclusion', no matter how sophisticated the classification is.[170] There are at least two reasons to support this point:

(1) The cooperative relationship between the tariff classification (as a result of tariff negotiations) and the *national treatment* obligation is less close than that between the tariff classification and the *MFN* obligation. It is true that one of the important purposes of the national treatment obligation is to prohibit members from circumventing tariff concessions through non-tariff barriers to import trade that might undermine the benefit of a tariff reduction. But one should be reminded that the broad purpose of Art. III is to avoid protectionism in the application of internal tax and regulatory measures and to provide a level playing field for imported goods *vis-à-vis* domestic like products.[171] This broad purpose needs a multi-dimensional determination of likeness based on comprehensive criteria, including not only tariff classification, but also physical properties, end-use, and the marketplace.

(2) Because the examiner of the GATT national treatment obligation does not need to be concerned about the matter of integrity of tariff classification nomenclature, the determination of likeness in such clauses can be freer from the tariff classification criteria.[172] In contrast, the determination in the case of MFN clauses often carries the burden of needing to pay attention to the integrity of the nomenclature.[173] In fact, this difference explains why the national treatment clause (as opposed to MFN clauses) includes, explicitly through the *Addendum*, the 'substitutable' product relationship in addition to the 'like' product relationship.

Therefore, in the first stage, the likeness determination in Art. III of the GATT depends upon a 'balanced' examination of the three objective elements, which will be subject to the *unavoidable discretionary judgement* of the tribunal.

Should the result of the objective factor examination create the same effect on the likeness or substitutability test when considering 'likeness' in the various paragraphs or sentences of Art. III? First of all, as regards the first sentence of Art. III:2, one could say that the result of the objective characteristics analysis alone creates a *presumption* regarding likeness. This point comes from the understanding that the 'like' concept here has the narrowest scope, of 'identical', combined with the fact that the sentence adopts a formalistic standard of 'in excess of' while no reference to the first paragraph is made.[174] This strict nature and formalistic approach in the first sentence would fit well with the formalistic approach (i.e. presumption) in the likeness determination.

This presumption based on the objective characteristic test can be rebutted by the party opposing it. For a successful rebuttal, the party needs to put forward a credible result of a demand substitutability analysis that shows the existence, or lack thereof, of 'sufficient' demand substitutability between the products at issue. In this process, the CVA-PCPDS may be employed, as discussed in Chapter II at 3.2.2. One should be reminded that by using the PMP Questionnaire, which includes questions with which to identify 'neutral' respondents, the party can internalize the 'potential substitution' factor into the outcome of the Analysis (see Chapter II, at 3.2.4). How much is the 'sufficient' demand substitutability in this context? Because 'identical' product relationships require the Quadruple-Price Standard (QPS), as suggested at 1.1.3 above,[175] if the hypothetical price change is given at 25 per cent, the entire demand for one product should switch to the other in question.

If a rebuttal is successful,[176] the tribunal moves to the second step of the demand substitutability analysis, because the likeness is determined after all in the market, as discussed in Chapter II. Sometimes, the tribunal itself may decide to proceed to the second step analysis: if the results of objective characteristic analysis are not good enough to produce the presumption ('tough case'), the tribunal may rely on the demand substitutability analysis. Again, in the second stage, in order to obtain a conclusion regarding likeness that is consistent and transparent across Art. III:2, first sentence cases, the tribunal may rely upon such analytical tools as the CVA-PCPDS, the PMP Questionnaire (including questions for identifying neutral respondents), and the QPS.

In contrast, as regards the second sentence of Art. III:2, Art. III:4, Art. III:5 (III:1), TBT Agreement, Arts 2:1, 5:1, 5:2, and Annex III:D, and the SPS Agreement, Annex C:1, it can be said that the result of objective characteristic analysis alone does not amount to creating a presumption as to likeness. These provisions adopt such broad concepts as 'directly competitive or substitutable', or 'remotely similar', respectively, and the flexible standard of 'not similarly taxed' or 'no less favourable treatment' (as opposed to 'in excess of' in the first sentence of Art. III:2). Thus, there is little reason for such an inflexible factor as objective characteristics to play a presumptive role in likeness determinations in those provisions. In determining 'directly competitive or substitutable' products, the complaining party should not be permitted to make an allegation of direct substitutability based only on the objective characteristics of the products concerned, succeeding because no rebuttal is raised by the defending party. Likeness, or direct competitiveness or substitutability, in those provisions should be analyzed through a comprehensive test, including an objective characteristics examination and a subsequent market-based end-use analysis.[177]

It should be restated that, when applying the CVA-PCPDS and the PMP Questionnaire including questions for identifying neutral respondents, the direct competitiveness or substitutability in the second sentence of Art. III:2 should be evaluated using the PSE Standard (see Chapter II, at 3.2.2). By comparison, 'like products' in Arts III:4 and III:5 (III:1), as well as in the TBT/SPS Agreements, should be determined using the Double-Price Standard (DPS), as in the case of MFN clauses (see 1.1 above). To assist the panel's judgement with regard to demand substitutability, the results of the direct view approach and/or the time-series analysis could be referred to (see Chapter II, at 3.2.2 and 3.2.3). Where the result of the demand substitutability analysis is not clear enough for the tribunal to reach a conclusion, supply substitutability could be examined to complement it by taking into account any mitigation effect. At this stage, the CVA-PCPSS combined with the IASR Standard could be employed (see 1.1 above and Chapter II, at 3.2.3). With the toughest cases, future competition analysis as well as the supply-side direct view and time-series analyses (see 1.1 above and Chapter II, at 3.2.4).

1.3. Prohibition of Quantitative Restrictions

1.3.1. *Article XI:2*

To the general prohibition of quantitative restrictions in the first paragraph of Art. XI, the second paragraph provides several exceptions. One of those is an import restriction on agricultural or fisheries products, imported in any form, necessary to enforce governmental measures that operate (1) to restrict the production or marketing of the 'like domestic product', or (2) to remove any temporary surplus of the 'like product'. Or if there is no substantial domestic production of the 'like product', this exception is extended to the 'directly substituted product' relationship.[178] These concepts, of 'like' and 'directly substituted' products based on comparison between imported goods and domestic goods in the importing state, should be analyzed.

As regards the 'like' product concept, negotiating records seem to oppose a broad understanding. During the London Conference, a Chilean delegate commented that the concept 'definitely does not mean merely a competing product'.[179] He took the example that restricted production of domestic apples did not justify importation limits imposed on foreign bananas merely by reason that they competed with apples.[180] This position was supported by a US delegate.[181]

The purpose of the prohibition of quantitative restrictions and the basic nature of Art. XI:2 as an exception from the general rule signal a narrow scope for the concept. One can argue that a narrow understanding of the like product concept would strike the best balance between the aim of providing a mechanism for stabilizing fluctuations in the supply of agricultural and fisheries products,[182] on the one hand, and the danger of generating the possibility of circumvention, on the other.[183] For the purpose of supporting price or removing any temporary surplus of domestic products, quantitative restrictions on foreign 'identical or closely similar' products would suffice in many cases. For example, domestic tomato prices (or surplus) would be substantially stabilized (or reduced) due to quota impositions on the importation of tomatoes. Such a restriction on imports of foreign tomatoes combined with no restriction on importing *tomato concentrates* would not be likely to result in a serious import surge of foreign tomato concentrates. However, if there is no substantial domestic production of tomato concentrates, so that the tomato price support (or surplus disposal) program of the importing country is in a vulnerable position because of an import surge of tomato concentrates, the importing country is entitled to extend the import restriction to foreign tomato concentrates.[184] Thus, a problem might arise only when there exists substantial domestic production of tomato concentrates. But in this case, the very existence of a substantial amount of domestic production of the product would substantially mitigate the effect of the surge, if any, in speed and in extent.[185] Hence, to support the price or remove the surplus of domestic tomatoes, there would not be much need to cover foreign *tomato concentrates* in addition to *tomato* imports. In a serious situation in which such a need arises, it could (and should) be dealt with by safeguard measures in GATT Art. XIX, in which a much broader scope of likeness—i.e., like *or directly competitive* products—is subject to the safeguard protection.[186]

A broad understanding of the 'like product' concept in Art. XI:2 would make the exception more susceptible to protectionist endeavors. Some quantitative restrictions taken so as to protect domestic products would be able to be justified as necessary measures to restrict production or to remove any surplus of domestic products, which are in fact merely 'remotely similar' to the imported products subject to the restriction. For instance, in the example above, a quota imposed on tomato concentrates as well as on tomatoes would be legitimized under the umbrella of broad 'likeness', even when there exists substantial domestic production of tomato concentrates. This consequence of a broad understanding of likeness in Art. XI:2 would engender more incentive for protectionist endeavors from the domestic *tomato concentrates* industry, with no great help in furthering the objective of price stabilization or surplus disposal of domestic tomatoes.

It is interesting to find that the text of the *waiver* given to the United States with respect to the Art. XI:2 exception includes only the term 'like product', without even mentioning the term 'directly substituted product' in the text[187] (Art. XI:2 itself includes both terms). The reason for such an omission seems obvious: the very 'anti-broad-likeness' sentiment explained above seems to have led GATT

Contracting Parties to eliminate the option (if only the conditional option) of import restrictions on 'directly substituted' products altogether from the policy options available to the United States, the party that obtained an extremely exceptional instrument of waiver.

Therefore, the concept of 'like' in Art. XI:2 should be taken to mean 'identical or closely similar'. It should be noted that this is broader than the scope of likeness in Art. III:2, first sentence. Putting aside the strict nature of the first sentence, one could explain this from the fact that Art. XI:2 is able to use the 'additional ammunition' of 'directly substituted' only when the original comparator ('like') is unavailable.[188] If one is able to use both originals and additions alternatively, as in the case of Art. III:2, one deserves to be checked (by tribunals) for any possible misuse of the original tool; without such an alternative usage, one would need to be allowed to use the original ammunition to the full extent to which it is supposed to function.[189] In this light, the ruling of the Panel in *EEC Apples from Chile* seems to be appropriate: Chilean apples, although of different varieties, were a like product to Community apples for the purposes of Art. XI:2(c).[190]

Turning to the concept 'directly substituted', one finds few clues in the negotiation records (as opposed to *Ad* Art. III:2, with regard to which ample records are available). Originally, the equivalent provision of the New York Conference draft of the GATT contained no reference other than 'like products'.[191] Naturally, there was discussion during the Conference about inserting a broader concept such as 'directly *competitive*' goods. Supporting a UK proposal that the draft should reflect references to the permissibility of using import restrictions in cases when 'directly competitive' products are involved, a Cuban delegate pointed out that products 'may be competing for the same market and yet may be entirely different in form'.[192]

These remarks by the Cuban delegate provide a good definition of 'directly competitive' products: products that are different in form, yet competing for the same market. An insight from this observation would be that the concept 'directly competitive' could include products that are entirely different in form. This definition and its inclusiveness may be utilized in defining the 'directly substituted' concept, despite the fact that ultimately GATT Art. XI:2(c) opted for the term 'directly substituted', rather than 'directly competitive'.[193] An inquiry into any possible difference of meaning between 'competitive' and 'substituted', or even between 'substituted' and 'substitutable', will be pursued below.

In relation to the definition of 'directly substituted', attention should be paid to the phrase 'in any form' in subpara (c) of Art. XI:2. According to this provision, the general prohibition on quantitative restrictions does not extend to 'import restrictions on any agricultural or fisheries product, *imported in any form*, necessary to the enforcement' of certain governmental measures.[194] The interpretive note in *Ad* Art. XI:2 indicates that the term 'in any form' covers the 'same products when in an early stage of processing and still perishable, which compete directly with the fresh product and if freely imported would tend to make the restriction on the fresh product ineffective'.[195] The consequence is to allow the importing state, which is undergoing a production control or surplus disposal program in the areas of domestic agricultural or fisheries products, to impose quantitative restrictions on imported foreign products that are 'like' products (or, in the absence of them, 'directly substituted' products) to the domestic products, even though those foreign products have already undergone an 'early' stage of processing, thus being at a different stage of processing from the domestic products under the program.

The negotiating records indicate that the reference in Art. XI:2(c) to the phrase 'in any form' has been included in the various versions of the ITO Charter and the GATT from the beginning.[196] With the adoption of the draft ITO Charter emerging from the Geneva Conference, the Interpretative Note, presently located in *Ad* Art. XI:2(c), made its first appearance.[197] The obvious intent was to prohibit importing states from imposing restrictions on incoming agricultural or fisheries products when these imports are in some 'advanced' stage of processing. A Geneva Conference confirms the intent by recording that the phrase 'in any form' was not seen as extending to such products so far along the processing spectrum as to be able to be 'tinned' or 'capable of being stocked'.[198] Havana Conference records indicate that the provision 'should not be construed as permitting the use of quantitative restrictions as a method of protecting the industrial processing of agriculture or fisheries products'.[199]

Judged from these records, Art. XI:2 does not aim at protecting the industrial processing sector of agriculture or fisheries products. The basic purpose of the provision is to empower importing states to deal with the 'capricious bounty of nature, which will sometimes give you a huge catch of fish or a huge crop', and the problem of 'a multitude of small unorganized producers that cannot organize themselves'[200] and so produce surpluses. Specifically, the provision is an endorsement that government regulations restricting production of domestic agricultural or fisheries goods can be buttressed by import restrictions on even processed foreign agricultural or fisheries goods which are in the early stage of the process and which could prove directly competitive therewith. If this responsive action were not permitted, the heightened domestic price of the regulated goods would lead to a surge of such early-stage processed imports, which would result in a circumvention of the import restriction on the unprocessed fresh products.[201]

Employment of the phrase 'in any form' in Art. XI:2(c) clarifies the proper understanding of the term 'directly substituted' rather than of the term 'like', because the narrow scope of the latter (as reasoned above) does not fit with the flexible (i.e., potentially broad) phrase of 'in any form'. This is confirmed by the language of the *Ad* Article, in which 'in any form' is located side by side with 'compete directly'.[202] When drafters located both of these terms together, they most likely wanted to snare as many kinds of goods as possible that might undermine the thrust of Art. XI:2(c). In other words, since the phrase 'in any form' could include various processing stages of goods, the concept 'directly substituted' should be understood to be, at least, as inclusive as that phrase in order to catch those stages of goods.

Thus, the concept 'directly substituted' is quite a broad one, reaching well beyond the term 'remotely similar' so far as products at issue are 'competing for the same market'. Indeed, the reason why the GATT, through *Ad* Art. XI, limited the scope of the provision only to early-stage processed and still perishable imports was because of the concern about this comprehensiveness of the concept 'direct substituted'.[203]

So, how broad is the scope of the 'directly substituted' product relationship? This inquiry provides a perfect stage for comparison with the phrase 'directly competitive or substitutable' in Art. III:2. Looking at the 'mysterious' language of 'directly substituted' employed in Art. XI:2, one might ask, 'Why did the drafters use the slightly different term 'substitut*ed*' in this provision instead of 'substitut*able*'?' Instead of raising the unanswered question of whether it was intentional or coincidental, one could draw a logical conclusion based on 'the ordinary meaning to be given to the terms in their context and in the light of [the provision's] object and purpose'.[204]

It is possible to argue that the term 'substituted' is equal to the term '*actually* competitive' or 'compet*ing*':[205] in other words, the drafters wanted to use the word 'substituted' as a term expressing an actual competitive phenomenon that was occurring in the market, not as a term (such as 'substitutable') that can accommodate any possibility of 'potential or future competition'. One could further argue that this potential or future competition factor makes a difference in scope between 'substituted' and 'substitutable'—the latter, holding time or opportunity factor, can become a broader (i.e., inclusive) concept than the former.[206]

Indeed, this interpretation is reinforced when one considers the different purposes of the two provisions concerned, i.e., Arts XI:2 and III. Since the nature of Art. XI:2 is an exception to the general elimination of quantitative restrictions, its application must be limited by narrowly interpreting the scope of the term 'directly substituted'. Furthermore, because the purpose of the provision is to provide relief in certain *current* situations, including a temporary surplus, there is little room for 'future competition or substitutability' to be considered. In addition, because Art. XI:2 will be invoked by the *importing* state to justify its imposition of quantitative restrictions, it is inconceivable that the state would introduce the potential competition factor by indicating that another measure *of its own* has blocked the potential substitutive relationship between the products at issue. Thus, one should understand the concept 'directly substituted' as being free from the potential or future competition consideration. In contrast, Art. III is a basic obligation, the purpose of which is to protect the 'expectation of competitive relationship'. Thus, as already discussed in Chapter II, one has to broaden its coverage by including potential and future (under certain conditions) competition factors in the term 'substitutable'. In this regard, it should be emphasized that a plain reading of the word 'substitut*able*' (compared with 'substitut*ed*') includes potentiality as well as future aspects.[207] Conditions of competition, or competitive relationships, can be fully protected by taking such factors into consideration.[208]

1.3.2. *Performance*

What is the appropriate modification of the Framework Analysis of GATT likeness or substitutability for the establishment of Art. XI:2 likeness?

The first point is that, different from the MFN context but similar to the national treatment context, the three elements of the objective characteristic factor should be taken into consideration with equal evidentiary weight. This point comes from the understanding that the cooperative relationship between tariff classification, on the one hand, and prohibition of quantitative restrictions or permission of certain exceptions, on the other hand, is less close than that between the tariff classification and the MFN obligation. By keeping the quantitative restriction, one of the non-tariff barriers, under control, the prohibition surely helps to maintain the benefits of tariff reduction. But it should be noted that Art. XI originates in the separate experience of widespread and escalating use of quotas during the 1930s that influenced GATT drafters to try to abolish this method of trade restraint. This experience also controls the exceptions set out in Art. XI:2, in that the provision obligates nations to give public notice, to guarantee previous access, and to avoid using quantitative restrictions in a manner that would have trade restricting effects.[209]

Furthermore, because the likeness determination in Art. XI, similar to the national treatment clause, has nothing to do with the integrity of the tariff classification system, a determination under the provision can be made relatively free from the tariff classification criterion.[210] Therefore, in the first stage of the examination of objective characteristics, the likeness interpretation in Art. XI:2 of the GATT should depend upon a 'balanced' examination of the three objective elements, which will be carried out under the *unavoidable discretionary judgement* of the tribunal.

What kind of practical effect should the first step analysis have in the likeness test? The result of the examination of the objective characteristics should not create a presumption with regard to likeness, as opposed to the case of the likeness test under the first sentence of Art. III:2, but similar to the case under the second sentence of Art. III:2, Art. III:4, and the TBT/SPS Agreements (see 1.2 above). Likeness in Art. XI does not necessitate the presumption, because neither a formalistic approach nor the narrowest scope of likeness applies in the provision.[211] Likeness or direct substitution in Art. XI should be subject to a comprehensive analysis, including an objective characteristic examination and subsequent market-based end-use analysis.[212]

In the second stage, when the examiner undertakes the CVA-PCPDS, the proper threshold standards are the Triple-Price Standard (TPS) for the 'like (closely similar)' product test, and the PSE Standard for the 'directly substituted' product test, as discussed.[213] It should be noted that there is no need to employ the PMP or the Future Competition Questionnaire because the potential and future competition factors are not relevant here, as discussed at 1.3.1 above.

Should supply substitutability be taken into consideration in the product likeness or substitutability test in Art. XI:2? The answer seems to depend on whether
high supply substitutability can generate the mitigation effect. Measures permitted
under the Art. XI:2 exception generally take the form of quantitative restrictions
against 'foreign-origin' like or directly substituted products (e.g., import restrictions
on *foreign* tomatoes or tomato concentrates as against no restriction on *domestic*
tomatoes). Thus, unless foreign producers subject to the restriction switch the
country of origin of products through, say, direct investment, a mere production
switch (supply substitution) would bring about no mitigation effect on their competitive opportunity in the market concerned.[214] Absent the mitigation effect,
there is no rationale to include the supply substitutability factor in the Art. XI:2
context.

The direct view approach or the time-series analysis may be used as necessary,
as explained already.

2. FAIR TRADE PROVISIONS

The 'like product' concepts in GATT Arts VI:1, VI:4, and XVI:4 call for a comparison between a category of imported products and a category of products sold in
the home market of the exporting country. Article VI:1 provides that the unfair
practice of dumping exists whenever a category of imported products is sold at less
than the normal price of the 'like product' in the exporting country, or, in the
absence of such a domestic price, of either the 'like product' in any third country
or the cost of production plus selling cost and profit (Antidumping Agreement,
Arts 2.1, 2.2).[215]

GATT Art. XVI:4 prohibits export subsidies on non-primary products resulting
in 'bi-level pricing', sales of exports at a price lower than that of 'domestic like
products'.[216]

Article VI:4 declares that neither dumping nor countervailable subsidies can be
asserted by reason of the mere existence of lower prices in the market into which
the product is imported than the price on its home market, if the price difference
is due to the exemption from or refund of duties or taxes borne by the 'like product' when destined for consumption in the 'exporting country'.[217] Although not
directly tied to Art. XVI:4, the obvious effect of Art. VI:4 is to insulate a certain
bi-level pricing (resulting from duty or tax exemption or refund) from a countervailing duty punishment.

This comparison of prices between imported and home products of the exporting country is designed to charge GATT members to refrain from maintaining
certain practices that place exports at a different price from that that would be
charged if they had been sold in the home market of the exporting state.[218] As a
result, exports are to carry an undistorted price that reflects the price of each sup-
plying state. Thus, the underlying principle of these provisions may be said to be

that of competition on a fair and non-discriminatory basis, with the winners determined through performance on the level playing field.[219]

Although, as discussed in 2.1 below, this bi-level pricing requirement has been subsequently altered in the subsidy context, fair trade provisions in general contribute to inhibiting government (or private) temptation to rely on short-term, *ad hoc* policies creating artificial competitive advantages, by requiring in a clear fashion uni-level pricing or the non-provision of prohibited subsidies. Frequently, these requirements are responsive to the political demands of domestic producers competing with importing products. Without such political considerations having influenced the GATT, the multilateral trading system would not have been able to obtain the necessary support in the international (or domestic) community.

It should be noted that the non-discrimination provisions and the dumping/subsidy provisions are geared up to serve different 'masters' in different economic contexts. The latter provisions protect *domestic firms* producing import-competing products that are *materially harmed*, through imports, by unfair artificial advantages enjoyed by foreign competitors.[220] The targeted advantages include subsidies to production or exportation, as well as protected home markets that generate dumping, i.e., lower prices for export-destined products than for home-market-destined products.[221] In contrast, the former provisions protect the *foreign competitors* from being deprived of legitimate *competitive benefits* obtained by tariff concessions, or of comparative advantages acquired by individual diligence or natural conditions.[222]

Of course, serving different masters requires different targets. The non-discrimination provisions aim to prevent intervention by the importing country, while the fair trade provisions are primarily concerned with depriving the exporting country or firms of unfair advantages.[223]

2.1. Antidumping and Subsidy Provisions

2.1.1. Article VI:1, and the Antidumping Agreement

Thanks to these different masters, targets, and economic contexts, the 'likeness' concepts in the antidumping/subsidy provisions and non-discrimination provisions are not guaranteed to have similar scopes. Even as between Art. VI:1 and Art. XVI:4, that seek to maintain the product's home market price, there could be subtle differences in the scope of likeness, as discussed below.

First of all, regard should be had to the fact that Art. VI embodies something of a digression from the general GATT rules: while the basic rule of the GATT deals with discriminatory treatment, this provision deals with non-discriminatory unfair practices. This suggests that the likeness concept in Art. VI should be interpreted narrowly so as to limit the coverage of the antidumping obligation.[224]

The negotiation records of GATT Art. VI give support to a narrow reading of 'likeness'. During the London Conference, contrary to the US draft text of the provision containing references not only to 'like' but also to 'similar' products, the

Australian Government proposed to delete the term 'similar' from the provision.[225] Subsequent deletion of the 'similar' concept from the text indicates the drafters' intention to restrict the scope of the likeness concept. It does not necessarily indicate, however, that the concept 'like' means 'identical' (the narrowest understanding). Rather, drafters could have worried about the consequences that the flexibility of the term 'similar' might bring about, which is in favour of the argument that they wanted to eliminate only the 'remotely similar' concept from the definition of 'likeness'. This understanding signals that the term 'like' should be read as meaning 'identical or closely similar'.[226] But an extract from a subsequent preparatory record shows that there was clear support for the 'narrowest' understanding of likeness. At the Havana Conference, an Australian delegate suggested that the like product concept used in the context of antidumping and countervailing duties referred to products that are 'the same'.[227]

The basic idea underlying Art. VI:1[228] is to permit such countervailing measures that negate unfair pricing advantages, upsetting the normal competitive relationship between two related markets. One might argue that this is subtly different from the basis of Art. XVI:4, that deals with the 'prohibition' of export subsidies. *Unfairness* is different from *illegality*, against which the General Agreement is fully geared up. The 'narrowest' understanding in Art. VI:1 and 'narrow' understanding in Art. XVI:4 (see 2.1.2 below) might be able to reflect this difference.

In fact, the determination of 'like products' has long been a controversial issue in the antidumping field. This is because defining the category of 'like products' is a critical preliminary step that will set the stage for the rest of the investigation and which will, if measures are imposed, govern the scope of their application.[229] From the very inception of an antidumping action, the determination of 'like products' can be a critical strategic choice. Complainants are faced with conflicting interests in this regard. There is a strong incentive to define broadly the category of 'like products' (thus, the scope of 'domestic industry') in Art. 4.1 of the Antidumping Agreement,[230] because in that way one can sweep a larger group of products into the scope of the investigation and any eventual antidumping duties (Antidumping Agreement, Arts 5.2, 5.4, 5.8, 6.11). On the other hand, by drawing too broad a category of 'like products', complainants can make it more difficult to meet the standing criteria and to prove injury (Antidumping Agreement, Arts 3.1, 3.2, 3.6).[231] Therefore, in many cases, the complainants and/or antidumping authorities would try to narrow the scope of the 'like product' definition so as to increase their success rate. This problem of system abuse (by the arbitrary interpretation) is well illustrated by the Panel in the *New Zealand—Imports of Electrical Transformers from Finland* case:

In its examination whether the New Zealand transformer industry had suffered injury from the imports in question, the Panel subsequently dealt with the argument put forward by New Zealand that this industry was structured in such a way that there existed four distinguishable range of transformers ... which for purposes of injury determination had to be considered separately. The Panel was of the view that this was not a valid argument, especially in light of the fact that the complaining company [represented]...the New Zealand transformer industry...It was thus, in the Panel's view, the overall state of health of the New Zealand transformer industry which must provide the basis for a judgement whether injury was caused by dumped imports. To decide otherwise would allow the possibility to grant relief through antidumping duties to individual lines of production of a particular industry or company—a notion which would clearly be at variance with the concept of industry in Article VI...[232]

It could generally be said that the main focus of antidumping law has been changed, from regulation of unfair trade practices (price differentiation practices) to prohibition of system abuse by antidumping authorities of member states. In this light, one might say that too narrow a scope of likeness would not be desirable because it would enable one to carve out a pocket of injury in an otherwise healthy industry. At the same time, an overly broad definition of likeness would make it possible to sweep a larger group of products into the scope of the investigation to make the foreign industries concerned suffer regardless of the result of the investigation.

Facing this dilemma and the subtle difference between the antidumping and subsidy contexts (as discussed further below), the WTO Agreement resolved the problem by adopting definitive interpretations that furnish the 'narrowest' interpretation ('identical') in the first place and the 'narrow' one ('closely similar') in the second place. Article 2.6 of the Antidumping Agreement and Art. 15.1 of the SCM Agreement employ exactly the same definitive interpretations of the like product concept; furthermore, they do not distinguish the concept in the domestic countervailing process from that in the multilateral process.[233] According to these provisions, the like product means the 'identical' product. But in the absence of such a product, one can utilize the 'closely similar' product concept.[234] This understanding applies 'throughout the Agreement'.[235]

Despite the lack of 'full delicacy',[236] this legislation deserves credit, at least in that the 'conditional (not alternative)' approach in the provisions—employing the narrow concept only in the absence of the narrowest concept—might be effective in preventing the respondent companies from circumventing antidumping orders by making minor changes to the dumped or subsidized product.[237]

2.1.2. *Article XVI:4, the SCM Agreement, and the Agreement on Agriculture, Art. 9.1(b)*

GATT Art. XVI:4 provides that:

...contracting parties shall cease to grant either directly or indirectly any form of subsidy on the export of any product other than a primary product which subsidy results in the sale of such product for export at a *price lower than* the comparable price charged for the *like product* to buyers in the domestic market...(emphasis added)

This provision indicates that 'bi-level-pricing' is a necessary requirement for the prohibition of export subsidies. It should be noted that this requirement is still relevant, if not fully, even though the SCM Agreement has subsequently altered the subsidy regulation regime to a substantial degree. According to Art. 1.1 of the SCM Agreement, 'a subsidy shall be deemed to exist if... there is a financial contribution by a government... *or... there is any form of income or price support in the sense of Article XVI of GATT 1994...*' (emphasis added). Based on this definition, the Agreement proceeds to the concept of 'prohibited subsidy': '... the following subsidies, *within the meaning of Article 1*, shall be prohibited: (a) subsidies contingent ... upon export performance, including those illustrated in Annex I...'[238] One of the export subsidies listed in Annex I of the SCM Agreement is '*any other charge on the public account constituting an export subsidy in the sense of Article XVI of GATT 1994*'.[239]

Logical combination of these provisions leads to the net result that the 'bi-level pricing' condition in GATT Art. XVI:4 is still alive as a requirement in a certain type of prohibited subsidy case, although it is no longer an absolute requirement across all cases. For instance, (1) if a government provides a 'financial contribution' conditional upon 'export performance' or 'domestic use' that is a prohibited subsidy (regardless of whether it results in bi-level pricing or not); (2) if a government grants 'any form of income or price support' (other than financial contribution) conditional upon 'export performance' or 'domestic use' then it is also a prohibited subsidy, *provided that the support results in 'bi-level pricing'*. This latter type of subsidy is what the above Annex language explicitly indicates as being one of the export subsidies prohibited by the GATT/SCM Agreement. Accordingly, to prohibit export subsidies in the latter type of cases, one should necessarily show the existence of bi-level pricing between products selling in the home market and 'like products' selling in the export market. For that purpose, one needs to clarify the concept 'like product' in Art. XVI:4, as follows.

With regard to the scope of likeness in Art. XVI, it should be noted that para 4 was added, along with paras 2, 3, and 5, in the form of section B, when the Contracting Parties amended the Article in 1955.[240] Paragraph 2 announces the principal objective of the amendment: to address 'harmful effects' and 'undue disturbance to normal commercial interests'.[241] Export subsidies are 'harmful' and 'undue' because they negate the effect of duties that have been legitimately established by the importing country after negotiations. This negation would create an artificial advantage for the subsidized exports, which would 'disturb normal commercial interests'. The artificial advantage would also be created in third country markets where the subsidizer and another non-subsidizer compete. Thus, what is important is to prohibit as many obstacles as possible that cause such effects. Indeed, not only 'similar' products, but also 'competitive' or 'substitutable' products can disturb normal commercial interests: any price support of the exporting product achieved through the export subsidization can cause harmful effects to its competitive or substitutable products. Thus, in the first instance, it seems appropriate to view the likeness concept in Art. XVI:4 broadly.

The drafting history of Art. XVI:4 seems to encourage this first impression. During the 1946 London Conference, a joint drafting subcommittee indicated that it would violate a state's undertakings if the state subsidized exports of a certain product and then argued it was permissible because the practice did not result in lower export prices than the home market price of the 'like product', when it actually resulted in a lower export price than the home market price of a product 'differing slightly' from the alleged 'like product'.[242]

This record indicates that the concept of like product in a subsidy context might encompass more than just 'identical' products, or even more than 'closely similar' products. Since Art. XVI:4 'hinges' the obligation of export subsidy prohibition on the concept of likeness, a broad interpretation could be the lifeblood of the obligation. Indeed, this 'broad-likeness sentiment' in Art. XVI:4, as opposed to the 'narrower-likeness sentiment' in Art. VI:1 (as discussed at 2.1.1 above), could be further buttressed by the fact that there exists a methodological difference between the two provisions in respect to calculating the price difference between the exported product and the like domestic product.[243] That is, the following methodological difference could be said to generate the need for different scopes of likeness between the two provisions.

According to Art. VI:1, the home market price is determined not only by the like product formula, but also, in the absence of a home market price, by the constructed price formula or the third market price formula.[244] In contrast, Art. XVI:4 does not provide alternative methods for determining bi-level pricing.[245] In order to compensate for the absence of the constructed price formula, one might say that the like product concept in Art. XVI:4 should be interpreted somewhat more broadly than that in Art. VI:1.[246] In the dumping context of Art. VI:1, even when no domestic sales of a like product exist, one can resort to the cost–profit formula to determine the dumping practices. Hence, a narrow interpretation of likeness does not increase the chance of any circumvention efforts. Indeed, the very juxtaposition of the constructed formula along with the like product formula in the text of Art. VI:1 suggests a strict interpretation of likeness: any broad interpretation might result in the non-use of the constructed formula, except in cases involving non-market economies. Only in very rare instances in which even remotely similar products do not exist, would one be reminded of the utility of the formula.

By the same token, it could be said that likeness in Art. XVI:4 should have broader coverage than in Art. VI:1, in that if the same narrow approach were to be taken with regard to subsidies, very often the price difference between the home market and the export market created by subsidies might be justified by a lack of close similarities between the two products in comparison.[247] No subsidy would exist without price comparison (in the second type of subsidies requiring 'bi-level pricing'). Thus, a broader interpretation of the likeness concept in the subsidy context would fill the vacuum created by the absence of the alternative formula, thereby making the subsidy system less vulnerable to any circumvention efforts.

However, as stated at 2.1.1 above, this broader understanding of Art. XVI likeness can exist only in theory and be relevant after a possible future amendment of the SCM Agreement. Under the strict (narrow) definition of 'like product' in the

Agreement,[248] the understanding cannot be sustained. In order to be in line with
the 'like product' concepts scattered throughout various provisions of the
Agreement,[249] the likeness concept in the subsidy provisions of the GATT should
be equally strict. It seems that the negotiators of the SCM Agreement gave more
credit to the structure of Art. VI, in which the antidumping and countervailing
processes are juxtaposed,[250] and to the historical context in which both processes
have been often considered together. The theoretical delicacy mentioned above
might have been thought of as unimportant, or might not have been noticed by
them at all.

In conclusion, the like product concept in Art. XVI:4 should be understood as
covering the 'identical' product and, in the absence of such a product, the 'closely
similar' product, i.e. a product which, although not alike in all respects, has characteristics closely resembling those of the product in comparison.

This understanding of likeness in the export subsidy provisions of the
GATT/SCM Agreement extends to a comparable provision of the Agreement on
Agriculture. One of the export subsidies subject to reduction commitments under
the Agreement on Agriculture is the 'sale or disposal for export by governments or
agencies of non-commercial stocks of agricultural products at a *price lower than* the
comparable price charged for the *like products* to buyers in the domestic market'.[251]
Considering that the term 'like product' is used in the same context of the bi-level
pricing requirement of export subsidies, one can say that 'like' means 'identical'
product and, in the absence of such a product, 'closely similar' product in accordance with the 'likeness' concept in the GATT/SCM Agreement. The fact that the
SCM Agreement conceded control over export subsidies on agricultural products
to the Agreement on Agriculture[252] cannot affect the point that the export subsidy
provision of that Agreement is on a logical continuum with comparable provisions
of the GATT/SCM Agreement.

2.1.3. *Article VI:4, Ad Art. XVI, and the SCM Agreement, Annex I*

Does the narrow understanding with regard to the likeness concept in Art. VI:1
extend to likeness in Art. VI:4?[253] Although both paragraphs share a common purpose, a fundamental difference arises from the fact that the likeness concept
employed in para 1 functions as a standard for price comparisons between the
products in question, whereas in para 4 it is utilized to identify the existence of a
duty/tax exemption or refund and to justify it. In other words, as regards the fourth
paragraph, in order to establish that an export product is tax-exempted and that the
exemption is legitimate, one should be able to identify the 'like domestic product'
which is subject to the same amount of tax obligation.

The basic purpose of Art. VI:4 is to prevent any tax/duty refund or exemption
that exceeds the tax/duty charged or to be imposed, as well as to distinguish
between direct and indirect taxes. A narrow reading of likeness in the provision is
necessary to achieve this purpose, because a broad understanding of the term

would give rise to the circumvention problem. Indeed, countries circumventing the provision would try to interpret the likeness concept as broadly as possible and justify their excessive tax/duty rebates, which would otherwise fall into the category of prohibited subsidies, by referring to the amount of tax imposed on merely 'remotely similar' categories of products.[254] In some cases, a country might earmark a certain category of product for export only and grant it tax/duty exemptions, and justify its actions by relying upon the broad likeness interpretation.[255] As a consequence, the usual productive efficiencies that other trading partners might possess on the subsidized product would be undercut. Only a narrow interpretation of the likeness concept can avoid this possibility that clearly contradicts the purpose of Art. VI. In practice, honest exporting states are not tempted to give exemptions or refunds of taxes or duties already collected unless the export product is identical, or very similar to domestic goods that are subject to tax.[256]

This reasoning is also relevant to the interpretation of 'like products' in *Ad* Art. XVI[257] and Annex I(g), (h) of the SCM Agreement.[258] In these provisions, the likeness concept is utilized to identify the existence of any excessive duty/tax exemption or remission; such 'excessive' exemption or remission would be defined as an export subsidy, subject to GATT discipline. Considering that any broad understanding of likeness is not in line with the purpose of the provisions (bringing about the same circumvention problem as mentioned above), one should give a narrow interpretation to the term.[259]

It should be noted, however, that this narrow interpretation of likeness (in Annex I(g) and (h) of the SCM Agreement) has no place in Annex I(d).[260] Illustrating a provision of goods and services for the domestic export industry on more favourable terms than those imposed on the domestic consumption industry, item (d) uses the term 'like or directly competitive', while other export subsidies items, such as (g) and (h), employ the term 'like' only. The reason might be that having broader coverage of likeness in item (d) would help to avoid circumvention, in contrast to items (g) or (h) situations in which a narrower coverage would do the same: should the term 'like products' alone be employed in item (d), governments could circumvent the export subsidy designation by providing 'directly competitive products' (not like products) for the export industry on more favourable terms than for the domestic consumption industry. Also, this is why the coverage of the likeness in the item reaches not only goods but also 'like or directly competitive *services*'. It is interesting to witness that exactly the same reasoning results in two very different scopes of likeness in the same list ((d) *versus* (g) and (h) in Annex I). Thus, here the coverage of 'like or directly competitive' need not shy away from being broad.

In any event, as a result of the definitive interpretation of the Antidumping and SCM Agreements, the like product concept in Art. VI:4 and *Ad* Art. XVI (and SCM Annex I(g) and (h)) should be understood as meaning the 'identical' product and, in the absence of such a product, the 'closely similar' product.

2.1.4. Articles VI:7 and XVI:3 (Note 2 of Ad Art. XVI:3)

The comparison between imported and home goods extends to Art. VI:7, which employs the slightly different term 'like commodity'. This provision declares that a commodity imported under certain price support plans for the *primary commodity* shall be 'presumed not to result in material injury' even though the export price is lower than the home market price of the like commodity.[261]

With regard to this concept of 'like commodity', one can think of possible differences in meaning between this term and the term 'like *product*', and of the possible impact such differences may have on the scope of 'like'. First of all, the term 'commodity' in Art. VI:7 should be considered in relation to Art. XVI:3 and its *Addendum* Note 2. Article XVI:3 prohibits export subsidies on *primary products*, which are applied in a manner resulting in more than an equitable share of world trade in that primary product.[262] The *Ad* Article to the paragraph prescribes that certain price support programs applied to *primary products* by the exporting country shall not be considered *under certain conditions* as prohibited subsidies within Art. XVI:3, even though they result in lower prices for the export than the price of the 'like product' in the home market.[263]

The term 'primary product' is defined by the *Ad* Article as any product in its 'natural form', or which has undergone 'customarily required' processing for marketing in substantial volume in international trade.[264] Thus, any products that have undergone more processing than customarily required would not qualify as primary products in the provision. Accordingly, any export subsidy on such products would be subject to Art. XVI:4 (prohibition of export subsidies; see 2.1.2 above) rather than to Art. XVI:3. Since the *Ad* Article exception does not apply to Art. XVI:4, the above-mentioned subsidy would be struck down.

One might argue that, in the same way that Art. XVI:3 and the *Ad* Article provide certain exceptions in the context of the *export subsidy prohibition*, Art. VI:7 arranges certain exceptions for the primary product in the *antidumping and countervailing duty* context. This view would suggest that there is no difference between the like 'product' concept in Art. XVI:3 and the like 'commodity' concept of Art. VI:7. However, considering that Art. VI deals with the situation of the imposition of a unilateral measure (the antidumping or countervailing duty), as opposed to the multilateral measure of Art. XVI, one would like to have more room for the application of the Art. VI:7 exception.

Also noteworthy is the fact that the Art. XVI:3 exception creates a 'conclusive exemption' from the obligation, whereas the Art. VI:7 exception creates a mere 'presumption' that the measure under consideration did not result in material injury.[265] Different from the conclusive exemption, the presumption can be overturned by adverse proofs. Thus, a broad presumption engendered by allowing a broad exception in Art. VI:7 would present no serious problem due to the existence of this opportunity for rebuttal.

An additional point in support of the broader exception in Art. VI:7 is that while Art. XVI:3 does not grant exemption in cases in which the price support measure is 'financed out of government funds',[266] the Art. VI:7 exception does not have such a limitation. This difference in the scope of the exception suggests that the drafters wanted to limit its application in Art. XVI:3 more than in Art. VI:7. Moreover, considering that the satisfaction of conditions for the Art. VI:7 exception is determined by consultation among the concerned parties,[267] one could say that the practical effect of broadening the coverage of that exception would be to encourage more dialogue while tempering preferences for unilateral action.[268]

The conclusion obtained from the above analysis regarding the relationship between Art. VI:7 and Art. XVI:3 is that a broader coverage of exceptions under the former provision should be encouraged. But how? What ramifications will this conclusion have for the comparison between the concepts of 'like commodity' in the former provision and 'like product' in the latter?

First, presuming that the concept 'like' in both provisions is exactly the same, one might be able to argue that the term 'commodity' is more inclusive than 'product' (at least more than 'product' as defined in the 'primary product' context of *Ad* Art. XVI:3).[269] As a result, the commodity concept could include certain products that have undergone *more processing* than is 'customarily required for marketing'.[270] A good example of the commodity would be pasta; i.e., pasta could be a primary commodity while not qualifying as a primary product (as defined in the *Ad* Article).[271] While wheat on its own is the primary product subject to the *Ad* Art. XVI:3 exception, wheat *and* pasta may be covered by the Art. VI:7 exception.

As a result of such an interpretation, certain price support programs outside of the narrow scope of the *Ad* Art. XVI:3 exception could be saved to the extent that the countervailing duty process is concerned.[272] Thus, the term 'primary commodity' is endowed with a flexibility that can include not only the original form of the primary goods but also processed goods that have undergone substantial transformation processes. This difference of meaning between 'primary commodity' and 'primary product' can be applied in the same way to the concepts 'like commodity' in Art. VI:7 and 'like product' in *Ad* Art. XVI:3.

Secondly, aside from the difference of meaning between 'product' and 'commodity', one should consider whether a broad or narrow understanding of likeness in the two provisions could make a difference to the scope of the exception. As regards Art. VI:7, one might think that since a broad interpretation of the like commodities concept would help in identifying any two commodities for comparison, one could easily establish the existence of a price difference through such a broad understanding of likeness in this provision. On the other hand, considering that the alternative methods (cost-construction or third-market price) set out in Art. VI:1 could be employed in para 7 as well, one would be able to establish the price difference through these alternative methods of comparison, even when there are no identical or closely similar commodities available.

In both cases, Art. VI:7 would give a presumption of no material injury provided that the other conditions were met. Thus, the scope of the 'like' concept in the provision makes little difference to the end result. What makes the difference to the scope of the exception is the scope of the 'primary *commodity*' (or 'like *commodity*') concept, as explained.

Since there is no significant practical value in having different scopes of 'likeness' as between Arts VI:7 and VI:1, the scope of 'like' in Art. VI:7 should be read in the same manner as in Art. VI:1, i.e. 'identical' or, in the absence of this, 'closely similar'. Article VI is designed to regulate practices resulting in unfair price advantages, and para 1 of the Article puts such practices under obligation whenever they involve goods that are identical or, in the absence of these, closely similar. Article V:7 supports this objective by granting exemption only to such domestic price stabilization plans as have been determined, through consultation, to have little protectionist effect and, thus, little possibility of unfair price advantage.

The same reasoning extends to the 'like product' concept in *Ad* Art. XVI:3. But here it could signal a subtly broader scope to the likeness concept. In contrast to the antidumping context of Art. VI:1, the subsidy provision of Art. XVI does not have any alternative methods of comparison, such as the constructed price method. A narrow scope for likeness would afford an opportunity to deny the existence of subsidies in cases in which there is no identical or closely similar product in the home market of the exporting state *and* certain income or price supports other than financial contributions are at issue.[273] But as far as the *Ad* Art. XVI:3 exception is concerned, the emphasis on the broader understanding of the 'likeness' concept has little practical value: the provision would give exemption from the obligation *anyway*, provided that the other conditions are met.

Despite these discussions about theoretical differences, the likeness concepts in Art. VI:7 and Note 2 of *Ad* Art. XVI:3 should be understood as meaning 'identical' or, in the absence of this, 'closely similar'. The legislative definition in the Antidumping and SCM Agreements governs here as well.

In sum, the 'likeness' concept employed in the fair trade provisions such as GATT Arts VI:1 (Antidumping Agreement 'like product' provisions), XVI:4 (SCM Agreement 'like product' provisions[274] and Agreement on Agriculture, Art. 9.1), VI:4, *Ad* Art. XVI, VI:7, and XVI:3 (*Ad* Art. XVI:3, Note 2) should be understood as meaning 'identical' or, in the absence of this, 'closely similar'.

2.2. Performance

How should we modify the Framework Model of Likeness or Substitutability in order to apply it to the likeness concepts in these fair trade provisions? The first point is that none of the three elements of the objective characteristics factor should be treated with special emphasis. The antidumping provisions historically have been developed separate from the tariff concessions and have little connection with them. Although the SCM provisions are historically related to tariff concessions, the purpose of prohibition of export subsidies, i.e., 'fair trade', is much broader than the protection of benefits from the concessions. Furthermore, the likeness determination in those provisions has nothing to do with the problem relating to the integrity of tariff classification nomenclature.[275] Hence, the tariff classification, no matter how sophisticated it is, does not provide a presumptive guideline for the likeness determination. In the first stage of determining 'like products' in the fair trade provisions, a 'balanced' examination of the three objective elements—physical properties, tariff classification, and end-use in general—should proceed.

It could be said that the result of the examination of objective characteristics creates a presumption with regard to likeness as far as the determination of 'identical' products is concerned, similar to the case of likeness in the first sentence of Art. III:2 (see 1.2.2 above). One should be reminded that, under the definition given in the Antidumping and SCM Agreements, 'identical' products denotes products that are 'alike in all respects'. Given its ordinary meaning in its context and purpose, this phrase could be said to suggest such presumptive effects when *objective characteristics alike in all respects* are found. Moreover, given the *narrowest* scope of 'identical' (alike in *all* respects), one can say that this presumption would seldom engender vulnerability to abuse or circumvention of the fair trade provisions.

As a consequence of the presumption, the party opposing it should put forward any results of the market-based analysis that contradict the results of the objective characteristic examination. If such a successful rebuttal is raised, or if the objective characteristic test does not yield a clear presumption (tough case), the tribunal could proceed to the second stage of examination.

Even if the examination of objective characteristics produces a clear result of absence of an 'identical' product relationship, the examiner must turn to look at 'another product which has characteristics closely resembling those of the product under consideration' as an alternative.[276] Does the objective characteristic test create the same presumption for the concept 'closely similar' as for the concept 'identical'? The ordinary meaning of the phrase 'having characteristics closely resembling' seems not to be strong enough to justify such a presumption: not only objective characteristics, but also market-based factors seem to have a stake in the phrase. This point was supported by the Panel in *Indonesia National Car*, which proceeded to the market-segment approach:[277]

> ...However, we do not see that the SCM Agreement precludes us from looking at criteria other than physical characteristics, where relevant to the like product analysis. The term 'characteristics closely resembling' in its ordinary meaning includes but is not limited to physical characteristics, and we see nothing in the context or object and purpose of the SCM Agreement that would dictate a different conclusion.[278] ...[279]

Moreover, there is no practical reason to accept such a presumption, because no formalistic approach was taken in the provisions and the scope of the 'closely resembling' product is not as narrow as that of the 'identical' product. In addition, in order to maintain a balance with the concept of likeness in Art. XI:2, which has the same scope ('closely similar'), such a presumption should be denied here (as in Art. XI:2). Hence, the concept of the 'closely resembling' product in the fair trade provisions should be analyzed through a comprehensive analysis, comprising an objective characteristic examination with a subsequent market-based end-use analysis.[280] Of course, the same can be said of the concept 'directly competitive' in the SCM Agreement, Annex I(d) (see 2.1.3 above).

In the second stage of market-based analysis, the proper thresholds for the CVA-PCPDS should be the QPS for the 'identical', TPS for the 'closely resembling (closely similar)', and the PSE for the 'directly competitive' product relationship test, as discussed at 1.1.3 above.

Is the potential competition factor relevant in the likeness test in fair trade provisions? Given the complexity of the provisions, this matter needs to be addressed with regard to each type of provision. First, in such provisions as GATT Arts VI:1, XVI:4, VI:7, XVI:3 (Note 2 of *Ad* Art. XVI:3), the Antidumping Agreement, Art. 2, and, Agreement on Agriculture, Art. 9.1(b), the likeness concept is used to identify 'bi-level pricing', as discussed at 2.1. Thus, in most cases, the existence of a like product relationship will be argued by the *importing* state (or its authority) so as to prove the use of a bi-level pricing scheme by the exporters, which will justify that state's imposition of certain relief measures. In this situation, it is hardly conceivable that the state (or its authority) would introduce the potential competition factor by indicating that another measure *of its own* has blocked a potential like product relationship between the products differently priced by the exporters. Thus, the only route open for those pressing the potential competition argument would be to represent that, due to the dumping and export subsidies at issue exercised by the exporting country, consumers of the importing country came to feel that the products in question were less substitutable products, i.e. 'but for the unfair dumping or illegal subsidies that generate price differences (bi-level pricing) between these two products, our consumers would have thought the two products to be sufficiently like'.[281] This is a valid argument, and to that extent potential competition between alleged like products should be examined.

Secondly, under GATT Art. VI:4, *Ad* Art. XVI, and the SCM Agreement, Annex I(g) and (h), the like product relationship is used to determine the nature of any duty/tax exemption or remission. Here, the like product relationship will generally be raised by the *exporting state* to show that there are like domestic products in the exporting state subject to the same amount of tax obligation as the amount exempted (or remitted) on the exported product.[282] The exporting state will use this evidence to attack an antidumping or countervailing duty imposed, or export subsidy designated, by the importing state. Since the exporting state is not likely to argue that another measure *of its own* has blocked a potential like product relationship between the products at issue, the only way of presenting arguments with regard to the potential competition factor would be to blame the importing country for its illegal measures, including the particular antidumping or countervailing duties, i.e. 'but for the illegal duties, the domestic price of the like products could have fallen substantially; then consumers would think that the two products were like products'. When this type of argument is put forward, the panel needs to proceed to examine the potential competition factor.

Thirdly, under the SCM Agreement, Annex I(d), 'direct competitiveness' will be argued by the *importing country* to show the existence of export subsidies. The importing country will focus on the relationship between product A, provided by the exporting country to its *export* industry, and product B, provided by the exporting country to its *domestic consumption* industry. Proving that A was provided on more favourable term than B, the importing country can refer to the potential competition between A and B to reinforce its argument that A and B are directly competitive products. In this case, the panel can examine whether the illegal subsidy (or other illegal measures considered together) of the exporting country has blocked the competitive relationship between A and B, and take into account the result of the examination.

In addition to the above cases, one should remember that the definition of 'domestic industry' in the Antidumping and SCM Agreements is based on the 'like product' concept, and that many provisions of these agreements use this definition to deal with various issues, including standing, determination of injury, and remedy.[283] For instance, under the first type of provisions discussed above, the concept of 'like product' is raised not only to prove a bi-level pricing, but also to determine the scope of the 'domestic industry' injured by the discriminatory pricing. Hence, it is possible that the importing country will put forward the potential competition factor to argue that the scope of the domestic industry should be larger than the range of firms that are *currently* injured, i.e. 'but for the dumping or export subsidy, the scope of the like product would have been larger'.[284] This argument is a valid one, and is also possible in other types of unfair trade provisions.

Therefore, generally it can be said that the potential competition factor is relevant in the like product determination under fair trade provisions. One caveat is that the potential competition factor could have more practical importance in the SCM context than in the antidumping context. Under the antidumping provisions, one can after all rely upon the alternative method of cost–profit construction if one is not able to find the like product due to illegal barriers.[285] In the SCM provisions (with regard to the type of subsidies requiring 'bi-level pricing'), this window is closed to the desperate seeker of a like product relationship: to him or her, the last resort will be the potential competition argument.

To take account of the potentiality factor in the likeness test under the fair trade provisions, the PMP Questionnaire may be employed. In contrast, there is no need to employ the Future Competition Questionnaire here. The purpose of fair trade provisions is not to protect the expectation of competitive relationships, but to provide relief in certain *current* situations. Thus, whether it is in the context of determining bi-level pricing or the appropriateness of duty remission, one should not take any possible future development of likeness into consideration. This is true not only when demonstrating dumping or subsidization, but also in the context of identifying the industry injured. Fair trade provisions provide relief for domestic industry producing *currently* like products in certain situations involving material injury, threat of material injury, material retardation of the establishment of domestic industry,[286] or adverse effects (including serious prejudice or the threat of serious prejudice) to the interest of the member.[287] Although *threat* of injury or *threat* of serious prejudice are included here, one should note that these refer to *threats to the present (existing) like product relationship.* This point is quite clear from the text itself: 'threat of material injury to (existing) domestic industry', or 'threat of serious prejudice to the (existing) interests of the Member'. Interpreting these phrases, if one tried to inject the future factor not only into the terms 'material injury' or 'serious prejudice', but also into such words as 'domestic industry' or 'interests', the resulting scope of each of these phrases would become too broad, which is clearly against the purpose or function of the fair trade provisions.[288]

Turning to the supply substitutability factor, should the above-mentioned purpose of the fair trade provisions, which is different from non-discrimination clauses, make a difference in the role played by supply substitutability? The general point is that the mitigation effect by way of supply substitutability should carry more weight with regard to the likeness determination in the fair trade context. Since fair trade provisions are geared towards protecting domestic industry—often sacrificing consumer welfare or efficiency as a consequence—one should be concerned about the possibility of 'overprotection'. If a certain firm can easily mitigate its injury through supply substitution, there is little reason to include such a firm under the umbrella of 'domestic industry'. Giving antidumping or countervailing duty protection to the products of such a firm would result in 'overprotection'.

Supply substitutability analysis using the CVA-PCPSS can help to identify the overprotection problem and solve it. Giving enhanced weight[289] to the supply substitutability factor in defining likeness will exclude more highly supply-substitutable products from the coverage of 'like product', which will limit the definition of 'domestic industry', thereby lessening the overprotection problem. Moreover, sometimes the tribunals could use the supply substitutability factor as an effective check against overly broad definitions of 'domestic industry' resulting from heavy reliance on the potential competition factor.[290]

For the sake of precision, the direct view approach or time-series analysis may be used, as necessary.

3. OTHERS

3.1. Transparency in Customs Valuation

The main purpose of GATT Art. VII and the Customs Valuation Agreement is to prevent an importing country overvaluing imported items and thereby wiping out the benefit of tariff concessions. As with classification, however, many problems are associated with valuation.[291] It has already been noted that differences in valuation methods make tariff-reduction negotiations more complex.[292] One objective of many countries in the Tokyo Round was to reduce the costs and delays associated with troublesome valuation systems; the result was the Valuation Code, and this (as revised) became the Customs Valuation Agreement.[293] The Valuation text establishes a series of definitions of value for customs purposes, with a ranking of how they are to be used.[294]

Given the historical development and the broadened focus of the provisions, they may be discussed under the rubric 'transparency in customs valuation'.

3.1.1. Article VII:2

GATT Art. VII and the Customs Valuation Agreement compare a category of 'imported goods' with a category of 'goods sold for export to the same country of importation and exported at or about the same time as the goods being valued'.[295] This type of comparison may be distinguished from the MFN type in that the imported product can be compared with the like product of the same exporting country, not with that of third countries; it may be distinguished from the fair trade type in that the like product to be compared is one that is already introduced into the importing country, not one that is sold in the home market of the exporting country.

According to Art. VII:2, the value for customs purposes of imported goods should be 'based on actual value of the imported merchandise or of *like merchandise*' and the value is generally the price at which such or like merchandise is 'sold or offered for sale in the ordinary course of trade under fully competitive conditions'. The value should 'not be based on the value of merchandise of national origin or an arbitrary or fictitious value'.[296] For the customs valuation purposes, the focus is therefore firmly on the 'imported' merchandise. Even in certain exceptional cases, in which one can refer to the price of domestic goods of the importing state, the reference is relevant only to disclose the value of the import.[297]

It should be noted that the provision uses a different term—'like merchandise'. *Webster's Dictionary* defines 'merchandise' as 'commodities or goods that are brought and sold in business'. For the purpose of conceptual differentiation, one could say that 'product' and 'commodity' are concepts that focus on inherent characteristics or utility, whereas 'merchandise' focuses on the present mode of transaction. In other words, merchandise is any product or commodity that is being sold by merchants, no matter how it is characterized.[298] In addition, accepting any possible difference of meaning between 'commodity' and 'product' as defined in Art. VI:7 and *Ad* Art. XVI:3 (as discussed at 2.1.4 above), one can say that the system of customs valuation of Art. VII is inclusive enough to encompass all goods sold in the course of business, whether considered as products (within the narrow meaning given in *Ad* Art. XVI:3) or as commodities. On the other hand, the concept of 'goods' seems a more 'generic' term, including all concepts of product, commodity, and merchandise. Is it just coincidence to encounter the term 'goods' in such 'generic' provisions as Art. V (Freedom of Transit)[299] and the Customs Valuation Agreement?[300]

It should be remembered that the distinction between the concepts 'product' and 'commodity', due to the narrow definition of 'primary product' in *Ad* Art. XVI, is valid only within the context of Art. VI:7 and the *Ad* Art. XVI:3 comparison.[301] Various GATT provisions show that the concept of 'product' is employed as a generic term, and the terms 'product', 'merchandise', and 'goods' are used interchangeably. By looking at the customs valuation context (Art. VII of the GATT), one can easily confirm this interchangeability: while the second paragraph employs 'merchandise', the other paragraphs (such as paras 3 and 5) fall back on 'product'. Accordingly, it could be said that the use of the word 'merchandise' in Art. VII:2 signals nothing in particular with regard to the distinction drawn with the term 'product'. There is no such practical value here comparable to the distinction between 'product' and 'commodity' as they appear in Arts VI:7 and XVI:3.

Turning back to the practical issue of interpreting 'likeness' in Art. VII:2, the initial focus should be on the basic purpose of the provision. The Article seeks to establish a uniform benchmark for the purposes of international customs valuation. In order to exclude arbitrary customs-valuation practices and to preserve benefits from tariff concessions, one needs transparent criteria with which to determine the value of imports. GATT Art. VII:2 and the Customs Valuation Agreement supply such criteria, with which one can calculate the value of products and compare it with the claimed price. Such price comparisons allow not only for the calculation of proper duty levels, but also for the determination of the existence of any unfair trading practices, including dumping and subsidies.

According to these provisions, the value of imported merchandise is an actual value (transaction value) of the merchandise or that of 'like merchandise'. The Customs Valuation Agreement provides a definitive interpretation of the concept of 'like merchandise' as meaning 'identical or similar goods', and Art. 15 of the Agreement defines the terms 'identical' and 'similar' as follows:

(a) 'identical goods' means goods which are the *same in all respects*, including physical characteristics, quality and reputation. Minor differences in appearance would not preclude goods otherwise conforming to the definition from being regarded as identical;

(b) 'similar goods' means goods which, although not alike in all respects, have *like characteristics and like component materials which enable them to perform the same functions and to be commercially interchangeable*. The quality of the goods, their reputation and the existence of a trademark are among the factors to be considered in determining whether goods are similar;

. . .

(d) goods shall not be regarded as 'identical goods' or 'similar goods' unless they were produced in the *same country* as the goods being valued;

(e) goods produced by a different person shall be taken into account only when there are no identical goods or similar goods, as the case may be, *produced by the same person* as the goods being valued. (emphasis added)

At the outset, one can see that the above definition of 'like' avoids broadness. It is clear from the text that the drafters intended to narrow down the scope of 'similar goods' as much as possible, in that at least four conditions are required to be fulfilled in order for goods to be 'similar goods':

(1) having like characteristics;
(2) having like component materials;

(3) performing the same functions; and
(4) being commercially interchangeable.

These four conditions are strengthened by additional requirements:

(5) produced in the same country;
(6) sold for export to the same country of importation;[302]
(7) exported at or about the same time;[303]
(8) sold or offered for sale in the ordinary course of trade under fully competitive conditions;[304]
(9) produced preferably by the same person;[305] and
(10) adopting the similar goods concept in the absence of identical goods.[306]

It may be said that this extreme narrowness functions in the first place as a precaution against any possible abuse of the customs valuation mechanism by the importing country. Imposition of such conditions and the resulting transparency will help to exclude arbitrary customs-valuation practices and to preserve benefits from tariff concessions. It will also act as a check against possible circumvention by the exporting country. If an exporting state could obtain a reduced duty rate for the exporting goods by referring to remotely similar goods, after simply modifying a few characteristics so as to distinguish the exporting goods from identical or closely similar goods or goods from third countries, the country would have an unfair competitive advantage. Moreover, too broad an understanding of likeness would not fit well with the structure of the Agreement, which provides such alternative methods as deducted or computed value calculation.[307]

On the other hand, an extremely narrow definition of likeness would result in heavy reliance on the time- and cost-consuming alternative methods, because quite frequently there might be no exactly 'identical' products. This might be one of the reasons why the Customs Valuation Agreement adopted the concept of 'similar goods' as an alternative to identical goods.

Thus, it seems that the 'identical' and 'similar' goods in the customs valuation context have the scopes of 'identical' and 'closely similar' products respectively. But it should be noted that in actual application, these 'identical' and 'similar' concepts are much narrower than those in all other provisions because of the aforementioned requirements of same country (in production and importation), time, manner (sold in an ordinary and competitive manner), and producer.[308] Thus, combined with an additional requirement that the 'similar' goods concept be utilized in the absence of 'identical' goods, the likeness concept in Art. VII:2 of the GATT could be said to be the narrowest in scope in the General Agreement.

3.1.2. Performance

The Framework Model of Likeness or Substitutability may be tailored for the use of likeness determinations under the customs valuation provisions.

The first point in this regard is that, in the first step of the examination of object-ive characteristics, balanced consideration should be given to the three elements of physical characteristics, tariff classifications, and general end-uses. In other words, although there is a close relationship between tariff concessions and customs valua-tion, the tariff classification criterion should not carry special evidential weight in the process of examination. It should be noted that customs valuation provisions play an important role in enhancing transparency (reducing costs and delay in customs procedure and encouraging tariff negotiations) in addition to their role of preserving the benefits of tariff concessions. Moreover, since the likeness deter-mination in these provisions cannot impair the 'physical integrity' of tariff classifi-cation nomenclature even in the worst case scenario,[309] the examiner need not be as concerned about that integrity as he need be in the case of GATT Art. I.

It could be said that the result of the examination of objective characteristics creates a presumption with regard to likeness so far as the determination of 'ident-ical' products is concerned, which is comparable to the cases of 'likeness' in the first sentence of Art. III:2 and of 'identical goods' in the antidumping and SCM provisions. Similar to the definition given in the Antidumping/SCM Agreements, 'identical' products here means products which are 'the same in all respects' (including physical characteristics, quality, and reputation).[310] Given its ordinary meaning within its context and purpose, this phrase could be said to suggest a pre-sumptive effect when *objective characteristics which are the same in all respects* (except for minor differences in appearance)[311] are found. Moreover, considering the nar-rowest scope of 'identical' (even narrower than likeness in the first sentence of Art. III:2 or the fair trade provisions, as in sections 1.2 and 2 above), one can say that accepting such a presumption would seldom engender vulnerability to abuse or circumvention with regard to the customs valuation provisions.

Hence, the party in opposition to the presumption has to rebut it with credible results of a market-based analysis that show otherwise. If such a rebuttal is successful, or the objective characteristic test does not yield such a presumption in the first place (tough case), the tribunal could proceed to the second stage of the examination.

The second stage of market-based analysis is also needed when the examination of objective characteristics clearly demonstrates the absence of an 'identical' goods relationship. In such an event, the examiner must turn to look at 'similar' goods, i.e. 'goods which, although not alike in all respects, have like characteristics and like component materials which enable them to perform the same functions and to be commercially interchangeable'. Looking at this definition, it is clear that the first stage of the examination should not produce any presumption regarding 'similar goods'. Hence, to find a 'similar' goods relationship, the market-based analysis, including examinations of the quality of the goods, their reputation, and the exist-ence of a trademark[312] should proceed and the results should be referred to.

It should be recalled that, in the second stage, the proper thresholds for the CVA-PCPDS are the QPS for the 'identical goods' and the TPS for the 'similar goods' (closely similar) relationship test. There is no need to employ the PMP or

Future Competition Questionnaire here. This is not just because the language of the above definition of 'identical' or 'similar goods' contains no hint of a potential or future competition factor. The purpose of the customs valuation provisions leads to such a conclusion as well. Indeed, in order to set a benchmark price for valuation purposes, inquiries into the *current* like product relationship would suffice: the objective is to obtain the *present* market value of the like product in the importing country. If one cannot find the market value (whether due to illegal barriers, or because of unavailability of current like merchandise), one can refer to the alternative methods of 'unit price' or 'computed value' at any time.[313] Indeed, to include within the likeness test such flexible and cross-temporal factors as potential or future competition would contravene the fact that the likeness is determined, in the absence of identical or similar goods, according to the alternative methods that are based on 'strict' and 'static' (present) cost–profit calculation. Thus, the 'like' product determination in the customs valuation provisions should exclude any potential or future competition factor.

Should one take into account the supply substitutability factor in determining 'like merchandise' in the customs valuation context? To answer this question, one needs to recall the role of the factor played in other contexts and to consider whether it is also relevant for present purposes. The role played by the supply substitutability consideration in 'non-discrimination provisions' is to take account of the mitigation effect in determining likeness, so that the scope of likeness (i.e., the scope of non-discrimination obligations) may be reduced to the extent to which the mitigation effect applies.[314] This role should be played more actively in the 'fair trade provisions' because of the possibility of overprotection, as explained at 2.2 above.[315] This rationale for including supply substitutability analysis scarcely exists in the likeness determination under the customs valuation provisions. Since comparisons are made between two categories of like imported products, not between favoured goods and discriminated goods, it does not have meaning to consider the mitigation effect between the two categories. Furthermore, because the primary purpose of these provisions is to enhance transparency in customs valuation, not to provide certain relief to producers, there is no overprotection concern. Indeed, given that, through many additional conditions,[316] the scope of 'like merchandise' is already narrowed enough to prevent circumvention by customs authorities, one need not further narrow it by considering supply substitutability.[317]

The direct view approach and the time-series analysis may be used, as necessary.

3.2. Safeguard

3.2.1. *Article XIX:1; Safeguard Agreement, Arts 2.1, 4.1;*
Agreement on Textiles and Clothing, Art. 6.2

Article XIX:1 of the GATT calls for a comparison between the imported product and the domestic product of the importing state, where 'injury' is being inflicted on the producers of the domestic product as a consequence of a surge in importation.[318] In particular, the provision and Art. 2.1 of the Agreement on Safeguards entitle an importing state to take safeguard measures, which would otherwise be inconsistent with GATT obligations, when increased imports cause or threaten serious injury to domestic producers of 'like' or 'directly competitive' products.[319] This safeguard right is extended to Art. 6.2 of the Agreement on Textiles and Clothing using similar language.[320]

The obvious purpose is to allow states to adopt protective measures whenever unanticipated increases in imports, accompanied by serious disruptive consequences to competitive domestic producers, occur. Since the exemption from the general obligations is granted wholly for safeguard purposes—i.e., it allows trade restrictive measures to be taken against a perfectly legitimate trade flow—the state invoking the exemption should pay the price. While one might appropriately act to protect endangered industries from imports, one must restore the overall standing of the trading relationship. To restore the *status quo ante*, any measures taken to protect domestic 'like or directly competitive' products should be offset by other compensatory measures through consultation. This concern for the restoration of competitiveness is further buttressed by the emphasis on the necessary and temporary nature of the safeguard measures and the notification obligation.[321]

The structure of this provision would seem to emphasize its exceptional character. Considering this character, coupled with concern for possible abuse of the provision, one might expect application of the narrow scope of the term 'like or directly competitive'. The drafting history of the GATT, however, does not seem to support this expectation. The history shows that Art. XIX was included in the Agreement mainly due to concerns by the United States that commitments to free trade might undermine economic health.[322] According to the record, the London draft of the ITO Charter employed the term 'like or similar products' in its emergency provision.[323] This language was replaced at the New York Conference with 'like or directly competitive' in both the draft ITO Charter and the draft GATT.[324] One might say that this signified that the term 'directly competitive' was designed to encompass even entirely dissimilar products.

This background demonstrates that the term 'like or directly competitive' should be broad enough to include products that are very different but which capture the attention of domestic consumers in the importing state. Borrowing the definition suggested by the Cuban delegate in the same Conference but in the Art. XI:2 context, the concept of 'directly competitive' attains the scope of 'different in form, but yet competing for the same market'.[325]

From the perspective of trade policy, a broad interpretation of 'like or directly competitive' products may guarantee safe and thorough protection from the possible fatal collapse of domestic industries of the importing state. Departing from this broad understanding might result in a situation in which economic well-being is threatened by compelling importing states to refrain from responding to increased shipments of foreign products that are dissimilar from certain domestic products but that continue to take away the market of the domestic product. Ironically, the very fact that the provision preserves the effective opportunity for the protection of domestic industry could drive home GATT's firm commitment to free trade and market openness; the escape clause might not have been needed had such an ambitious goal not been set.[326] Article XIX is a critical provision that sets out this guarantee.

It might be thought that a broad understanding of the terms might, as circumstances arise, assist efforts to abuse the safeguard system by abetting a broad scope of domestic industry. However, given that safeguard measures are adopted in the end by the decision-makers of the state who must take account of the following considerations, one should not attach too much weight to this concern. First, it should be noted that the state invoking the clause always has to provide equivalent concessions to the other state; and if no compensation is agreed upon, the former state may have to tolerate retaliation by the latter in certain circumstances.[327] Certainly, because of this mechanism, the possibility of abuse by the invoking state would be generally less than in other exceptional provisions containing no such compensatory obligation. Secondly, one more factor that reduces the possibility of abuse is that safeguard measures should be applied to a product being imported irrespective of its source.[328] This MFN obligation would burden the states invoking the safeguard measure—especially, those risking the abuse—with additional concerns.

In contrast to the above proposition, there could exist a tendency for the state invoking the safeguard measures (or the supporting domestic industry) to try to define the 'like or directly competitive' concept as narrowly as possible to take account only of those sectors severely affected by increased imports. This problem will matter, in particular, if the products are somehow divided into separate industries, as they often are in the case of steel. This sort of 'gerrymandering' would make it easier to establish the existence of 'serious injury', one of the most difficult conditions for the safeguard measure to meet. This tendency could be dealt with by adopting a broad understanding of the phrase 'like or directly competitive'.

With regard to the scope of the 'like' concept, any lengthy discussion would have little merit. In the context of Art. XIX:1, whether or not the products concerned are 'like' or 'directly competitive' makes no difference to the end result, whereas it has a practical value in the contexts of Art. III:2 and Art. XI:2. Unlike Art. XI:2, the safeguard provision possesses two concepts applied *concurrently* (like *or* directly competitive); unlike Art. III:2, the provision does not distinguish the requirements to apply the provision in regard to 'like' products from those in regard to 'directly competitive' products.[329]

For the sake of conceptual classification, one might be able to say that the 'like' product concept should be understood as meaning the 'identical' product. This understanding would be in line with previous interpretations regarding the comparison of Art. III:2 and Art. XI:2.[330]

To examine the scope of 'directly competitive' in Art. XIX provides the perfect stage for comparison between 'directly competitive or substitutable' (Art. III:2), 'directly substituted' (Art. XI:2), and 'directly competitive' (Art. XIX:1). Based on points made in earlier sections of this book, this matter may be concluded as follows.

First of all, it should be restated that the term 'substituted' is equal to the term '*actually* competitive' or 'compet*ing*', and any potential or future competition factor is excluded from the scope of the concept. In fact, as indicated already, this potential or future competition factor effects a difference in scope between 'substituted' and 'substitutable'—the latter, connoting a time (or potentiality) factor, can be seen as being a broader concept than the former.[331]

As regards the 'directly competitive' concept in Art. XIX:1, one could argue that in general it has a scope similar to the term 'directly substituted'.[332] Although Art. XIX has the 'ambitious' objective of providing escape from system collapse, it should not be allowed to be too far-reaching in achieving its objective; the potential or future competition factor should be excluded from the likeness test under the provision. The reasons are quite similar to those indicated with regard to the 'directly substituted' concept of Art. XI:2. First, the future competition factor is not relevant in the safeguard context. The purpose of Art. XIX is not to protect the expectation of a competitive relationship, but to provide relief in certain situations causing or threatening serious injury to domestic producers of like or directly competitive products.[333] One might try to include the future (or potential) competition concept under the term 'threaten' in the text, but the term in this context is used to denote 'injury' and, thus, to accommodate certain 'non-existing' serious injuries. It is hardly reasonable to see that in this context 'threaten' is used to indicate that 'like or directly competitive products' means not only (1) *currently* like or directly competitive products, but also (2) products expected to be like or directly competitive *in the near future*, or (3) products expected to be like or directly competitive *in the hypothetical case of any constraints being removed*. In other words, the term 'threaten' means threats to the *present (existing)* like product relationship.[334] Secondly, the potential competition factor is not relevant here either. In general, the existence of potential competition between the two products under consideration will be raised by the party claiming likeness of the products. This means that the factor could possibly be used as a tool for the *importing* state that imposes safeguard measures. But it is not likely that, justifying its safeguard measure, the importing state would introduce the potential competition factor by indicating that another measure *of its own* has blocked a like product relationship between the products in its own market.[335]

Even if one were to accept the introduction of the potential or future competition factors into Art. XIX's likeness test, it would be unlikely that mere potentially or prospectively substitutable products could 'cause or threaten *serious injury*' to each other. If GATT member countries were permitted to invoke the Art. XIX justification based on the potentiality or future theory, the possibility of abuse would become too great. The safeguard door remains open: member countries would be able to take action whenever the potentiality was realized.

To summarize, one can conclude that in general the concepts of 'directly substituted' in Art. XI:2 and 'directly competitive' in Art. XIX:1 have the same scope and concede the 'throne of broadness' to the broadest concept in the GATT—'directly competitive or substitutable'—residing in the National Treatment Kingdom.

3.2.2. *Performance*

How might one tailor the likeness or substitutability analysis to fit GATT Art. XIX:1, the Safeguard Agreement, Arts 2.1 and 4.1, and the Agreement on Textiles and Clothing, Art. 6.2?

The first point is that none of the three elements of the objective characteristic factor should be treated with special evidentiary weight. With regard to the tariff classification element, it should be noted that not only do the safeguard provisions have little functional connection with tariff concessions, but also the likeness determination in Art. XIX:1 has nothing to do with the problem of integrity of the tariff classification system.[336] Therefore, in the first stage, the likeness determination in the safeguard provisions should depend upon a 'balanced' examination of the three objective elements—physical properties, tariff classification, and end-use in general.

The result of the examination of objective characteristics does not create a presumption of likeness, in contrast to the first sentence of Art. III:2, the 'identical products' in the fair trade provisions, and the 'identical goods' in the customs valuation provisions. This is because neither a formalistic approach nor the narrowest scope of likeness is adopted in the provision (compare with 1.2.2, 2.2, and 3.1.2 above). Likeness or direct substitution here should be analyzed through a comprehensive examination of objective characteristics and the market-based end-use.[337]

In the second stage, the proper threshold for the CVA-PCPDS is the PSE Standard because the 'like or directly competitive' relationship is involved. It should be noted that there is no need to employ the PMP Questionnaire or the Future Competition Questionnaire here because the potential or future competition factor is not relevant, as indicated at 3.2.1 above.

With regard to the supply substitutability factor, the mitigation effect by way of supply substitutability should be given more consideration here. Since the primary purpose of the safeguard provisions is to protect domestic industry against injury regardless of its efficiency,[338] one should be concerned about the possibility of 'overprotection'. If a certain firm can easily mitigate its injury through supply substitution, the 'like or directly competitive' product concept should be narrowly tailored so as to exclude such a firm from the umbrella of 'domestic industry'. Supply substitutability analysis by the CVA-PCPSS can help in identifying the overprotection problem and solving it. Giving enhanced weight to the supply substitutability factor within the analysis can reflect this consideration in the outcome of the likeness or substitutability analysis.

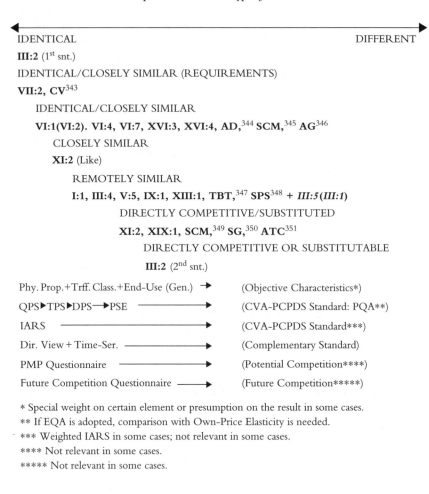

IDENTICAL   DIFFERENT

III:2 (1st snt.)

IDENTICAL/CLOSELY SIMILAR (REQUIREMENTS)

VII:2, CV[343]

　IDENTICAL/CLOSELY SIMILAR

　VI:1(VI:2). VI:4, VI:7, XVI:3, XVI:4, AD,[344] SCM,[345] AG[346]

　　CLOSELY SIMILAR

　　XI:2 (Like)

　　　REMOTELY SIMILAR

　　　I:1, III:4, V:5, IX:1, XIII:1, TBT,[347] SPS[348] + *III:5(III:1)*

　　　　DIRECTLY COMPETITIVE/SUBSTITUTED

　　　　XI:2, XIX:1, SCM,[349] SG,[350] ATC[351]

　　　　　DIRECTLY COMPETITIVE OR SUBSTITUTABLE

　　　　III:2 (2nd snt.)

Phy. Prop.+Trff. Class.+End-Use (Gen.) →　　(Objective Characteristics*)

QPS▶TPS▶DPS→PSE ——————→　　(CVA-PCPDS Standard: PQA**)

IARS ——————→　　(CVA-PCPDS Standard***)

Dir. View+Time-Ser. ——————→　　(Complementary Standard)

PMP Questionnaire ——————→　　(Potential Competition****)

Future Competition Questionnaire ——→　　(Future Competition*****)

* Special weight on certain element or presumption on the result in some cases.
** If EQA is adopted, comparison with Own-Price Elasticity is needed.
*** Weighted IARS in some cases; not relevant in some cases.
**** Not relevant in some cases.
***** Not relevant in some cases.

Figure III.1: Likeness or Substitutability Analysis in Each Provision of GATT

In the context of supply substitutability analysis, it would be interesting to compare *safeguard* cases with *fair trade* cases. First of all, it should be restated that the general role played by the supply substitutability factor is to reduce the scope of likeness as determined by demand-side analysis, and thereby to reduce the scope of GATT/WTO obligations to the extent of the mitigation effect (see Chapter II, sections 3 and 3.2.3). So, as between the fair trade and safeguard provisions, which demand more narrowly tailored 'likeness'?

Conveniently, this question returns us to the considerations raised to determine the basic scope of the term 'like or directly competitive'. As was mentioned at 3.2.1 above, since safeguard measures are taken against the perfectly legitimate trade of

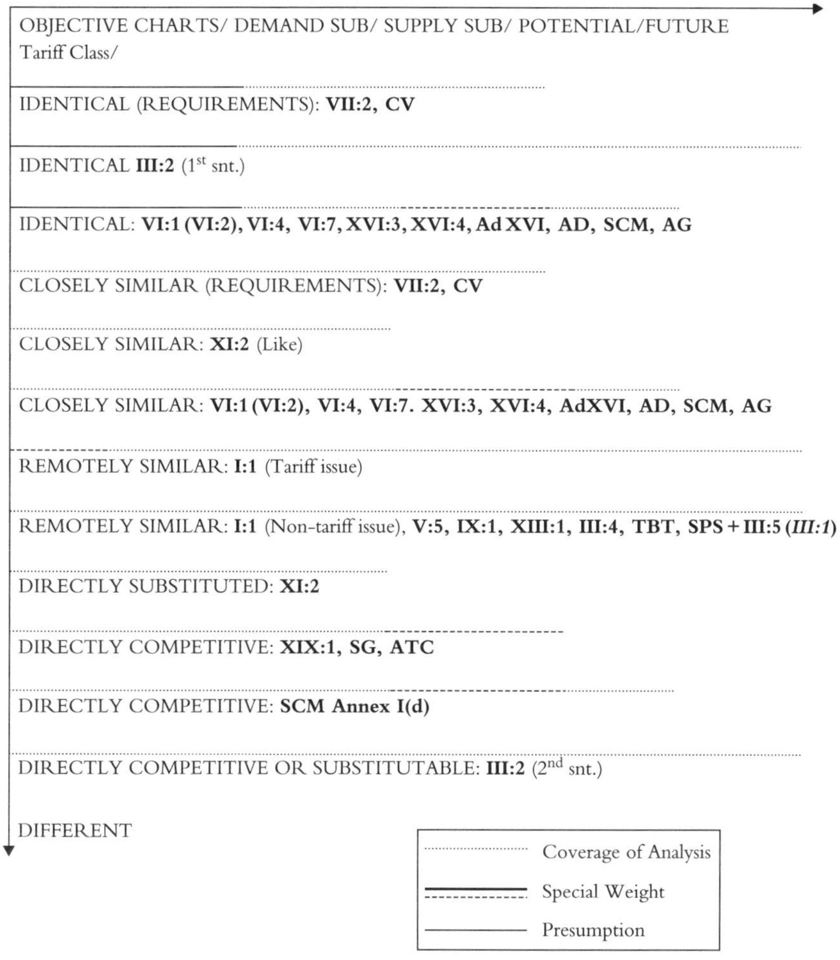

OBJECTIVE CHARTS/ DEMAND SUB/ SUPPLY SUB/ POTENTIAL/FUTURE
Tariff Class/

IDENTICAL (REQUIREMENTS): **VII:2, CV**

IDENTICAL **III:2** (1st snt.)

IDENTICAL: **VI:1 (VI:2), VI:4, VI:7, XVI:3, XVI:4, Ad XVI, AD, SCM, AG**

CLOSELY SIMILAR (REQUIREMENTS): **VII:2, CV**

CLOSELY SIMILAR: **XI:2** (Like)

CLOSELY SIMILAR: **VI:1 (VI:2), VI:4, VI:7. XVI:3, XVI:4, AdXVI, AD, SCM, AG**

REMOTELY SIMILAR: **I:1** (Tariff issue)

REMOTELY SIMILAR: **I:1** (Non-tariff issue), **V:5, IX:1, XIII:1, III:4, TBT, SPS + III:5 (*III:1*)**

DIRECTLY SUBSTITUTED: **XI:2**

DIRECTLY COMPETITIVE: **XIX:1, SG, ATC**

DIRECTLY COMPETITIVE: **SCM Annex I(d)**

DIRECTLY COMPETITIVE OR SUBSTITUTABLE: **III:2** (2nd snt.)

DIFFERENT

··········	Coverage of Analysis
- - - - -	Special Weight
————	Presumption

Figure III.2: Likeness or Substitutability Analysis in Each Provision of GATT

foreign producers, in contrast to the 'unfair trade' regulated by the fair trade provisions, one would like to reduce the range of import products subject to safeguard measures as much as possible. This can be done by narrowing down the scope of 'like or directly competitive' products, giving greater consideration to supply substitutability. But, on the other hand, the multilateral nature (as well as the MFN obligation) of the safeguard provision,[339] as opposed to the antidumping and SCM provisions, mitigates against such a 'narrow-coverage sentiment' in the safeguard clause. Moreover, this 'narrowing down' would make it easier to take safeguard measures against the imports, because the regulators could more easily satisfy the requirement for 'serious injury'.[340]

Thus, after all, it is hard to say that more consideration of supply substitutability (through narrowing down the scope of likeness obtained after demand substitutability analysis) is needed in Art. XIX than in the antidumping or SCM provisions. What is clear, though, is that more consideration should be given to the supply substitutability factor in the likeness analysis under the *safeguard* provisions than is given in the likeness test under the *non-discrimination* provisions. After all, the sole purpose of the former provisions is to provide relief to domestic producers, while the latter provisions have the comprehensive purpose of preserving economic and political efficiency.[341] Thus, the 'weighted' IASR Standard[342] can be used in the CVA-PCPSS for the present purpose.

The direct view approach or time-series analysis may be used, as necessary.

All of discussions in this chapter may be summarized in two figures: Figure III.1 is one-dimensional; Figure III.2 is two-dimensional.

IV

Conclusion

Having finished our performance and confirmed its value through the review process, we have finally reached the point at which we may ask the last question: What common characteristics of the likeness concept can be found in the history of GATT likeness cases referred to in the previous chapters?

The first characteristic is that the likeness concept has been *modified* in its application to various likeness provisions. Starting from the single definition of the term, 'practically identical', offered by the League of Nations,[1] the 'like product' concept during the early stages of the GATT seems to have been understood as having more or less the same scope in all those provisions (*Australia Ammonium Sulphate; Japan Wine and Liquor*).[2] After the WTO system was successfully launched, however, the panel and the Appellate Body made it clear that the likeness concept had different scopes depending on the provision concerned, hence the image of an accordion: even within one provision, the accordion of likeness is meant to be played differently.[3]

One might say that such diversification reflects the 'judicialization' process of international trade law and the changing environment of the world trading system. The WTO Dispute Settlement Understanding represents a 'thickening of legality'.[4] In the 'symbiosis of diplomacy and litigation',[5] the DSU represents a decided move by the GATT/WTO dispute settlement system toward litigation. As this 'lawyers triumph over diplomats'[6] has progressed, the international tribunal has been asked to tailor its deliberations to strict legal interpretations of each provision of likeness, or even of each paragraph of a provision, thereby generating more diverse interpretations.

The judicialization process is not alone in demanding narrowly tailored decisions. As the international tribunal has increasingly encountered a variety of ingenious non-tariff barriers, as well as more close cases, it has needed more precision in the reasoning of its decisions, and thus more diversification in the likeness interpretation. This necessity might have also justified the tribunal's increased discretion.

The second characteristic is that the scope of likeness in basic non-discrimination provisions has been gradually expanded over time. Not only through the sneaky attachment of the *Addendum* to Art. III:2 by the 1948 amendment and the resulting enlargement of scope of the paragraph,[7] the scope of the likeness concept has been generally broadened through interpretations by the tribunal. One notable example: in 1949, conhaque and cognac were considered as being different products due to additives and aromatic differences (*Brazilian Internal Taxes*);[8] in 1996, shochu, vodka, whisky, brandy, rum, gin, genever, and liqueurs were all considered 'like or directly competitive or substitutable products' (*Japan Alcoholic Beverages*).[9] Organoleptic differences that formerly played a role were largely ignored in modern times![10]

The aim-and-effect theory put a brake on this expansion drive. In the period 1992–1994, the ever-expanding scope of the likeness concept seemed to be reined in in the context of the national treatment obligation. Relying upon the attractions emanating from the aim-and-effect approach, the likeness concept seemed to achieve a balance between free trade and regulatory autonomy, wearing off the 'surplus fat' of the 'incidental (non-inherent) discriminatory effect'.[11]

This 'fitness' effort was overruled, however, by subsequent WTO tribunals. Rejecting the aim-and-effect approach out of concern over circumvention of the national treatment obligation (*United States Gasoline, EC Banana, Japan/Korea/ Chile Alcoholic Beverages*),[12] the tribunals resumed the drive for expansion of the likeness concept, notably in the national treatment context. Introducing the potential or future competition factor as another 'regular-entry accordion' (*Korea Alcoholic Beverages*),[13] the tribunals have marched deep into the territory of traditional regulatory autonomy.

Of course, what made this march possible was the necessity of furthering the 'judicialization' process so as to deal with the variety of newly-emerging non-tariff barriers, and the altered environment of the international trading system in which the GATT/WTO was empowered with much stronger credibility and authority. Finally, free from the *German Sardine*-type hesitation,[14] the WTO tribunals are able to announce the existence of two accordions[15], tuned to the *unavoidable elements of individual discretionary judgement* of the tribunals.

All of this diversification and expansion of the likeness concept share a common justificatory source—the 'judicialization' of international trade law, which indeed provides an excellent justification. Yet can this judicialization also provide justification for the panels' emphasis on *discretion* and the *accordion* in likeness analysis? Do we need more accordions and greater discretion in order to allow the judicialization process to progress? The WTO tribunals seem to think so, probably hoping that the justification of judicialization will cover all substantive issues (definition and scope of likeness) as well as methodological issues (discretion and use of the accordion in likeness tests).

This justification does not excuse their lack of methodology, however. Despite its handiness, the traditional *Border Tax Adjustment* Report approach lacks the precision and flexibility that are necessary to face changes in specific social contexts not contemplated in the original GATT. Thus, in close cases involving new areas, the approach often fails (see Chapter II, at 3.3). On the other hand, in spite of its attractiveness in dealing with *de facto* discrimination and regulatory autonomy, the aim-and-effect approach collapses because of the greater danger of circumvention. Facing an increasing number of close or *de facto* cases, the WTO tribunals have put forward the potential and future competition concept. But this merely offers old wine in new bottles. The tribunals, other than emphasizing accordion-like discretionary judgements put forward by themselves on a case-by-case basis, have shied away from indicating what the general tone of the accordion is supposed to sound like in relevant contexts, or even what its general mechanism is. This lack of guidance is clear with regard to the traditional likeness factors, not to mention the potentiality factor. As a consequence, consistency, transparency, and predictability— the very values that the judicialization has sought to promote—have been put in peril. GATT tribunals might have won each battle in court, but they emerged defeated in the war of judicialization.

The search for 'likeness' must be undertaken and pursued with relentless clarity. It is, in essence, an economic task put to the uses of the law.[16] Unless this task is well done, the results will be distorted in terms of the conclusion whether the law has been violated and what the recommendation of implementation should contain.[17]

Why should only physical properties, tariff classification, or end-use in general be relevant in the likeness determination? When 99 per cent of consumers in the relevant market consider that two products are no longer 'like' due to certain subjective perceptions on, e.g. process or production methods (PPMs), why should the tribunal stick to the old approach and rule against the predominant perception? When an increasing number of close and controversial disputes appear in the world trading system, involving new and more politically sensitive subject matters, how persuasive can this old approach be as regards the recalcitrant losers and their constituency?

The market-based economic analysis suggested in this book rescues the methodological justificatory source from the oxymoronic excuse of judicialization (or any other poor excuse of, say, the 'nature' of the term 'likeness') and restores it to the genuine power of the self-determination rule of democracy. This rule offers the simple proposition: what the people see as being 'like' ought to be 'like'; what the people consider to be 'potentially like' ought to be 'potentially like'; and what the people believe will be 'like in the near future' ought to be considered 'like in the near future'. In this light, the recent case of *EC Asbestos*, in which consumer preferences were taken into account as a legitimate and indispensable factor, indicates the possible development of a welcome trend in likeness determinations.[18]

Under the self-determination rule, the democratic tribunals are entitled only to act as 'umpires' in the dispute, not to 'govern' it: they must listen to what people say. For future tribunals, which will necessarily have to be requested to identify and exploit a middle ground between free trade and domestic regulatory autonomy, the various standards and criteria suggested in the market-based economic analysis provide the ideal tools for the development of democracy and transparency, with which the tribunals can function as trusted umpires. Indeed, taking the worst-case scenario, an imperial umpire is better than most umpire-like emperors for the sake of stability of people's lives. The good news for the tribunals is that acting in this way does not deprive them entirely of their discretion. A certain degree of discretion is always readily available to an umpire. Of course, this discretion is functional in nature, not tyrannical.

Truly, the GATT system has witnessed remarkable changes. Again, the most basic change has been the shift in focus from diplomacy to legality. This started from the resolution of a dispute in a way that laid down GATT's first thin layer of legality. The addition of a multitude of further layers over the years has established today's rather remarkably thick system of legality as the basis for settling international trade disputes.

In the area of 'likeness or substitutability' determination, this process should progress, if only belatedly. In the past, the tribunals laid down the first thin layer in the *Border Tax Adjustments* Report, sealing it with a cover made from the *unavoidable elements of individual discretionary judgement*. As a result, not being able to penetrate the hard cover, something important seems to have been left out: the theory of comparative advantage that continues to provide the focus of liberal trade policies and the rules of the international trade law system. Cut off from the theory, the first layer has been contaminated with intellectual inconsistency. While we may have made progress in the development of trade law for over 50 years, the relationship between that law and its intellectual underpinnings remains enigmatic in this subject area. This enigma will most likely remain as long as the likeness determination is kept out of the marketplace.

One response to this enigma might be to continue to live with the intellectual inconsistency between accepted economic theory and existing rule. Perhaps the system under the rule might continue to evolve in an *ad hoc*, reactionary fashion. But for those who prefer a legal system consistent with the fundamental concepts justifying its existence, discomfort is then inevitable. For them, two other choices are available: (1) either to change the rule to make it consistent with the economic theory; or (2) to find a new statement of economic theory that justifies the existing rule. For these diligent people, it is clear that as long as this evolutionary process remains incomplete, one must continue to inquire whether the existing rule tallies with the economic theory underpinning the international trade system as a whole. In other words, in order to complete the evolutionary process, it would be preferable to adjust the rule to make it consistent with economic theory.

This simple dynamic seems to have been overlooked by the tribunals, scholars, and practitioners of our 'dismal science', although they have been living alongside economics and watching its brilliant application to the field of antitrust law. Its absence (or willful blindness to it) seems to have been covered by such theoretical excuses as the unique soil of international society and the imperfection of the science of econometrics, as well as by such practical ones as the strict time-limits on panel procedures, the lack of resources for panels' fact-finding processes, and/or considerations of judicial economy. But in the era of electronic commerce, in which electronic sales data as well as Internet market surveys are easily and credibly available for the use of econometric methodology, and in the second stage of the WTO's *drive-to-maturity*, in which the tribunal, through its transparent and consistent standard-setting efforts, has to prepare for its own mature demise (making the meaning of WTO law so predictable that litigation will not be needed),[19] those excuses will continue to lose validity (if they ever had any).

The WTO tribunal has crossed the Rubicon halfway,[20] but is still hesitating to land on the other side.[21] Once it has crossed, it should conquer Rome as quickly as possible. Otherwise, it will end up being conquered by 'enemies', who are mostly strangers to GATT drafters. Moreover, even if the tribunal does not cross, such enemies might themselves ford the river. Indeed, to Caesar, who had not been in control of Rome, time must have been the enemy's ally.

Similarly, for *you*, the tribunal, accustomed to old excuses while suffering from an outdated, two-culture syndrome between law and economics,[22] time will only be on the side of your virulent 'enemies' or so-called moralists, who are poised to hide behind environment, labor, or human rights shields: it will make you a convenient target. Alas! The emperor was right: attack is the best defense.

Cast the die! Take your seat of glorious umpireship at the Colosseum of Rome, giving signals to the winner of fair and transparent games—for the peace of world citizens, not to mention for your own survival!

Appendix I

The historical origin of the term 'like product' in the field of international economic law seems to date back to the MFN clause of the 'Jay Treaty' between the United States and the United Kingdom in 1794.[1]

According to Art. 3 of the Treaty, all goods and merchandise from one party 'shall be subject to no higher or other Duties than would be payable [by the other party] . . . on the Importation of *the same* from Europe . . .' (emphasis added). Furthermore, Art. 15 of the Treaty states that:

No other or higher Duties shall be paid by the Ships or Merchandize of the one Party in the Ports of the other, than such as are paid by the *like vessels or Merchandize* of all other Nations. Nor shall any other or higher Duty be imposed in one Country on the importation of any articles, the growth, produce, or manufacture of the other, than are or shall be payable on the importation of the *like articles* being of the growth, produce or manufacture of any other Foreign Country. (emphasis added)

Hence, one could say that the term 'like product' first appeared in the provisions of the MFN treatment, using the words 'the same [goods and merchandize]' or 'like merchandize or like articles'.

Before this Treaty, the MFN clause had been inserted in various bilateral commercial treaties.[2] But the clause employed the terms 'Subjects', 'Inhabitants', 'Merchants', 'Most Favoured Nations', or 'Citizens', because the MFN obligation was understood as meaning equal treatment between 'subjects', 'people', or 'vessels', not between 'products'.[3] Commencing with the Jay Treaty, states began to understand the MFN obligation in terms of 'product' relationships (rather than producers' relationships), which seemed to make the MFN rule more strict. If the MFN were interpreted as applying to the producers' relationship, some discriminatory treatments of some *products* might be permitted, provided the overall *producer* relationship was not harmed. For instance, suppose a producer in country X produces products A and B (A and B have the same price) and another producer in country Y produces the same (like) two products; both of them export A and B to country Z. In this example, country Z may be allowed to impose a 5 per cent tariff on A imported from X and a 7 per cent tariff on A imported from Y, provided that Z imposes a 7 per cent tariff on B imported from X and a 5 per cent tariff on B imported from Y. One might argue that this is not a violation of the MFN because, despite the existence of tariff discrimination on each product, the *overall* competitive relationship between the *producer* in X and the *producer* in Y is unaffected. Thus, whether the MFN is understood in the context of product relationship or producer relationship could result in there being different scopes of the obligation: according to the former understanding, country Z would violate the MFN obligation in the above example.

With regard to the term 'product' relationship, another interesting issue may be raised: does the Art. I MFN obligation apply only on the GATT *member-to-member* basis? In fact, this issue was raised in 1989 by Canada in the *Japan SPF Lumber* case.[4] Canada contended that the prohibition of discrimination between member countries was only a part of the larger obligation requiring that '*all* products' considered to be 'like' be treated in the same way.[5]

The significance of this claim appears in the possibility that discrimination between like products imported from the 'same' country could violate the MFN obligation. Although the plain text of the provision seems to contain a seed of support for the Canadian argument,[6] most panel decisions seem to suggest the requirement for country-of-origin discrimination.[7] Considering the basic purpose and historical development of the provision, and that its title is the 'General Most-Favoured-*Nation* Treatment', one could conclude that discrimination with regard to the country of origin should be required as a precondition of the MFN challenge.[8]

At any rate, going back to the discussion of the Jay Treaty's language, it should be noted that many bilateral treaties since the Jay Treaty have adopted the *product*-relationship-based MFN and/or national treatment clause by including such terms as (1) 'same articles';[9] (2) 'same merchandize';[10] (3) 'like articles';[11] (4) 'like articles, the produce or manufacture';[12] (5) 'like articles, being the growth, produce, or manufacture';[13] (6) 'articles of like nature, the growth';[14] (7) 'same articles, being the produce, or manufacture';[15] (8) 'similar articles' or 'similar native productions';[16] (9) 'same merchandise or produce';[17] (10) 'same or like articles, the produce, growth or manufacture';[18] (11) 'same merchandise or articles of commerce';[19] (12) 'same or similar merchandize';[20] (13) 'similar goods' or 'same goods';[21] (14) 'articles of like nature, the growth';[22] (15) 'articles of like nature, the products of the soil or industry';[23] (16) 'like goods and merchandize',[24] etc.

Before 1934, MFN clauses in commercial treaties negotiated by the United States generally were conditional in nature,[25] although this was not universally the case.[26] It was not until after World War I that the United States began negotiating unconditional MFN clauses routinely with its trading partners, primarily under the authority of the Reciprocal Trade Agreements Act of 1934.[27] The typical unconditional MFN clause in a bilateral US trade treaty relating to trade in goods used the following boilerplate language:[28]

Any advantage of whatsoever kind which either High Contracting Party may extend, by treaty, law, decree, regulation, practice or otherwise, to any article, the growth, produce or manufacture of any other foreign country shall simultaneously and unconditionally, without request and without compensation, be extended to the *like article, the growth, produce or manufacture* of the other High Contracting Party.[29]

The Reciprocal Trade Agreements Act of 1934, which added s 350 to the Tariff Act of 1930 (the Smoot-Hawley Tariff Act), moved the unconditional MFN principle to center stage by requiring the non-discriminatory application to all countries of tariff and trade concessions granted in bilateral agreements, regardless of whether those countries had agreements with the United States containing an MFN clause.[30]

What was the reason for this 'depersonalization' of the MFN likeness clause that brought more strictness to the obligation? It may have been just an unintentional change; or one might say that this trend reflected the altered industrial environment. Consequent upon specialization and the mass production system, one-producer-one-product systems have been the trend (multiple-goods producers, as in the above example, have substantially disappeared). Thus, it seems natural that MFN has come to be understood on a products basis.

It is no wonder that this understanding was adopted by the standard League of Nations MFN clause.[31] During the discussions of the clause at the end of the 1920s and the beginning of the 1930s, the Economic Committee of the League of Nations raised questions concerning the interpretation of 'like products'.[32] The conclusion was, in essence, that whether or not products were 'like' should be decided on the basis of the 'intrinsic qualities' of the products, and that 'any endeavour to find a more precise formula . . . appears to be Utopian'.[33] (In this context, one should note that the concept of 'like product' was discussed in relation to the customs treatment of goods, and that attempts were being made at establishing a general tariff nomenclature at the time.[34] Also noteworthy is the fact that during the drafting of the Havana Charter, it was proposed to elaborate a general definition of the concept together with other key terms, but this attempt was abandoned.[35])

From this moment, the 'orphan' GATT (or its tribunals) has traveled a long way away from its 'dead parents', who left no formula except for a definition of 'practically identical with another product'[36]—a journey toward the Utopian home!

Appendix II

Q = Original Equilibrium
Q* = Short-run Equilibrium

Q**, Q₊** = Long-run Equilibrium
S/sub = Supply Curve under Supply Substitution
D/sub(+) = Demand Curve under Demand Substitution
S/tax = Supply Curve under Tax Imposition
D or S = Demand or Supply Curve under no Substitution

★ SITUATION I ★

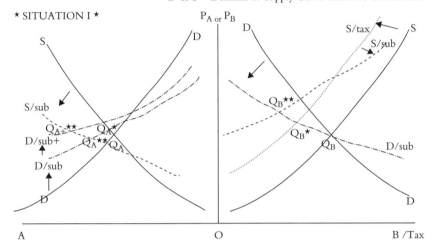

★ SITUATION II ★

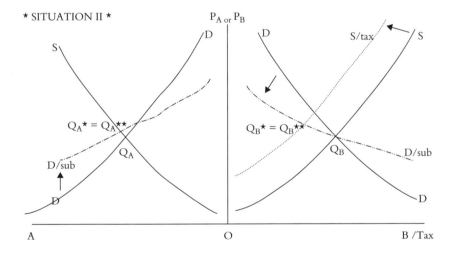

★ SITUATION III ★

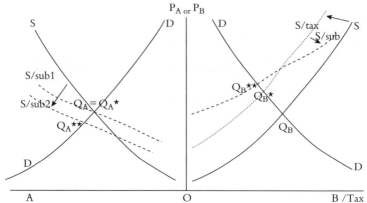

S/sub1 = Domestic Producer's Supply Curve under Supply Substitution
S/sub2 = Domestic +Foreign Producers' Supply Curve under Supply Substitution

★ SITUATION IV ★

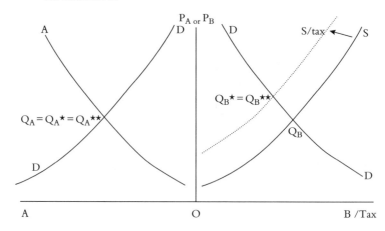

Appendix III

If the original market price of product X has been set at an extremely high level because of the existence of a strong monopoly, or at an extremely low level due to severe dumping practices, the assumption of proportionality (assuming that a 2.2 per cent switching rate under the 3.3 per cent price change hypothetical is the same degree of substitution as a 4.4 per cent switching rate under the 6.6 per cent price change hypothetical) might not hold. The reason is because cross-price elasticity could differ depending on relative price level (see Figures X and Y, below). One can think of the example that a demand curve has many different own-price elasticities depending on the relative price level (each point on the curve can have a different elasticity). In general, it could be said that in high price levels, the elasticity would be larger than in a lower price level. In case of a linear and proportionally down-sloping demand curve (as shown in Figure X), the elasticity in the middle (center) point of the curve would be 1; above the center price level, the elasticity would be larger than 1; and below the center price level, the elasticity would be less than 1. Thus, one can see that own-price elasticity differs depending on relative price levels.

Attention may be paid to 'cross-price elasticity' to draw similar insights. Figure Y shows that products X and Y are good substitutes. It should be noted, however, that, at too low a price level for X, its consumers would not bother to switch to Y, in spite of the modest price increase of X (because the price is still too cheap). Also, at too high a level of price, they would not switch either (because most consumers of X have already switched to Y and only loyal consumers of X or extremely rich people would remain as X consumers). Hence, if the 'base-price level', starting from which the hypothetical price change is given to respondents, is set at too high or too low a level in the first place, the resulting cross-price elasticity of demand might not reflect the reality.

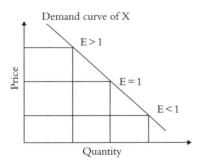

Figure X: Own-price elasticity

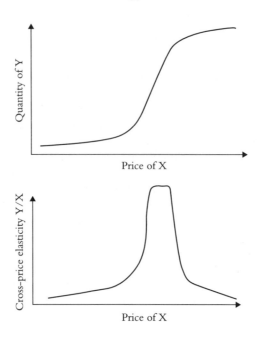

Figure Y: Cross-price elasticity

By the same token (reasoning), one can say that if the 'price change' is given at too large a rate (for instance, an 80 per cent hypothetical price rise) or a negligible rate (e.g., 0.3 per cent price rise), a similar failure may occur.

In these cases, the assumption of proportionality might not hold, and thus the credibility of the CVA on *Proportional* CPDS would fall to that extent. Therefore, the hypothetical price change should be a *small* (but not too small) variation from the *current price* of product X.

It should be noted that sometimes the current price does not reflect a legitimate competitive relationship between X and Y due to the existence of discriminatory measures in the market. In this case, the 'potential competition factor' should be taken into account, as discussed in Chapter II at 3.2.4. Because the 'potential substitutability' means a substitution rate that would exist 'but for' an allegedly discriminatory measure, one can calculate the specific degree of potential substitutability by referring to consumer response according to hypothetical changes in the 'Pre-Measure Price' (PMP).[1] In other words, by using the *pre-measure price* standard, not the *current price* standard, in composing the questionnaire of the CVA-PCPDS, one could remove the protective effect, created by the discrimination, from the outcome of the analysis.[2]

All of these conclusions can be transferred to a '*supply* substitutability' context, as follows. Although products X and Y are good sectors for supply substitution, supply substitutability can differ depending on specific points of relative price levels. The reason is, of course, because at too low a price level for product X, producers of product Y would not bother to switch to X, in spite of the modest price increase of X (because the price increase is too small to bring about meaningful profits); and conversely, at too high a price level for X, no supply substitution would occur (most of the supply substitutions legally or practically feasible have already arisen). Hence, if the base-price level, starting from which the hypothetical price change is given to respondents, is set at too high or too low a level in the first place, the resulting cross-price elasticity of supply might not reflect the reality. With the same reasoning, one can say that if the price change is given at too large or negligible a rate, a similar failure can occur.

In these cases, the assumption of proportionality might not hold and thus the credibility of the CVA on *Proportional* CPSS would fall to that extent. Thus, the hypothetical price change should be a *small* (but not too small) variation from the *current price* for product X.[3]

Where the current price does not reflect a legitimate competitive relationship between X and Y due to the existence of discriminatory measures in the market, the potential competition (supply-side) factor should be taken into account using the PMP Standard in the questionnaire of the CVA-PCPSS.

References

I BOOKS AND ARTICLES

Bermann, G. A. *et al.* (1993), *European Community Law* (St. Paul, Minn.: West Publishing Co.)—*understanding of European Community law.*

Bhagwati, J. (1998), *A Stream of Windows: Unsetting Reflections on Trade, Immigration and Democracy* (Cambridge, Mass.; London: MIT Press)—*understanding the role of the international trading system.*

——and Hirsch, M. (eds) (1999), *The Uruguay Round and Beyond: Essays in Honor of Arthur Dunkel* (Ann Arbor: University of Michigan Press)—*understanding the WTO agreements.*

——and Hudec, R. (eds) (1996), *Fair Trade and Harmonization* (London: MIT Press)—*understanding of primary objectives of the WTO Agreement.*

Bhala, R. and Kennedy, K. (1998), *World Trade Law: The GATT-WTO System, Regional Arrangements and US Law* (Charlottesville, Va: Lexis Law Publishing)—*understanding of principles of the international trading system.*

Cottier, T. and Mavroidis, P. C. (eds) (2000), *Regulatory Barriers and the Principle of Non-discrimination in World Trade* (Ann Arbor: University of Michigan Press).

Frankel, J. A. (1997), *Regional Trading Blocs: in the World Economic System* (Washington DC: Institute for International Economics)—*understanding a trend of regionalism in the world trading system.*

GATT (1970), '*A Study by the GATT Secretariat, the Most-Favoured-Nation Clause in GATT*', *Journal of World Trade Law*, vol. 4, No. 6.

—— (1995), *GATT Analytical Index: Guide to GATT Law and Practice*, 6th edn (Geneva: WTO Secretariat)—*useful guidance to GATT/WTO cases.*

Handler, M. *et al.* (1993), *Trade Regulation*, 3rd edn (University Casebook Series)—*understanding of US antitrust laws.*

Hudec, R. E. (1990), *The GATT Legal System and World Trade Diplomacy*, 2nd edn (Salem, Mass: Butterworth)—*understanding the relationship between law and politics in the international trading system.*

—— (1993), *Enforcing International Trade Law: the Evolution of the Modern GATT Legal System* (Salem, Mass: Butterworth)—*understanding the evolutionary process of the GATT law.*

Jackson, J. H. (1969), *World Trade and the Law of GATT* (Charlottesville, Va: Bobbs–Merrill Co. Inc.)—*basic approach of the like product issue.*

—— (1998a), *The World Trade Organization: Constitution and Jurisprudence* (London: The Royal Institute of International Affairs)—*understanding the role of the WTO.*

—— (1998b), *The World Trading System: Law and Policy of International Economic Relations*, 2nd edn (Cambridge, Mass, London: MIT Press)—*basic understanding of various GATT provisions.*

——*et al.* (1995a), *Legal Problems of International Economic Relations* (St. Paul, Minn.: West Publishing Co.)—*general understanding of the WTO Agreement and relations between international trade and diplomacy.*

——*et al.* (eds) (1995b), *1995 Documents Supplement to Legal Problems of International Economic Relations* (St. Paul, Minn.: American Casebook Series)—*comprehensive texts of the WTO Agreement and comparison between the WTO Agreement and US trade law.*

——and Sykes, A. O. Jr (1997), *Implementing the Uruguay Round* (Oxford: Clarendon Press)—*understanding the UR process.*

McGovern, E. (1995), *International Trade Regulation* (Exeter: Globefield Press)—*comprehensive analysis of various GATT provisions.*

Mendoza, M. R. *et al.* (eds) (1999), *Trade Rules in the Making: Challenges in Regional and Multilateral Negotiations* (Washington DC: Brookings Institution Press)—*understanding Art. XXIV of GATT and the relationship between regionalism and multilateralism.*

Palmeter, D. and Mavroidis, P. C. (1999), *Dispute Settlement in the World Trade Organization: Practice and Procedure* (The Hague, London, Boston: Kluwer Law International)—*understanding procedural aspects in the WTO dispute settlement system.*

Polinsky, M. (1989), *An Introduction to Law and Economics* (Boston and Toronto: Little, Brown and Company)—*understanding of the desirable relationship between law and economics.*

Posner, R. A. (1976), *Antitrust Law: An Economic Perspective* (Chicago: University of Chicago Press)—*understanding of the necessity of an economic approach in antitrust law.*

Zedalis, R. J. (1994), 'A Theory of the GATT "Like" Product Common Language Cases' 27 Vand. J. Transnat'l L. 33—*basic idea of classifying various like product provisions and proceeding with provision-by-provision analysis.*

II GATT PREPARATORY RECORDS

Record of Preparatory Committee of the International Conference on Trade and Employment, Committee II: General Observations of the Czechoslovak Delegation on the Agenda of Committee II (UN Doc. E/PC/T/C.II/24, 28 October 1946).

Record of Preparatory Committee of the International Conference on Trade and Employment, Committee II—Fifth Meeting (UN Doc. E/PC/T/C.II/36, 31 October 1946).

Record of Preparatory Committee of the International Conference on Trade and Employment, Committee II—Twelfth Meeting (UN Doc. E/PC/T/C.II/65, 22 November 1946).

Record of Preparatory Committee of the International Conference on Trade and Employment, Committee II—Verbatim Report of the Twelfth Meeting (UN Doc. E/PC/T/C.II/PV/12, 22 November 1946).

Summary Record of the Fifth Meeting of the Third Committee: Commercial Policy (UN Doc. E/Conf.2/C.3/SR.5, 4 December 1947).

Summary Record of the Thirtieth Meeting of the Third Committee: Commercial Policy (UN Doc. E/Conf.2/C.3/SR.30, 31 January 1948).

Tentative and Partial Draft Outline of General Agreement on Tariffs and Trade (UN Doc. E/PC/T/C.II/58).

Record of Preparatory Committee of the International Conference on Trade and Employment, Committee II—Twelfth Meeting (continued) (2nd Part) (UN Doc. E/PC/T/C.II/65 Add 1, 23 November 1946).

Record of Preparatory Committee of the International Conference on Trade and Employment, Committee II—Report of the Technical Sub-Committee (UN Doc. E/PC/T/C.II/64, 22 November 1946).

Record of Preparatory Committee of the International Conference on Trade and Employment, Committee II—Part III: Recommended Text of Chapter IV Commercial Policy (UN Doc. E/Conf.2/C.3/59).

Record of Third Committee: Commercial Policy—Report of Sub-Committee A (UN Doc. E/Conf.2/C.3/59, 16 February 1948).

Summary Record of the Eleventh Meeting of the Third Committee: Commercial Policy (UN Doc. E/Conf.2/C.3/SR.11, 16 December 1947).

Corrigendum to Summary Record of the Eleventh Meeting of the Third Committee: Commercial Policy (UN Doc. E/Conf.2/C.3/SR.11/Corr.1, 17 December 1947).

Corrigendum to Summary Record of the Eleventh Meeting of the Third Committee: Commercial Policy (UN Doc. E/Conf.2/C.3/SR.11/Corr.2, 23 December 1947).

Corrigendum to Summary Record of the Eleventh Meeting of the Third Committee: Commercial Policy (UN Doc. E/Conf.2/C.3/SR.11/Corr.3, 14 January 1948).

Summary Record of the Thirtieth Meeting of the Third Committee: Commercial Policy (UN Doc. E/Conf.2/C.3/SR.30, 31 January 1948).

Report of the Second Session of the Preparatory Committee of the United Nations Conference on Trade and Employment (UN Doc. E/PC/T/186, 10 September 1947).

Report of the Drafting Committee of the Preparatory Committee of the United Nations Conference on Trade and Employment (UN Doc. E/PC/T/34/Rev.1, 29 May 1947).

The Transition From War to Peace Economy, Report of the Delegation on Economic Depressions—Part I (C.6.M.6. 1943.I, League of Nations, Geneva, 1943).

Commercial Policy in the Post-War World, Report of the Economic and Financial Committees (C.31.M.31.1945.II.A., League of Nations, Geneva, 1945).

Recommendations of the Economic Committee Relating to Commercial Policy (C.138.M.53.1929.II, League of Nations, Geneva, 1929).

Consultative Committee Application of the Recommendations of the International Economic Conference (C.130.M.45.1929.II, League of Nations, Geneva, 1929).

Report by the German Representative, Work of the Thirty-Fifth Session of the Economic Committee (C.511.1931.II.B., League of Nations, Geneva, 1931).

Economic Committee Report to the Council on the Work of the Thirty-Fifth Session (C.427.M.177.1931.II.B, League of Nations, Geneva, 1931).

Economic Committee Report to the Council on the Work of the Thirty-Fourth Session (C.180.M.68.1931.II.B, League of Nations, Geneva, 1931).

Economic Committee Report to the Council on the Work of the Thirty-Third Session (C.641.M.260.1930.II.B, League of Nations, Geneva, 1931).

Report by the Danish and Portuguese Governments, Application of the International Convention for the Abolition of Import and Export Prohibitions and Restrictions (C.L.8.1931./II.B, League of Nations, Geneva, 1931).

Proposals for Expansion of World Trade and Employment (*United Nations Review* Vol.V-No.7, 31 December 1945).

Endnotes

INTRODUCTION: PURPOSE AND SCOPE

[1] The General Agreement on Tariffs and Trade, as amended and in force on 1 January 1994, 55 UNTS 187; BISD Vol. IV. This is a legally separate instrument from the original GATT 1947, which can be found at 55 UNTS 194.

[2] Jackson, John H., *World Trade and the Law of GATT* (Bobbs-Merrill Company, Inc., 1969) 259.

[3] Ibid.

[4] GATT Arts I.1, *Ad* I.4, II.2(a), III.2/4, *Ad* III, *Ad* V.5, VI.1/4, IX.1, XIII.1, XVI.4, *Ad* XVI, *Ad* XVI.3; Agreement on Implementation of Article VI of the GATT 1994 (*hereinafter* Antidumping Agreement), Arts 2.1, 2.2, 2.6, 3.1, 3.2, 3.3, 3.6, 4.1, 5.2, 5.4, 5.8, 6.11; Agreement on Subsidies and Countervailing Measures (*hereinafter* SCM Agreement), Arts 6.3, 6.4, 6.5, 6.7, 11.2, 11.4, 12.9, 15.1, 15.2, 15.3, 15.6, 16.1, 27.9, 27.10, Annex I(g) and (h); Agreement on Agriculture, Art. 9.1; Agreement on Rules of Origin, Art. 1.2, fn1; Agreement on Technical Barriers to Trade (*hereinafter* TBT Agreement), Arts 2.1, 5.1, 5.2, Annex 3.D; Agreement on the Application of Sanitary and Phytosanitary Measures (*hereinafter* SPS Agreement), Annex C.1(a) and (f).

[5] GATT Art. VI.7.

[6] GATT Art. VII.2, *Ad* VII.4.

[7] GATT Art. XIX.1; Safeguard Agreement, Arts 2.1, 4.1; Agreement on Textiles and Clothing, Art. 6.2; SCM Agreement, Annex I(d) ('like or directly competitive products or services').

[8] GATT Art. XI.2(c).

[9] GATT *Ad* Art. III:2.

[10] Agreement on Implementation of Article VII of the GATT 1994 (*hereinafter* Customs Valuation Agreement), Arts 2, 3, 5.1, 5.2, 7.2, 15.2, 15.3, Note to Arts 2/5/7, General Introductory Comment 2/3; SCM Agreement, Art. 15.1, fn 46.

[11] *See* Appendix I, where the origin and development of the 'like product' concept are also discussed.

Before examining these concepts, one needs to ponder the basic definition of 'product (commodity/merchandise/good)' as opposed to 'service'. The basic distinction is that products are tangible, while services are not. Although this distinction is workable in most circumstances, sometimes it is not easy to operate because services are closely related to products (for example, services are reflected in the added value of products). Thus, the rules concerning non-tariff barriers (notably GATT Art. III:4) had to cover to some extent product-related services such as sale, purchase, transportation, and distribution. There was discussion by a GATT preparatory committee of whether electric power should be considered a product or a service, and it was ultimately decided not to constitute a product. *See* UN Docs. E/PC/T/C.6/41 (p. 5) and 89 (p. 4). It is clear that raw materials (as long as they are removed from their natural environment and thus distinguished from natural resources) are products covered by GATT. With regard to 'waste', the European Court of Justice has ruled that waste should be 'regarded as a product the movement of which must not in principle, pursuant to Article 30 EEC, be impeded' (*Commission v Belgium (Wallonia Waste)*

(Case C-2/90) [1992] ECR I–4431, para 28). *See also* Kramer, L., 'Environmental Protection and Article 30 EEC Treaty' (1993) 30 CML Rev 115–16. It should be noted that, mainly because of possible conflict between trade law and international agreements restricting trade in hazardous waste, the OECD has expressed some concern about including waste among 'normal free-tradable products'. *See* OECD, *Environmental Policy, How to Apply Economic Instruments* (OECD, 1991) 43. One case in this regard was brought to GATT concerning export restrictions on 'copper scrap'. Although the Panel never got to discuss the merits of the case (the dispute came to a settlement), the fact that the exportation of copper scrap was restricted and the issue was brought before GATT by a potential importing country show that copper scrap was considered by both the exporting and the importing countries as valuable raw material: *EEC—Restrictions on Exports of Copper Scrap*, BISD 37S/200 (adopted on 20 February 1990). *See* Fauchald, Ole Kristian, *Environmental Taxes and Trade Discrimination* (Kluwer Law International, 1998) 89–92.

[12] Terms such as 'commerce' and 'product' sometimes give rise to such implication. *See* GATT Arts II.1, III.1. In addition, Art. XXIV.5(b) speaks of 'corresponding duties', giving rise to the classification problem of which duties correspond. Furthermore, there are the classification problems referred to in Art. II, and particularly in para 5 of that Article. *See* Jackson, *supra* note 2. The product relationship problem under Arts II.1 and XXIV.5 is concerned with the 'classification' issue rather than with the product likeness issue, which is beyond the subject matter of this book. The 'implicit' likeness in Art. III:1 is discussed in Chapter III, at 1.2.

[13] The accordion of 'likeness' stretches and squeezes in different places as different provisions of the WTO Agreement are applied. The width of the accordion in any one of those places must be determined by the particular provision in which the term 'like' is encountered, as well as by the context and the circumstances that prevail in any given case to which that provision may apply. *See Japan—Taxes on Alcoholic Beverages (hereinafter 'Japan Alcoholic Beverages')* Appellate Report, sec. H(1)(a), WT/DS8/AB/R, WT/DS10/AB/R, WT/DS11/AB/R (1996). There was a GATT case regarding a similar subject matter, which will be called *'Japan Wine and Liquor'*, *see* Chapter II, note 65.

[14] *See* UN Doc. E/PC/T/C.II/65 at 2, 3; EPCT/C.II/PV.12 at 7. *See also* Chapter III, note 1; Appendix I, note 36. At the same sub-committee, a proposal to include a provision defining 'like products' and 'similar products' was rejected. *See* E/PC/T/C.II/64 at 7 and E/PC/T/C.II/PV/12 at 5–8.

[15] The International Convention on the Simplification and Harmonization of Customs Procedures (the Kyoto Convention) represents a multilateral attempt to move toward the harmonization of rules of origin. Annex D.1 of the Convention set forth guidelines based on the principles of wholly obtained goods and last 'substantial transformation' that countries were to use in drafting their rules of origin. According to the Annex, origin of goods should be determined by the last or final country in which 'substantial transformation' of the goods took place, and the 'substantial transformation' could be determined by applying one of three different methods: percentage of value added, change in tariff heading, or specified process of manufacture. *See* the Kyoto Convention, 18 May 1973, 1975 Gr. Brit. TS No. 36 (Cmnd 5938) (entered into force 25 September 1974).

Having a primary aim of ensuring that rules of origin will not themselves create unnecessary obstacles to trade, or impair the rights of GATT members, the WTO Agreement on Rules of Origin provides that WTO members will attempt to harmonize international non-preferential rules of origin within three years of its implementation; the WTO 'Work

Programme' has been initiated for the task. *See* Agreement on Rules of Origin, Annex 1A, Agreement Establishing the World Trade Organization (15 April 1994), reprinted in H.R. Doc. No. 316, 103rd Cong., 2nd Sess. 1515 (1994). For details, *see also* Chapter III, note 50.

[16] The GATT was not intended to be an organization. The negotiators expected the International Trade Organization (ITO) that was to be created by their draft treaty-charter to be the institutional framework to which the GATT would be attached. When the US Congress refused to approve the ITO Charter and that charter was declared dead by 1951, the GATT, which came into (provisional) force in 1948, became the focus of attention as a possible institution through which nations could solve some of their trade problems. *See* Jackson, John H., *The World Trade Organization: Constitution and Jurisprudence* (The Royal Institute of International Affairs, 1998) 12.

[17] The World Trade Organization, established on 1 January 1995 as a result of Uruguay Round negotiations (1986–94). As of June 2001, 141 countries are members of the WTO. *See Members and Observers* **<http://www.wto.org/english/thewto_e/whatis_e/tif_e/org6_e.htm>**.

[18] This function, however, gives rise to many questions, including: What constitutes an interpretative decision? When should such a recommendation (under Art. IX:2 of the WTO Establishing Agreement) be made? Is there not a danger that interpretation could result in creeping legislation that could undermine the amendment provisions? And is there any clear procedure to transfer interpretative issues from the Dispute Settlement Body (DSB) to the Ministerial Conference or the General Council? For detailed discussion in this regard, *see* Asif Qureshi, *The World Trade Organization Implementing International Trade Norms* (Manchester University Press, 1998).

[19] *See* Jackson, John H., 'Strengthening the International Legal Framework of the GATT–MTN System: Reform Proposals for the New GATT Round', in Ernst-Ulrich Petersmann and Meinhard Hilf, eds, *The New GATT Round of Multilateral Trade Negotiations: Legal and Economic Problems* (Kluwer Law International, 1988) 16.

[20] Akakwam, Philip A., 'The Standard of Review in the 1994 Antidumping Code: Circumscribing the Role of GATT Panels in Reviewing National Antidumping Determinations', 5 *Minn. J. Global Trade* 285 (1996).

[21] *See*, e.g., Art. 3.2 of the Understanding on Rules and Procedures Governing the Settlement of Disputes (DSU), 15 December 1994, Marrakesh Agreement Establishing the World Trade Organization, Annex 2, (1994) 33 ILM 112.

[22] McGovern, E., *International Trade Regulation* (Globefield Press, 1995) 8.11–1.

[23] In para 2 of Art. III, this general standard is expressed by such phrases as 'in excess of' and 'not similarly taxed'. This difference in language could bring about delicate distinctions in dealing with *de facto* discrimination cases. *See* Chapter II, at 3.2.3.

[24] As regards para 2 of Art. III, the meaning of 'directly' should be also clarified. In the end it is important to achieve a harmonious interpretation between likeness, which is basically a legal concept, and competitiveness and substitutability, which are basically economic concepts.

[25] If two products are not 'meaningfully related' to each other, different treatment itself imposed on one product causes little harm to the other, which hardly gives reason for the treatment to be condemned by the GATT. It should be noted that a vague definition of likeness could cause excessive regulation of the allegedly discriminatory measures.

[26] The term 'economic analysis' can have different meanings in different contexts. The author would like to define this term as 'an analysis that is based on efficiency and a

welfare-maximizing way of thinking and that employs econometric tools to the utmost extent possible and concepts developed in the science of economics'. In general, 'economic analysis' proceeds with a cost–benefit approach, to achieve not only economic efficiency (*see* Chapter I, note 8) but also diplomatic and legal efficiency. In other words, the analysis puts due emphasis on legal aspects as well as policy orientation. In this light, '*economic* analysis' is a broader concept than '*econometric* analysis'.

[27] In *Japan Alcoholic Beverages*—against the Japanese Liquor Tax Law that had divided the entire spectrum of alcoholic beverages into a large number of separate categories (with different tax rates and tax formulae for each) and in which most domestic products had ended up in low tax categories as opposed to most imports in high tax categories—the Panel and the Appellate Body ruled that domestic shochu and imported vodka are 'like' products under the first sentence of Art. III:2 and that shochu, on the one hand, and whisky, brandy, rum, gin, genever and liqueurs, on the other, are 'directly competitive or substitutable products' under the second sentence of Art. III:2. In the latter test on 'directly competitive or substitutable' products, the tribunals explicitly endorsed examination of the 'marketplace', which could be implicitly extended to the former test on 'like' products. *See* Chapter II, notes 92–101 and accompanying texts.

Marco Bronckers and Natalie McNelis name this approach the 'Market-based Approach'. They explain that this is a 'new' approach and suggest that it be employed throughout GATT 'like' provisions, where the purpose is to protect or improve competitive conditions. As an illustration of the benefit of the approach, they show that its application to antidumping law could substantially reduce arbitrariness or inconsistency in antidumping determinations. *See* Bronckers, M. and McNelis, N., 'Rethinking the "Like Product" Definition in WTO Antidumping Law', *Journal of World Trade* (Kluwer Law International, 1999) 33(3).

[28] The facts in *Korea—Taxes on Alcoholic Beverages* (hereinafter '*Korea Alcoholic Beverages*') resemble those in *Japan Alcoholic Beverages*, except for differences in consumer habits between Korea and Japan; and different source materials, manufacturing methods, and comparative price levels between Japanese shochu and Korean soju. According to the Korean tribunal, these differences were not enough to render a different ruling from that in the Japanese case. *See* WT/DS75/AB/R; WT/DS84/AB/R (18 January 1999).

The factual situation in *Chile—Taxes on Alcoholic Beverages* (hereinafter '*Chile Alcoholic Beverages*') was quite distinct from the Japanese or the Korean cases, in that the Chilean tax discrimination was based on alcoholic strength and value (*ad valorem*), whereas the Japanese and Korean liquor tax was imposed discriminatorily, based on specific type of alcoholic beverages. The Chilean measure was designed to afford protection to domestic pisco in relation to certain imported products (whisky, brandy, rum, gin, vodka, liquors, tequila, etc.) by applying steeply graduated progression of the tax rates between 35° (where most pisco was located) and 39° alcoholic content (where most imports were located). Despite this distinction, it was not difficult for the tribunal to find *de facto* discrimination in 'discrimination based on alcoholic strength', similar to the previous two 'type discrimination' cases. *See* WT/DS/87/AB/R; WT/DS/110/AB/R (13 December 1999).

[29] I.e. Art. III:2 of GATT.

[30] *See* Chapter II, notes 92 and 141 and accompanying texts. The 'market segment analysis' in *Indonesia National Car* could be illustrated as an indication of such broader application. In this case, referring to the like product definition in *Japan Alcoholic Beverages*, the Panel based its decision on two considerations: physical characteristics; and whether there existed distinct 'market segments' between domestic and imported automobiles. This case strongly

shows that the like product concept under the SCM Agreement should also be based on the marketplace. For details, *see* Chapter II, notes 128, 129, and 254–257 and accompanying texts.

Also to be noted is the *EC Asbestos* case, in which such market-based factors as consumer preferences and habits were heavily taken into account in the context of Art. III:4 of the GATT. *See* Chapter II, note 97.

[31] This will generate predictability.

I RELATIONSHIP BETWEEN LAW AND ECONOMICS: DOES 'RUBICON' EXIST BETWEEN THEM?

[1] *See* Introduction, note 13. Of course, our ultimate goal is 'playing harmonious melody using the tuned accordion'.

[2] This necessity becomes greater, especially when too many complicated repertoires need to be played before mastering the instrument.

[3] *See* Introduction, note 16.

[4] If one has a certain common tool (methodology) for interpreting 'likeness', it will help to compare each likeness with others and adjust its scope according to the different purposes of each provision. Especially when dealing with various 'likeness' terms scattered over the many provisions of GATT with little guidance in the texts, the necessity for this tool becomes greater. In the absence of this common tool, the GATT tribunals, even dealing with the same provision, have failed to produce a consistent methodology to determine 'likeness' (e.g., the *Border Tax Adjustment* (BTA) Report approach *versus* the aim-and-effect approach in Art. III of the GATT; *see* Chapter II, at 2 and 3). In order not to repeat this inconsistency in the future, a tribunal needs a common methodology with which it can proceed to coherent interpretation of likeness in cases involving the same provision, as well as interpreting likeness across different provisions.

[5] *See* Cass, R., 'Economics and International Law', 29 NYUJ Int'l L. & Pol. 474 (1997).

[6] Webster defines 'Rubicon' as 'a bounding or limiting line; one that when crossed commits one irrevocably'. The Rubicon symbolized a tradition which prevented generals from bringing their troops into Rome, and Julius Caesar, by crossing the river in 49 BC, signaled a war between Rome and Gaul. For the purpose of this book, Rubicon can be rephrased as a division line between law (especially international trade law) and economics; it symbolizes such traditional tendencies of the international trade tribunals (or some countries) as (1) emphasis on independent characteristics between law and economics, (2) efforts to preserve the discretionary area in undertaking the likeness test, notwithstanding the resulting loss in credibility or justification of the tribunal's decisions, and (3) lack of a systemic approach or econometric analysis in the likeness test. Hence, the term 'Crossing the Rubicon' represents a challenge against the traditional dichotomy.

[7] 'The supreme difficulty of our generation . . . is that our achievements on the economic plane of life have outstripped our progress on the political plane to the extent that our economics and our politics are perpetually falling out of gear with one another. On the economic plane, the world has been organized into a single-embracing unit of activity. On the political plane, [nation-states] have been growing . . . more numerous and the national consciousness more acute. The tension between these two antithetical tendencies has been producing a series of jolts . . . in the social life of humanity.' *See* Cohen, Stephen D., *The Making of United States International Economic Policy* (Praeger Publishers, 1994) 3.

[8] In general, economic efficiency can be defined as meaning three concepts: the degree to which (1) enough output is produced to satisfy all the demand of consumers who value the product in excess of its cost of production (allocative efficiency); (2) output is produced at minimum cost (productive efficiency); and (3) sellers reduce their costs and design new and superior products to satisfy consumer preferences (dynamic efficiency). *See* Milton Handler *et al.*, *Trade Regulation* 3rd ed. (The Foundation Press, Inc., 1990).

[9] Cohen, *supra* note 7, at 4.

[10] Ibid.

[11] Ibid., at 7.

[12] Ibid.

[13] Ibid.

[14] Ibid.

[15] In addition to this political economy, some international trade negotiators might have been baffled by the complexity and technicality of economic analysis, which has assisted development of the two-culture syndrome.

[16] *See* Cass, *supra* note 5, at 475.

[17] *See*, e.g., Bowman, Ward S., Jr, *Patent and Antitrust Law: A Legal and Economic Appraisal* (University of Chicago Press, 1973); Bork, Robert H., *The Antitrust Paradox: A Policy at War with Itself* (Free Press, 1978); Posner, Richard A., *Antitrust Law: An Economic Perspective* (University of Chicago Press, 1976); Areeda, P. and Turner, D.F., 'Predatory Pricing and Related Practices Under Section 2 of the Sherman Act', 88 Harv. L. Rev. 697 (1975).

[18] *See* Cass, *supra* note 5, at 476.

[19] Panel Report in *Korea Alcoholic Beverages*, para 7.4. This view was followed by the Panel in *Chile Alcoholic Beverages*. *See infra* note 38 and accompanying text.

[20] In other words, whereas the emphasis of competition law ought to be on 'preserving a desirable degree of competition' against action by the market participants, that of GATT Art. III is on preventing members from applying internal taxation so as to afford protection to domestic production.

[21] When applying GATT Art. III, panels must take into account the 'potential' competition which would materialize between the products concerned in the absence of the tax differential in dispute, in addition to the 'actual' competition existing under current taxation conditions. In contrast, competition authorities tend to consider tax differentials as a permanent barrier to competition and disregard any additional competition which may arise from removing that barrier. As a result, the scope of the 'relevant product' markets defined for competition purposes will generally be narrower than the scope of 'directly competitive products' defined for the purposes of Art. III. *See Korea Alcoholic Beverages* Panel Report, para 7.4. For details, *see* Chapter II, at 3.2.

[22] *See* the Preamble of the GATT. *See also* Chapter II, notes 154 and 158–162 and accompanying texts. There is no doubt that the guiding economic premiss that underlies the entire GATT/WTO system is 'open trade'. In a liberal economic system, government does not thwart private parties in their attempts to enter voluntary transactions, and taxes are stable, predictable, and non-prohibitive. The General Agreement is liberal in this sense. Interventions by government in liberal exchange across frontiers to make fair may be the political price of liberalism, but such interventions are themselves its antithesis. *See* Wolf, M., 'Why trade liberalization is a good idea', in J. Michael Finger and Andrzej Olechowski, eds, *The Uruguay Round, A Handbook on the Multilateral Trade Negotiations* (World Bank, 1987) 14. By exploiting the law of comparative advantage, liberal trade policies permit the unrestricted

flow of the best goods and services at the lowest prices, thereby increasing total world wealth. Under the law of comparative advantage, resources are allocated efficiently across and within industries in response to competitive pressures from imports. Both of these phenomena lead to product specialization and increased firm size that in turn lowers the unit cost of goods and services. The role that international trade rules play in fostering liberal trade manifests itself in two important ways. First, specialization and economies of scale become possible because of secure access to a barrier-free international market. Secondly, increased international competition leads to product and process innovation, further reducing costs and expanding consumer choices. *See* Bhala, R. and Kennedy, K., *World Trade Law, The GATT-WTO System, Regional Arrangements and US Law* (Lexis Law Publishing, Charlottesville,Va, 1998) 3, 4.

[23] The Preamble of the GATT bears this out: '. . . Being desirous of contributing to these objectives by entering into reciprocal and mutually advantageous arrangements directed to the substantial reduction of tariffs and other barriers to trade and *to the elimination of discriminatory treatment in international commerce*, Have through their Representatives agreed as follows . . .' (emphasis added)

[24] *See infra* note 29 and accompanying text.

[25] Some views on antitrust law even argue that minimization of deadweight losses, and indifference to the transfer of wealth resulting from the monopoly overcharge, should provide the exclusive focus of antitrust policy. *See* Handler *et al.*, *supra* note 8, at 200. For a more general and theoretical treatment, *see* Posner, *supra* note 17. Concerning the concept of 'deadweight loss', *see* Chapter II, note 166.

[26] Judge Posner's statement in an antitrust (monopoly) case confirms this assertion: 'Opinion about the offense of monopolization has undergone an evolution. Forty years ago it was thought that even a firm with a lawful monopoly . . . could not be allowed to defend its monopoly against would-be competitors by tactics otherwise legitimate; it had to exercise special restraint—perhaps, indeed, had to hold its prices high, to encourage new entry. . . . Later, as the emphasis of antitrust policy shifted from the protection of competition as a *process of rivalry* to the protection of competition as *a means of promoting economic efficiency* . . . It became recognized that the lawful monopolist should be free to compete like everyone else; otherwise the antitrust laws would be holding an umbrella over inefficient competitors . . . Today it is clear that a firm with lawful monopoly power has no general duty to help its competitors, whether by holding a price umbrella over their heads or by otherwise pulling its competitive punches . . .' (*Olympia Equipment Leasing Co. v Western Union Telegraph*, 797 F.2d 370, 375–76 (7th Cir. 1986), cert. denied, 480 US 934 (1987) (emphasis added)).

[27] In this light, one might be able to say that, whereas the GATT is at a stage of protecting the 'process of rivalry' between competitors, the competition law goes one step further to protect competition as a 'means' of promoting economic efficiency. *See* ibid. It could be said that competition 'means' flexibility, thus, a more efficiency-oriented latitude than the rigid GATT non-discrimination path is created.

Of course, the GATT (or the 'trade law') includes not only non-discrimination provisions but others as well, notably fair trade provisions. It is difficult to say that the non-discrimination → efficiency path for the non-discrimination provisions is equally relevant for the fair trade provisions which aim at providing domestic industry with a certain relief against material injury. These fair trade provisions in antidumping or subsidy law focus on *injury to domestic competitors*, rather than on *injury to competition* as required under competition law.

Despite this mixed formula of the trade law, considering that non-discrimination provisions rather than fair trade provisions represent the main purpose of the trade law, one could generalize the above path as that of the trade law and use it for comparison with the path of competition law.

[28] Regardless of whether the competing producers or products are domestic or foreign.

[29] *See* League of Nations, *Recommendations of the Economic Committee Relating to Commercial Policy* (Geneva, June 1929), LN Docs. C.138.M.53.1929.II, pp.1–3.

[30] In order to realize free trade through market openness, protection of the producers' competitive relationship is indispensable. This protection will lead to an increase of consumer welfare.

[31] In the United States, the notion of consumer welfare has been an undefeatable primary focus of antitrust law, especially since the late 1970s and 1980s when the 'Chicago School' became the mainstream of jurisprudence. Such a position is well expressed in Richard Posner's *Antitrust Law* (*supra* note 17), and Robert Bork's *The Antitrust Paradox* (1978) and numerous US Supreme Court decisions since *Continental T.V., Inc. v GTE Sylvania Inc.* 433 US 36 (1977). Several times, the US Supreme Court has declared that the purpose of antitrust laws is the furtherance of consumer welfare. *See*, e.g., *National Collegiate Athletic Ass'n v Board of Regents of Univ. of Okla.*, 486 US 85, 107 (1984); *Reiter v. Sonotone Corp.*, 442 US 330, 343 (1979). In the antitrust legal literature, consumer welfare has been used synonymously with the combination of productive and allocative efficiency and the sum of producer and consumer surplus. *See* the following statement by the US FTC: 'Antitrust policy wisely disfavors monopoly, but it also seeks to promote vigorous competitive behavior. Indeed, the essence of the competitive process is to induce firms to become more efficient and to pass the benefits of the efficiency along to consumers...' (*Re E.I. Dupont De Nemours & Co*, 3 Trade Reg. Rep. (CCH) π 21,770 (FTC Oct. 20, 1980)).

In contrast, EU competition law has been known to include diverse aims other than maximization of consumer welfare. Because Arts 81 and 82 (ex 85 and 86) arise as a part of the Treaty of Rome, they have been developed within the broader contexts that the Treaty creates, such as elimination of structural constraints on competition including territorial restrictions, bolstering small or regional firms by permitting cooperation, single-market integration, etc. In general, EU law considers such aspects as loss of jobs, impact on exports, or public interest other than economic efficiency.

This difference between the two competition laws seems to arise mostly from the different stage of development of the two regions. As Sir Leon Brittan stated, the Chicago School approach is not directly relevant to EC competition policy because the approach presupposes the existence of an integrated market, something the European Union still seeks to develop. *See* Brittan, L., *European Competition Policy: Keeping The Playing-Field Level* (The Brasseys, Inc., 1992). *See also* Jebsen, P. and Stevens, R., 'Assumptions, Goals And Dominant Undertakings: The Regulation of Competition Under Article 86 of The European Union', 64 Antitrust L.J. 443 (1996).

Despite this difference of coverage, if asked to pick only one aim of competition law, both the US and the EU will not hesitate to choose 'consumer welfare'.

[32] *See* Gifford, Daniel J. and Matsushita, M., 'Antitrust or Competition Laws Viewed in a Trading Context: Harmony or Dissonance?', in Jagdish Bhagwati and Robert Hudec eds., *Fair Trade and Harmonization*, vol. 2 (MIT Press, 1996) 298. *See also Korea Alcoholic Beverages* Panel Report, para 10.81 ('It is not illogical that markets be defined more broadly when implementing laws primarily designed to protect competitive opportunities than when implementing laws designed to protect the actual mechanisms of competition.'). For an excellent debate concerning the difference between the two laws, *see* Elzinga, Kenneth G.,

'The Interface of Trade/Competition Law & Policy: An Economist's Perspective', 56 Antitrust L.J. 439 (1987) and Eckes, Alfred E., 'The Interface of Trade/Competition Law & Policy: An Economist's Perspective: An ITC Commissioner's Perspective', 56 Antitrust L.J. 417 (1987).

[33] As international trade and financial exchange have increased, the law regulating international business and financial transactions has gained added significance. The changed environment of international business has affected a number of domestic legal issues. Antitrust considerations, for example, cannot sensibly be framed solely in terms of domestic competition when businesses compete in a global market. Securities fraud cannot be a matter of purely domestic concern in a world market for securities, linked electronically and operating around the clock. Private international law, international trade law (and other bodies of quasi-public international law relating to finance and commerce), and cognate areas of domestic law have been affected by the growth of international commercial and financial dealings. In this environment, competition policy focused on only one state's welfare cannot be beneficial, at least in the long run.

[34] The International Trade Organization Charter was developed under the auspices of the Economic and Social Council of the newly-formed United Nations, which appointed a Preparatory Committee of 19 nations in February 1946, to draft a convention to be considered at an International Conference on Trade and Employment. The Draft Convention was considered at sessions in London ('London Conference') (*Report of the First Session of the Preparatory Committee of the United Nations Conference on Trade and Development*, UN Doc.E/PC/T/33 (1946), reprinted as *Preliminary Draft Charter for the International Trade Organization of the United Nations*, Department of State Pub. 2728, Commercial Policy Series 98 (1946)) and Geneva ('Geneva Conference') from 10 April to 22 August 1947 (*Report of the Second Session of the Preparatory Committee of the United Nations Conference on Trade and Employment*, UN Doc. E/PC/T/186 (1947), reprinted as *Draft Charter for the International Trade Organization of the United Nations*, Department of State Pub. 2927, Commercial Policy Series 106 (1947)). This Draft followed a prior revision of the 'London Draft' by the Drafting Committee of the Preparatory Committee in New York ('New York Conference') which met from 20 January to 25 February 1947 (*Report of the Drafting Committee of the Preparatory Committee of the United Nations Conference on Trade and Employment*, UN Doc. E/PC/T/34/Rev.1 (1947)). A final conference in Havana ('Havana Conference'), from 21 November 1947 to 24 March 1948, produced the 'Havana Charter', the Charter for an International Trade Organization (*Report of Committees and Principle Sub-Committees of the United Nations Conference on Trade and Employment*, UN Doc. ICITO 1/8 (1948); *United Nations Conference on Trade and Employment, Final Act and Related Documents*, UN Doc. E/Conf.2/78 (1948)).

[35] 'REALIZING the aims set forth in the Charter of the United Nations, particularly the attainment of the higher standards of living, full employment and conditions of economic and social progress and development ... TO THIS END they pledge ... to promote national and international action designed to attain the following objectives: ... 4. To promote on a reciprocal and mutually advantageous basis the reduction of tariffs and other barriers to trade and the elimination of discriminatory treatment in international commerce ... 6. To facilitate through the promotion of mutual understanding, consultation and co-operation, the solution of problems relating to international trade in the fields of employment, economic development, commercial policy, business practices and commodity policy....' (Art. 1 of Charter for the International Trade Organization (Havana Charter), Final Act and

Related Documents, United Nations Conference on Trade and Employment, Havana, Cuba, 21 November 1947–24 March 1948; UN Doc. ICITO/1/4 (1948).)

[36] 'Each Member shall take appropriate measures and shall co-operate with the Organization to prevent, on the part of private or public commercial enterprises, business practices affecting international trade which restrain competition, limit access to markets, or foster monopolistic control, whenever such practices have harmful effects on the expansion of production or trade and interfere with the achievement of any of the other objectives set forth in Article 1.' (Art. 46:1, Havana Charter, Chapter V)

[37] This point is borne out by the relationship between antidumping law and competition law. *See* the following remarks (Gifford and Matsushita, *supra* note 32, at 298–9): 'If the trading nations broadly agree on efficient resource allocation as an objective, then they should be willing to consider reforming their domestic laws to confirm to that objective. Their antitrust laws largely conform to this efficiency objective. Their trade laws do not conform to that objective. ... It is not impossible to rethink the premises of antidumping and countervailing duty laws. Such a reexamination of premises carries the potential for a thorough revamping of current trade laws. Were new trade legislation designed with conscious attention to the efficiency norms which underlie antitrust laws, that legislation would be both revolutionary and paradoxically a return to the efficiency concerns implicitly underlying the predatory-pricing provisions of the 1916 Antidumping Act. It would also bring coherence into the laws governing domestic and international trade. ... The 1916 Antidumping Act clearly took the form of an antitrust law. Subsequent legislation, beginning with the 1921 Antidumping Act, has traceable roots in the earlier legislation. It is now time to reconsider the policies underlying the trade laws and to bring them into line with the efficiency norms underlying antitrust law.' The authors argue that existing antidumping legislation should switch the focus from protection to efficiency and open markets as the guiding principles.

[38] *Chile Alcoholic Beverages* Panel Report, para 7.87.

[39] In this light, one should note that, these days, in competition law heavy focus is given to identifying potential sources of competition and to preventing possible distortions in the future (in addition to correcting current distortions of competitive relationships). In other words, even though competition law does not look at 'potential competition' as defined in the GATT, it still pays attention to latent sources of competition (this is 'potential competition' as defined in competition law context) and market development factors in the near future. Policy consideration in these aspects is one of the important criteria in competition law decisions, especially in the merger context. The issue of protecting consumer 'expectation' is becoming more important in the jurisprudence of competition law. *See supra* notes 25 and 26. *See also* Kauper, Thomas E., 'The Problem of Market Definition Under EC Competition Law', 20 Fordham Int'l L.J. 1682, 1726–7 (1997).

[40] *See* Chapter II, notes 122–127 and 344, and Chapter IV, notes 7–13 and accompanying texts.

[41] One good thing about a universal language of economics is that, in many cases, it could be value neutral. Cultures could have different goals. Without intervening in the goal-setting process, the language could reveal a relationship between the goal and its means. It provides a useful tool for examining whether specific measures, allegedly taken to implement the goals, are really honest ones or, rather, disguised ones under the cloak of false justification. In this light, it can be said that what economics does in most cases is to 'translate',

not to 'judge'. The latter function is usually reserved for a more appropriate entity, such as the GATT panel. For instance, in likeness or substitutability analysis, what economics shows is how much elasticity exists between two products in comparison (translating complicated market factors into a single economic language). Whether the specific amount of elasticity is enough to define the relationship between the products or not is determined by the judgement of the panel in charge. For details, *see* Chapters II and III.

[42] *See* Chapter II, note 69.

[43] *See* Cass, *supra* note 5, at 484.

[44] An interesting question that arises is whether drafters want to give discretion to panels or to contracting parties? It is possible to think that drafters might not have wanted panels to brood over discretion, but they could not have agreed on less vague substantive positions. Indeed, the vagueness might have been the only choice that would accommodate the conflict of interests among parties. Another question that is worthy of consideration is whether the discretion is necessary if the WTO Agreement itself is inconsistent and incoherent?

[45] *See supra* note 41 and accompanying text.

[46] This is why Milton Friedman emphasizes the idea that economic analysis takes as the measure of its success the accuracy of its descriptions and predictions. *See* Friedman, M., *Essays in Positive Economics* (University of Chicago Press, 1953) 30–43.

[47] This is true unless a comprehensive amendment of relevant GATT provisions, or a definitive interpretation of 'likeness' concepts in each provision, is provided by the legislative function of the WTO.

It should be noted that such a value judgement by the tribunals is exercised, in particular, in determining or considering such phrases as '*sustainable* development', '*optimal* use of resources'. Value judgements are also exercised with regard to the prevention of circumvention, further negotiation of trade liberalization, etc.

[48] This analysis, while not fully determinate, is built on certain propositions that almost any competent economist would accept. For instance, demand curves will be negatively sloped, price declines for one product will lead to a decreased demand for substitutable goods, and one has to make decisions in order that benefits exceed costs. This relatively well developed set of accepted propositions and tools for transparent analysis exerts a steady pull on decisions made through this analysis; objective evidences obtained through the economic analyses provide clear proof regarding definitions of benefit and cost, thus enabling thorough cost/benefit analysis. *See* Cass, *supra* note 5, at 490.

[49] Ibid.

[50] *See* Plato, *Protagoras* (Benjamin Jowett and Martin Ostwald trans., Liberal Arts Press 1965) 20–21.

[51] Ibid.

[52] *See* Bell, J. and Schokkaert, E., 'Interdisciplinary Theory and Research on Justice', in Klaus R. Scherer, ed., *Justice: Interdisciplinary Perspectives* (Cambridge University Press, 1992) 237.

[53] With regard to the role of 'justification' in acquiring states' 'observance of international law', Professor Thomas Franck suggests that states are likely to obey norms of international law that have a high degree of 'legitimacy'. Franck defines legitimacy as 'a property of a rule or rulemaking institution which itself exerts a pull toward compliance on those addressed normatively because those addressed believe that the rule or institution has come into being

and operates in accordance with generally accepted principles of right process' (Franck, T., *The Power of Legitimacy Among Nations* (Oxford University Press, 1990) 24 (emphasis omitted)). *See also* Franck's earlier article, 'Legitimacy in the International System', 82 AJIL 705 (1988).

[54] 'An international institution can provide an additional buffer for national policy officials to make arguments in favor of the goals of an international institution. They can say that their nation is constrained by the international law and must obey these obligations' (Jackson, John H., *The World Trading System—Law and Policy of International Economic Relations*, 2nd ed. (The MIT Press, Cambridge, Mass, London, 1998)) 349.

[55] *See infra* note 58, and Chapter II, note 100 and accompanying texts.

[56] *See supra* note 6. In 60 BC, Julius Caesar established a triumvirate with Pompei and Crassus to rule the Roman world. After Crassus' death, disputes led to civil war between the followers of Caesar and Pompei. Caesar defeated Pompei in Spain in 45 BC. Julius Caesar returned to Rome and broke the tradition which prevented generals from bringing their troops into the city, i.e. 'crossing the Rubicon River'. Caesar was declared perpetual dictator of Rome in February 44 BC. Although he was assassinated in 44 BC by a conspiracy of senators who feared that his dictatorship would destroy the republic, Caesar's kingdom continued under the rule of his adopted son and heir, Octavius, who later became the first emperor of Rome under the name Augustus.

[57] *See* Chapter II, note 56.

[58] The Appellate Body in *Japan Alcoholic Beverages* prescribed that: 'The Panel did not say that cross-price elasticity of demand is '*the* decisive criterion' for determining whether products are 'directly competitive or substitutable'... We agree. And, we find the Panel's legal analysis of whether the products are 'directly competitive or substitutable products'... to be correct.' (*Japan Alcoholic Beverages* Appellate Report, sec. H2(a))

Similarly, the Panel in *Korea Alcoholic Beverages* stated that: 'Quantitative analysis, while helpful, should not be considered necessary.' Also, in *Japan Alcoholic Beverages* the Appellate Body 'approved the examination of the economic concept of substitution as one means of examining the relevant markets... the use of cross-price elasticity of demand was approved...'. *See Korea Alcoholic Beverages* Panel Report, paras 10.42; 10.44. *See* further Chapter II, notes 110–112 and accompanying texts.

But it should be noted that the tribunal started accepting the 'important evidential force' of the economic analysis, especially as to the results of high demand substitutability. *See* Chapter II, notes 113–115 and accompanying texts.

[59] *See* Vermulst, E., Mavroidis, P.C. and Waer, P., 'The Functioning of the Appellate Body After Four Years: Towards Rule Integrity' [1999] *Journal of World Trade* 32–33.

[60] Ibid.

[61] *See* Franck, T., *Fairness in International Law and Institutions* (Clarendon Press, 1995) 26–46.

[62] *See supra* note 58.

[63] With regard to the nature of political and economic order in international relations, *see* generally Keohane, R.O. and Nye, J.S., *Power and Interdependence* (Addison-Wesley Publishing Co., 1989); Boyle, F.A., *Foundations of World Order: The Legalist Approach to International Relations 1898–1921* (Duke University Press, 1999); Bull, H., *The Anarchical Society: A Study of Order in World Politics* (Columbia University Press, 1995); Cox, R.W. and Sinclair, T.J., *Approaches to World Order: Cambridge Studies in International Relations* (Cambridge University Press, 1996).

II APPLYING THE RELATIONSHIP TO GATT LAW: ACROSS THE RUBICON!

[1] In undertaking the interpretation of likeness or substitutability, Art. 31 and Art. 32 of the Vienna Convention should be closely referred to: Vienna Convention on the Law of Treaties (VCLT), UN Doc. A/CONF.39/27 (1969), reprinted in (1969) 8 ILM 679. Among the three possible ways of treaty interpretation—i.e. 'subjective' (focusing on intentions of the drafting parties), 'objective' (focusing on text), and the 'teleological' (focusing on object or purpose) approach—it seems that the Vienna Convention adopts the textual approach complemented by the teleological approach. *See Yearbook of the International Law Commission*, Vol. II, p. 220, 1966 (in its commentary to the provision, the International Law Commission suggests the textual approach as a starting point for interpretation). Thus, although interpretations of the phrase in one context can have an influence by analogy on an interpretation of the phrase in another context, it is important to relate the interpretation to the purposes of the GATT provision being construed (*see* VCLT Art. 31.1). On the other hand, the principle that the object and purpose are to be referred to in determining the meaning of the terms of the treaty and not as an independent basis for interpretation should also be borne in mind. *See* Jennings, R., *Oppenheims' International Law*, Vol. I, 9th ed. (Jennings and Watts, eds, Longman 1992); *International Status of South West Africa* [1962] ICJ Rep 128, at 336. As the Appellate Body confirmed in *United States Gasoline*, it should be noted that one of the corollaries of the general rule of interpretation in the Vienna Convention is that interpretation must give meaning and effect to all the terms of the treaty (*United States—Standards for Reformulated and Conventional Gasoline*, WT/DS2/R 1996).

In reality, it is not easy to draw any clear distinction among those approaches. Further, throughout the GATT history, the solutions of disputes have often been founded on compromises based on the object and purpose of the provisions and the Agreement as a whole, and not necessarily on the wording of the relevant provision. Also, reference must be made to the principle of 'effective interpretation', that one should choose the interpretation that most effectively ensures the fulfilment of the objective or purpose of the treaty. *See Yearbook of the International Law Commission, supra*, p. 219; Brownlie, I., *Principles of Public International Law* (Clarendon Press, 1990) 631; Jennings, and Watts, *supra*, pp. 1278–81. *See also Japan Alcoholic Beverages* Appellate Report, sec. F. Further regard deserves to be had to such practical considerations as the incoherent wording of several provisions, the lack of treaty amendment despite fast changes in international trade environment, etc. These factors advocate object and purpose as an important source of treaty interpretation.

Nonetheless, this does not deprive the textual approach of status as a fundamental starting point for treaty interpretation. The clear wording of a provision should prevail, even when this may undermine what may be regarded as the objects and purposes of GATT or the provision in question. Within this limitation, one can raise the question of what weight should be attributed to such sources as 'objective and purpose' and 'intention' (as recorded in preparatory works) to complement the primary source of 'textual meaning' of the treaty. This 'text-based teleological' approach forms the basis of the interpretation of likeness or substitutability in this book.

[2] This thought process may be transformed into the series of questions that follow. Answers to these questions will be needed to complete the task of the present chapter. The issue in question is whether Products A and B are 'like' or 'directly competitive or

substitutable' products. Proper steps to answering these questions are:

(1) *Step 1 (preliminary understanding of the concepts and generalization)*
—What is the general meaning of 'like', or 'substitutable'?
—In general, what is the distinction between the terms 'like' and 'substitutable'?
—What does the term 'directly' mean? What role does the term play in the various GATT texts of 'directly competitive' or 'directly substitutable' (or substituted)?
—What is the ordinary meaning of the terms 'identical', 'similar', and 'directly competitive or substitutable'?

(2) *Step 2 (identifying evidential elements to define likeness)*
—Which elements should be considered in order to determine identical, similar, or directly competitive or substitutable relationships, as defined by their ordinary meaning?
—Do such elements as products' properties, nature, quality, end-use, and tariff classification suggest that the two products are sharing an identical, similar, or directly competitive or substitutable relationship?

(3) *Step 3 (grouping evidential elements into several factors; setting up model for analysis)*
—What is the marketplace? In the marketplace, how can such evidential elements be systematically grouped?
—What are the relevant factors by which 'likeness' or 'substitutability' could be identified and evidenced? Are there any other factors to be included in the Model?
—What effects do demand- or supply-side constraints in the market have on the scope of the concepts?
—What is the appropriate methodology used to find out such 'likeness' or 'substitutability'?
—What are the possible standards (threshold) to be used by the methodology to determine a sufficient degree of 'likeness' or 'substitutability'?
—How much discretion does the tribunal have in applying this methodology?

(4) *Step 4 (application of the model to specific context of relevant provision)*
—Are there certain types of provision that may be grouped together?
—What is the nature of the provision concerned? Is it a general (or fundamental) provision, or an exceptional provision? Is the provision primarily aimed at facilitating free trade?
—Does a broad interpretation of 'like' or 'substitutable' help to achieve the purpose of the provision?
—Is there any indication by the GATT drafters in this regard?
—Is it necessary to adjust the general scope of 'likeness' or 'substitutability', obtained in *Step 1*, according to the specific needs of broadness or narrowness of the concept deducted here?
—How does one weigh each factor established in *Step 2* in the specific contexts of each provision?
—What is the result of applying the model to each provision?

[3] Again, these concepts largely depend on the purpose of each provision in which they are employed, or on the specific context in which the product relationship is invoked. This point is examined in Chapter III. Here, since our task is to lay an initial basis for the term 'likeness', the various terms indicating product relationship may be divided into several conceptual categories according to the ordinary meaning of the language used. Of course there still remains the question of with which tool these conceptual divisions should be measured;

this is why we need the section 2 of this chapter, evidential factors to define likeness or sub-stitutability, in that it provides the necessary tools to define 'likeness' or 'substitutability'.

[4] *See* Art. 2.6 of the Antidumping Agreement and Art. 15.1, fn 46 of the SCM Agreement: 'Throughout this Agreement the term "like product" ("produit similaire") shall be interpreted to mean a *product which is identical, i.e. alike in all respects to the product under consideration*, or in the absence of such a product, another product which, although not alike in all respects, has characteristics closely resembling those of the product under consideration.' (emphasis added)

[5] Ibid.

[6] Sometimes this one characteristic could be significant enough to outweigh the others.

[7] Since these concepts will be used for defining likeness in each provision of the GATT, too broad a range of concept, such as 'similar', has less utility as a conceptual tool because it may be unable to reflect delicate differences of likeness among relevant provisions.

The Appellate Body seems to agree with the necessity of this conceptual division. In *EC Asbestos* it stressed that 'products may share only very few characteristics or qualities, or they may share many. Thus, in the abstract, the term "like" can encompass a spectrum of differing degrees of "likeness" or "similarity"' (*EC—Measures Affecting Asbestos and Asbestos-containing Products*, WT/DS135/AB/R (12 March 2001), para 92).

[8] In other words, the concept of 'similar' as one of our analytical tools is much narrower than the term 'similar' which is used in daily life. For instance, being asked to purchase an item 'similar' to beef, many people would end up buying pork at the supermarket in the absence of beef.

[9] Emphasis added.

[10] *See Korea Alcoholic Beverages* Panel Report, para 10.40.

[11] 'One could say that woollen sweaters and coal can be substituted for each other. If you are cold, you could either put on a sweater or throw another lump of coal on the fire. Washing machines and socks could be substitutable. The easier and cheaper the availability of laundry facilities, the fewer socks a person needs in order to have a constant clean supply. With this view of substitutability, baby carriages and wheelbarrows could be substitutable!' Ibid. para 6.246.

'For every product, substitutes exist. But a relevant market cannot meaningfully encompass that infinite range. The circle must be drawn narrowly to exclude any other product to which, within reasonable variations in price, only a limited number of buyers will turn; in technical terms, products whose "cross-elasticities of demand" are small.' *Times-Picayune Publishing Co. v United States*, 345 US 594 (1953), 612 (antitrust case)).

[12] When consumers buy a certain product or service, they have a certain primary purpose of the consumption. In other words, they consume the product because they believe the main utility of the product can satisfy their particular needs or tastes. Directly substitutable goods should be able to serve the purpose and satisfy the needs or tastes. The Appellate Body in *EC Asbestos* emphasizes this point in the context of Art. III:4: *see EC Asbestos* Appellate Report, para 101. The difference of consumption purposes between a vacation ticket and a car; a meal in a restaurant and shoes/TV set, and an exercise machine and kitchen paper is evident (unless a substantial number of consumers tend to waste money randomly without purpose). Concerning the relationship between an exercise machine and a skimmed milk product, *see infra* note 38.

[13] In *Canada Periodicals*, Canada submitted that Canadian magazines had many functions, including as an advertising medium and a communication medium; and that US magazines might be directly substitutable for Canadian magazines as regards the former function, but

not substitutable at all as regards the latter function because of their different editorial content. *See infra* note 117.

[14] But, *see infra* note 14 and accompanying text.

[15] That is, P can be consumed for two different purposes and in two different ways (each purpose and way should be statistically meaningful enough to be a dominant reason to buy the product).

[16] The same thing could be said concerning the relationship between an exercise machine and skimmed milk, illustrated above. The reasons why people go to a health club would be various: to become fit, to have access to very expensive equipment, even to meet friends, etc. Of course, if two particular products in comparison are overwhelmingly in one market, i.e. a vast majority of the product is used for one of its multiple uses, they can be in a direct relationship of substitution despite their multiple uses.

[17] In general, if the demand for B increases as the price of A rises (or vice versa), A and B are substitute goods. If the demand for X decreases as the price of Y rises, X and Y are complementary goods.

[18] If tea prices rise, the demand for tea will decrease while the demand for coffee increases. As a result of this increasing coffee demand, the demand for sugar will go up as well.

[19] Wagons and automobiles could be another example.

[20] This shows that the likeness concept can be changed according to technological innovations and resulting business cycles.

[21] If one interprets the term 'directly' as being 'above a certain *de minimis* level', this problem of overbroad coverage would become serious unless the *de minimis* standard was established at quite a high level.

[22] *See* Introduction, notes 7, 8 and 9, and *infra* note 25 and accompanying texts.

[23] The US proposal presented at the Geneva Conference referred to 'competitive products' only in the national treatment clause. *See* Chapter III, note 112. The proposal was controversial and, during the initial discussions, one delegate suggested that the term should be clarified. *See* UN Doc. E/PC/T/A/PV/9, at 14; UN Doc. E/PC/T/C.II/32, at 4. The proposal was subsequently referred to a sub-committee which redrafted the provision. The sub-committee added the terms 'directly' and 'substitutable', and this revision of the wording was accepted without comment. *See* UN Docs. E/PC/T/174, at 5–6 and 20, and E/PC/T/A/PV/43, at 19–28. The GATT preparatory records thus indicate that the terms were included to clarify the meaning of the provision, and possibly to restrict its scope of application. *See* Fauchald, Introduction, note 11, at 148–9.

[24] In order to examine 'demand substitutability', three methods are available in general: 'cross-price elasticity of demand', 'constant-price elasticity of demand', and 'own-price elasticity of demand'.

Cross-price elasticity between products X and Y is the responsiveness of demand for product X to percentage change in the relative price of product Y. If a slight decrease in the price of X causes a considerable number of customers of Y to switch to X, it would be an indication that a high cross-elasticity of demand exists between them, that the two products are good substitutes, and that the products compete in the same market.

Constant-price elasticity between X and Y is the responsiveness of demand between X and Y, when the relative price between the two is constant. A 'non-availability test' examines the constant-price elasticity of demand. *See infra* notes 106 and 107, and accompanying texts. *See also* Appendix III at the end of this book.

Own-price elasticity of demand for product X is a measure of the responsiveness of demand for X to percentage change in its own price. *See supra* note 11.

In general, elasticity of substitution is measured by the cross-price elasticity.

[25] *See* the French version of GATT; Fauchald, Introduction, note 11, at 148 (emphasis added).

[26] *See supra* notes 21 and 22, and accompanying texts.

[27] The plain meaning of 'competitive' involves an objective assessment of the marketing relationship, which is often referred to by producers (or suppliers). The plain meaning of 'substitutable' involves a consumption–utility concept. Consumers tend to view products based on this concept.

[28] GATT Art. XIX:1(a) reads: 'If [there are] increased quantities and . . . serious injury to domestic *producers* in that territory of *like or directly competitive* products, the contracting party shall be free . . . . to suspend . . .' (emphasis added).

[29] By the same token, one could argue that the term 'directly competitive' in Annex I of the SCM Agreement is used to reflect *producers'* (export goods producers and domestic goods producers) perspective. The Annex illustrates a list of export subsidies prohibited by the Agreement. One of these export subsidies is 'the provision by governments . . . of imported or domestic products or services for use in the production of exported goods, on terms or conditions more favourable than for provision of like or *directly competitive* products or services for use in the production of goods for domestic consumption, if . . . such terms or conditions are more favourable than those commercially available . . .' (Annex I(d) of the SCM Agreement). *See* Chapter III, note 260.

In the same light, a series of US statutes having a purpose of producer protection are employing the same term, 'like or directly competitive': (1) Escape Clause of the US Trade Act of 1974 adopts almost the same language as above (19 USC 2251 (a)); (2) Generalized System of Preferences provision of the US Trade Act of 1974 reads '. . . [exercising authority to extend Generalized System of Preferences] . . . the President shall have due regard for . . . [among others] . . . the anticipated impact of such action on United States *producers* of *like or directly competitive* products . . .' (19 USC 2461(3)); and (3) Market Disruption provision of the Act prescribes (in the context of protection of domestic industry against imports from Communist countries) that market disruption exists whenever 'imports of an article, *like or directly competitive* with an article produced by such domestic industry, are increasing rapidly . . .' (19 USC 2436(e)(2)(A)).

[30] Early in the development of modern price theory it was recognized that the conduct and performance of firms and industries does not depend solely on the character of the demand, cost–output, and similar controlling relationship, plus the character of the firms' motivation (for example, profit maximization), but also on the *structure of the market* in which the firm sells. *See* Handler *et al.*, Chapter I, note 8, at 152. *See also infra* note 39 and accompanying text.

Hence, it should be noted that in some cases, the producers' consideration of the other factors, including substitutability of supply, antidumping, and relationship with competitors, can make the difference between the scope of 'directly competitive' and 'directly substitutable' products. In these cases, the broader scope between the two will determine the coverage of the national treatment obligation because the two phrases are linked by 'or' in Art. III of the GATT.

[31] GATT Art. XI:2 reads: 'The provisions of paragraph 1 of this article shall not extend to . . . (c) Import restrictions on any agricultural or fisheries product, imported in any form, necessary to enforcement of governmental measures which operate: (i) to restrict the quantities of the like domestic product or . . . a domestic product for which the imported product can be *directly substituted*; or (ii) to remove a temporary surplus of the like domestic product, or . . . *directly substituted* [product]' (emphasis added).

[32] Whisky is a grain-based spirit, whereas pisco is a fruit-based spirit (made from grapes).

[33] *See* Lancaster, Kelvin J., 'A New Approach to Consumer Theory', in *Journal of Political Economy*, Vol. LXXIV (April 1966), pp. 132–57.

[34] *Chile Alcoholic Beverages* Panel Report, para 7.82.

[35] *Korea Alcoholic Beverages* Appellate Report, para 115.

[36] The first and the second conditions follow from the texts of the decisions above. The third condition is obtained from the logical corollary that, in order to 'yield satisfaction' or to become 'alternative' ways of satisfying a need or taste, there should not be a significant reduction of consumption utility. Of course, the problem of defining the degree of 'significance' remains.

[37] Unless there happens to be another 'directly competitive' relationship between X and Y or tea and sugar.

[38] Moreover, it is still doubtful whether the two products satisfy the first factor because of the non-reciprocal nature of substitution. (Can an exercise machine substitute for skimmed milk? Yes, but only for rich people.) *See supra* notes 19 and 20, and accompanying texts.

[39] *See supra* note 30.

[40] Paying attention to this difference has little practicality for Art. III of the GATT, in which the second paragraph covers *either* 'directly competitive' or 'directly substitutable' product relationships. But it can have practical value, as can be seen in (say) Art. XIX, in which only the term 'directly competitive' is used.

[41] *See supra* note 31.

[42] *See supra* note 28.

[43] *See Japan Alcoholic Beverages* Panel Report, para 6.22. In the case of Art. III:4, one can raise the issue of whether the coverage of 'like' could be the same as that of 'directly competitive or substitutable'. *See* Chapter III, at 1.2.4.

[44] The wording of Art. III and of the Interpretative Note *Ad* Art. III makes it clear that a distinction must be drawn between, on the one hand, 'like', and, on the other, 'directly competitive or substitutable' products. Such an approach is in conformity with the principle of 'effective treaty interpretation' as laid down in the 'general rule of interpretation' of the Vienna Convention on the Law of Treaties. *See Japan Alcoholic Beverages* Panel Report, para 6.22.

[45] It is interesting to think of the relationship between Korean and Chinese ginseng in different marketplaces. Korean and Chinese ginseng can be considered as being directly substitutable products in the United States; this would not be true at all in the Korean market, because most Koreans have a very strong and persistent historical belief in the effects of their own ginseng. If someone opened a Chinese ginseng shop in Korea, he or she would go bankrupt immediately because, except, perhaps, for some foreign travelers in Korea, no one would shop at a store selling Chinese ginseng.

Indeed, although it was in the context of the aim-and-effect approach, this same issue arose in *US Automobiles* and *US Malt Beverages*. In the former case, the Panel found that vehicles of the same model, year, and even colour could be considered 'unlike' merely because they were sold at different prices; and that vehicles with fuel efficiency below the threshold were unlike those with fuel efficiency above the threshold, in spite of the physical similarity. *See* the Panel Report, *infra* note 201, paras 6.23, 6.1. In the latter case, the Panel found that beers above and below a certain level of alcoholic content were not 'like products', despite the fact that they were found to be 'similar' on the basis of their physical characteristics. *See* the Panel Report, *infra* note 332, paras 5.70–5.77. In the latter case, one might say that measurable physical differences (certain level of alcoholic content) existed between the individual products. Nonetheless, the differences would be microscopic when one approached the threshold.

[46] In this light, the *Japan Alcoholic Beverages* Panel (as confirmed by the Appellate Body) ruled that only vodka and shochu are 'like' products: 'Substantial noticeable differences in physical characteristics exist between the rest of the alcoholic beverages [other than vodka] at dispute and shochu that would disqualify them from being regarded as like products...[Such differences are]...the use of additives...the use of ingredients...appearance [arising from manufacturing processes]'. *See* the Panel Report, para 6.23.

This definition of 'like product' reappears in the *EC Asbestos* case, in which like products are defined as products that share a number of identical or similar characteristics or qualities. *See EC Asbestos* Appellate Report, paras 90–92.

[47] It is interesting to see that the US National Cattlemen's Association announced that China's accession to the WTO should satisfy certain conditions specific to red meats and red meat products. One of these conditions is that China should reduce the tariff for beef from the current level of 40 per cent to 20 per cent, which is the current tariff level for pork. *See China's Accession to WTO and 1999 WTO Negotiations*, <**http://hill.beef.org/files/FSPP/catw9wn.htm**>.

[48] *See infra* notes 220–222, and accompanying texts.

[49] As regards the processed goods problem, the phrase 'in any form' in Art. XI:2 of GATT provides a good start. *See* Chapter III, notes 194–203, and accompanying texts.

[50] For definitions of, and distinctions among, these concepts, *see* this chapter at 1.1 and 1.2 (notes 4–8 and accompanying texts).

[51] Article 32 of Vienna Convention on the Law of Treaties provides that:
'Recourse may be had to supplementary means of interpretation, including the preparatory work of the treaty and the circumstances of its conclusion, in order to confirm the meaning resulting from the application of article 31, or to determine the meaning when the interpretation according to article 31:
   (a) leaves the meaning ambiguous or obscure; or
   (b) leads to a result which is manifestly absurd or unreasonable.'

[52] The Appellate Body prescribes that in the 'like' products case of the first sentence, the third element, 'so as to afford protection', is not separately required and the *de minimis* exception is not applied, as opposed to the 'directly substitutable' products case in the second sentence. *See Japan Alcoholic Beverages* Appellate Report, sec. H1(a). This has little effect on the results of the case because the difference in a *de minimis* exception generates literally a *de minimis* difference and the element, 'so as to afford protection', is easily satisfied through an objective examination of the 'design, architecture and revealing structure' of the measure in question. *See* Chapter III, notes 55, 58, and 59, and accompanying texts.

[53] However, there could be a more practical point of contention when distinguishing 'like' from 'substitutable' in Art. III:2, depending on circumstances; this point will be discussed later. *See* this chapter at 3.2.5 and Chapter III, at 1.2.

[54] As opposed to Art. XIX, in which the two concepts are utilized in a complementary manner. *See* Chapter III, at 3.2.

[55] This classification of concepts is based on the standard meaning of the language and rational inference, as elaborated above. It is natural and reasonable to draw such conceptual divisions when the various provisions of GATT use the same terms as 'identical', 'similar', 'directly', 'competitive', and 'substitutable' to describe the common subject of product relationship.

[56] 'With regard to the interpretation of the term "like or similar products", which occurs some sixteen times throughout the General Agreement, it was recalled that considerable

discussion had taken place...but that no further improvement of the term had been achieved. The Working Party concluded that problems arising from the interpretation of the terms should be examined on a case-by-case basis. This would allow *a fair assessment in each case of the different elements* that constitute a "similar" product. Some criteria were suggested for determining, *on a case-by-case basis*, whether a product is "similar": the product's end-uses in a given market; consumers' tastes and habits, which change from country to country; the product's properties, nature and quality.' (The Report of *Working Party on Border Tax Adjustments*, BISD 18S/97, para 18 (emphasis added).) It should be noted that these factors indicated by the Report explicitly covered all uses of the term throughout the GATT; this was confirmed by the Appellate Body in *Japan Alcoholic Beverages*. *See* the Appellate Report, sec. H1(a).

[57] *See Japan Alcoholic Beverages* Panel and Appellate Report, WT/DS8/R, 1996, paras 6.20 *et seq.* and WT/DS8/AB/R, 1996, sec. H.; Report of the Panel in *United States Gasoline*, para 6.8.

[58] It is possible that 'end-use *in general*' (or general end-use) could be different from 'end-use *in the given market*'. The former may be said to be a more objective concept than the latter; the former concept is defined according to the universal utility of the product, while the latter is determined according to the particular market condition. Furthermore, consumer tastes and habits (or preferences) can affect end-uses in a given market. In this case, the subjectivity of the concept 'end-use in the given market' becomes greater.

It is possible that two products which boast of a perfect substitutable relationship in market A may be 'not substitutable', or at least 'not directly substitutable', in market B because the substitutability is decided in the market in question and the condition of each market is usually different. Consumers' tastes and habits cannot be properly examined separate from the market in which they are rooted. *See infra* notes 85, 93, and 100, and *supra* note 45 and accompanying texts.

[59] Ibid. *See also* McGovern, Introduction, note 22, at 8.12–3.

[60] The tariff classification factor belongs to the 'objective factor group'. Adopting the Harmonized System (including General Rules of Interpretation) that classifies goods mainly according to product properties, most countries are maintaining more transparent and similar tariff classification systems. Relying on the tariff classification factor, GATT likeness determination will become much more objective. For details, *see infra* notes 237–239 and accompanying texts.

[61] *See EEC—Measures on Animal Feed Proteins (hereinafter 'EEC Animal Feed Proteins')* Panel Report, BISD (25th Supp.) paras 4.1–4.3 (1978). Concerning end-use, *see infra* note 72 and accompanying text. *See also infra* note 367.

[62] *See Spain—Tariff Treatment of Unroasted Coffee ('hereinafter Spain Unroasted Coffee')* Panel Report, paras 4.5–4.8, L/5135—28S/102, BISD (28th Supp.) 102, 112 (1981). For details, *see infra* note 220.

[63] The Panel noted that 'one of the possible methods for determining whether two products were like products' was to compare their end-uses: 'The domestic products subject to the tax are: crude oil, crude oil condensates, and natural gasoline. The imported products subject to the tax are: crude oil, crude oil condensates, natural gasoline, refined and residual oil, and certain other liquid hydrocarbon products. The imported and domestic products are thus either identical or, in the case of imported liquid hydrocarbon products, serve substantially identical end-uses. The imported and domestic products subject to the tax on petroleum are therefore in the view of the Panel "like products" within the meaning of Article III:2.' *See* BISD (34th Supp.) 136, 153 (1990).

[64] *See United States—Standards for Reformulated and Conventional Gasoline, supra* note 1. The Panel did not proceed to Art. I examination for the reason of judicial economy.

[65] *Japan—Customs Duties, Taxes and Labelling Practices on Imported Wines and Alcoholic Beverages*, L/6216-34S/83 (1987). In this case, the Panel found that: (1) imported and Japanese-made gin, vodka, whisky, spirits, brandy, classic liqueurs, and wines are like products between each other; (2) imported vodka and Japanese shochu are like products; and (3) all the above products are directly competitive or substitutable products among each other. Accordingly, the Panel ruled that the mixed tax system of Japan violated Art. III of the GATT by discriminating between those like or directly competitive or substitutable products, through such measures as (1) imposing varied excise rates according to alcoholic strength and raw material content; and (2) adopting an arbitrary grading system, non-taxable thresholds, and the simplified method of tax base assessment. *See* section 5 of the Panel Report in *Japan Wine and Liquor.*

[66] *See infra* note 75 and accompanying text.

[67] In the Japanese case, Japan submitted that the differences in the product's properties, nature, and quality; its end-uses; consumers' tastes and habits; and the HS classification between shochu and vodka prevented the two categories from qualifying as 'like' products.

Against the above submission, the Panel noted: '. . . vodka and shochu *shared most physical characteristics*. In the Panel's view, except for filtration, there is virtual identity in the definition of the two products. The Panel noted that a difference in the physical characteristic of alcoholic strength of two products did not preclude a finding of likeness especially since alcoholic beverages are often drunk in diluted form.' According to the Panel, this dilution mitigates alcoholic strength among different alcoholic beverages having different strengths.

The Panel then reinforced its conclusion with the same reasoning in the 1987 Panel Report: '. . . Japanese shochu (Group A) and vodka could be considered as "like" products in terms of Article III:2 because they were both white/clean spirits, made of similar raw materials, and the end-uses were virtually identical.'

Recalling its conclusions concerning the relationship between Arts II and III, the Panel noted that (1) vodka and shochu were currently classified under the same heading (HS 2208) in the Japanese tariffs; and (2) vodka and shochu were covered by the same Japanese tariff binding at the time of its negotiation. The Appellate Body accepted this approach with an additional note about the tariff classification. With regard to the interpretation of end-use, *see infra* note 75 and accompanying text.

See Japan Alcoholic Beverages Panel Report, paras 4.54, 4.58, 4.59, 5.7, 6.23, and the Appellate Report, sec. H (emphasis added).

In *Korea Alcoholic Beverages* and *Chile Alcoholic Beverages*, the issue of identifying factors concerning the interpretation of the first sentence of Art. III:2 did not arise because the complainants failed to establish a prima facie violation of Art. III:2, first sentence (in the Korean case) or dropped the claim on the first sentence violation, originally contained in the request of the Panel, from the contents of the first complainant's submission to the Panel (in the Chilean case). *See Korea Alcoholic Beverages* Panel Report, para 10.104. *See Chile Alcoholic Beverages* Panel Report, paras 1.9, 3.1–2 (fn 39). With regard to the Art. III:2, second sentence issue, *see infra* notes 111,112 and this chapter at 2.2.

[68] Panels have tended to take account only of 'end-uses in general'. They have inquired about the product's end-use according to the general (universal) use of the product, not according to the market-based end-use reflecting unique consumer preferences or habits. Indeed, panels have maintained a broad and abstract understanding of the end-use concept.

For instance, in *Japan Alcoholic Beverages*, Japan argued that there was a difference between the end-uses of shochu and vodka in that: (1) 60 per cent of consumers drink shochu during meals, but 63 per cent drink 'spirits' after meals; (2) 42 per cent of shochu consumers drink the product in question with hot water, but only 4 per cent, 1 per cent, and none of vodka, gin, and rum consumers, respectively, do so; and (3) no shochu consumers drink the product in question with tonic water, while 26 per cent, 32 per cent, and 15 per cent of vodka, gin, and rum consumers, respectively, do so. *See Japan Alcoholic Beverages* Panel Report, para 4.54. Against this argument, the Panel, noting essentially the same conclusion as in the 1987 *Japan Alcoholic Beverages* Panel Report, prescribed that the end-uses were virtually identical in that the traditional Japanese consumers' habits with regard to shochu provided no reason for not considering vodka to be a 'like' product and that the flexibility in the use of alcoholic drinks and their common characteristics often offered an alternative choice for consumers. *See* ibid., para 6.23.

With regard to end-uses between shochu and whisky, Japan put forward similar arguments that: (1) according to a study in Japan, 60 per cent of shochu consumers drink shochu during meals, while 72 per cent of whisky consumers drink whisky after meals; (2) according to a study submitted by the Community, only 8 per cent of people who consume shochu drink the beverage 'on the rocks', while 68 per cent of bourbon whisky consumers do; none of the bourbon whisky consumers mix their drinks with hot water or juice, while 42 per cent and 37 per cent of shochu consumers do, respectively. *See* ibid., para 4.79. But this argument seems to have been rejected due to the Panel's silence on the matter.

More discussion will follow on this point.

[69] The Appellate Body in *Japan Alcoholic Beverages* justified the above approach as a 'discretionary', not arbitrary, decision: 'In applying the criteria cited in the *Border Tax Adjustments* to the facts of any particular case, and in considering other criteria that may also be relevant in certain cases, *panels can only apply their best judgement* in determining whether in fact products are "like". This will always involve an *unavoidable element of individual, discretionary judgement*. We do not agree with the Panel's observation in paragraph 6.22 of the Panel Report that distinguishing between "like products" and "directly competitive or substitutable products" under Article III:2 is "an arbitrary decision". Rather, we think it is a *discretionary decision* that must be made in considering the various characteristics of products in individual cases. . . . The concept of "likeness" is a relative one that evokes the image of an accordion. The accordion of "likeness" stretches and squeezes in different places as different provisions of the WTO Agreement are applied. The width of the accordion in any one of those places must be determined by the particular provision in which the term "like" is encountered as well as by the context and the circumstances that prevail in any given case to which that provision may apply.' (*Japan Alcoholic Beverages* Appellate Report, sec. H(1)(a) (emphasis added))

The Panel in the same case took a more frank approach: '. . . previous panels had not established a particular test that had to be strictly followed in order to define likeness. Previous panels had used different criteria in order to establish likeness, such as the product's properties, nature and quality, and its end-uses; consumers' tastes and habits, which change from country to country; and the product's classification in tariff nomenclatures. In the Panel's view, "like products" need not be identical in all respects . . . Japan offered no further convincing evidence that the conclusion reached by the 1987 Panel Report was wrong, not even that there had been a change in consumers' preferences in this respect.' (*Japan Alcoholic Beverages* Panel Report, paras 6.21, 6.231)

[70] Cultural autonomy advocates would argue that this trend is not desirable. According to them, more balanced considerations should be given to subjective factors; subjective elements including consumer habits and preferences, traditional consumption patterns, domestic goods preferences, and special uses of the products should not simply be ignored in the name of discretion or judicial economy. In general, consumer habits and preferences are formed throughout a long period. This is especially true in the case dealing with countries having long histories. A variety of combinations of materials, production methods, and strengths are experimented on during this period, but most of them are weeded out through a competitive process. After a long history of trial and error, only particular combinations of product categories can survive and come to be favoured by consumers. Usually these socially established product boundaries have their roots in history, and they tend to remain stable over the years. *See Japan Alcoholic Beverages* Panel Report, para 4.120.

[71] For definition, *see supra* note 58.

[72] *See* the Panel Report, para 4.3.

[73] *See* the Panel Report, para 4.7. The Panel furthermore found it relevant to its examination that unroasted coffee was mainly, if not exclusively, sold in the form of blends, combining various types of coffee. *See infra* note 220 and accompanying text.

[74] *Canada—Certain Measures Concerning Periodicals*, WT/DS31/AB/R (30 June 1997). *See* the Appellate Report, sec. VI B and Panel Report, paras 3.113–9.

[75] *Japan Wine and Liquor* Panel Report, para 5.6.

[76] Ibid. para 5.7.

[77] Article 90 (ex 95) of the Treaty Establishing The European Community (as amended by the Treaty on European Union). *See infra* note 83.

[78] *Commission v United Kingdom* (*Wine and Beer taxes*) (Case 170/78) [1983] ECR 2265.

[79] In this case, the United Kingdom excise tax on light wine, which was calculated per gallon, was about five times that levied on beer, and represented about 38 per cent of the consumer sale price for light wine, versus 25 per cent for beer. The UK produces almost no wine, but substantial amounts of beer. As regards the question of competition between wine and beer, the Court considered that: 'To a certain extent at least, the two beverages in question were capable of meeting identical needs, so that it had to be acknowledged that there was a degree of substitution for one another.... For the purpose of measuring the possible degree of substitution, attention should not be confined to consumer habits in a Member State or in a given region. Those habits, which were essentially variable in time and space, could not be considered to be immutable; *the tax policy of a Member State must not therefore crystallize given consumer habits so as to consolidate an advantage acquired by national industries concerned to respond to them.*' (emphasis added) After comparing the UK tax on the basis of volume, alcoholic content, and product price, the Court determined that the UK's tax system had the effect of subjecting wine imported from other Member States to an additional tax burden so as to afford protection for domestic beer production. *See* Bermann, George A. et al., *European Community Law* (West Publishing Co., 1993) 334–5.

[80] The GATT Preamble mentions 'raising standards of living' and 'expanding the production and exchange of goods'. This is in line with the goals of the EC Treaty as prescribed in the Preamble: 'to ensure the economic and social progress', 'constant improvement of the living and working conditions', and 'steady expansion, balanced trade and fair competition'.

[81] *See* the Preamble of GATT (Chapter I, notes 27–29 and accompanying texts) and the Preamble of the Agreement Establishing the WTO.

[82] EU Members are 'determined to lay the foundations of an ever closer union among the people of Europe', 'anxious to strengthen the unity of economies of people of Europe and to ensure their harmonious development by reducing the differences existing between the various regions and the backwardness of the less favoured regions', and 'desiring to contribute, by means of a common commercial policy, to the progressive abolition of restrictions on international trade'. *See* the Preamble of the EC Treaty.

[83] *See* Chapter III, note 78 and 1.2. *Compare with* Art. 90 (ex 95) of the EC Treaty, which reads: '*No Member State shall impose*, directly or indirectly, on the products of other Member States any internal taxation of any kind in excess of that imposed directly or indirectly on similar domestic products. Furthermore, *no Member State shall impose* on the products of other Member States any internal taxation of such a nature as to afford indirect protection to other products. Member States shall, not later than at the beginning of the second stage, repeal or amend any provisions existing when this Treaty enters into force which conflict with the preceding rules. (emphasis added)

The general interpretation of this provision is that the first paragraph prohibits discriminatory internal taxation and that the second forbids protectionist internal taxation. *See* Bermann *et al.*, *supra* note 79, at 325.

[84] The concept of '*de facto* or *de jure* discriminations' goes back to a pre-GATT period. One can easily find it in the League of Nations documents. *See* e.g., League of Nations, *Recommendations of the Economic Committee Relating to Commercial Policy* (Geneva, June 1929), LN Docs. C.138.M.53.1929.II, p. 2 ('There is one fact which the world does not seem to have fully realized—that for many years past bilateral agreements have been powerless to arrest the progress of protectionism. In certain cases, indeed, the treaty-making methods that have been employed since the war have seemed to encourage this tendency; the exaggerated margin between autonomous tariffs and the tariffs which States contemplate introducing as the ultimate outcome of their negotiations, the deliberately restrictive rates in the minimum tariffs established by certain countries, have produced pernicious results in this respect, and the more so because the general tariffs were put into operation before any negotiations whatever had taken place and their severity was sometimes further aggravated by *de facto* or *de jure* discriminations').

[85] *See* UN Doc. EPCT/A/PV.9, at 7 (1947); Chapter III, note 127 and accompanying text.

[86] The Art. XX 'health exception' is put aside here. Recall that the Japanese Panel's statement quoted above is concerned wholly with the issue in Art. III (it did not touch on the Art. XX issue). (*See supra* note 76 and accompanying text.)

[87] It is doubtful that Hindus would ever consume beef as a substitutable food for pork. It is equally doubtful that Americans or Europeans would eat dog meat as a regular food. Is a dog a substitutable product for beef, or cat?

[88] There are some Asian countries where dog meat is normally consumed as traditional nutritional food. For many consumers in those countries, a live dog and dog meat could be directly substitutable. But the 'general' end-use between a dog and dog meat is clearly different. If the general end-use became a central criterion in determining 'likeness', these Asian countries might be permitted to take discriminatory measures to protect the domestic dog meat industry by imposing 1,000 per cent tax on dogs and 10 per cent tax on dog meats. The results would be: (1) foreign dog-feeding industries could no longer export their products (dogs) to the Asian countries (unless they killed the dogs before exporting, which is not plausible); (2) domestic dog-feeding industries would be relatively all right because they would kill most dogs before sending them to the market; and (3) domestic dog meat

industries would enjoy perfect protection; in fact many of them would cooperate or merge with dog-feeding industries. The overall result would be that in the market of the Asian countries, there would be no more dogs from foreign countries. Is this not crystallizing traditional consumer habits? The point is that the Japanese Panel's ruling (in *Japan Wine and Liquor*), based on the combination between the 'end-use-in-general approach' and the 'no-crystallization-of-traditional-preferences policy', would not work in some circumstances. An end-use should be sought from the market concerned.

[89] But one might criticize this point in that the preference itself can be a valuable source of trade from which comparative advantages spring forth. Often, exchanging the cultural or traditional preferences of one society enriches the tastes and human relations of the other society. Trade devoid of such an exchange might result in 'dry societies', just as adding salt to fish would dry the fish out by dehydrating it.

[90] As a result, the 'command system' would only lose its credibility.

[91] This dangerous assumption, if extended to the territory of the 'directly competitive or substitutable' product relationship, would invalidate the subsequent admission by another Japanese Panel, in *Japan Alcoholic Beverages*, that exactly the same products could be considered to be directly substitutable in *market A*, but not in *market B*. *See infra* note 100 and accompanying text.

[92] 'The Panel emphasized the need to look not only at such matters as physical characteristics, common end uses, and tariff classifications, but also at the "market place". This seems appropriate. The GATT 1994 is a commercial agreement, and the WTO is concerned, after all, with markets.' (*Japan Alcoholic Beverages* Appellate Report, H2(a))

[93] *See infra* note 100 and accompanying text.

[94] 'The Panel stated the following: 'In the Panel's view, the decisive criterion in order to determine whether two products are directly competitive or substitutable is whether they have common end-uses . . . We agree.' (Ibid.)

[95] It should be noted that in general, the objective factors, such as physical characteristics and tariff classification, reflect end-use in general, not specific usage in relevant markets.

[96] Since the early days, US antitrust law has developed a similar market-based approach to define the 'relevant market'. According to this approach, a 'reasonable interchangeability of use' or 'cross-elasticity of demand' test determines the boundaries of a relevant product market. *See United States v E.I. Du Pont De Nemours & Co.* (*Cellophane*), 351 US 377, 76 S.Ct. 994, 100 L.Ed. 1264 (1956); *United States v Grinnell Corp.* (*Grinnell*), 384 US 563, 88 S.Ct. 1698, 16 L.Ed.2d 778 (1966). For details, *see infra* note 142. Because of the two-step legal approach of first defining the market and then deciding whether a monopoly power exists, this test was criticized in that it may lead to the understatement of a defendant's market power because, for example, not enough consideration is given to the cost advantages of producers of distinctive substitutes. *See* Turner, Donald F., 'Antitrust Policy and The Cellophane Case', 70 Harv.L.Rev. 281, 282–3, 308–13 (1959). *See* Judge Learned Hand's opinion in *United States v Corn Products Refining Co.*, 234 F.964 (S.D.N.Y. 1916).

[97] Although the Appellate Body in *Japan Alcoholic Beverages* endorsed the Panel's market-based approach in the Art. III:2, second sentence context (*see supra* note 92), this does not mean that the 'likeness test (the first sentence)' is excluded from a market-based approach. This point becomes clear by referring to the Panel's original ruling: '. . . in the Panel's view, the wording makes it clear that the appropriate test to define whether two products are *"like"* or *"directly competitive or substitutable"* is the marketplace. The Panel recalled in this respect the words used in the Interpretative Note ad Article III, paragraph 2, namely "where

competition exists": competition exists by definition in markets.' *See Japan Alcoholic* Panel Report, para 6.22 (emphasis added). *Indonesia National Car* supports this broad application. *See infra* note 130 and accompanying text.

To confirm this trend, the Appellate Body in *EC Asbestos* examined the Panel's ruling on the likeness relationship between the products concerned (chrysotile asbestos and PCG fibres; and cement-based products containing chrysotile asbestos fibres and cement-based products containing PCG fibres) in the context of Art. III:4 of the GATT. The Body ruled that the Panel did not take into consideration all the necessary elements. In particular, what was missing from the Panel's analysis was the examination of such a market-based element as consumer tastes and habits (health risk to consumers, in particular). *See EC Asbestos* Appellate Report, paras 104–132.

[98] *See EC Asbestos* Appellate Report, paras 109–120 and 139. But it should be noted that this market-based approach in the *Asbestos* case was opposed by a member of the Appellate Body in a roundabout way. *See* the 'concurring statement' by the member, *op. cit.*, para 149.

[99] *Japan Alcoholic Beverages* Panel Report, para 6.22.

[100] Ibid. (emphasis added).

[101] The Panel and the Appellate Body shied away from suggesting a full set of methodology with regard to the market-based approach. All they prescribed was that economic analysis based on elasticity of substitution can be used, but that this analysis should not be *the* decisive criterion in determining what is 'directly competitive or substitutable': 'The Panel did not say that cross-price elasticity of demand is "*the* decisive criterion" for determining whether products are "directly competitive or substitutable" . . . We agree. And, we find the Panel's legal analysis of whether the products are "directly competitive or substitutable products" . . . to be correct.' (*Japan Alcoholic Beverages* Appellate Report, sec. H2(a)).

[102] Fell from 26.7 per cent in 1988 to 19.6 per cent in 1990. *See Japan Alcoholic Beverages* Panel Report, para 6.30.

[103] The Panel noted that this rise was short-lived, since as of 1992 the Japanese economy entered into a recession and there was a shift of demand towards the less expensive categories of liquors. Ibid.

[104] Ibid.

[105] The Panel and the Appellate Body relied on a static study, such as the ASI study, in which data were taken from 'contemporary reactions of a representative sample of shochu drinkers to a series of thirty-six different combinations of price levels for shochu and five brown spirits', while discounting the value of the historical study by the Institute for Social Study of Japan, which was based on household survey statistics from the past 20 years. The complaining parties criticized the latter study, stating that the methodology used was flawed. This criticism was accepted by the Panel since Japan did not rebut it. *See Japan Alcoholic Beverages* Panel Report, paras 6.28–6.32.

[106] The survey conducted based on consumer opinion showed that (1) if shochu were not available, 6 per cent of the consumers would switch to spirits, whereas only 4 per cent would switch to whisky; (2) if whisky were not available, 32 per cent of the consumers would choose brandy and only 10 per cent would choose shochu (*Japan Alcoholic* Panel Report, para 6.31). The result of this survey shows the 'constant-price elasticity of demand', which is different from the 'cross-price elasticity of demand' shown by the results of the ASI Study. *See supra* note 24.

[107] It seems that the Appellate Body accepted the Panel's approach: 'We find the Panel's legal analysis of whether the products are "directly competitive or substitutable products" in

paragraphs 6.28–6.32 of the Panel Report to be correct.' (*Japan Alcoholic Beverages* Appellate Report, sec. H2(a)).

[108] *Japan Alcoholic Beverages* Panel Report, paras 6.22, 6.31.

[109] One should recall that in *Japan Alcoholic Beverages* in 1997, the market-based end-use approach was explicitly endorsed. *See supra* notes 92–96 and accompanying texts.

[110] It should be noted that the Appellate Body held that 'the context of the competitive relationship is necessarily the marketplace since this is the forum where consumers choose between different products' (*Korea Alcoholic Beverages* Appellate Report, para 114).

[111] Complaining parties submitted the Dodwell Study, in which 500 Korean consumers of spirits were surveyed. In this Study, employing basically the same research methods as those of the ASI study, respondents were allowed to choose (1) between soju and brown spirits (standard scotch, premium scotch, cognac) and (2) between soju and white spirits, according to nine different price combinations. The switching rate turned out to be: (1) 8 per cent demand increase of brown liquors according to 10 per cent price increase for soju; and (2) 72 per cent demand increase of white spirit according to 20 per cent increase in the price of soju combined with 20 per cent reduction in the price of white spirits, etc. These changeover rates were considered to be much lower in actuality because of the methodological defects of the study that were effectively revealed by Korea (*see infra* note 354 and accompanying text). Despite these defects, however, according to the Panel, 'there is a merit' to this study and the result showed 'evidence of the beginnings of substitutability and common end-uses by imports'. *See Korea Alcoholic Beverages* Panel Report, paras 5.143–5.149, 10.74, 10.91–4.

[112] *See Korea Alcoholic Beverages* Panel Report, paras 10.56–11.2. Concerning the Korean Panel's consideration of the potential competition, see this chapter, at 2.2.

[113] This survey (the 1998 SM Survey), submitted by the EC, was performed by Search Marketing SA at the request of the EC spirits industry. The surveyors put two questions to a representative sample comprising over 400 consumers who had purchased both pisco and at least one other spirit during the last six months. The first question was to measure the rate of product changeover between pisco and other distilled spirits in circumstances when one was not available (non-availability analysis). The rate of switching products turned out to be very high at 43–70 per cent. The second question aimed to measure the respondents' reaction to changes in the relative price of pisco and other distilled spirits (cross-price elasticity of demand analysis). Where the price of pisco rose 1.7 per cent and, simultaneously, the prices of whisky and other spirits fell by 25.3 per cent and 2.3 per cent respectively, the share of respondents choosing whisky and other spirits instead of pisco increased by 123.8 and 42.6 per cent respectively; this substantial increase took place at the expense of the consumption of all the categories of pisco (15.5 per cent reduction rate). *See Chile Alcoholic Beverages* Panel Report, paras 4.186–4.194.

[114] For details, *see infra* note 300.

[115] *See Chile Alcoholic Beverages* Panel Report, para 7.71.

[116] According to Canada, the study (Task Force Report) characterized the relationship as one of 'imperfect substitutability'—far from the direct substitutability required by Art. III of GATT. *See Canada Periodicals* Appellate Report, sec. B1.

[117] 'US magazines can probably provide a reasonable substitute for Canadian magazines in their capacity as an advertising medium, although some advertisers may be better served by a Canadian vehicle. In many instances however, they would provide a very poor substitute as an entertainment and communication medium.' (*Canada Periodicals* Panel Report, para 3.119.)

[118] 'The statement by the economist, Leigh Anderson, quoted by Canada and the Task Force Report's description of the relationship as one of *"imperfect substitutability" does not modify our appreciation. A case of perfect substitutability would fall within Article III:2, first sentence, while we are examining the broader prohibition of the second sentence.* . . . newsmagazines, like TIME, TIME Canada and Maclean's, are directly competitive or substitutable in spite of the "Canadian" content of Maclean's.' (*Canada Periodicals* Appellate Report, sec. B1 (emphasis added)).

[119] *See supra* notes 24, 106, and 107, and accompanying texts.

[120] For example: consumer A has bought only diamonds all her life; hence, no other stones could substitute for diamonds for her. A presumption of the non-availability of diamonds might lead her to buy (say) gold based upon an arbitrary decision. The 10 per cent could include such a 'forced switch'.

[121] *See supra* note 24.

[122] The Panel Report, para 10.78 (emphasis added).

[123] The definition of and distinction between potential and future competition or substitutability is given at 3.2.4. *See infra* note 340 and accompanying text.

[124] *See* 3.2.4.

[125] *See supra* note 69.

[126] *See* Introduction, note 13.

[127] Several previous panels, such as those in *Japan Alcoholic Beverages* and *Canada Periodicals*, used the concept of potential competition. But the usage was confined to a complementary role. In *Korea Alcoholic Beverages*, the concept broadens its coverage even to 'future' competition and emerges as a 'star', not a 'supporting actor', making its appearance 101 times throughout the performance. *See infra* notes 344, 336–338 and accompanying texts.

[128] In this case, examining whether the Indonesia National Car and certain imported light cars were 'like products' under the SCM Agreement and Art. III of the GATT, the Panel first looked at basic properties, nature and quality, and end-use in general, and then proceeded to a market segment approach, which was basically a market-based end-use analysis.

According to the result of the objective characteristic test and the market segmentation approach, the Panel ruled that the National Car (Timor) was a 'like' product to Japanese light cars (Corolla, etc.) as well as several US/EC models (Ford Escort, Peugeot 306 and Opel Optima), but not a 'like' product to the Vectra and Rolls Royce. *See Indonesia National Car* Panel Report, paras 14.104–14 and 14.163–93.

[129] *Op. cit.*, para 14.175.

[130] *See op. cit.*, paras 14.110–1, 14.141.

[131] GATT Interpretative Note *Ad* Art. III:2.

[132] It seems that this interpretation puts member nations in a more vague and unpredictable situation in the 'competitive or substitutable' product cases than in the 'like' product cases. When the Appellate Body determines 'like products', it can place stress on 'narrowness' (*see* Chapter III at 1) and turn to the historical development of what constitutes a 'like product', thus rendering some predictability. In contrast, when it undertakes the 'directly competitive or substitutable' test, it leaves member nations and panels, with no historical understanding of how to test the market at issue, bewildered as to how broadly to apply the rule. *See* Gupta, R., 'Appellate Body Interpretation of the WTO Agreement: A Critique in Light of Japan-Taxes on Alcoholic Beverages', 6 *Pacific Rim Law & Policy Journal* 710 (1997).

[133] The Panel made its decision based on four pieces of evidence: (1) the finding of the 1987 Panel Report; (2) a study submitted by the complainants done by ASI market research, an independent research institution ('the ASI Study'); (3) a survey submitted by Japan; and (4) evidence concerning the '1989 Japanese tax reform which showed that whisky and shochu are essentially competing for the same market'. Factors (2) through (4) were explicitly held by the Panel to display a significant elasticity of substitution. *See Japan Alcoholic Beverages* Panel Report, para 6.

[134] *See* Introduction, note 21 and accompanying text.

[135] *See* this chapter at 3.2.4.

[136] *See supra* notes 61–68 and accompanying texts.

[137] *See supra* note 105.

[138] *See* Jackson, J. *et al.*, *Legal Problems of International Economic Relations* (West Publishing Co., 1995) 530–31.

[139] 'Panels may seek information from any relevant source and may consult experts...may request an advisory report...from an expert review group...' (DSU Art.13:2).

[140] This term 'relevant market' has started to be employed by the Appellate Body. *See Japan Alcoholic Beverages* Appellate Report, sec. H2(a) ('It does not seem inappropriate to look at competition in the *relevant markets* as one among a number of means of identifying the broader category of products that might be described as "directly competitive or substitutable". Nor does it seem inappropriate to examine elasticity of substitution as one means of examining those *relevant markets*.'); *Canada Periodicals* Appellate Report, sec. VIB1 ('Our conclusion that imported split-run periodicals and domestic non-split-run periodicals are "directly competitive or substitutable" does not mean that all periodicals belong to the same *relevant market*, whatever their editorial content. A periodical containing mainly current news is not directly competitive or substitutable with a periodical dedicated to gardening, chess, sports, music or cuisine.') (emphasis added)

[141] *See Japan Alcoholic Beverages* Appellate Report, sec. H2(a); *Canada Periodicals* Appellate Report, sec. VIB1.

[142] *See* the European Commission, *Commission Notice on the Definition of the Relevant Market for the Purpose of Community Competition Law* (hereinafter Commission Notice), p. 2, published in (1997) OJ C 372/5; <**http://europa.eu.int/comm/dg04/entente/en/relevma.htm**>.

Market definition is a threshold question in dominant position or merger analysis in the field of antitrust law. A market may be defined as an area of trade (product or service, and geographic) in which a hypothetical single firm would be so insulated from competition that it could exercise market power. If transportation costs of production factors are high, the scope of a geographic market would be much narrower than the product market.

The United States definition of the relevant market for competition law purposes appears in many decisions since the landmark case of *Cellophane*. *See supra* note 96.

In *Cellophane*, the Supreme Court articulated a definition of a product market as being 'products that have reasonable interchangeability for the purpose for which they are produced—price, use and qualities considered'. (The Court found that cellophane, over which du Pont has a monopoly position, was not the relevant product market, which was all flexible packaging material.)

Since *Cellophane*, US courts have focused on 'reasonable interchangeability,' emphasizing product uses and physical characteristics and, relatedly, cross-elasticity of demand. *See Brown*

Shoe, infra note 157 ('The outer boundaries of a product market are determined by the reasonable interchangeability of use or the cross-elasticity of demand between the product itself and substitutes for it.'); *Edward J. Sweeney & Sons, Inc. v Texaco*, 637 F.2d 105, 117 (3d Cir. 1980) (stressing that the product in question, Texaco gasoline, was not considered interchangeable with other branded and non-branded gasoline by a significantly large number of consumers); *Eastman Kodak Co. v Image Technical Services, Inc.*, 112 S. Ct. 2072 (1992) (ruling that because service and parts for Kodak equipment are not interchangeable with other manufacturers' service and parts, the relevant market is composed only of those companies that service Kodak machines); *Grinnell, supra* note 96 ('In case of a product it may be of such a character that substitute products must also be considered, as customers may turn to them if there is a slight increase in the price of the main product.').

Starting from the 1980s, the US Justice Department has used merger guidelines that have similar content to the Commission Notice. *See infra* note 263.

It is no wonder that this notion of 'reasonable interchangeability' (restated as 'limited interchangeability') and the method of cross-elasticity of demand recur in the EU jurisprudence. In the *Continental Can* case the ECJ set forth the market test as being defined by the products with which there is only limited interchangeability: *Continental Can v Commission* [1973] CMLR 199. Since then, the EU courts have repeated this principle with some frequency. *See*, e.g., *United Brands v Commission* [1978] 1 CMLR 429 (ruling that bananas had unique characteristics which made them a distinct product market from other fruits and there was no long-term (apparently meaning year-long), cross-elasticity between bananas and other fruits); *Michelin v Commission* [1985] 1 CMLR 282 ('absence of interchangeability between tires for heavy vehicles and tires for light vehicles'); *Hoffmann-La Roche v Commission* [1979] 3 CMLR 211.

By the same token, the Commission made the following statement in its Telecommunications (Antitrust) Guidelines: 'A product market comprises the totality of the products which, with respect to their characteristics, are particularly suitable for satisfying constant needs and are only to a limited extent interchangeable with other products in terms of price, usage and consumer preference. An examination limited to the objective characteristics only of the relevant products cannot be sufficient: the competitive conditions and the structure of supply and demand on the market must also be taken into consideration.' (Commission Notice, *Clarifying the Application of Community Competition Rules to the Market Participants in the Telecommunications Sector* [1991] 4 CMLR 946.)

Later, by issuing the Commission Notice, the European Communities made it clear that the market-based economic analysis should be a central tool for defining 'relevant markets'.

In general, although the languages used by the US and the EU's approach to determine 'relevant market' share many similarities, the EU definition tends to draw comparatively narrow markets and assert the existence of monopoly power within such markets mainly on the basis of market shares. For detailed comparison, *see* Jebsen and Stevens, Chapter I, note 31.

[143] What is referred to is the 'basic concepts' and 'criteria' of the relevant 'product' market. The specific 'scope' of the relevant market in the context of GATT could be substantially different from that of competition law: with regard to this point, *see* Chapter I, notes 19–21 and accompanying texts. The concept of relevant 'geographic' market has importance in the field of competition law, because geographic location or surroundings can bring about differences in the competitive conditions between geographical areas, in spite of similarity in product markets; this difference should be taken into account when identifying competitors, setting the threshold level of competition, and assessing market impact, etc.

In general, the relevant geographic market is determined by such factors as legal limitations, transportation costs, consumer preferences, buyer convenience, entry barriers, etc. *See* such US cases as *L.A. Drafter & Sons v Wheelabrator-Frye*, 735 F.2d 414, 423 (11th Cir. 1984) and *United States v Eastman Kodak Co.*, 63 F.3d 95, 109 (2d Cir. 1995); such EU cases as *Gemeenschap BV v Esso Netherland BV* [1977] 2 CMLR D1 and *Napier Brown & Co. v British Sugar Plc* [1990] 4 CMLR 196. The basic purpose of the GATT is to prevent protectionist measures from being taken by member states, rather than to maintain competition in the market. Thus, the extent to which the geographic market concept plays a role in the GATT may not be as great as in competition law. In the GATT jurisprudence, the geographical market is usually set at the national level; each state has different geographic conditions. But according to the increasing necessity for more precise and justifiable GATT determinations, more narrowly tailored geographic markets (e.g., sub-national level) could be set. This narrow definition of the geographic market could be combined with the market-based end-use approach: specifically with supply substitutability analysis or market segment analysis.

[144] *See* Commission Notice, *supra* note 142, p. 7.

[145] Ibid.

[146] For example, 'smell' is important to liquor, but not to a ball.

[147] For instance, in *Japan Alcoholic Beverages*, with regard to whether the products concerned (whisky, brandy, gin, genever, rum, and liqueurs) were directly competitive or substitutable products to shochu, Japan argued that the differences in physical characteristics between whisky/brandy and shochu were sufficiently large to prevent the two categories from qualifying as directly substitutable products, i.e. differences (1) in materials, (2) in the post-distillation processing, (3) in alcoholic strength, (4) in colour, and (5) in containers. Then Japan moved on to end-use arguments: (1) shochu consumers usually drink shochu during meals, while most consumers of whisky drink whisky after meals; (2) while it is very rare to add ice to shochu, most bourbon whisky consumers drink the beverage 'on the rocks'; and (3) shochu consumers often mix the beverage with hot water or juice while no whisky consumers would do so.

Against these Japanese submissions, the Panel first noted that the 1987 Panel Report that dealt with this issue concluded that both 'white' and 'brown' spirits were directly competitive or substitutable products to shochu, all the products concerned being distilled spirits. The Panel mainly relied on the analysis of product characteristics and intended uses, the results of which were accepted by the 1996 Panel and Appellate Body. *See Japan Alcoholic Beverages* Panel Report, para 4.79.

[148] *See* Commission Notice, *supra* note 142, p. 7.

[149] *See* Commission Notice, *supra* note 142, p. 10.

[150] In this regard, the following questions should be addressed. Why are these groups separate? Are there any illegitimate constraints (both in demand and supply side) that lead to this separation? Without those constraints, what would happen? These questions are related to subsequent inquiries on supply substitution and potential competition factors.

[151] It is known that Japanese 'shochu' and Korean 'soju' differ, in addition to a slight difference in name, in taste, and in composition. Although the Panel in *Korea Alcoholic Beverages* declined to give significant meaning to this difference, one might still question, under the full-fledged market-based end-use analysis, what kind of effect these differences, combined with differences in consumer habits and market conditions, may have on the likeness or substitutability tests.

[152] *See* Commission Notice, *supra* note 142, p. 10.

[153] Professor John Jackson commented that GATT obligations could change consumer preferences and/or at least have an effect on consumer preferences by educating the process of the free trade.

[154] *See* the Preambles of the WTO Agreement and GATT. *See also* Chapter I, notes 22 and 23 and accompanying texts. It is interesting to see that the term 'optimal use' presents a contrast with the term 'full use' employed in the Preamble to the GATT 1947.

[155] In other words, account should be taken of one more factor—'time or potentiality of change' in substitutive relationships.

[156] Supply substitutability may be defined as being the 'ability or willingness of *producers* to switch their production factors from one product sector to the other'. Here, *supply* substitutability means *production* substitutability. That is, the focus is on 'producers': wholesalers or retailers who are also related to the 'supply' process are beyond our concern for the purpose of this book.

[157] It should be noted that in the context of 'relevant market' determination for antitrust purposes, several US cases took the supply substitutability factor into consideration: *Brown Shoe Co. v United States (Brown Shoe)*, 370 U.S. 294, 82 S. Ct. 1502, 8 L. Ed.2d 510 (1962) (stating that 'cross-elasticity of production facilities may also be an important factor in defining a product market within which a vertical merger is to be viewed'); *Virtual Maintenance, Inc. v Prime Computer, Inc.*, 995 F.2d 1324, 1328 (6th Cir. 1993); *Kaiser Aluminum & Chem. Corp. v FTC*, 652 F. 2d 1324, 1330 (7th Cir. 1981) ('cross-elasticity of supply, or production flexibility among sellers, is another relevant factor to be considered in defining a product market for antitrust purposes'); *Equifax v FTC*, 618 F. 2d 63, 66 (9th Cir. 1980). In EU antitrust law, *Michelin v Commission* [1985] 1 CMLR 282 took account of the supply substitution factor in ruling that new replacement tires for heavy vehicles constituted a relevant market: the ECJ relied, among others, on the fact of the absence of cross-elasticity of supply for new replacement tires for heavy and light vehicles because of the 'significant differences in production techniques and in the plant and tools needed for their manufacture'.

For theoretical support for the inclusion of the supply substitution factor in the definition of relevant markets, *see* the following remarks (criticizing the reasonable interchangeability test in *Cellophane* case) by Richard Posner (*op. cit. supra*, Chapter I, note 17, at 127–8):'. . . This formulation is deficient in two respects. First, it ignores substitution in production. A folding carton produced for one soap company is not interchangeable with a folding carton produced for another company, due to differences in the advertising copy printed on the carton and to other minor design and production differences stemming from the carton manufacturer's efforts to custom-design his cartons for each user; an air-conditioner designed for a Volkswagen "Beetle" will not fit into a Mercedes (or for that matter another Volkswagen model); a computer terminal designed to plug into an IBM computer won't plug into a Burroughs. Yet in all of these examples the two products are made with the same components, facilities, equipment, workers, etc., and an increase in the price of one product above the competitive level would result in a prompt switch into its production by firms producing the other product'. Criticizing the *Brown Shoe* decision (above), Judge Posner adds that the court was 'right to add a production-substitutability test to the test of the cellophane case but wrong to limit it to vertical-merger cases; it is equally applicable in a horizontal case' (ibid., at 129). He continues to criticize lack of consideration of supply substitution in such subsequent cases as *United States v Aluminum Co. of America*, 377 U.S. 271 (1964); *United States v Continental Can Co.* 378 U.S. 441 (1964); *United States v Pabst Brewing Co.*, 384 US 546 (1966). Ibid., at 130. According to Judge Posner, the very geographical dimension considered in market definition is implicitly a matter of substitution in supply. Ibid., at 132.

[158] *See* Chapter I, notes 22–26.

[159] '...A large and steadily growing volume of real income and effective demand... the substantial reduction of tariffs and other barriers to trade and to the elimination of discriminatory treatment in international commerce...' (*see* the Preamble of the GATT).

[160] *See* Chapter I, notes 30–32 and accompanying texts.

[161] '...Raising standards of living, ensuring full employment... large and steadily growing volume of real income...' (*see* Chapter I, notes 27–29, and *supra* note 80).

[162] '...Developing the full use of the resources of the world and expanding the production and exchange of goods...' (*see* ibid.).

[163] This assumption is made to be in line with a typical case of *de facto* discrimination, which has become a predominant trend of discriminatory measures since the late 1980s.

[164] As defined here the distinction between 'long run' and 'short run' depends on factor mobility, i.e. these concepts are not related to a particular time frame. 'Long run' means a period sufficient to transfer production factors from one sector to the other, no matter how short it is. Hence, 'short-run' analysis focuses primarily on the examination of demand substitutability. By contrast, long-run analysis includes the supply-substitutability consideration in addition to the short-run effect.

[165] The examination proceeds on the assumption of 'competitive' market structure. It is generally known that free trade increases competition, while monopoly is frequently a result of protection.

[166] The higher price eliminates consumption by those consumers who value units of the product at more than the (marginal) cost of production. Those consumers lose the 'benefit of the bargain' they might have received on those units no longer purchased. This consumer loss amounts to the difference in the dollar value the consumer places on those foregone units ('willingness to pay') less the competitive price paid for them; this excess of value over price is referred to by economists as 'consumer surplus'. The loss in consumer surplus is called a '*deadweight loss*' to denote the fact that the consumer loss is not gained by others (e.g., producers or government). It is not a wealth transfer, but rather represents wasted resources—that is, an irrecoverable loss in economic efficiency.

An analogous loss in 'producer surplus' occurs when output is restricted below the efficient, competitive level. The sellers lose the incremental profit (or 'surplus') they earned by selling some units of output at the competitive price that were produced at a lower 'marginal' cost. This reduction in producer surplus harms the seller as well as society, because the loss is not a wealth transfer, but a non-recoverable waste of resources. *See* Handler, *Chapter I*, note 8, at 199.

In the case of tax imposition as in the present hypothetical situation, a price increase generated by the tax and a subsequent reduction in consumption and production levels causes a 'deadweight loss', in the first place, for consumer and producer surpluses. But this initial impact can be worsened or mitigated as the demand or supply substitution process goes on.

[167] The rate of price increase depends upon the slopes of B's demand and supply curves. The higher the demand substitutability is, the smaller the price increase becomes.

[168] If the market structure of sector A is monopoly, the domestic producer of A would be able to maintain the current level of production and gain a monopoly profit generated by higher prices. But without certain protection, this high profit will most likely induce market entry from others to result in an increased number of transactions.

[169] The margin of surplus depends upon slopes of demand and supply curves of product A.

[170] This export is possible because the discriminatory measure is based on origin–neutral criteria (this assumption will be removed later). Combined with the possible entry by a third producer, this switch by the foreign company would increase competition in A product market of country X.

[171] This degree will be determined by slopes of demand and supply curves in both sectors.

[172] *See supra* note 166.

[173] Some might indicate certain damages, including (1) loss in possibility of choice (to consumers); and (2) loss in arbitrage chance between highly substitutable goods and sunk cost, e.g., advertisement expense (to exporters, importers, or intermediate retailers). But it should be noted that the definition of high demand and supply substitutability has already internalized these losses.

To illustrate SITUATION I, if a much higher tax is imposed on concentrated lemon than on lemon juice, the competitive relationship between foreign concentrated lemon exporters will be damaged because their products will become much more expensive than lemon juice, which will result in many consumers switching to lemon juice. But since foreign producers of concentrated lemon can easily reconfigure their production facilities to make lemon juice, the net result of protection in the long run would be that the importation of concentrated lemon would be replaced by lemon juice imports. In the world industry, lemon juice production is increased as much as reduction in concentrated lemon production.

The same might be said with regard to the relationship between vodka and shochu. It is a known fact that the only difference in manufacturing methods between the two is the medium used for filtration (shochu uses white birch charcoal as filtering material). *See Japan Alcoholic Beverages* Panel Report, para 6.23 ('In the Panel's view, only vodka could be considered as like product to shochu since, apart from commonality of end-uses, it shared with shochu most physical characteristics. Definitionally, the only difference is in the media used for filtration.').

[174] According to Preambles of the Agreement Establishing the WTO and the GATT, full employment is one of the objectives of the WTO.

[175] This new market search would incur additional expenses. Even if the market is found, the increases in supply of B in the market would push down the price of B in it, which will affect the gain of the foreign producer.

[176] Due to the increased price of A, a third party may enter the market of product A. If such an entry occurs to the extent that it returns the increased price of A to the original price level, the deadweight loss in sector B could be substantially compensated by the increased deadweight gain in sector A. Of course, this effect has nothing to do with the 'mitigation effect', which is a concept based on relationships between the domestic and foreign producers.

[177] Given the low supply substitutability, the increased transaction in sector A combined with the decreased transaction in sector B cannot mean a 'neutral' impact on distribution of resources. Moreover, it should be noted that there is only small increase of transaction in sector A (compare with SITUATION I).

One possible example of SITUATION II could be the relationship between sparkling water and natural spring water. These products are considered to be directly substitutable by consumers because of their similarity in properties and end-use. Suppose that the price of natural spring water soared due to the tax discrimination. Then, many spring water consumers would switch to sparkling water, thereby generating short-run benefits to sparkling water producers. But it is very difficult for sparkling water producers to switch to natural spring water, because natural water production facilities (including geographical requirements) are very different from those of sparkling water production facilities. This will cause high losses for natural water producers because they cannot export as much as before. Hence, the only choice they have is to reduce their production following the shrinking demand. On the other hand, in the sparkling water industry, increasing demand will be met mostly by production increase by existing producers or by newcomers, not by switching natural water producers.

[178] The higher price eliminates consumption by those consumers who value units of the product at more than the (marginal) cost of production. Those consumers lose the 'benefit of the bargain' they might have received on those units no longer purchased. *See supra* note 166.

[179] Producers will lose unless B's demand curve is perfectly vertical. In other words, if the price elasticity of demand of product B is null, producers would effectively transfer all tax burden to consumers and no reduction of production would happen because consumers would buy the same amount of product B as before despite the increase in price.

[180] Because there will be little increase in transaction in sector A (low demand substitution).

[181] Whether this switch is profitable depends on the slope of demand and supply curves in both sectors. Assuming supply curves in sectors A and B would be similar (which can be largely inferred from 'high supply substitutability'), the profitability of the switch would mainly depend upon demand curves in both sectors. In general, the condition that the switch of resources is profitable is that A's demand curve is more price elastic than that of B *in the range where the switch occurs*. One could say that in most cases the switch would be profitable because the condition would most likely be satisfied: note that a new price of A would be formed at a much lower price than a new price for B (compare price level at Q_A^{**} with that at Q_B^{**}) and that, in a lower price range, demand is more price elastic because more poor people tend to consume in that range. Rich people, on the other hand, tend to pay less attention to changes in price and, in a higher price range, one could identify more rich consumers (recall that in general the demand curve is not a straight line!).

[182] Because of this increase of price in sector B, foreign producers of B would stop switching to sector A at a certain point. A third producer might enter sector B in country X in order to fill the supply gap. But even if third parties enter sector B, the price would not go down below the price level at Q_B^* because they have to pay taxes anyway.

[183] It largely depends on the consumption pattern of consumers in country X: if they consume product A more than product B, they could be better off.

[184] Unless demand curve of A has an infinite price elasticity, A's domestic producers would suffer.

[185] An example would be the relationship between imported light oil and domestic heavy oil. Despite higher prices in light oil caused by the discriminatory tax, domestic light oil consumers would not switch their consumption to heavy oil because each type of oil has its own specific usage. Due to the price increase, the consumers of light oil would be forced to reduce their consumption of light oil. Accordingly, foreign gasoline producers would start to reduce production up to the profit maximization point. Since there is no big difference in the production facility and technologies used in light and heavy oil production, some producers of light oil would switch to the production of heavy oil, if the increasing supply

of heavy oil did not result in a notable price reduction in the sector, while reduction of production in light oil could drive up its price. This profit generated by the production switch would compensate a part of their falling profit in the gasoline sector. As this switch goes on, the price of heavy oil would go down. No matter how small the price decrease is, the domestic heavy oil industry would suffer, whereas heavy oil consumers would enjoy the benefit. At any rate, the deadweight loss of efficiency (caused by a smaller number of transactions) lies in the light oil sector, and this loss would mostly be paid by importers.

[186] This conclusion is *not invalidated* by taking account of the third party market entry or monopolistic/competitive market structure. If such entry occurs, or if a monopolistic market structure is presumed, the degree of mitigation effect could only become smaller. *See supra* notes 168, 170, 176, and 182.

[187] Such as higher taxes or tariff rates on *foreign origin* goods and quantitative restrictions imposed on *imports from certain countries*.

[188] This would generate not only distortion of the product/producer relationship, but also a lot of X-inefficiencies, i.e., monopoly power acted as a narcotic, depressed energy, led to luxurious management perks, and created slack, etc.

[189] Article 31 of the Vienna Convention on the Law of Treaties.

[190] *See* Introduction, notes 4–11 and accompanying texts.

[191] Producers tend to have a perspective more concerned with the long term with regard to understanding *demand* substitution than consumers do. Responding to questions asking whether two products are demand substitutable, consumers would reply positively if they think that those products are interchangeable 'now' (spot orientation). There is no guarantee that producers, who think the current demand substitutability in the market is transient (flow orientation), would give the same answer.

[192] One should be reminded that GATT provisions dealing with likeness issues articulate their obligations based on 'product' relationships, not 'producer' relationships. With regard to the historical evolution of the language, *see* Appendix I.

[193] Thereby letting the discriminatory measure survive.

[194] It should also be noted that the point that a third party entry in SITUATION I can 'mitigate' the mitigation effect weakens the strength of an argument relying upon the mitigation effect.

[195] The number of consumers is larger than that of producers. Furthermore, the consumer's perspective is apparent in the market, whereas the producer's perspective is hidden and/or needs longer to be realized.

[196] *See* Chapter II, at 1.3.

[197] What about other situations, such as SITUATIONS II and III? One could compare these with SITUATION VI. In SITUATION II, in which *more* distortion (high demand substitution) and the *same* low mitigation effect (low supply substitution) are generated, the need for protecting foreign producers becomes greater. In SITUATION III, in which *less* distortion (low demand substitution) and a *larger* mitigation effect (high supply substitution) are expected, such a need becomes smaller. Hence, it can be concluded that the likeness should be positive in SITUATION II and negative in SITUATION III. It should be noted that the same answer can be obtained *anyway* through the demand-substitutability-only approach. Thus, in SITUATIONS II and III, taking account of the supply substitutability factor does not have practical importance; supply substitutability cannot play a meaningful role in the final outcome.

[198] In this era of mass production and high specialization, it is generally very difficult for a business enterprise to switch its production facility from one product sector to the other.

This is true mainly because of high initial fixed costs plus subsequent sunk costs (in distribution lines, advertisements, product reputation, labor specialization, risk, etc.). High supply substitutability can be expected, for instance, in such a limited field as the agricultural industry, which is mainly operated by small farms. For example, farmers would switch their production sectors from potato to sweet potato if the latter price soared. This is possible because their sunk costs and entry barriers are not large and no great specialization is necessary.

[199] In general, with respect to the matter of product substitution, consumers are constrained only by budgetary limitations, whereas producers are confronted by many other constraints including sunk costs, climate, marketing strategy, and various risks (*see supra* note 198). This difference tends to keep demand substitutability much higher than supply substitutability. Furthermore, general trends of mass production and specialization make supply substitution much more difficult. In addition, in many cases supply substitutability will reflect demand substitutability because producers tend to take account of the switching rate of consumers who consume products of the producers.

[200] Recognizing the supply substitutability test might necessitate a consideration of certain non-violation situations; requiring foreign producers to modify their products, as this test would, in essence deprive them of markets that they previously enjoyed.

[201] *See* Report of Panel in *United States—Taxes on Automobiles (hereinafter 'United States Automobiles')*, DS31/R, 1994 (unadopted). In this case, the Panel ruled that certain provisions of the US fuel economy legislation (CAFE law) were inconsistent with Art. III:4, while certain excise taxes (luxury tax, gas-guzzler tax) did not violate Art. III:2. The Panel reasoned that Art. III need only invalidate taxes with the 'aim and effect' of protecting domestic production. Looking at the 'wording of the legislation as a whole', the Panel found a lack of protectionist aim; determining the effect of the measures, the Panel focused on the 'qualitative factors', indicating that the differentiation by the measures did not engender a disadvantage '*inherent* to EC or other foreign automobiles' and that 'the threshold did not appear arbitrary or contrived in the context of the policies pursued'. Thus, the Panel concluded that the effect of the tax measures was not protectionist.

[202] Ibid., paras 5.12–5.15.

[203] Ibid., para 5.14.

[204] Examining the effect of the gas-guzzler tax, the Panel disregarded quantitative evidence that European automobiles bore the brunt of the tax, because 'the technology to manufacture high fuel economy automobiles ... was not inherent to the United States, nor were low fuel economy automobiles inherently of foreign origin'. The distinction was thus not protectionist in effect. *See* ibid., at para 5.25.

In addition, with regard to the distinction based on the model-type averaging method (it was alleged that this method discriminated against foreign cars), the distinction's effect was not to alter the conditions of competition in favor of domestic production in that foreign manufacturers were not 'inherently' limited to offering a smaller number of model variations than domestic manufacturers. *See* ibid., at para 5.31.

[205] The Big Three auto manufacturers of the United States produced the overwhelming majority of light trucks sold in the United States. These trucks were subject to a lower rate of gas-guzzler tax despite their relatively lower fuel economy. Applying the inherency test consistently, the Panel concluded that, because light trucks were not inherently of domestic manufacture, the effect of the distinction was not to afford protection to domestic production. The gas-guzzler tax was thus consistent with Art. III. *See* ibid., paras 5.34–5.36.

[206] *See* Farber, D.A. and Hudec, R.E., 'GATT Legal Restraints on Domestic Environmental Regulations', in Jagdish Bhagwati and Robert Hudec, eds, *Fair Trade and Harmonization* (MIT Press, 1996) 75–76.

[207] *See* ibid.

[208] *See* ibid. It is interesting to see that the inherency test is also used in the GATS, but in quite a different way. The GATS excuses competitive burdens that are inherent in the regulatory process in the sense that they cannot be avoided by regulation in any other form. *See* Art. XVII of the GATS. An example might be that of the risk of multiple regulation inherent in any business that operates in more than one jurisdiction. The *United States Automobiles* decision, on the other hand, looks to whether a regulation has been shaped to seize upon some inherent (unavoidable) characteristic of the foreign producer, thereby imposing a competitive disadvantage that could easily have been avoided by using a different form of the same regulation. In the former case, the inherent characteristic is causal, while in the latter case it is the regulation that is the active cause of commercial disadvantage—or so one could say. *See* Farber and Hudec, *supra* note 206, at 78. *See also* Chapter III, note 144.

[209] *See supra* note 45 and more generally at 3.2.5.

[210] A panel could find 'useful guidance in the reasoning' of an unadopted report that it considered to be relevant. *See Japan Alcoholic Beverages* Panel Report, para 6.10. It could be an 'important interpretive material'. *See* Jackson, Introduction, note 16, at 87.

[211] For details, *see* 3.2.5.

[212] *See* 3.2.5. Concerning the concept of domestic policy autonomy, *see* Roessler, F. 'Diverging Domestic Policies and Multilateral Trade Integration', in Bhagwati and Hudec, *op. cit. supra* note 206.

[213] Subsequently, these effects could just as easily, and often do, turn out to be disproportionately burdensome to domestic interests. This would appear to have been the case, for example, with the general luxury tax law in *US Automobiles*, in which the original tax law turned out to have such a seriously adverse impact on US furriers, jewelers, and luxury boat builders that Congress was forced to repeal those parts of the tax shortly thereafter.

[214] With regard to the aim-and-effect theory, *see* 3.2.5. Concerning the over-inclusiveness problem, *see supra*.

[215] 'GATT Panel Rejects Key EU Challenges to US Fuel Conservation Measures', *Int'l Trade Daily* (BNA) (4 October 1994).

[216] The author owes this idea to Mr Fauchald. *See* Fauchald, Introduction, note 11, at 142–3.

[217] It is interesting to consider how this factor of supply substitutability could play a role in interpreting the terms 'like service' or 'like service supplier' in the GATS. *See* Chapter III, note 144 and accompanying text.

In general, the combination of broad definitions of 'like service (supplier)' together with MFN or the national treatment for foreign service (supplier) would extend substantial rights to foreign corporations. On the other hand, a narrow definition would lead to more deference to domestic regulatory autonomy.

These days, the role of GATS is discussed in the context of regulating new areas, including electronic commerce and trade and investment. Dealing with these new areas, can the factor of supply substitutability carry more weight in defining the 'like service (supplier)' concept than in defining the concept of 'like product' in the GATT? For instance, there could be two different types of service, which result in similar utility to consumers: selling music by disc and selling music by electronic transmission. Are these 'like services (suppliers)'? Might the answer be different depending on the supply substitutability of the supplier? That is, if the supplier is already equipped with traditional as well as e-commerce sales networks (high supply substitutability), can this be taken into consideration to make those two types of services 'not like'?

Certainly, these questions necessitate further study. One possible argument: compared to trade in goods, trade in services is subject to more supply-side constraints (e.g., geographical distance, market conditions, service providers' willingness); and since the GATS takes a more cautious approach (regulating more limited areas) than the GATT does, the likeness concept in the GATS should be more cautious (narrower) than that in the GATT, suggesting more weight on the role of the supply substitution factor in undergoing the determination of what is a 'like service (supplier).'

[218] *See* 3.2.4.

[219] If its customers are in a position to switch easily to available substitute products or to suppliers located elsewhere, a firm or group of firms cannot have a significant impact on the prevailing conditions of sale, such as prices. *See* Commission Notice, *supra* note 142.

[220] *See Spain Unroasted Coffee* Panel Report, paras 4.6–4.7. This case involved a dispute between Brazil and Spain concerning the latter's imposition of a 7 per cent *ad valorem* duty on coffee classified as 'unwashed Arabica', 'Robusta', or 'other'. In contrast, 'Colombian mild' and 'other mild' entered duty free. As a result of a change of tariff system in 1979, that replaced the former unbound 22.5 per cent tariff on all items classified simply as 'coffee', Spain came to have a sophisticated tariff classification system in which all coffees were divided into five distinct categories. In examining Spain's alleged Art. I violation, the Panel paid particular attention to arguments about the physical characteristics of the various types of coffees involved, only to reject them. The Panel held that 'organoleptic differences resulting from geographical factors, cultivation methods, the processing of the beans, and the genetic factor were not sufficient reason to allow for a different tariff treatment'.

[221] The Panel Report, para 6.23. This ruling was accepted by the Appellate Body. *See* the Appellate Report, sec. H1(a).

[222] *See Korea Alcoholic Beverages* Panel Report, para 10.64. This position was accepted by the Appellate Body.

[223] This point was raised by the Korean side in *Korea Alcoholic Beverages*. The Panel Report, para 7.17.

[224] *See supra* notes 45, 97, and 130, and accompanying texts.

[225] *See* Chapter III, particularly notes 174 and 310–311, and accompanying texts.

[226] It should be noted that the *Border Tax Adjustments* Report indicated not only product 'properties' and 'nature' as being valid factors in deciding objective characteristics, but also '*quality*' and such subjective factors as 'consumers' *tastes and habits, which change from country to country*' and 'end-use *in a given market*'. *See supra* note 56.

In *Indonesia—Certain Measures Affecting The Automobile Industry* (hereinafter '*Indonesia National Car*'), WT/DS64/R (2 July 1998), the Panel paid attention to a variety of non-physical characteristics including brand loyalty, brand image/reputation, status, after-sales service, and resale value. But since Indonesia provided almost no evidentiary support for its view that there were differences in non-physical characteristics (except for a single sentence in a newspaper article, stating that 'dealers say consumers ask a lot of questions about the quality of the Timor and the after-sales service'), the Panel did not rule either way. Nonetheless, it could be said that these non-physical characteristics were internalized into the market segment approach, adopted by the Panel. *See Indonesia National Car* Panel Report, para 14.191. For a case summary, *see supra* notes 128–130 and accompanying texts.

[227] *See* the Panel Report on *Italian Discrimination Against Imported Agricultural Machinery*, adopted on 23 October 1958, BISD 7S/60 at p. 64, para 15; *see also Japan Alcoholic Beverages* Appellate Report, sec. H1(a).

[228] *See* Report of the Working Party, *Australian Subsidy on Ammonium Sulphate (hereinafter 'Australia Sulphate')*, GATT Doc. C.P.4/39 (1950), 2 BISD 188, para 8. In this case, Chile complained that an Australian subsidy scheme designed to stimulate the purchase and use of fertilizer by Australians violated, *inter alia*, Art. I by subsidizing the sale of domestic and foreign ammonium sulphate, but did not do so for the sales of domestic and foreign sodium nitrate, a product Chile considered to be like ammonium sulphate. The Panel found these products not to be 'like' products. Although it was found that these two types of fertilizer were closely related and had been distributed in Australia through the same agency and sold at the same price, the Panel ('without trying to give a definition of "like products" and leaving aside the question of whether the two fertilizers were directly competitive') concluded that they were 'not to be considered "like" products within the terms of Article I' of the GATT. The principal reason for this conclusion was that in the Australian tariff, and in the tariffs of other countries, the two products were listed as being separate items and were subject to different treatment.

Unlike a GATT or WTO 'panel' proceeding, which is adversarial, a 'Working Party' is an *ad hoc* inquisitorial body open to all interested WTO members and established to study and report on the issues submitted to it for its consideration. A Working Party submits reports of its investigation to the General Council. *See* Bhala and Kennedy, Chapter I, note 22, at 66.

[229] Interestingly, some argue that this agreement between parties with regard to tariff binding negotiations should be seen as one of the important criteria for *likeness in Art. III* (not to mention in Art. I of the GATT) as long as it does not harm the interests of a third party: 'When the complaining party has taken part in such negotiations and accepted the result, it can expect the classification to be respected not only in relation to tariffs, but also in relation to internal taxes and government regulations. On the other hand, one should bear in mind that the agreement is often based on other circumstances than those that are relevant to the dispute in question. Moreover, issues related to internal taxes and government regulations are often of great importance to third parties. Third parties may for example be exporters of products that enjoy favourable treatment under the tax arrangement. Under such circumstances, it would not be desirable to base the findings with regard to the GATT-consistency of the arrangement on a previous agreement between the parties to the dispute.' (*see* Fauchald, Introduction, note 11, at 137–8).

[230] *See* Report of the Working Party in *Australia Sulphate, supra* note 228, at para 8.

[231] *See Treatment by Germany of Imports of Sardines (hereinafter 'Germany Sardines')*, GATT Doc. G/26 (31 October 1952) (*Nor. v F.R.G.*), BISD 1S 53, at 57, para 13. In this case in which Germany imposed a higher duty on Norwegian sardines (one species of the clupeoid family of fish) than on sprats and herrings (the other species of the family), the Panel concluded that Art. I had not been violated, in spite of the fact that the products of the various varieties of clupeae were closely related and were considered by many interested parties as directly competitive, in that: 'Although the Norwegian complaint rested to a large extent on the concept of "like" products as set out in the Agreement and the German reply addressed itself also to that concept, the Panel was satisfied that it would be sufficient to consider

whether in the conduct of the negotiations [between Norway and Germany in 1948] at Torquay the two parties agreed expressly or tacitly to treat these preparations [of fish] as if they were "like products" '(at para 12).

The Panel found that the evidence indicated that the parties involved understood the products to be different for tariff purposes (at para 13). Thus, the Panel stated that any argument supporting Norway's position had to be based on 'assurances which it considered it had obtained in the course of the negotiation rather than on the automatic operation of the most-favored-nation clause' (at 7–58, para 13). Ultimately, the Panel found nullification and impairment under Art. XXIII:1(b), because Germany had assured Norway that, though sprats and herrings were different from sardines, they would be accorded similar tariff treatment (at 58–59, paras 16–17).

[232] *See* Zedalis, Rex J., 'A Theory of the GATT "Like" Product Common Language Cases', 27 Vand. J. Transnat'l L. 33 (1994).

[233] *Japan—Tariff on Imports of Spruce, Pine, Fir (SPF) Dimension Lumber (hereinafter 'Japan SPF Lumber')*, GATT Doc. L/6470 (1989), BISD 36th Supp. 167, 198.

[234] *See* Zedalis, *supra* note 232, at 83–85.

[235] *See* Bhala and Kennedy, Chapter I, note 22, at 67.

[236] *See Spain Unroasted Coffee* Panel Report, para 4.11.

[237] The Harmonized System is a uniform system for classification of products for customs purposes that was adopted by the United States and most of the world's major trading nations by 1988. Correct classification of merchandise is necessary for the assessment of import duties, application of import quotas, compilation of accurate international trade statistics, and a variety of other purposes. It is self-evident that the use of a single classification system worldwide, rather than different systems on a country-by-country basis, facilitates international trade by eliminating uncertainties with regard to duty rates and simplifying the classification of merchandise traded among nations. The international HS has 22 sections divided into 97 chapters, and contains over 5,000 article descriptions (nomenclature), as well as six General Rules of Interpretation, and Section and Chapter Notes. The nomenclature is organized into a six-digit numerical coding system, of which the first two digits represent the 'chapter', the second two digits are referred to as 'headings', and the third two digits as 'subheadings'. The sections generally group commodities by industrial or commercial sectors. The HS headings in each chapter are designed, as much as possible, to progress from crude products to those based on increasingly sophisticated processing. *See* International Convention on the Harmonized Commodity Description and Coding System, 14 June 1983; Protocol for the International Convention on Harmonized Commodity Description and Coding System, 24 June 1986 (deposited at Customs Cooperation Council in Brussels, effective 1 January 1989).

[238] *See* Irish, M., 'Interpretation and Naming: The Harmonized System in Canadian Customs Tariff Law', *Canadian Yearbook of International Law* Vol. 31, pp. 90–91 (1993). But it should be noted that the physical features of goods are not the only criteria on which the HS was drafted. Other considerations, including function and purpose ('footwear', 'headgear', etc.), are relevant for some chapters. *See* ibid.

[239] *See* ibid.

[240] In this light, it can be noted that the Appellate Body in *Japan Alcoholic Beverages* cautioned that there was a major difference between tariff classification nomenclature and tariff bindings or concessions made by WTO members under GATT Art. II. *See Japan Alcoholic Beverages* Appellate Report, sec. H1(a).

[241] *See GATT Analytical Index: Guide to GATT Law and Practice*, Vol. 1, pp. 106–108 (GATT, 1995).

[242] In the Art. III context, *see Japan Alcoholic Beverages* Panel Report, para 6.21.

[243] For the definition, *see supra* notes 58 and 68.

[244] *See Korea Alcoholic Beverages* Panel Report, para 10.78.

[245] *See* following statement by the *Korea Alcoholic Beverages* Panel: 'There is a considerable degree of overlap between the questions of common end-uses and common channel of distribution. Often, consumer products will be distributed in a manner that reflects their intended end-uses. Channels of distribution tend to reveal present market structure while end-uses deal with both the current overlap, if any, and potential for future overlap. In the present case, it is evident that soju and western-style beverages are currently sold through similar retail outlets in a quite similar manner for off-premise consumption.' (Panel Report, para 10.83.)

[246] *See* ibid., para 10.69.

[247] 'All the beverages described are utilized for socialization purposes in situations where the effect of drinks containing relatively high concentrations of alcohol is desired. They may be used in a variety of social settings, including with food, either meals or otherwise. Korea's attempts to rebut this argument ultimately were unpersuasive. The distinctions that Korea would have us draw are too narrow and transitory'. (Ibid., at para 10.82.)

[248] *See supra* note 75 and accompanying text.

[249] *See supra* notes 117 and 118, and accompanying text. But one should take note of the other part of the Appellate Body's statement, that 'a periodical containing mainly current news is not directly competitive or substitutable with a periodical dedicated to gardening, chess, sports, music or cuisine', although this statement is an *obiter dictum. See supra* note 140.

[250] *See* Chapter III, particularly notes 174 and 310, and accompanying texts.

[251] *See Korea Alcoholic Beverages* Panel Report, para 10.78.

[252] Ibid.

[253] Consumer surveys on usage patterns and attitudes, data from consumers' purchasing patterns, views expressed by retailers and generally, market research studies submitted by the parties and their competitors can be taken into account to establish whether an economically significant proportion of consumers consider two products as substitutable, taking also into account the importance of brands for the products in question. *See* the Commission Notice, *supra* note 142, pp. 9–11.

[254] *See Indonesia National Car* Panel Report, para 14.177.

[255] The Panel relied for its interpretation of likeness upon a market segmentation analysis undertaken by DRI's Global Automotive Group, a company whose clients include all major auto manufacturers, including KIA, PT, TPN's national car partner. This analysis was submitted by the United States and the European Communities. *See* the Panel Report, para 14.177.

[256] This categorization was designed to identify sets of products that car consumers would recognize as falling within competing categories.

It is interesting to compare this 'market segmentation' approach with a sort of parallel concept of 'submarket' in the United States antitrust law. In *Grinnell*, the Supreme Court noted that some buyers had a special preference for 'accredited' central station protective service (CSPS) as opposed to non-accredited central station protection for which others have shown a preference. It defined CSPS as a separate product market, using the concept of 'submarket'. *See Grinnell, supra* notes 96 and 142.

In *Brown Shoe* (*supra* note 157), the US Supreme Court held that 'within this broad market, well-defined submarkets may exist which, in themselves, constitute product markets for antitrust purposes.... Boundaries of such a submarket may be determined by examining such practical indicia as industry or public recognition of the submarket as a separate economic entity, the product's peculiar characteristics and uses, unique production facilities, distinct customers, distinct prices, sensitivity to price changes, and specialized vendors'. Accordingly, the Court ruled that, despite a common category of shoes, men's, women's, and children's shoes constitute separate relevant markets.

A more complete description comes from a Fifth Circuit decision: 'Antitrust law recognizes that economically significant submarkets may exist which themselves constitute relevant product markets. The fact finder may determine a submarket exists by examining such practical indicia as industry or public recognition of the sub-market as a separate economic entity, the product's peculiar characteristics and uses, unique production facilities, distinct customers, distinct prices, sensitivity to price changes, and specialized vendors.' (*Domed Stadium Hotel, Inc. v Holiday Inns, Inc.*, 732 F.2d 480, 487–88 (5th Cir.1984))

[257] *See supra* notes 128–130, 226, and 254, and accompanying texts. The Panel drew the conclusion of likeness by combining the results of direct view analysis and judgements on objective characteristics.

[258] Channels of distribution and points of sale were examined in *Korea Alcoholic Beverages*. The Nielsen Survey submitted by Korea concluded that while all Korean restaurants, Chinese restaurants, and mobile street vendors deal in standard soju, most cafes/western-style restaurants and bars deal in whisky. But this conclusion was effectively attacked by the United States, which argued that soju and western-style beverages are currently sold through similar retail outlets in a quite similar manner for off-premise consumption. *See Korea Alcoholic Beverages* Panel Report, paras 10.71, 10.83.

A similar study (the 1997 SM Survey) was submitted by the EC in *Chile Alcoholic Beverages*, indicating that all types of premises market both pisco and the imported distilled spirits together. For both categories, the preferred outlets were the same, supermarkets and liquor stores. By the Panel, this fact of sharing shelf space was taken as 'supportive of a finding that the domestic and imported products were directly competitive or substitutable' (*Chile Alcoholic Beverages* Panel Report, paras 7.55–7.59).

[259] *See supra* notes 30 and 39, and accompanying texts.

[260] Another example might be found in the SCM Agreement. In interpreting the terms 'like product' or 'like or directly competitive product' in Annex I of the Agreement, the producer's view of likeness or competitiveness could play a significant role in the case of Annex 1(d), where the issue is whether the provision of intermediate goods by the government to export *industry*, compared to domestic like or directly competitive *industry*, could be an export subsidy prohibited by the Agreement.

[261] Parties involved in disputes often carry out various consumer surveys or other studies to justify their positions. These studies are submitted to panels if the results are favorable to the party in question, but not if they are unfavorable. Such studies, especially undisclosed ones, can provide useful information to panels.

[262] Commission Notice, *supra* note 142, pp. 4–5.

[263] During the 1980s, the US Justice Department adopted merger guidelines, which set forth an analytical framework for defining relevant markets. According to the 1992 Merger Guidelines, adopted by the Department of Justice (DOJ) and the Fair Trade Commission (FTC) and amended in 1997, the investigation begins by taking the product of one of the

merging firms and asking whether a coordinated, significant price increase above the current level by all the firms making the product would be profitable. The hypothesized increase usually is a 5 per cent price rise lasting one year. If the hypothesized increase would be profitable, those firms constitute a relevant market. Later, the use of 'current' level of price as a standard of hypothetical price increase was criticized and other alternatives were suggested, such as using marginal cost as the standard price or referring to both results of price-increase and price-decrease hypothetical. *See* Handler *et al.*, Chapter I, note 8, at 218 and Chapter 9.

[264] These consumers who are subject to the hypothetical questions are called 'respondents'.

[265] *See* Appendix III.

[266] Since 'directly competitive or substitutable' is the broadest scope of product likeness or substitutability (*see* this chapter, at 1.3), one should first deal with the threshold for this concept. Individualization of thresholds in each scope of likeness or substitutability (i.e. 'identical', 'closely similar', 'remotely similar', 'directly substituted', 'directly competitive') is discussed in Chapter III.

[267] Posner, *supra* Chapter I, note 17, at 126 (emphasis added).

[268] *See Rothery Storage & Van Co. v Atlas Van Lines Inc.*, 253 U.S. App. D.C. 142, 792 F.2d 210 (1986).

[269] *See supra* notes 96, 142, and 157, and accompanying texts.

[270] In general, a price increase of one product, *ceteris paribus*, would change the relative price between products, which would stimulate consumer efforts to maintain the same level of expenditure by reducing consumption of the product of which the price has been increased, and by increasing consumption of other products which became relatively cheaper.

[271] *See infra* notes 340 and 348, and accompanying texts.

[272] *See* Chapter I, notes 19 and 21, and accompanying texts.

[273] *See infra* note 348. The European case of *Guinness/Grand Metropolitan* provides an excellent illustration of this difference. The parties in the merger had provided to the Commission consumer surveys, which suggested that all spirits were within the same relevant market. The Commission, however, disregarded those surveys because most of them were originally aimed at addressing 'taxation issues' and, thus, the results of the surveys were not appropriate to be used by competition authorities as an aid to market definition in a competition law context. *See* Commission Decision of 15 October 1997, declaring a concentration to be compatible with the common market and the functioning of the EEA Agreement (Case No IV/M.938—*Guinness/Grand Metropolitan*) (notified under document number C (1997) 3169).

In a merger or dominant position context, the relevant market definition is mostly needed to measure the market share of the dominance. *See* Handler *et al.*, Chapter I, note 8, at 155. Competition authorities could maintain a high level of competition in the market by narrowly defining the scope of the relevant market (so as to allow for the dominance to be assessed in the narrowly-tailored market).

[274] *Korea Alcoholic Beverages* Panel Report, para 10.44 (emphasis added).

[275] *See* the Pre-Measure Price (PMP) criterion in Appendix III, or more generally at 3.2.4 of this chapter.

[276] Shochu, on the one hand, and five brown spirits (scotch whisky, Japanese whisky, Japanese brandy, cognac, and North American whisky) and three white spirits (gin, vodka, and rum), on the other. *See Japan Alcoholic Beverages* Panel Report, para 6.29.

[277] *See* ibid.

[278] This model can still be called the CVA-PCPDS, although it adopts the EQA instead of the PQA.

[279] *See supra* note 120 and accompanying text.

[280] *See Japan Alcoholic Beverages* Appellate Report, sec. H2(c). In addition, it should be noted that the European Court of Justice has established a certain range of threshold points with respect to interpretation of the second paragraph of Art. 90 (ex 95) of the EC Treaty. Since the paragraph prohibits 'protectionist' measures (other than 'discriminatory' measures), it had always been controversial as to how sizable a tax differential needed to be in order to be considered protectionist. It is generally understood that the range is about 10 to 16 per cent. *See Commission v Belgium (Wine vs. Beer)* (Case 356/85) [1987] ECR 3299 (against the Commission's argument that Belgium's 25 per cent value added tax rate on wine (largely imported) versus the 19 per cent rate on beer (substantial domestic production) violated what was then Art. 95, the Court held that the 6 per cent difference was not sufficient to have a protectionist effect); *Commission v Greece (Alcohol excise tax)* (Case C-230/89) [1991] ECR 337 (the Court ruling a 36 per cent value added tax on whisky, gin, rum, etc. (largely imported) as opposed to a 16 per cent rate on ouzo and brandy (largely domestic) to have a protectionist effect).

Another example of the standard-setting efforts may be seen in the definition of monopoly under the US antitrust law (section 2 of the Sherman Act). US courts have made continuous efforts to establish threshold percentages of market share to be determined as 'monopoly'. *See Domed Stadium Hotel, Inc. v Holiday Inns, Inc.* 732 F.2d 480, 489–90, 5th Cir. 1984 (setting 50 per cent market share as the threshold); *Syufy Enterprises v American Multicinema, Inc.* 793 F.2d 990, 9th Cir. 1986 (holding 60–69 per cent is sufficient to show monopoly power when coupled with other factors, including the fragmentation of competition and the presence of entry barriers); *Reazin v Blue Cross and Blue Shield* 899 F.2d 951, 967, 9th Cir. 1990 (quoting *dicta* that courts generally require a minimum market share between 70 and 80 per cent). Today, it is generally accepted that companies holding more than 70 per cent of a market are regarded as having monopoly power.

In regard to the *prima facie* unlawfulness of mergers (Clayton Act, section 7), the US Supreme Court held that a 30 per cent market share presents the threat of undue concentration. Despite the Court's note that this figure does not reflect a minimum threshold point, this figure has subsequently worked as a litmus test on the illegality of the horizontal merger: *United States v Philadelphia National Bank*, 347 U.S. 321, 83 S.Ct. 1715, 10 L.Ed.2d 915 (1963). In fact, this decision was an authoritative interpretation on the issue of *prima facie* illegality of merger that had been controversial for many years. Before this decision, many scholars had expressed their opinion on the threshold. For example, Kaysen and Turner suggested that 20 per cent should be the division line of *prima facie* unlawfulness (*Antitrust Policy* (Harvard University Press, 1959) 133); Stigler suggested that any acquisition by a firm controlling 20 per cent of the market after the merger was presumptively unlawful ('Mergers and Preventive Antitrust Policy', 104 U. of Pa. L.Rev. 176, 182, 1955); Marham mentioned 25 per cent ('Merger Policy Under the New Section 7: A Six-Year Appraisal', 43 Va.L.Rev. 489, 521–22, 1957).

This 30 per cent threshold is also used to determine the illegality of a 'tying arrangement'. In general, 30 per cent of the market share in the tying product market is the minimum requirement for the supplier of a tying product to have sufficient market power over the tied product market. *See* Song, H-S, and Chung, C.S. *The US Antitrust Law Guide* (Korean Embassy in Washington DC, 1998) 156.

Use of the standard of market concentration (Herfindahl-Hirschman Index; HHI) in the merger guidelines by the antitrust authority represents another effort at standard setting based on economic analysis. In general, HHI over 1,000 and HHI increase (*ante* and *post* merger) over 50 tend to be challenged by the authority. *See* Song and Chung, *op. cit.*

[281] *See supra* note 107 and accompanying text.

[282] *See supra* note 115 and accompanying text. The elasticity of 0.26 means that a 10 per cent rise in the price of whisky leads to an increase of 2.6 per cent in the demand for pisco. For details, *see infra* note 299.

[283] *See* Chapter III, notes 71 and 72, and accompanying texts; and, more generally, Chapter III at 1.2.3.

[284] *See infra* notes 296–299 and accompanying texts.

[285] Usually, the purpose of the survey is not disclosed to respondents.

[286] *See* Viscusi, W. Kip, *Valuing Life and Other Nonmonetary Benefits, Economics of Regulation and Antitrust* (MIT Press, 2000) 685–707.

[287] This tendency often leads to the misleading quantification.

[288] In *Korea Alcoholic Beverages*, Korea successfully attacked the validity of the Dodwell Study by indicating defects in the sampling process of age, occupation, income, and region. It seems this success forced the Panel to rely upon the potential competition factor. *See Korea Alcoholic Beverages* Panel Report, paras 5.217–5.224.

[289] If consumers think of it as a transitory rise in price, any speculative factors can intervene, thus the result does not reflect a change in consumption *habit* (pattern) of consumers. Therefore, any impression of transitory change should not be implied in the questions.

[290] The time-series models examine the past behavior of a time series in order to infer something about its future behavior. This method used to produce a forecast might involve the use of a *simple deterministic model* such as a linear extrapolation, or the use of a *complex stochastic model* for adaptive forecasting: an example of the former is the examination of past trends in predicting population growth; an example of the latter is the examination of passenger loads for an airline to forecast the demand for airline capacity, seasonal telephone demand, the movement of short-term interest rates, as well as other economic variables. Time-series models are particularly useful when little is known about the underlying process that one is trying to forecast. The limited structure in time-series models makes them most reliable only in the short run, but they are nonetheless rather useful. *See* Pindyck, R.S. and Rubinfeld, D.L., *Econometric Models and Economic Forecasts*, 2nd ed. (McGraw-Hill Book Co., 1981) XV–XVI.

[291] *See Canada Periodicals* Panel Report, para 3.119. In general, market shares between substitutable products tend to be in inverse proportion.

[292] The Appellate Body said: 'This argument would have weight only if Canada had not protected the domestic market of Canadian periodicals through, among other measures, the import prohibition . . . and the excise tax'. *See* the Appellate Report, sec. B1.

[293] *See Japan Alcoholic Beverages* Panel Report, paras 6.30, 6.31.

[294] *See* ibid. This factor of 'competing for the same market' plays a significant role in determining direct substitutability. It seems that this criterion was suggested for the first time in one of the drafting committees of the 1947 New York Conference by a Cuban delegate regarding the interpretation of the concept of 'directly competitive (substituted)' in Art. XI, who pointed out that products 'may be *competing for the same market* and yet may be entirely different in form'. *See* U.N.Doc. E/PC/T/C.VI/17 at 4 (1947).

[295] The study was based on data taken from a national household survey for the 20-year period of 1975 through 1994, which, in Japan's view, confirmed that there was no cross-price elasticity between shochu and other distilled imported liquors. *See Japan Alcoholic Beverages* Panel Report, para 4.167.

[296] The development of the different variables is driven by factors that cannot be explained by an econometric model, but happen due to autonomous factors. For instance, consumption of a product may change simply due to fashion, economic growth, population growth, etc. When a large portion of the changes in consumption is influenced by factors of this nature, it will be difficult to separate statistically the influence of price movements from that of trends. *See* ibid., para 4.88.

[297] When the error terms from different (usually adjacent) time periods are correlated, we say that the error term is autocorrelated. Autocorrelation (or serial correlation) occurs in time-series studies when the errors associated with observations in a given time period carry over into future time periods. For example, if we are predicting the growth of stock dividends, an overestimate in one year is likely to lead to overestimates in succeeding years; an advertising campaign in one year that pushed up consumption of the product will also have an impact on consumption of the following year. If it is not corrected, autocorrelation decreases the precision of the econometric estimates. *See* Pindyck and Rubinfeld, *supra* note 290, at 152; *Japan Alcoholic Beverages* Panel Report, para 4.88.

[298] If there exists an exact linear relationship between the independent variables in the model, we say that the independent variables are perfectly collinear. By contrast, multi-collinearity arises when two or more variables (or combinations of variables) are highly (but not perfectly) correlated with each other. The coefficient of a variable is an estimation of change between the variable and the outcome factor, *with all other variables constant*. Since under the multicollinearity it is impossible to keep all other variables constant, we are not able to interpret the regression coefficient. *See* Pindyck and Rubinfeld, *supra* note 290, at 87–9. In particular, variables may move in parallel over time without necessarily implying any causal relationship. An often cited example is that of cumulative rainfall and the consumer price index, which both rise over time. *See Chile Alcoholic Beverages* Panel Report, paras 4.232–7. One of the reasons could be that the variables can in actuality be closely related because of outside factors (i.e., those not measured directly) that may affect the markets that are examined jointly. For instance, changes in the consumption of one type of liquor are related to changes in the consumption of another liquor: a hot summer will increase the consumption of all beverages. Again, this effect shows how difficult it is statistically to separate the influence of one variable from that of another. *See Japan Alcoholic Beverages* Panel Report, para 4.88.

[299] Using nominal prices instead of deflated ones can bring about over/undervaluation problems. Changes in income can affect demand in all of the product markets studied, and this effect may vary systematically across the markets. *See* ibid., paras 4.3, 6.31.

[300] The EC had access to a study carried out in 1995 by the Gemines consulting group, at the request of Chile's pisco industry. According to this study, the estimated elasticity rate was 0.26, indicating that if the price of whisky went up by 10 per cent, the sales volume of pisco would increase by 2.6 per cent. According to Gemines, that rate of cross-price elasticity was sufficient to conclude that pisco and whisky were 'substitutes, albeit to a moderate extent'. By contrast, on the basis of similar regressions, Gemines reached the conclusion that neither wine nor beer could be considered as substitutable with pisco. The EC submitted another Gemines study done in 1996, which concluded that a reduction in the tax on

whisky by 50 per cent would lead to a 47 per cent drop in the price of whisky, which would in turn lead to a 17 per cent drop in the demand for pisco. *See Chile Alcoholic Beverages* Panel Report, paras 4.217–20.

[301] According to the study, the elasticity was 0.07–0.128. *See* ibid., paras 4.223–9.

[302] *See supra* note 298.

[303] If A and B are substitutes, the price increase of A will lead to an increase in demand for B; thereby, the price of B will go up as well.

[304] Sometimes, data for the price comparison study cannot be available, especially in case of door-to-door sales.

[305] A similar attack was exercised by the US Supreme Court in an antitrust case. In this case, against the majority opinion that 'cellophane' composes a same relevant market with 'glassine, waxed paper, or sulphite paper', the dissenting opinion emphasized, as its basis for dissent, an 'indifferent' price movement between the two product categories with the following statement: '. . . Yet throughout this period the price of cellophane was far greater than that of glassine, waxed paper or sulphite paper. . . . Finding. . . states that Sylvania, the only other cellophane producer, absolutely and immediately followed every du Pont price change, even dating back its price list to the effective date of du Pont's change. Producers of glassine and waxed paper, on the other hand, displayed apparent indifference to du Pont's repeated and substantial price cuts. DX-994 shows that from 1924 to 1932 du Pont dropped the price of plain cellophane 84%, while the price of glassine and waxed paper remained constant. And during the period 1933–1946 the prices for glassine and waxed paper actually increased in the face of a further 21% decline in the price of cellophane. If "shifts of business" due to "price sensitivity" had been substantial, glassine and waxed paper producers who wanted to stay in business would have been compelled by market forces to meet du Pont's price challenge just as Sylvania was.' *See Cellophane, supra* note 96, dissenting opinion.

[306] *See supra* notes 17–20 and accompanying texts. For all the market-based economic studies, the bar-coding system can provide a useful tool. Because these days many retail goods are bar-coded, one can obtain, by pursuing the records, credible evidence of change in consumption according to a change in price. *See* this chapter at 3.3.

[307] *See supra* note 156.

[308] In the broadest sense, the supply substitutability includes following categories: (1) existing manufacturers who make a slightly different product can modify their manufacturing process to compete in an adjacent product market (narrowest definition of supply substitution); (2) manufacturers currently serving a remote market can divert their production into the monopolist's market ('geographic diversion'); (3) firms actively competing in the market but operating at less than full capacity can expand their operations; (4) lastly, companies entirely outside the product and geographic market may be able to invest quickly in new facilities and become competitors ('new entrants'). *See* Handler *et al.*, Chapter I, note 8, at 221.

[309] In general, the more reliable approach is to analyze 'existing' data or information contained in *ex ante* studies. *Ex post* studies are usually carried out by parties in dispute or other neutral institutions for the purpose of settlement of specific disputes.

[310] *See supra* notes 30 and 39, and accompanying texts.

[311] Not too large or small, typically in the range 5–10 per cent. *See* Appendix III.

[312] Or, the criteria could be 'profit change' rather than price change. The question can be constructed to ask whether the respondents would switch their production from the sector where a certain percentage of tax is imposed, to another sector where less tax is imposed.

[313] *See* Appendix III.

[314] Infinite demand of Y (or X) is assumed.

[315] Product price is known as the most important consideration to suppliers of the product. It is reasonable to assume that if X price rises twice as much as before, twice as many suppliers would switch their supply to this sector, *ceteris paribus. See* Appendix III.

[316] *Compare with supra* notes 266–270 and accompanying texts.

[317] In the case of a likeness test between a Timor and a Rolls Royce, the IASR would be the average supply substitution rate of the 'automobile manufacturing industry'.

[318] Shochu and vodka are basically similar type of liquors with regard to material, process, and technique. *See supra* note 173. Thus, the supply substitution rate between them would be relatively high. But shochu and whisky are quite different in all of the aspects listed above.

[319] Given similarity in source material, taste, color, etc., the demand substitutability between shochu and vodka will likely be higher than it would be between shochu and whisky.

[320] Concerning the origin-neutral-cases limitation, *see supra* note 197 and accompanying text. With regard to contextual analysis of whether or not supply substitutability should be considered in the likeness test of each provision, *see* Chapter III.

[321] *See supra* note 265 and accompanying text.

[322] The questionnaire can be structured to examine switching rate where production of one product is prohibited (non-availability analysis on supply substitutability). *Compare with supra* note 106.

[323] *See supra* notes 158–217 and accompanying texts.

[324] *See supra* notes 284–289 and accompanying texts.

[325] *See supra* notes 246–299.

[326] There was discussion of whether such products as tramways and buses or coal and fuel oil could be considered as categories of directly competitive or substitutable products. There seems to be some disagreement with respect to these products. One delegate asked if 'coal vs. fuel oil' and 'tramways vs. buses' could be considered directly competitive or substitutable. Another delegate noted the need for actual cases in order to interpret the provision, but opined that such products were not substitutable. A third delegate, however, stated that decisions could not be made except in relation to a particular factual situation, but that a tax on coal in a particular case might be designed to protect the fuel oil industry. *See* E/Conf.2/C.3/SR.40 at p. 2.

[327] *See* ibid.

[328] Ibid.

[329] *See* Report of the GATT Panel, *United States—Measures Affecting the Importation, Internal Sale and Use of Tobacco (hereinafter 'United States Tobacco')*, BISD, DS44/R (1994) paras 92–93, 95–98.

[330] Another good example is Art. XI of the GATT. The following paragraph of the *Oilseed* case explains this point: 'A previous panel pointed out that Articles III and XI are to protect expectations of the contracting parties as to the competitive relationship between their products and those of other contracting parties. Both articles are not only to protect current trade but also create the predictability needed to plan future trade.' *See* Report of the Panel, *EEC— Payments and Subsidies Paid to Processors and Producers of Oilseeds and Related Animal-Feed Proteins (hereinafter 'EEC Oilseeds')*, BISD 37S/86 para 150, adopted on 25 January 1990. *See also United States—Taxes on Petroleum and Certain Imported Substances*, BISD 34S/136 (report adopted on 17 June 1987). This does not mean, however, that the likeness test in Art. XI:2

should include potential or future competition analysis: Art. XI:2 prescribes 'exceptions' to the general prohibition of quantitative restriction in Art. XI. *See* Chapter III at 1.3.

[331] *See Brazilian Internal Taxes*, BISD II/181, para 16 (1949) (ruling that Art. III was intended to *prevent* damage (not merely to provide means of redress), and thus Art. III:2, first sentence was equally applicable whether imports from other contracting parties were substantial, small, or non-existent); *US—Taxes on Petroleum and Certain Imported Substances*, BISD 34S/136, para 5.1.9 (1988) (holding that the purpose of Art. III is to protect expectations of the competitive relationship); *Japan Alcoholic Beverages* Appellate Report, sec. F ('Article III protects expectations not of any particular trade volume but rather of the equal competitive relationship between imported and domestic products').

See also the following ruling based on 'inherency'-type reasoning: 'However, beyond the immediate circumstance of a higher assessment on imported flue-cured tobacco than on like domestic tobacco, the Panel considered that the US statutorily prescribed averaging method for calculation of the BDA on imported tobacco *contained an inherent risk of a higher assessment* on some types of imported tobacco than on like domestic tobacco.... The Panel noted that an internal regulation which merely *exposed* imported products to a risk of discrimination had previously been recognized by a GATT panel to constitute, by itself, a form of discrimination, and therefore less favourable treatment within the meaning of Article III...' (*United States Tobacco* Panel Report, paras 92–93, 95–98 (1994) (emphasis added).)

Indicating the above ruling of the *US Tobacco* Panel, some scholars argue that future substitutability should be included in the likeness test of Art. III: '*Moreover*, even if a given regulation in its application does not currently discriminate against imports, if the regulation poses the risk of discrimination *in the future* it violates the national treatment obligation'. (Bhala and Kennedy, Chapter I, note 22, at 93; emphasis added).

[332] *United States—Taxes on Petroleum and Certain Imported Substances*, para 5.1.9 (1987) (3.5 cent per barrel tax differential between imported and domestic oil violates Art. III); *United States—Measures affecting Alcoholic and Malt Beverages (hereinafter 'United States Malt Beverages')*, BISD 39S/206, 270–71, at para 5.6 (1992) (national treatment violation even though only 1 per cent of domestic beer benefited from tax reduction).

[333] *See* Report of the GATT Panel, *United States—Section 337 of the Tariff Act of 1930*, BISD, 36S/345, 387, at para 5.14 (1989).

[334] It is interesting to see that the concept of 'potentiality' was also used in regard to the 'standing' issue. In *EC Bananas*, the European Community claimed that the United States did not have standing to bring its claim under GATT 1994 because the United States is not a banana exporter. The Panel and Appellate Body disagreed on the grounds that 'A member has broad discretion in deciding whether to bring a case against another member... The United States is a producer of bananas, and a *potential* export interest by the United States cannot be excluded. The internal market of the United States for bananas *could be affected* by the EC banana regime, in particular, by the effects of that regime on world supplies and world prices of bananas.' *See EC—Regime for the Importation, Sale and Distribution of Bananas (hereinafter 'EC Bananas')*, WT/DS27/AB/R paras 14–15, 135–6 (1997).

[335] *See supra* notes 291–292 and accompanying texts.

[336] *See Korea Alcoholic Beverages* Panel Report, para 10.48 (emphasis added).

[337] *Ibid.*, para 10.64.

[338] *Korea Alcoholic Beverages* Appellate Report, secs 114, 115.

[339] 'We agree that Panels should look at evidence of trends and changes in consumption patterns and make an assessment as to whether such trends and patterns lead to the

conclusion that the products in question are either directly competitive or substitutable now or can reasonably be expected to become directly competitive or substitutable in the near future. In the case before us, as in the Korea case, potential competition is relevant for several reasons. Until 30 November 1997, whisky faced very high rates of taxation (45 percentage points higher than pisco). We must take into consideration the possibility that the current level of actual competition between pisco and other spirits is less than the level that could have developed under equal tax conditions. It is possible that the tax system in question (in conjunction with other measures not at issue, such as previously higher duties) may have inhibited consumers from choosing imports.' (*Chile Alcoholic Beverages* Panel Report, paras 7.24–5.)

340 The *ordinary* meaning of *potential competition* could include, in the broadest sense, all four categories above. To distinguish this ordinary meaning from the specific meaning of 'potential competition' in a narrow sense, the author would use quotation marks only for the latter, *i.e.* 'potential competition' is used to express the narrow sense, while potential competition (without quotation marks) is used to express the ordinary and broadest meaning.

341 Krugman, P.R. and Obstfeld, M., *International Economics: Theory and Policy*, 4th ed. (Addison-Wesley Longman, Inc. 1997) 41.

342 'One influential study finds that when a US state hits economic difficulties, workers quickly begin leaving for other states; within six years the unemployment rate falls back to the national average. . . . So labor is certainly a less specific factor than most kinds of capital.' Ibid.

343 Thus, 'potential competition or substitutability' is a *retrospective* flow concept, while 'future competition or substitutability' is a *prospective* flow concept.

344 The *Korea Alcoholic Beverages* Panel used the words 'potential/potentially/potentiality' 77 times and the word 'future' 24 times in its report. *See supra* note 127.

345 *See Korea Alcoholic Beverages* Panel Report, paras 10.49, 10.81.

346 As an economic analysis, submitted by Korea, presents a low co-relationship between Korean soju and foreign whisky, and the validity of the Dodwell Study, submitted by the complainants, was effectively attacked by Korea, the Panel turned its attention to the Japanese market, which is, according to the Panel's view, a 'comparable' foreign market to the Korean market. *See infra* note 355 and accompanying text.

347 *See supra* note 338 and accompanying text. *See also* Chapter III, note 206 and accompanying text.

348 Competition law also takes into consideration a 'potential competition' factor in relevant market determination. But it should be noted that, despite the similarity in the 'idea' itself, the potential competition concept in competition law and its namesake in the GATT have different meanings. In competition law, potential competition is basically an extension of supply substitutability. Since the existence of potential entrants may constrain the market power of the existing dominant entity, these entrants should somehow be encompassed within the definition of the relevant market, even though they have no current market share. *See* Handler *et al.*, Chapter I, note 8, at 221. Thus, in competition law, a longer timeframe is given for the consideration of potential competition than that given for supply substitutability. The longer the period is, the more supply substitution would occur because a higher potential entry would be realized as supply substitution. But in the GATT, the potential competition concept presupposes legal barriers and examines what would happen in a hypothetical case in which there are no such barriers. By contrast, the supply substitution concept does not have such a presupposition. Thus, in the GATT it is not proper to think that the former concept is a mere extension of the latter.

This difference in meaning of potential competition between the two legal fields happens because competition authorities, as opposed to GATT tribunals, tend to consider legal barriers such as tax differentials as permanent barriers to competition and disregard any additional competition that may arise from removing those barriers. *See supra* notes 272 and 273. *See also* Chapter I, notes 19 and 21. Accordingly, inquiry points of the potential competition factor between the two laws should be different.

With respect to the scope of the potential competition in the competition law context, it seems that there is a little difference between the United States and the European Communities. United States law often includes the very near potential competitors in the market on the theory that strong near potential competition is likely to cause incumbents to behave responsibly. European Communities law is less likely than United States law to treat potential competitors as though they were in the market. *See* Bermann *et al.*, *supra* note 79, at 811.

In the antitrust law context, the area where the potential competition concept is most utilized is the conglomerate merger. Since this type of merger constitutes neither horizontal nor vertical constraints, the competition authorities tend to examine any 'potential' impediments in horizontal or vertical competitive relationships. *See*, e.g., *United States v Penn-Olin Chemical Co.*, 378 U.S. 158, 84 S.Ct. 1710; *FTC v Proctor & Gamble Co.*, 386 US 568, 87 S.Ct. 1224; *United States v Falstaff Brewing Corp.*, 410 U.S. 526, 93 S.Ct. 1096; *United States v Marine Bancorporation*, 418 U.S. 602, 94 S.Ct. 2856.

[349] One can reasonably infer future likeness between products from the current trend of increasing consumer use of the products. But the future is always uncertain. Who can predict without fault that this trend will lead to likeness in the end? A massive economic crisis or natural disaster could occur and change this trend fundamentally. With regard to the future, only reasonable *speculation* is possible at best.

[350] These possibilities are more serious in competition law, where it takes longer to litigate. *See* Handler *et al.*, Chapter I, note 8, at 221.

[351] This issue was discussed in the context of the US antidumping law. *See* Holmer, A.F. and Bello, J.H., 'US Trade Law and Policy Series #9: The Scope of "Class or Kind of Merchandise" in Antidumping and Countervailing Duty Cases', *The International Lawyer*, Vol. 20 No. 3, pp. 1015–18 (Summer 1986).

[352] The future substitution factor is concerned not only with the definition of the likeness concept, but also with the determination of whether there exists 'discrimination' prohibited by the GATT, as indicated at the beginning of the discussion on this issue. In particular, the factor raises an interesting question concerning *de facto* discrimination. In this transient environment of competitive relationships, one might argue that a measure that leads to '*de facto*' discrimination may nevertheless be compatible with the GATT if there exists strong evidence that this *de facto* discriminatory effect is only temporary and would be quickly eroded because of a change in consumption patterns or other market conditions. If such strong and stable evidence is shown through the future substitution test, there is little reason why the tribunal would stick to the *current* effect of *de facto* discrimination; after all, the *de facto* discrimination is based on the 'burden (or effect) on competitive relationship' test. In order to assess the full implications of the *de facto* discrimination, therefore, it is necessary to assess the likelihood of all relevant aspects, including such possible changes in the future in consumption patterns and market conditions.

[353] *Korea Alcoholic Beverages* Panel Report, para 10.50. This paragraph was cited and fully accepted by the *Chile Alcoholic Beverages* Panel. *See* the Panel Report, paras 7.23–4.

[354] *See supra* note 111.

[355] Ibid., para 0.80.

[356] Panel Report on *Japan Alcoholic Beverages*, para 6.28, citing, Panel Report on *Japan Wine and Liquor*, para 5.9.

[357] *See Korea Alcoholic Beverages* Panel Report, para 10.44 (emphasis added).

[358] A good example is the Adimark Survey submitted by the EC in *Chile Alcoholic Beverages*. In order to assess the reactions of the different socio-demographic segments of the Chilean population to the proposed price changes, the survey covered four 'focus groups', high income group, low income group, high age group, and low age group. The survey concluded, *inter alia*, that the section of Chilean society most reluctant to switch from pisco to imports was the group with least exposure to such products. Those with the greatest experience already with imports showed the willingness to switch more readily; young consumers, in particular, considered that the reduction in the tax applied to whisky would provide a 'good alternative to replace pisco'. Despite the small number of respondents, the survey was highly referred to as 'qualitative' evidence by the Panel. *See Chile Alcoholic Beverages* Panel Report, paras 4.249–53, 7.41–5.

[359] By comparing answer sheets of the experienced with those of the inexperienced, one could calculate how much is due to the 'frozen preferences' effect.

With regard to this potential competition methodology, one could pose an interesting question: how far can the inquiry into potentiality reach? In actuality, product substitutability is hindered due to various supply-side impediments in the market. Such impediments include not only *illegal barriers* (such as quotas, discriminatory taxes, or tariffs) but also many *legitimate practical barriers* (such as market distribution system, price regulation, etc.). For example, the price difference between manufacturers' suggested retail prices and actual on-shelf prices can impede substitutability: even though products X and Y are actually substitutable, the price discount of product X by the producer would not affect the demand for product Y if the discount could not affect actual on-shelf prices. Local presence requirements, conditions of access to distribution channels, or costs associated with setting up a distribution network can have an influence on product substitutability by hindering consumers' access to the goods (thus reducing their availability). Further examples of such hindrance could include technical standards, packaging regulations, and monopolies.

Among these, the focus of the potential competition or substitutability test (for the purpose of the GATT likeness analysis) should be limited to the 'illegal' barriers under consideration. For example, in *Canada Periodicals*, the Appellate Body considered the tariff protection effect, which was one of the issues under consideration. When a complaining party files a complaint about a discriminatory tax measure, the potential competition issue should be examined only in the hypothetical situation in which the tax measure is removed. Other issues beyond the subject matter issue should not be allowed to intrude into this stage of the potential competition examination. Otherwise, the 'unbridled horse' of potential competition may reach too far.

This point could provide for another delicate difference between the GATT and competition law.

[360] As already discussed, once the examiner obtains the results from demand and supply substitution analysis and adjusts those results to take into account potential substitution and competition considerations, there is not much reason to consider future effect too. Thus, only limited situations would be witness to the utility of the future effect. For example, if the overall outcome of the PMP Questionnaires (CVA-PCPPDS complemented by

CVA-PCPSS) turned out to be somewhat unsatisfactory in meeting the threshold rate of substitution (PSE Standard complemented by IASR), the examiner could turn to future effect tests, provided the situation on which the future effect is based is clearly supposed to occur (as in hi-tech goods).

[361] Once a complaint is submitted, it takes usually about one to one and a half years to determine it. Sometimes it takes two years. Thus, one could argue that, if it is proven that certain future competition or substitution will occur during this period, it is better to take it into account in the likeness consideration. Otherwise, the losing party should file the complaint again as soon as it is rejected.

The US Horizontal Merger Guidelines (*supra* note 263) set two years as the timeframe of the 'timeliness' element for the purpose of examining market entry barriers. It seems that the one year timeframe is also used in other contexts. If new firms, within two years after certain mergers and acquisitions under investigation, can enter the market, this will be used as negative evidence of the illegality of the merger. *See* Song *supra* note 280, at p. 105. *See also* Kauper, Chapter I, note 39, at 1707–8.

One of the EU antitrust cases, *Elopak Italia v Tetra Pak* [1992] 4 CMLR 551, gives some indication in that regard. The Commission rejected the assertion that the relevant product market was the packing market for liquid foods, but instead narrowed the product market to the packing market for aseptic and nonaseptic machines and cartons. The rejection arose because of the judgement that the market should be assessed merely over the short term, and that the possibility of substitutability between various packing types over the long term was not relevant. The Commission explained that 'a short period corresponds more to the economic operative time during which a given company exercises its power on the market and, consequently, on which one must concentrate in order to assess that power'. The Commission, however, did not bother to expound upon the boundaries between the short, medium, and long term. *See* Jebsen and Stevens, Chapter I, note 31.

[362] Sometimes, one can use these answers to compare with answers to other questions concerning demand and supply substitutability or potential competition; this comparison will be helpful to judge the sincerity of the respondent or to reveal inconsistency in the respondent's answering.

[363] *See* McGovern, Introduction, note 22, paras 8.12–4.

[364] *See supra* notes 200, 208, and 214, and accompanying texts.

[365] Another case might possibly be *EEC Animal Feed Proteins. See infra* note 367. In this regard, it should be noted that the *Automobile* report was not adopted by the Contracting Parties, and *Malt Beverages* used traditional tests as well as the aim and effect approach.

[366] *See* Panel Report of *United States Malt Beverages*, paras 5.25, 5.71; Panel Report of *United States Automobiles*, paras 5.8 *et seq.* In those cases, whether or not the purpose of the measures was to afford protection to domestic production was considered, and it was concluded that there were no such purpose and effect, thus determining that (1) high-alcohol and low-alcohol beers, and (2) luxury vehicles and ordinary vehicles are not like products. For further details, *see supra* notes 45 and 201.

[367] Thus, interestingly, the initiator of the aim and effect type approach, although it was not to the full extent, seems to be the Panel in *EEC Animal Feed Proteins* (1978). Examining whether vegetable proteins and skimmed milk powder were 'directly competitive or substitutable' products within the meaning of Art. III:2, the Panel clearly considered, among others, the purpose and effect of the measure, as the following statement demonstrates (*EEC—Measures on Animal Feed Proteins*, BISD 25S/49 (14 March 1978), para 4.3

(emphasis added)): '*Substitutable products* The Panel noted that the General Agreement made a distinction between "like products" and "directly competitive and substitutable" products. The Panel therefore also examined whether these products should be considered as directly competitive and substitutable within the meaning of Article III. In this regard the Panel noted that both the United States and the EEC considered most of these products to be substitutable under certain conditions. The Panel also noted that the *objective of the EEC Regulation* during the period of its application, in its own terms, was to allow for increased utilization of denatured skimmed milk powder as a protein source for use in feedingstuffs for animals other than calves. Furthermore, the Panel noted that the security deposit had been fixed at such a level as to make it economically advantageous to buy denatured skimmed milk powder rather than to provide the security, thus making denatured skimmed milk powder competitive with these products. The Panel concluded that vegetable proteins and skimmed milk powder were technically substitutable in terms of their final use and that the *effects of the EEC measures* were to make skimmed milk powder competitive with these vegetable proteins.'

[368] With regard to the definition of 'aim and effect', the United States seems to suggest that 'aim' is 'purpose' ('aim and purpose are interchangeable') and 'effect' is 'impact on competitive relationship' between the products in question ('the effects-only test would imply that all internal measures maintained by the Community and its Member States should be reviewed and judged solely in relation to whether they happen to disadvantage imports'). Emphasizing that its suggested test is not 'aim *or* effect' but 'aim *and* effect', the United States argued that *both* the 'aim' and 'effect' of the measure should be examined. *See Japan Alcoholic Beverages* Panel Report, para 4.50.

[369] 'Whether two products that are not identical are nevertheless considered to be like products depends on the perspective from which they are viewed. *A fox and an eagle are like animals to a hare but not to a furrier...* Article III:1 prescribes the perspective from which products are to be compared by declaring that domestic taxes and regulations should not be applied "so as to afford protection to domestic production". The term "so as to" suggests that both the intent and the effect of the regulation or tax are relevant. In determining whether two products are alike, the central issue thus is whether the product categories under which they fall have been distinguished with the intent and effect of affording protection.' (Roessler, *supra* note 212, at 29.)

This view suggests that a measure could be said to have the 'aim' of affording protection if the analysis of the circumstances in which it was adopted, in particular an analysis of the instruments available to achieve the declared policy goal, demonstrated that a change in competitive opportunities in favor of domestic products was a desired outcome and not merely an incidental consequence of the pursuit of a legitimate policy goal. *See Japan Alcoholic Beverages* Panel Report, para 4.17.

The examination of the 'effect', according to this view, should focus on the qualitative alteration of the conditions of competition, such as the targeting of imports and any evidence of cross-elasticity of demand between the favored and disfavored categories. This view further emphasizes that the aim-and-effect test would apply only to a small subset of Art. III cases that involve origin-neutral legislation. *See* Roessler, *op. cit.*

[370] *See* Chapter III at 1.1 and this chapter at 3.2.3.

[371] Certain provisions under Art. XX except only those measures that are 'necessary' to further the approved policy goal. Once a complaining party has shown that the challenged measure is inconsistent with the GATT, the burden of showing that the inconsistency is

justified under Art. XX shifts to the depending party. *See*, e.g., *United States Malt Beverages*, para 5.41. Hence, the regulating nation bears the burden of showing the 'necessity' condition.

[372] Professor Roessler wrote that this result was 'probably not intended by the drafters of the General Agreement and that would hardly be acceptable to the contracting parties' (*see* Roessler, *supra* note 212, at 30).

[373] Thereby enhancing the 'regulatory autonomy'. *See* ibid., at 31; *see also* Roessler, F., *Regulatory Reform and International Market Openness* (OECD, 1996) 118.

In *Japan Alcoholic Beverages*, the United States referred the Panel to the reasoning of the *United States Malt Beverages* Panel Report, as it specifically addressed the issue of product differentiation based on facially-neutral criteria: 'The purpose of Article III is ... not to prevent contracting parties from using their fiscal and regulatory powers for purposes other than to afford protection to domestic production. Specifically, the purpose of Article III is not to prevent contracting parties from differentiating between different product categories for policy purposes unrelated to the protection of domestic production'. (The Panel found under these criteria that beer with a high alcoholic content is not like beer with a low alcoholic content. *See United States Malt Beverages* Panel Report, para 5.25; *Japan Alcoholic Beverages* Panel Report, para 4.33.)

In the US view, the *Malt Beverages* Panel sought to avoid a result that would make even an unintentional coincidence between domestic regulation and the presence or absence of foreign competition in the market, a violation of Art. III:2. Such a result would force policy harmonization and encroach on the policy options available to legislators and regulators to an extent unanticipated when the GATT was drafted. The United States noted that the WTO Agreement recognizes that origin-neutral regulatory distinctions can be compatible with WTO principles although these distinctions do not appear in Art. XX of GATT 1994.

Examples taken by the United States are policies protecting historic buildings not in the 'national treasure' class, policies protecting foreign art, non-protectionist food labelling rules, and Sunday closing laws. Japan pointed to differentiated treatment between unleaded gasoline and leaded gasoline as an example of legitimate policy. *See Japan Alcoholic Beverages* Panel Report, paras 4.3, 4.18, 4.40.

[374] Under the Agreement on Technical Barriers to Trade ('TBT Agreement'), technical regulations are permitted when they fulfil 'legitimate objectives'. The Agreement includes a 'not exhaustive' list of such legitimate objectives (i.e., national security requirements, prevention of deceptive practices, protection of human health or safety, animal or plant life or health, or the environment). *See* Art. 2.2. According to the United States, there are many other legitimate objectives, and even those specifically listed in the TBT Agreement are not all found in Art. XX; no one could read the TBT Agreement as prohibiting technical regulations, or find that they are, *per se*, inconsistent with Art. III of GATT 1994 whenever imports are disproportionately affected, simply because the regulations in question are based on criteria other than those in Art. XX. *See Japan Alcoholic Beverages* Panel Report, para 4.25.

[375] *See* ibid., paras 4.26–4.28.

[376] The United States submitted that if national treatment obligations in the GATT and the GATS were to be interpreted consistently, a discrimination test linked only to enumerated general exceptions would lead to difficult conclusions in the case of GATS which has a narrower exceptions list than that of GATT. *See* ibid., para 4.40.

[377] *See* Chapter III, notes 100–104 and 143.

[378] *See supra* note 371.

[379] The adoption of the aim-and-effect test would have important repercussions on the issue of burden of proof. According to the aim-and-effect test, the complainant has the burden of showing not only the effect of a particular measure, which is in principle discernible, but also its aim, which sometimes can be indiscernible. *See Japan Alcoholic Beverages* Panel Report, paras 4.13, 6.16.

These risks involved in the aim-and-effect approach should be avoided. In this regard, the European Community's argument in *Japan Alcoholic Beverages* is noteworthy: '... the aim-and-effect test could open the door to claims that the extraterritorial application of environmental regulations concerning non-product related processes and production methods is not contrary to Article III.... one could argue that the imposition of a higher sales tax rate on products which have been manufactured by workers whose wages are below a certain level or who are required to work on Sundays does not infringe Article III:2 ... because the tax differential is based on non-protectionist social considerations.... Moreover, there is a risk that the aim-and-effect test could contaminate other GATT provisions and, more generally, the entire WTO system by substituting for some of the hard-and-fast rules at the heart of the system the unpredictable balancing of ill defined "legitimate policy objectives". The Community concluded that if the general opinion were that the exceptions provided for in Article XX are not sufficient in relation to Article III:2, first sentence, the only approach consistent with the WTO Agreement would be to amend Article XX in order to add new grounds of justification and/or to relax the conditions for their application. Articles 3.2 and 19.2 of the DSU make clear that panels cannot add to or diminish the rights and the obligations of the Members under GATT. Thus, panels are precluded from engaging in the creation of new exceptions to existing obligations even when this appears to be necessary in order to fill GATT lacunae.' (*Japan Alcoholic Beverages* Panel Report, para 4.42.)

Moreover, if a determination of likeness depends upon the aim of the measure in question, several practical problems arise:

(1) very often, there is a multiplicity of aims that are sought through the enactment of legislation and it would be difficult to determine which aims should be determinative for applying the aim-and-effect test (*see* ibid., para 6.16.);

(2) access to the complete legislative history, which according to the arguments of the proponents of the aim-and-effect test, is relevant to detect protective aims, could be difficult or even impossible (*see* ibid.: 'The records of treaty negotiations can be in many cases incomplete or misleading, so that too much discretion has to be exercised in determining their value as an element of interpretation ... in the Panel's view, the analysis and reasoning of the International Law Commission could be relevant even in the context of preparatory work of domestic legislation'); moreover, that history could be manipulated by both proponents and opponents of the legislation; and

(3) it can be argued that the 'supplementary means', such as preparatory work and the circumstances of its conclusion, do not have the same authentic character as an element of interpretation. Although differences exist between international treaties and domestic legislation, the Vienna Convention on the Law of Treaties can be elucidating. The Convention limits the role of supplementary means to confirm or determine the meaning of the text when the interpretation leaves the meaning ambiguous or obscure, or manifestly absurd or unreasonable (*see* Art. 32 of the Vienna Convention on the Law of Treaties, UN Doc. A/CONF.39/27 (1969), *reprinted in* (1969) 8 ILM 679).

[380] *See Japan Alcoholic Beverages* Appellate Report, sec H2.

[381] In addition, it should be noted that although the aim of the measures in question cannot change, consumer tastes and preferences can. As a result, most consumers may come to consider that two products in question are no longer like or substitutable. In this case, the aim-and-effect test will still rely on the unchanged aim.

Furthermore, the interpretation of aim and effect is not free from controversy: in *Japan Alcoholic Beverages*, both the United States and Japan made opposing arguments using the same concept of aim and effect. Japan submitted that the discriminatory tax had the legitimate aim and effect of achieving horizontal tax equity by taxing according to the tax-bearing ability of domestic consumers. By contrast, the United States countered that the Japanese tax scheme had the aim and effect of protecting domestic goods by using carefully defined separate product categories. *See Japan Alcoholic Beverages* Panel Report, secs. III, IV.

[382] *See Japan Alcoholic Beverages* Panel Report, para 4.7.

[383] The Appellate Body in *Japan Alcoholic Beverages* excluded from the interpretation of like or substitutable products any extraneous considerations including the 'aim and effect' of the regulation in question; the examination of the aim of the measure becomes relevant only in order to determine whether the infringement of Art. III:2, first sentence may be justified under one of the general exceptions of GATT Art. XX. *See Japan Alcoholic Beverages* Appellate Report, sec. H.

This approach was followed by the confirmation of the Appellate Body in *Korea and Chile Alcoholic Beverages*: 'In our Report in Japan—Alcoholic Beverages, we said that examination of whether a tax regime affords protection to domestic production "is an issue of how the measure in question is applied", and that such an examination "requires a comprehensive and objective analysis".' *See Korea Alcoholic Beverages* Appellate Report, WT/DS75/AB/R; WT/DS84/AB/R, para 149 (1999). *See also Chile Alcoholic Beverages* Panel Report, sec. VII.

But one might still raise doubts as to whether the Korean and Chilean cases rejected the aim-and-effect approach because the 'genuine' issue of the approach—i.e. the issue of the first sentence of Art. III:2—did not arise in those cases. *See supra* note 67.

In *United States Gasoline*, while it did not deal with this issue specifically, the Panel stressed that the proper test should be confined to physical properties, and warned of the dangers of relying on extraneous factors. *See United States Gasoline* Panel Report, para 6.7.

In *EC Bananas*, the Appellate Body indirectly accepted a previous decision of *Japan Alcoholic Beverages*, which rejected the aim-and-effect test. *See EC Bananas* Appellate Report, sec. C6 (1997).

[384] In the antitrust law context, *see* Handler *et al.*, Chapter I, note 8, at 219.

[385] Ibid.

[386] Ibid.

[387] *See* Sullivan, L.A. *Handbook of the Law of Antitrust* (West Wadsworth, 1977) 72.

[388] In the US antitrust law context, the comparable approach is the 'price–characteristics–use' test of the *Cellophane* case. *See supra* notes 96 and 142.

[389] Consumer choice is largely dependent upon the physical characteristics of products.

[390] Demand substitutability is one of the considerations that producers take into account when making supply substitution decisions.

[391] Current barriers to trade could be a reason why there is a difference between the general end-use and the end-use in the market.

[392] Sangria is a mixture of wine, water, sugar, and fruit extracts. Cider, perry, and mead are fermented beverages.

393 *See* Handler *et al.*, Chapter I, note 8, at 219.

394 Ibid., at 222–3.

395 Ibid.

396 *See* Art. 13 of DSU. Due to this provision, WTO panels are not confined to the factual record provided by the parties in dispute. One can say that this authority reflects the civil law tradition of courts, as opposed to the common law tradition in which such authority of the court does not exist.

397 These panels include *EC Measures Concerning Meat and Meat Products* (*Hormones*; WT/DS26/R/USA, WT/DS48/R/Can, paras 8.7–8.9), *United States—Import Prohibition of Certain Shrimp and Shrimp Products* (WT/DS58/R, para 5.1), *Australia—Measures Affecting Importation of Salmon* (*Australia Salmon*; WT/DS18/R, paras 6.2–6.5) and *Japan—Measures Affecting Consumer Photographic Film and Paper* (WT/DS44/R, paras 1.9–1.10).

398 Not only the DSU, in general, but also the SPS Agreement and the TBT Agreement, in particular, give the panel authority to establish an advisory experts group for technical matters. *See* Art. 11.2 of the SPS Agreement; Art. 14.2 of the TBT Agreement.

399 A good example is the Permanent Group of Exports (PGE) under the SCM Agreement, which renders advisory opinions and consults parties concerning the issue of the existence of prohibited subsidies. *See* Arts 4.5, 24.3, 24.4 of the SCM Agreement. In addition, the Customs Valuation Agreement enables panels to request the Technical Committee on Customs Valuation to carry out an examination of any questions requiring technical consideration. *See* Art. 19.4 of the Customs Valuation Agreement.

400 This comment in turn can be subject to counter response by the experts. This process is well exemplified in *Australia Salmon. See supra* note 397.

401 As in cases of DSU, SPS and TBT experts.

402 As in the case of Customs Valuation experts.

403 As in the case of SCM PGE. It should be noted that the use of experts has not been without controversy. *See*, e.g., *EC Hormone Beef*. It could end up with a battle of the experts, and the experts' opinions may be less independent than those of the panellists. But more sophisticated reasonings tailored to a specific context of WTO agreements cannot be given in the end without participation of experts in the specific field.

404 Often, this first-step examination could be decisive in the entire likeness test, in which adequate data for economic analysis do not exist, or time-series trends cannot yet be modeled, or in which the process being examined subsequently operates in such a manner that it is not susceptible to the conventions of prediction and verification.

405 This does not mean that the objective-characteristics examination creates a presumption as to likeness together with rebuttal right for the opposing party; what it means is the '*de facto* completion' of the procedure in manifest cases. Different from the 'presumption-rebuttal' mechanism, the tribunal can have more freedom in this '*de facto* conclusion' system: the panel may well proceed to a second-step analysis despite the result of the first-step examination, especially if the result is not clear enough. By contrast, in the presumption-rebuttal system, if the opposing party fails to rebut the presumption, the panel is obliged to determine likeness based on the results of the first-step examination, no matter how marginal the result is. It should be noted that this proposal of the *de facto* conclusion of process is a 'general' one. That is, in several exceptional provisions of the GATT, the objective characteristics examination can create *presumptions* with regard to 'likeness' (e.g., the likeness test in Art. III:2, first sentence: *see* Chapter III, notes 174–176 and accompanying texts), in which case the party opposing the presumption will have the right to rebut.

III PROGRESSIVE INTERPRETATION OF 'LIKE' AND 'DIRECTLY
COMPETITIVE OR SUBSTITUTABLE' PRODUCTS IN THE PROVISIONS
OF THE GATT/WTO AGREEMENT: PLAYING THE ACCORDION!

¹ The following GATT preparatory work records show that there was serious discussion of this matter (including the historical background of the concept); it seems that due to the abortion of the ITO any subsequent discussion was stopped: 'Mr VIDEIA (Chile) referred to a report by the United States Delegate on the subject of defining "like products". That report indicated that the expression had been used for many years in most-favoured-nation clauses without a precise definition. The League of Nations had once made a report on the matter to the effect that a "like product" was one that was practically identical with another. But, the ITO would want to give continued study on the matter. The expression had different meanings in different contexts of the Draft Charter. He said that the Technical Sub-Committee had considered the question of definitions and had proposed that the ITO should work on that matter.' *See* UN Doc. EPCT/C.II/65, at 2 (1946). *See also* Introduction, note 14 and Appendix I, note 36.

² Jackson *et al.*, Chapter II, note 138, at 449.

³ Ibid.

⁴ *See* the Report of Working Party in *Australia Ammonium Sulphate*, BISD II/188 (1952), paras 8, 9 (between Arts I and III:4); *EEC Animal Feed Proteins*, paras 4.1, 4.2 (between Arts I and III:4). The Panel in *Japan Wine and Liquor* also seems to suggest the same scope. *See* the Panel Report, para 5.5(b) (among Arts I:1, III:2, III:4).

⁵ *See* Introduction, note 13.

⁶ Ibid.

⁷ 'The Article VI exception exists because it is felt by many that dumped and subsidized imports are unfair, suggesting a broader interpretation.' (Ibid.)

⁸ *See* Vienna Convention on the Law of Treaties, Art. 31.

⁹ Ibid.

¹⁰ Ibid., Art. 32.

¹¹ *See* Chapter II, note 1.

¹² *See* Zedalis, Chapter II, note 232. Using the four types of classification, Mr Zedalis approached the like product concept in each provision of GATT and concluded that the interpretation of the different scopes of the concepts was in line with the basic theme of the General Agreement, i.e. keeping any possible intervention efforts away from a natural comparative economic advantage. The author owes him credit for the initial idea and specific facts with regard to the provision-by-provision analysis on the likeness concept discussed below.

¹³ Articles I:1, XIII, IX, V:5.

¹⁴ Articles III:2, III:4, XI:2, and XIX:1, and Antidumping Agreement, Art. 4:1.

¹⁵ Articles VI:1, XVI:4, VI:4, VI:7, XVI:3 (Note 2 of *Ad* Art. XVI:3), *Ad* Art. XVI.

¹⁶ Article VII:2.

¹⁷ Except XIX:1 and the Antidumping Agreement, Art. 4:1 in the second type. The former provision will join the 'other provisions' category, and the latter will be classified as the 'fair trade provisions'.

¹⁸ Bhala and Kennedy, Chapter I, note 22, at 59. For detailed economic arguments, *see* Jackson, Chapter I, note 54, at 157–60.

[19] In this light, the following address is noteworthy: 'This obligation prevents the grant to favored nations to undercut the prices of their competitors in foreign markets and thus to shift the currents of world trade and cause untold injury. In its essence it means the rule of minimum disturbance in international trade and economic peace.' (Francis B. Sayre, *Most-Favored-Nation vs. Preferential Bargaining* (address before the United States Junior Chamber of Commerce at Columbus, Ohio, on 28 June 1935) p. 5 (US Department of State Commercial Policy Series No. 15, US GPO, Washington, 1935).)

[20] *See* Jackson, *op. cit. supra* note 18, at 159.

[21] With regard to works at several rounds of GATT preparatory conference meetings, *see* Chapter I, note 34.

[22] *See* UN Doc. E/PC/T/C.II/65 at 2 (1946).

[23] 'As regards the applicability of Article I to the Australian measure, the working party noted that the General Agreement made a distinction between "like products" and "directly competitive or substitutable products". This distinction is clearly brought out in Article III, paragraph 2, read in conjunction with the interpretative note to that paragraph. The most-favoured-nation treatment clause in the General Agreement is limited to "like products". Without trying to give a definition of "like products", and leaving aside the question of whether the two fertilizers are directly competitive, the working party reached the conclusion that they were not to be considered as "like products" within the terms of Article I.' (*Australia Sulphate* Working Party Report, para 8.) Regarding the case summary and ruling, *see* Chapter II, note 228.

[24] 'The Panel noted also that the General Agreement made a distinction between "like products" and "directly competitive or substitutable products" and that the most-favoured-nation treatment clause in the General Agreement was limited to "like products".' (*Germany Sardines* Working Party Report, para 12.) Regarding the case summary and ruling, *see* Chapter II, note 231.

[25] The broad meaning of wheat cereal could include wheat powder as well as wheat grain.

[26] *See Third Committee: Commercial Policy, Summary Record of the Fifth Meeting*, UN Conference on Trade and Employment, 3d Comm., 5th mtg., U.N.Doc. E/Conf. 2/C.3/SR.5 at 4 (1947). In the record, no explanation was given in that regard: 'Answering an enquiry of Mr ZORLU (Turkey) concerning the interpretation of the term "like product" the CHAIRMAN used the example of two categories of automobile, those weighing less than 1,500 kilos and those weighing more than that. A reduction of the tariff on automobiles in the former category would if granted to country X also have to be granted to other countries for automobiles in the *same* category: but in such a case the term "like product" would not, as he understood it, include automobiles weighing *more* than 1,500 kilos.' (Ibid.)

It is interesting to encounter this 1,500 kg standard in an old document of the League of Nations. A report submitted by the Danish and Portuguese Governments shows that automobiles with bodies weighing more than 1,500 kg (use for the conveyance of persons) had been subject to an import prohibition, and this restriction was abolished as of 1929 to implement the International Convention for the Abolition of Import and Export Prohibitions and Restrictions. *See* League of Nations, *Application of the International Convention for the Abolition of Import and Export Prohibitions and Restrictions*, C.L.8.1931./II.B (Geneva, 22 January 1931). It seems that in the 1920s, European countries had maintained quantitative restrictions based on the distinction between automobiles above 1,500 kg and those below 1,500 kg.

[27] *See* Zedalis, Chapter II, note 232, at 69.

[28] It should be noted, however, that this second inference could be vulnerable to attacks when one does not know the exact meaning of the communication between delegates. In addition, the usage of weight as a criterion for differentiating automobiles might have had a different nuance in the 1940s when automobiles were not so dominant a means of mass traffic as is the case these days. *See supra* note 26.

[29] *See Commercial Policy in the Interwar Period: International Proposals and National Policies*, League of Nations Doc. II Economic and Financial 1942 II.A.6, at 15 (1942). *See also* Jackson, Introduction, note 2, at 11.1. It should be noted that the idea of the MFN obligation in the United States can be traced back to the time of George Washington. In his famous Farewell Address, the first President of the United States stated that 'Harmony, and a liberal intercourse with all nations are recommended by policy, humanity, and interest. But even our commercial policy should hold an equal and impartial hand, neither seeking nor granting exclusive favors or preferences; consulting the national course of things; diffusing and diversifying by gentle means the streams of commerce, but forcing nothing.' *See* Sayre, *supra* note 19.

[30] *See* U.N.Doc. E/PC/T/PV.2 at 2 (1947); *see also US Proposals for Expansion of World Trade and Employment*, Dep't of State Pub. No. 2411, ch. III(A)(3), at 11.

[31] *See* U.N.Doc. E/PC/T/TAC/PV.2 at 29, 46; U.N.Doc. E/PC/T/TAC/PV.23 at 8 (1947).

[32] *See* generally U.N.Doc. E/PC/T/C.II/3 at 6, 7 (1946); U.N.Doc. E/PC/T/C.II/PV.2 at 10, 12 (1946); U.N.Doc. E/PC/T/TAC/PV.2 at 12, 23 (1947).

Concerning the historical development of the MFN obligation and the concept of 'like product' in the obligation, *see* Appendix I.

[33] Detailed tariff classification makes it possible to deny the benefit of tariff concessions to those who refuse to pay with reciprocal concessions.

[34] In *Japan SPF Lumber*, Japan contended that the concept of 'like' should be interpreted to exclude SPF dimension lumber, because otherwise sub-classifications could be used to undermine negotiated tariff concessions. Compelling Japan to extend the same favorable treatment to unbargained SPF lumber as to the non-SPF variety, which is a bargained-for concession, would discourage successive GATT tariff negotiations. *See* the Panel Report, para 3.20.

Professor Hudec speculates that in addition to the *Lumber* case, *German Sardines* hints at a narrow likeness. See Hudec, R., '"Like Product": The Differences in Measuring in GATT Articles I and III', in Thomas Cottier and Petros C. Mavroidis, eds, *Regulatory Barriers and the Principle of Non-discrimination in World Trade Law* (University of Michigan Press, 2000) 116–17 ('The case provides another good illustration of the type of tariff distinction that the author has suggested is common practice among GATT member countries—a practice that would support a uniquely narrow concept of "like product" for product distinctions made in tariffs.')

[35] The average tariff level for the world economy has been substantially reduced and most countries in the world have already exchanged comprehensive tariff concessions through many rounds of multilateral cross-sector negotiations. Furthermore, the single undertaking idea of the WTO agreements system helped in reducing the free-rider problem; every member of WTO is obliged to accede to every agreement annexed to WTO agreements except plurilateral agreements.

[36] *Spain Unroasted Coffee* and *Japan SPF Lumber* confirm this obligation. *See Spain Unroasted Coffee*, para 4.4.; *Japan SPF Lumber*, paras 5.8–5.10 (warning against national governments' abuse of tariff classification authority).

[37] In *EEC Duty on Grain-fed Beef from Canada*, GATT Doc. L/5099 (1981), BISD 28S 92, 98, para 4.2(a), the Panel ruled that Canadian grain-fed beef and US grain-fed beef certified as to quality by the US Department of Agriculture are like products, and the EEC, by imposing different duties on these two, violated Art. I. In this case, the EEC imposed about 20 per cent *ad valorem* tariff on high quality grain-fed beef from Canada, while permitting duty-free entry of high quality grain-fed beef from the United States. EEC Commission Regulation No. 2972/79 provided a description for such duty-free beef which would automatically be met if the relevant certification of grades was provided by the US Department of Agriculture. Since the automatic duty-free treatment was designed to reflect a concession negotiated between the EC and the United States during the Tokyo Round, the effect of the requirement for US certification was that Canadian beef otherwise within the described tariff category was subject to the import duty.

[38] Bhala and Kennedy, Chapter I, note 22, at 62–3.

[39] The MFN obligation applies equally to bound or unbound tariffs. It also applies to non-tariff matters. With regard to matters that are not related to tariff negotiations, the MFN obligation functions mainly as a tool for protecting natural comparative advantage (rather than securing the benefit of the bargain). *See* ibid.

[40] Ibid.

[41] Ibid.

[42] An important factor in considering whether the discretion was abused is to examine whether the classification is consonant with general practices of international society. *See* Chapter II, notes 228–234 and accompanying texts.

[43] *See* Art. 32 of Vienna Convention on the Law of Treaties, Chapter II, note 51. However, although it is rare, one could imagine a certain situation in which this compelling reason might exist. If an explicit agreement was reached in tariff negotiations that two merely substitutable products should be considered as being 'like' under Art. I (subject to the same tariff classification and duty rate), and if this agreement were supported by international practice, one might be able to witness the broadest understanding of likeness with regard to the product relationship.

[44] As indicated at the beginning of section 1 of this chapter, the four primary legal commitments of the GATT are MFN, national treatment, tariff binding commitments, and prohibition of quantitative restrictions.

[45] Article XIII of GATT reads: 'No prohibition or restriction shall be applied by any contracting party on the importation of any product of the territory of any other contracting party or on the exportation of any product destined for the territory of any other contracting party, unless the importation of the like product of all third countries or the exportation of the like product to all third countries is similarly prohibited or restricted'.

[46] Article IX:1 of GATT provides: 'Each contracting party shall accord to the products of the territories of other contracting parties treatment with regard to marking requirements no less favourable than the treatment accorded to like products of any third country.'

The WTO Agreement of Rules of Origin defines non-preferential rules of origin as rules which are used for purposes of: (1) determining status for granting most-favoured-nation treatment; (2) application of antidumping and countervailing duties pursuant to Art. VI of the GATT; (3) application of national safeguard measures pursuant to Art. XIX of the GATT; (4) country of origin marking on imported products or products with foreign components; (5) specifications for government procurement; (6) imposition of quantitative restrictions or tariff-based quotas; and (7) collection of trade statistics. *See* the Agreement on Rules of Origin, Art. 1.2.

[47] In the areas of tariff classification and valuation of goods for customs purposes, there have been several endeavors for harmonized international rules, and the results are reflected in the Uniform HS and the Customs Valuation Agreement. With respect to rules of origin, the Agreement on Rules of Origin concluded in the Uruguay Round represents a significant concerted attempt to bring the issue into the international trade regime. Concerning the Kyoto Convention, *see* Introduction, note 15.

[48] *See* the Preamble of the Agreement on Rules of Origin. Article 9.1(d) of the Agreement confirms this goal: 'notwithstanding the measure or instrument to which they may be linked, rules of origin should not be used as instruments to pursue trade objectives directly or indirectly. They should not themselves create restrictive, distorting or disruptive effects on international trade. They should not pose unduly strict requirements or require the fulfillment of a certain condition not relating to manufacturing or processing as a prerequisite for the determination of the country of origin.'

[49] The United States statute for the country of origin marking rules provides that: 'Except as hereinafter provided, every article of foreign origin (or its container . . .) imported into the United States shall be marked . . . in such a manner as to indicate to an ultimate purchaser in the United States the English name of the country of origin for the article.' *See* 19 U.S.C. § 1304(a) (Supp. 1996). Administrative regulations promulgated under this statute are provided in 19 C.F.R. § 134.0 (1996).

[50] *See* Introduction, note 15. Major components of the WTO work programme are directed to such tasks as: (1) developing harmonized definitions of goods to be considered 'wholly obtained in one country' and of 'minimal operations or processes' that do not by themselves confer origin to a good; (2) considering, on the basis of the criterion of substantial transformation, the use of tariff shift rule; and (3) for those products or sectors in which a change of tariff classification does not allow for the reflection of substantial transformation, developing supplementary or exclusive origin criteria based on value, manufacturing or processing operations, or on other standards. *See* Art. 9 of the Agreement on Rules of Origin. *See also* International Harmonization of Customs Rules of Origin, USITC Inv. No. 332–360, 60 Fed. Reg. 19,605 (1995).

[51] *See* Arts 2–8 of the Agreement on Rules of Origin.

[52] Article V:5 prescribes that: 'With respect to all charges, regulations and formalities in connection with transit, each contracting party shall accord to traffic in transit to or from the territory of any other contracting party treatment *no less favourable* than the treatment accorded to traffic in transit to or from any third country.' Interpreting this provision, *Ad* Art.V: 5 stipulates that: 'With regard to transportation charges, the principle laid down in paragraph 5 refers to *like products* being transported on the same route under *like conditions*.' (emphasis added)

[53] *See* this chapter at 1.2.6, in particular, note 169.

[54] But not losing physical similarity (thus easily interchangeable by nature).

[55] *See supra* note 52.

[56] *See* McGovern, Introduction, note 22, para 8.122.

[57] *See EEC Animal Feed Proteins* Panel Report, paras 4.1–4.2.

[58] Ibid. *See also* Bhala and Kennedy, Chapter I, note 22, at 66–7.

[59] *See* Fauchald, Introduction, note 11, at 144–5.

[60] Ibid. ('in cases concerning tariff classifications, the panels did not refer to the interpretation of the concept of "like products" in Article III. *Spain Unroasted Coffee*, para 4.8; *Japan*

SPF Lumber, para 5.14. On the other hand, in a case concerning non-tariff-related measures applied to animal feed proteins, the panel did not distinguish between Articles I and III when applying the concept "like products". *EEC Animal Feed Proteins*, paras 4.1–4.2'.) *See also* Hudec *op. cit. supra* note 34, at 112.

[61] *See* Chapter II, note 51.

[62] *See* Art. I:1 of the GATT. *See also EEC Animal Feed Proteins*, para 4.20.

[63] *See supra* note 40.

[64] If two countries negotiated tariff bindings for certain products and classified those products in different product categories (subject to different duty rates) despite their close similarity, this classification should be respected when interpreting 'likeness' under Art. I. Otherwise, the negotiated difference in duty rate will be meaningless due to an 'excessive' role by the MFN obligation.

[65] *See* Chapter II, note 242.

[66] Ibid.

[67] *See First Session of the Preparatory Committee of the United Nations Conference on Trade and Employment*, E/PC/T/C.II/PV/12, at 7–8 (1946).

[68] *See* Chapter II, notes 230–236 and accompanying texts.

[69] Ibid.

[70] Concerning MFN clauses of TBT and SPS Agreements, *see infra* note 169.

[71] *See supra* note 56 and accompanying text.

[72] Thus, in constructing the CVA-PCPDS, it is better to set the hypothetical price change at a moderate rate, probably less than 25 per cent. If the change is set at more than 50 per cent, for instance, 100 per cent substitution is required to qualify as being 'remotely similar' products. Then, this threshold would negate any differentiation effort between the stages, 'remotely similar', 'closely similar', and 'identical', because no more substitution rate above 100 per cent is possible. Indeed, if the price change is set at too high a rate, the resulting substitution rate could reflect not only a pure substitution effect, but also an *overly high* income effect (a sort of 'forced switch'). On the other hand, if the hypothetical price change is set at too low a rate (e.g., 0.2 per cent), no consumers would pay attention. *See* Chapter II, note 120 and Appendix III. It would be a good idea if the questionnaire provides 'multiple sets' of price changes, each set being made by small increments of change. This type of questionnaire would enhance the credibility of analysis of the responses.

[73] *See* Chapter II, note 280.

[74] This provision allows destination-principle adjustments on imports when goods are taxed in the country of consumption. Taxes can be required on imported goods, and their components, at the same rate as domestically produced goods of the same kind, provided that taxes are not applied so as to protect domestic production, and provided that MFN is respected. For further discussion, *see* Hufbauer, G.C., *Fundamental Tax Reform and Border Tax Adjustments* (Institute for International Economics, 1996) Vol. 43, pp. 50–56.

[75] *See* Jackson *et al.*, Chapter II, note 138, at 501.

[76] *Japan Alcoholic Beverages* Appellate Report, sec. F.

[77] *United States—Section 337 of the Tariff Act of 1930*, BISD 36S/345, para 5.10; *Japan Alcoholic Beverages* Appellate Report, sec. F.

[78] Article III:1 prescribes *inter alia*, that: 'The contracting parties recognize that internal taxes and other internal charges, and law, regulations and requirements affecting the internal sale, offering for sale, purchase, transportation, distribution or use of products...should not be applied to imported products so as to afford protection'.

[79] *United States—Taxes on Petroleum and Certain Imported Substances*, BISD 34S/136, para 5.1.9; *Japan Wine and Liquor*, para 5.5(b); *Japan Alcoholic Beverages, supra* note 76.

[80] *Japan Alcoholic Beverages, loc. cit.*

[81] Roessler, Chapter II, note 212, at 24. Also Professor Jackson states that 'Paragraph 2 of Article III requires national treatment in respect of international taxation (such as sales, excise or value added taxes), while paragraph 4 requires it in respect of regulations affecting the sale and use of goods generally'. *See* Jackson *et al.*, Chapter II, note 138, at 501.

[82] Roessler, *loc. cit.*

[83] *See* Chapter II, notes 331–333 and accompanying texts.

[84] Provided that they do not do so in a way that violates any other commitments they have made in the WTO Agreement.

[85] *Japan Wine and Liquor*, para 5.5(b); *Canada—Import, Distribution and Sale of Certain Alcoholic Drinks by Provincial Marketing Agencies*, BISD 39S/27, para 5.30.

[86] Jackson *et al.*, *supra* note 81, at 502.

[87] Ibid.

[88] *Japan Alcoholic Beverages* Appellate Report, sec. F.

[89] Ibid.

[90] *Brazilian Internal Taxes*, BISD II/181, para 4; *United States—Taxes on Petroleum and Certain Imported Substances*, BISD 34S/136, para 5.1.9; *EEC—Regulation on Imports of Parts and Components*, BISD 37S/132, para 5.4.

[91] *See Japan Alcoholic Beverages* Appellate Report, sec. F. At the Geneva Conference, delegates in the Tariff Agreement Committee addressed the issue of whether to include the national treatment clause from the draft Charter for ITO in the GATT 1947. One delegate noted: 'This Article in the Charter had two purposes, as I understand it. The first purpose was to protect the items in the Schedule or any other Schedule concluded as a result of any subsequent negotiations and agreements . . . But the Article in the Charter had an additional purpose. That purpose was to prevent the use of internal taxes as a system of protection . . . we are also ensuring that those countries which become parties to the Agreement undertake not to use internal taxes as a system of protection'.

This view is reinforced by the following statement of another delegate: '. . . [Article III] is necessary to protect not only scheduled items in the Agreement, but, indeed, all items for all our exports and the exports of any country. If that is not done, then every item which does not appear in the Schedule would have to be reconsidered and possibly tariff negotiations re-opened if Article III were changed to permit any action on these non-scheduled items.' *See* EPCT/TAC/PV.10, pp. 3 and 33.

[92] Bhala and Kennedy, Chapter I, note 22, at 237.

[93] Roessler, *supra* note 81, at 25.

[94] *See* Jackson *et al.*, *supra* note 81, at 523–7; *Japan Alcoholic Beverages* Panel Report, para 6.11.

[95] Panel Report, para 6.11.

[96] *See Japan Alcoholic Beverages* Appellate Report, sec. G; the Panel Report, para 6.12.

In addition, it can be noted that Art. I of the GATT refers only to paras 2 and 4 of Art. III, and not to para 1. This, combined with the fact that the general statement of the national treatment clause of Art. III:1 is more precisely elaborated in the subsequent paragraphs of Art. III, gives Art. III:1 the appearance of being hortative. *See* Fauchald, Introduction, note 11, at 110–111.

This does not mean, however, that para 1 plays no 'role' in Art. III. It is obvious that the provisions of Art. III must be interpreted in the light of the principle stated in para 1. In terms of Art. 31 of the Vienna Convention, Art. III:1 is part of the 'context' in which the other paragraphs of the provision must be interpreted. Paragraph 1 should be considered to state the general 'object and purpose' of Art. III. *See* ibid.

[97] *Japan Alcoholic Beverages* Panel Report, para 6.12.

[98] Ibid.

[99] Ibid.

[100] The reference is also made in the fifth paragraph of Art. III. It shows a clear textual contrast between the second and fifth paragraphs, on the one hand, and the fourth paragraph, on the other, which rejects any possible argument that omission of the reference in the fourth paragraph was done by mistake.

[101] *Japan Alcoholic Beverages* Appellate Report, sec. H2. Professor Jackson states that 'the language of Article III:1 . . . is in some sense hortatory. It is mandatory, however, when it is incorporated into paragraphs 2 and 5 and made applicable to internal taxes and mixing requirements' (Jackson *et al.*, Chapter II, note 138, at 518).

[102] *See Japan Alcoholic Beverages* Appellate Report, sec. H1. *See* Jackson *et al.*, Chapter II, note 138, at 525.

[103] *See* GATT *Ad* Art. III:2, 'only in cases where competition was involved'.

[104] *See Japan Alcoholic Beverages* Appellate Report, sec. H2. *See* Jackson *et al.*, Chapter II, note 138, at 525.

[105] *Japan Alcoholic Beverages* Appellate Report, sec. H2(c). Professor Roessler emphasized its case-by-case nature in his lecture at Georgetown.

[106] *Japan Wine and Liquors*, BISD 34S/83, para 5.11.

[107] *See supra* note 91.

[108] *See* Jackson *et al.*, Chapter II, note 138, at 525. Professor Jackson questions why, if Art. III is simply a matter of protecting expectations generated during tariff negotiations, the national treatment article does not then grandfather certain pre-existing discriminatory policies. Ibid. at 530.

[109] *See* Draft Report of the Technical Subcomm. of Committee II (16 November 1946), U.N. Doc. E/PC/T/C.II/54 at 4–5 (1946) (US Suggested Charter, Arts 9(1)–(2), as redrafted by the Subcommittee).

[110] *See* U.N. Doc. E/PC/T/TAC/PV.10 at 37 (Mr Winthrop Brown), 40 (Mr Shackle) (1947).

[111] *See* ibid. (Shackle arguing that a state importing natural products should not be able to tax in such a way as to allow untaxed domestic synthetics an economic advantage); *see also* U.N. Doc. E/PC/T/TAC/PV.10 at 14–15 (1947) (comments of Chinese delegate, Mr Wunsz King).

[112] *See* ibid. This effort to broaden the coverage of Art. III:2 seems to have been initiated by the United States. During the Geneva Conference, the US proposed including a provision corresponding to the second sentence of Art. III:2 in the draft Charter. *See* Chapter II, note 23. In fact, the broad concept of 'competitive product' was already put forward in the US Suggested Charter for ITO (UN Doc. E/PC/T/33, art. 9:2), reading '. . . imposition of internal taxes on the products of other countries for the purpose of affording protection to the domestic production of *competitive products*, would be contrary to the spirit of this Article, and they agree to take such measures as may be open to them to prevent in the future the adoption of new or higher taxes of this kind *within their territories*' (emphasis added).

There was some confusion as to the purpose and meaning of the provision when it was discussed during the London Conference. Some delegates emphasized that 'paragraph 1 of Article 9 would apply mainly to member (central) governments, while paragraph 2 would apply to state, provincial, or local governments', while other delegates 'felt that competitive products were not the same as like products,' and that 'the purpose of paragraph 1 . . . was to prohibit higher taxes on imported products than on like domestic products, while the purpose of paragraph 2 was to guard against the more concealed types of discriminatory taxation'. *See* UN Doc. E/PC/T/C.II/W.2, pp. 4, 5. The focus on the distinction between central authorities and local governments seems to have been the reason why the provision was left out of the draft Charter by the time of the London Conference. *See* Fauchald, Introduction, note 11, at 147.

Thus, the US proposal to broaden the coverage of the national treatment clause meant the revival of the original text of its Suggested Charter, and it was closely related to a proposal to delete the general provision of Art. III:1. *See* UN Doc. E/PC/T/A/PV/9, p. 3 and E/PC/T/TAC/PV/ 10, p. 37. *See also* Fauchald, *op. cit. supra.*

The proposal seems to have been met with numerous questions and much debate before being accepted: several countries, including China, Chile, Cuba, and Norway, reserved their positions on this provision at the Second Session of the Preparatory Committee. *See* UN Doc. E/PC/T/186 Corr.1, p. 18; E/PC/T/W/309; E/PC/T/W/280, pp. 1–2; E/PC/T/186 Corr.1, pp.18–19.

[113] 55 UNTS at 264.

[114] *See* GATT Doc. GATT/CP.2/22/Rev. 1, report adopted 2 September 1948; Protocol Modifying Part II and Article XXVI of the GATT.

[115] *See supra* note 113 and *infra* note 137. *See also* U.N.Doc. E/Conf.3/78, Havana ITO Charter Art. 18 (1948):

> '1.   The Members recognize that internal taxes and other internal charges, and laws, regulations and requirements affecting the internal sale, offering for sale, purchase, transportation, distribution or use of products, and internal quantitative regulations requiring the mixture, processing or use of products in specified amounts or proportions, should not be applied to imported or domestic products so as to afford protection to domestic production.
>
> 2.   The products of any Member country imported into any other Member country shall not be subject, directly or indirectly, to internal taxes or other internal charges of any kind in excess of those applied, directly or indirectly, to like domestic products. Moreover, no Member shall otherwise apply internal taxes or other internal charges to imported or domestic products in a manner contrary to the principles set forth in paragraph 1. . . .'

[116] *See supra* note 113 and accompanying text.

[117] Thus, theoretically, it is possible that although an importing country A accords *no less favourable* treatment as between domestic products (substantially produced in A) and foreign 'like' products, the foreign country B can bring a complaint of Art. III:2 violation if its *another* 'directly substitutable product' is treated less favourably than the domestic product of A. But in such a case, most likely the complainant would fail because one additional element ('so as to afford protection' to domestic products in Art. III:1) would hardly be satisfied.

[118] It is not clear whether this modification to the concurrent relationship between the two sentences was done knowingly by the drafters.

[119] *See Japan Alcoholic Beverages* Appellate Report, sec. H.

[120] *See Japan Alcoholic Beverages* Appellate Report, sec. H2(c); *Korea Alcoholic Beverages* Appellate Report, para 147; *Chile Alcoholic Beverages* Appellate Report, para 56.

[121] The Appellate Body in *Japan Alcoholic Beverages* held that: 'Unlike that of Article III:2, first sentence, the language of Article III:2, second sentence, specifically invokes Article III:1. The significance of this distinction lies in the fact that whereas Article III:1 acts implicitly in addressing the two issues that must be considered in applying the first sentence, it acts explicitly as an entirely separate issue that must be addressed along with two other issues that are raised in applying the second sentence.' (*Japan Alcoholic Beverages* Appellate Report, sec. H2).

[122] That is, the obligation of national treatment between 'directly competitive or substitutable' products in addition to that between 'like products'. *See supra* note 118.

[123] *See* Chapter II, note 280 and accompanying text. Since the only difference is whether *de minimis* tax discrimination is permitted, the complaining party will have only *de minimis* difference of preference in deciding whether it will invoke the first or the second sentence violation in that regard. In practice, every party would prefer to raise the second sentence claim which is more likely to succeed. *See infra* note 124.

[124] In *Korea Alcoholic Beverages*, despite the complainants' failure to establish a like product violation of the first sentence of Art. III:2, the Panel and the Appellate Body determined Korean soju and imported vodka to be 'directly competitive or substitutable' products within the coverage of the second sentence of the provision. *See Korea Alcoholic Beverages* Panel Report, paras 10.56–11.2.

In *Chile Alcoholic Beverages*, the complaining party dropped the claim on the first sentence violation, and concentrated its effort on the second sentence violation. *See* Chapter II, note 67.

[125] For the full text of the Geneva version, *see supra* note 113 and accompanying text. It should be recalled that before the Havana Conference, the actual language of what became Art. III clearly juxtaposed 'like' and 'directly competitive or substitutable' in the main text.

[126] *See* Zedalis, Chapter II, note 232, at 72, 73.

[127] *See* U.N.Doc. E/PC/T/A/PV.9 at 7 (1947). The rationale was not provided.

[128] An item occasionally used in finishing furniture.

[129] *See* E/Conf.2/C.3/SR.11, p.1 and Corr. 2. (The US delegate illustrating that tung oil and linseed oil are competitive and substitutable and that the US should impose equal taxes on both products in the absence of domestic production of tung oil—this obligation is what the second sentence means.)

[130] *See* Chapter II, notes 326–328 and accompanying texts.

[131] *See* E/Conf.2/C.3/SR.11, p. 3. (Answering a question whether it was permissible for the US to impose a tax on imported natural rubber in order to assist the production of synthetic rubber, the US delegate replied in the negative.) But concerning the relationship between 'tramways' and 'buses', there seems to have been some disagreement. *See* Chapter II, note 326.

[132] *See supra* note 22 and accompanying text.

[133] For instance, if no alcoholic beverages, priced over $30, were permitted to be sold, expensive whiskys (over $30) effectively would be excluded from the market.

[134] *See* McGovern, Introduction, note 22, at 8.12–1: 'In particular, the narrow interpretation appropriate in the first sentence of paragraph 2 . . . does not necessarily apply in the context of paragraph 4 . . . , and it was possible that "like product" in paragraph 4 might even have the same scope as "directly competitive and substitutable product" in paragraph 2.'

The Panel in *United States Gasoline* seems to signal an equal scope in interpretation of the two paragraphs: 'The Panel proceeded to examine this issue in the light of the ordinary meaning of the term "like". It noted that the word can mean "similar", or "identical".... Some criteria were suggested for determining, on a case-by-case basis, whether a product is "similar": the product's end-uses in a given market; consumers' tastes and habits, which change from country to country; the product's properties, nature and quality.... These criteria had been applied by the Panel in the 1987 Japan Alcohol case in the examination under Article III:2 of internal taxation measures.... The Panel considered that *those criteria were also applicable to the examination of like products under Article III:4*... The Panel... noted that chemically-identical imported and domestic gasoline by definition have exactly the same physical characteristics, end-uses, tariff classification, and are perfectly substitutable. The Panel found therefore that chemically-identical imported and domestic gasoline are like products under Article III:4.' (*See* Panel Report on *United States Gasoline*, paras 6.8, 6.9; the Appellate Body Report, sec. IC (emphasis added).)

But this statement by the Panel might also be understood as merely suggesting the application of the same criteria between the two paragraphs. Applicability of the same criteria does not necessarily guarantee an equal interpretation.

The Appellate Body in *Japan Alcoholic Beverages* did not make a clear determination on this matter. It stated that '... we agree with the Panel that the first sentence of Article III:2 must be construed narrowly so as not to condemn measures that its strict terms are not meant to condemn. Consequently, we agree with the Panel also that the definition of "like products" in Article III:2, first sentence, should be construed narrowly'. It continued: 'We note the argument on appeal that the Panel suggested in paragraph 6.20 of the Panel Report that the product coverage of Article III:2 is not identical to the coverage of Article III:4. That is not what the Panel said. The Panel said the following: [*"*]*If* the coverage of Article III:2 is identical to that of Article III:4, a different interpretation of the term 'like product' would be called for in the two paragraphs. Otherwise, if the term 'like product' were to be interpreted in an identical way in both instances, the scope of the two paragraphs would be different.[*"*] [*emphasis added*] This was merely a hypothetical statement.' (*Japan Alcoholic Beverages* Appellate Report, sec. H1(a) (including footnote 44).)

135 The Appellate Body in *EC Asbestos* stated that: 'As products that are in a competitive relationship in the marketplace could be affected through treatment of *imports* "less favourable" than the treatment accorded to *domestic* products, it follows that the word "like" in Article III:4 is to be interpreted to apply to products that are in such a competitive relationship. Thus, a determination of "likeness" under Article III:4 is, fundamentally, a determination about the nature and extent of a competitive relationship between and among products. In saying this, we are mindful that there is a spectrum of degrees of "competitiveness" or "substitutability" of products in the marketplace, and that it is difficult, if not impossible, in the abstract, to indicate precisely where on this spectrum the word "like" in Article III:4 of the GATT 1994 falls. We are not saying that *all* products which are in *some* competitive relationship are "like products" under Article III:4. In ruling on the measure at issue, we also do not attempt to define the precise scope of the word "like" in Article III:4. Nor do we wish to decide if the scope of "like products" in Article III:4 is co-extensive with the combined scope of "like" and "directly competitive or substitutable" products in Article III:2. However, we recognize that the relationship between these two provisions is important, because there is no sharp distinction between fiscal regulation, covered by Article III:2, and non-fiscal regulation, covered by Article III:4. Both forms of regulation can often be

used to achieve the same ends. It would be incongruous if, due to a significant difference in the product scope of these two provisions, Members were prevented from using one form of regulation—for instance, fiscal—to protect domestic production of certain products, but were able to use another form of regulation—for instance, non-fiscal—to achieve those ends. This would frustrate a consistent application of the "general principle" in Article III:1. For these reasons, we conclude that the scope of "like" in Article III:4 is broader than the scope of "like" in Article III:2, first sentence. Nonetheless, we note, once more, that Article III:2 extends not only to "like products", but also to products which are "directly competitive or substitutable", and that Article III:4 extends only to "like products". In view of this different language, and although we need not rule, and do not rule, on the precise product scope of Article III:4, we do conclude that the product scope of Article III:4, although broader than the *first* sentence of Article III:2, is certainly *not* broader than the *combined* product scope of the *two* sentences of Article III:2 of the GATT 1994.' *See EC Asbestos* Appellate Report, Chapter II, note 7, para 99.

[136] *See supra* note 56 and accompanying text.

[137] The negotiating history of Art. III:2 confirms that the second sentence and the *Ad* Article were added during the Havana Conference, along with other provisions and interpretative notes regarding Art. XVIII of the draft ITO Charter. While these amendments were introduced to delegates, the relevant Sub-Committee reported that: 'The new form of the Article makes clearer than did the Geneva text the intention that internal taxes on goods should not be used as a means of protection. The details have been relegated to interpretative notes so that it would be easier for Members to ascertain the precise scope of their obligations under the Article.' (E/CONF.2/C.3/59, P. 8) Article 18 of the draft ITO Charter subsequently became Art. III of the GATT pursuant to the Protocol Modifying Part II and Article XXVI, which entered into force on 14 December 1948.

[138] 'Any *internal tax or other internal charge*, or any *law, regulation or requirement* of the kind referred to in paragraph 1 which applies to an imported product and to the *like domestic product* and is collected or enforced in the case of the imported product at the time or point of importation, is nevertheless to be regarded as an internal tax or other internal charge, or a law, regulation or requirement of the kind referred to in paragraph 1, and is accordingly subject to the provisions of Article III'. (*Ad* Art. III, chapeau (emphasis added).) *See EC Asbestos* Appellate Report, paras 92–99.

[139] *See* GATT Art. XIX:1.

[140] *See* GATT Art. XI:2(c).

[141] *See supra* note 113 and accompanying text.

[142] More precisely, if tax or regulation of 'identical' products is involved, Art. III:2, first sentence and Art. III:4 will apply. If tax or regulation of 'closely similar' or 'remotely similar' products is concerned, Art. III:2, second sentence and Art. III:4 will impose the national treatment obligation. Thus, the results are the same.

[143] This is because the second sentence of Art. III:2 has the Art. III:1 factor as an additional requirement, as opposed to Art. III:4 in which no such additional requirement exists.

[144] GATS Art. XVII adopts the flexible standard of 'less favourable treatment' rule identical to GATT Art. III:4. It then makes clear that the obligation reaches facially neutral measures: the prohibition applies both to 'formally identical and formally different' measures whenever they 'modify conditions of competition' in favour of domestic suppliers. The provision then goes on to add that the prohibition does not apply to 'inherent competitive disadvantages which result from the foreign character of the relevant services or service

suppliers'. With respect to the meaning of 'inherent', Professors Hudec and Farber suggest an aim-based good-faith test: 'The word "inherent" is synonymous with "inevitable", the idea being to describe a situation in which there is no way that a regulation, even if enacted with the best of good faith and pure motives, can avoid disadvantaging the foreign supplier. In short, by introducing the all-purpose concept of causation, the drafters of the Uruguay Round Services Agreement may, in fact, have succeeded in introducing the issue of valid regulatory purpose into the legal definition of "less favourable treatment".' *See* Farber and Hudec, Chapter II, notes 206 and 208.

See Farber, D.A. and Hudec, R.E., 'Free Trade and the Regulatory State: A GATT's-Eye View of the Dormant Commerce Clause', *Vanderbilt Law Review*, vol. 47, 1401 at 1429.

[145] *See* TBT Art. 2.2; SPS Arts 2, 3, 7.

[146] However, although those terms lead to a very broad coverage of para 4 compared to para 2 in which such terms are absent, the scope of paras 2 and 4 might not be as large as it may seem from the wording of the provisions. Consider the following statement: 'It is difficult, in practice, to draw a clear line between internal taxes applied to the product itself and those that in some way or other also cover services related to the product. Taxes can either be set at a fixed rate per item or per weight of a product, or they can be calculated on the basis of the value of the product. The first category would clearly fall within the scope of paragraph 2, since it relates directly to the product, while the second category necessarily includes taxes on services that have added value to the product, even if they have not led to any modification of the product itself. (In general, transportation and distribution of a product may increase its value independently of whether the properties of the product are influenced.) A narrow reading of paragraph 2 would exclude the second alternative, but it is clear both from relevant practice and the preparatory works that paragraph 2 applies both to taxes applied to the value of products, and to some extent to services closely related to the products.' (Fauchald, Introduction, note 11, at 87–8.)

[147] To take a metaphor, despite a lack of reinforcement and back-up from the surroundings, Napoleon's army went all the way to Moscow only to fail.

[148] In several preparatory committees, several states (developing countries) raised this opposition. UN Doc. E/PC/T/A/PV/9 at 6, 11, 16–17, 47 (statements by Cuba, India, China). This view seems to have been shared with some developed states in relation to internal quantitative regulations. UN Doc. E/PC/T/W/309, pp. 2–3 (statement by Norway).

[149] In this regard, it could be noted that one reason for not adopting the Panel Report in a case concerning the compatibility of Spanish restrictions on domestic sale of soyabean oil with Art. III:4 was that the Panel applied a narrow interpretation of 'like products'. *See Spain—Measures Concerning Domestic Sale of Soyabean Oil* ('noted' panel report, 1981), GATT Doc. L/5142 Corr.1, paras 4.6 and 4.7. *See* GATT Docs. C/M/152, pp. 10–19, L/5161, pp. 9–10, and L/5188, pp. 5–6.

[150] As Art. III concerns conditions of competition between domestic and imported products, the actual negative impact on the imported product need not be shown. It should also be noted that since Art. III:4 makes no reference to Art. III:1, the latter acts implicitly, not independently, in addressing these three issues. *See supra* note 101 and accompanying text.

[151] *See supra* notes 75–77 and accompanying texts.

[152] 'No contracting party shall establish or maintain any internal quantitative regulation relating to the mixture, processing or use of products in specified amounts or proportions which requires, directly or indirectly, that any specified amount or proportion of any product which is the subject of the regulation must be supplied from domestic sources. Moreover,

no contracting party shall otherwise apply internal quantitative regulations in a manner contrary to the principles set forth in paragraph 1.' (Art. III:5.)

[153] One should be reminded that the first paragraph itself does not create a legal obligation. *See supra* note 96 and accompanying text.

[154] 'Regulations consistent with the provisions of the first sentence of paragraph 5 shall not be considered to be contrary to the provisions of the second sentence in any case in which all of the products subject to the regulations are produced domestically in substantial quantities. A regulation cannot be justified as being consistent with the provisions of the second sentence on the ground that the proportion or amount allocated to each of the products which are the subject of the regulation constitutes an equitable relationship between imported and domestic products'. (*Ad* Art. III:5.)

[155] *See supra* note 138 and accompanying text.

[156] *See* Panel Report in *United States Tobacco*, para 72 (ruling that 'The Panel noted that both Article III:5 and Article III:4 deal with internal regulations, but that Article III:5 is the more specific of the two provisions').

[157] These provisions are concerned with measures by the central government bodies of members. *See* TBT Agreement, Arts 2 and 5.

[158] Annex C is about control, inspection, and approval procedures which include, *inter alia*, procedures for sampling, testing and certification.

[159] 'Sometimes it is alleged that agencies or industry groups that set standards consciously try to "gerrymander" those standards to make it comparatively more difficult for foreign producers to comply. In this way a market for electronic components might be protected for domestic producers by certain quality or standards specifications. Likewise drug or cosmetic standards might be "shaped" to allow domestic manufacturers to accommodate them easily. The process of obtaining clearance of a product subject to inspection, for health or safety reasons, may also add enough of a burden to the importation of goods as to "afford protection" to domestic manufacturers'(Jackson, Chapter I, note 54, at 222).

[160] Ibid., at 223.

[161] Ibid.

[162] *United States Statement of Administrative Action, Uruguay Round Agreement Act*, pp. 742–86.

[163] TBT Arts 2.4, 2.5, 2.6, 5.4, 5.5; SPS Art. 2.2.

[164] TBT Arts 2.7, 5.5, 6, 9; SPS Arts 3, 4, 6.

[165] SPS Art. 5; TBT Arts 5.4, 5.5.

[166] TBT Arts 2.9, 2.11; SPS Art. 7.

[167] (Emphasis added.)

[168] *See* Chapter II, notes 4 and 5, and this chapter at 2 and 3.

[169] *See* the quoted texts, *supra* notes 157 and 158, and accompanying texts.

[170] *Compare with supra* notes 65–68 and accompanying texts.

[171] *See supra* notes 89–92 and accompanying texts.

[172] *See supra* note 92. *Compare with supra* note 64.

[173] This burden should be felt when MFN applies against discriminatory tariff measures.

[174] *See supra* notes 100 and 102, and accompanying texts.

[175] *See supra* note 72 and accompanying text.

[176] In many cases, the defendant, against a *prima facie* case of likeness established by the complainant, has to show that since there is less demand substitutability than the QPS threshold, the products are not 'like' products within the meaning of the first sentence. But

if a presumption of 'unlikeness' is established through the objective factor test, the complainant has to put forward a rebuttal that the QPS is satisfied.

[177] In actuality, there are many 'easy cases' in which the first-step analysis yields a conclusion on likeness manifest enough for the panel to complete the procedure (*see* Chapter II, note 405 and accompanying text). In tough cases, however, the second-step analysis becomes indispensable and more influential.

[178] *See* Art. XI:2(c). It should be noted that given the Agreement on Agriculture, Art. XI:2 is of limited importance.

[179] The language commented on was that of the US version of the ITO Charter which became GATT Art. XI(2)(c)(i)–(ii). Its thrust and terminology were largely similar to those of the GATT provision. *See* US Suggested Charter for an International Trade Organization of the United Nations, Dep't of State Pub. No. 2598 (1946), at 13; London Conference, U.N.Doc. E/PC/T/C.II/48, at 1 (1946). *See also* U.N.Doc. E/PC/T/C.II/PV.12, at 6 (1946); U.N.Doc. E/PC/T/C.II/36, at 8 (comment to same effect made by Mr Hawkins, United States, at the 5th meeting of Committee II).

[180] *See* U.N.Doc. E/PC/T/C.II/PV.12, at 6.

[181] *See* U.N.Doc. E/PC/T/C.II/PV.2, at 20 (Speekenbrink's inquiry); U.N.Doc. E/PC/T/C.II/PV.5, at 27 (US delegate, Hawkins' response to an inquiry from Mr Speekenbrink, of The Netherlands, regarding whether like meant 'products used for the same purpose').

[182] In the primary product sector, there is a tendency for both oversupply and undersupply arising from crop and animal production cycles. Overproduction can lead to underproduction in the next season as farmers adjust their efforts, with consequences for prices that are not so attractive. The problem of overproduction is compounded by the fact that lower prices do not necessarily lead to increased consumption. The special nature of this sector and its volatility have led governments in most countries to intervene in the market in order to stabilize prices in the interests of both consumer and farmer. In the interest of food security, governments have also been concerned to ensure that adequate supplies exist domestically. Moreover, by avoiding large-scale imports, domestic production and a healthy balance of payments can go hand in hand. *See* McDonald, B., *The World Trading System: The Uruguay Round and Beyond* (Macmillan Press Ltd, 1998) 189.

[183] *See* Report of Conference, United Nations Conference on Trade and Employment, U.N.Doc. ICITO/1/8, at 91–92 (1948) (noting the basis for invoking Art. XI(2)(c) related to supply rather than price fluctuations); *see also* The Geneva Charter for an International Trade Organization, Dep't of State Pub. No. 2950, at 6 (1947).

[184] Article XI:2 permits utilization of the concept of 'directly substituted' products where there is no substantial domestic production of the like product. *See* the provision and following discussion.

[185] A substantial portion of the increasing demand for tomato concentrates generated by the measure could be absorbed by domestic tomato concentrates suppliers.

[186] Article XIX does *not* contain the condition that, *only in the absence of substantial domestic production*, can one take protective measures with regard to 'directly competitive' products. *See* this chapter, at 3.2. Furthermore, many primary products are subject to the special safeguard provision of the Agreement on Agriculture. *See* Art. 5 of the Agreement.

[187] *See Decision of 5th March, 1955 Granting a Waiver to the United States in Connection with Import Restrictions Imposed Under Section 22 of the United States Agricultural Adjustment Act (of 1933), As Amended*: 'Having Also Received the statement of the United States: that there

exist in the United States governmental agricultural programmers . . . which from time to time result in domestic prices being maintained at a level in excess of the prices at which imports of the *like products* can be made available for consumption in the United States and that under such conditions imports may be attracted into the United States in abnormally large quantities . . .' (emphasis added). With this decision, the United States obtained a waiver from the Art. XI (and Art. II) obligation with regard to its import restriction program on agricultural products.

[188] *See supra* note 184. *See also* Chapter II, note 54; this chapter, note 118; and accompanying texts.

[189] Thus, the issue of defining 'like' here is of great practical value. Since the 'directly substituted' product concept can never be used to justify the quantitative restriction as long as there exists substantial domestic production of 'like' product, the scope of likeness, whether narrow or broad, can make a difference in justifying the invocation of Art. XI:2, and thereby in the result of the dispute. Such practicality cannot be found in Art. III:2 where 'like' and 'directly competitive or substitutable' are alternative options for the party invoking the provision.

[190] Despite a Chilean submission that Chilean apples were different varieties to those in surplus in the Community ('Golden Delicious') and that they were bought by selective consumers looking and willing to pay a premium for a fresh and high quality product, the Panel so held. *See EEC Restrictions on Imports of Apples from Chile*, L/5047 (1980), paras 3.10, 4.4.

[191] Report of the Drafting Committee of the Preparatory Committee, UN Conference on Trade and Employment, U.N.Doc. E/PC/T/34/Rev. 1, UN Sales No. 1947.11.3 (1947), Art. IX(2)(e), at 70.

[192] *See* U.N.Doc. E/PC/T/C.VI/17, at 4 (1947).

[193] There seems to have been debate as to whether the terms 'substituted' or 'competitive' should be adopted. The Geneva Conference draft of the ITO Charter provided the first reference to the broader concept of 'substitutable'. *See* U.N.Doc. E/PC/T/186, UN Sales No. 1947.11.4, Art. 20(2)(c)(i), at 20. In the context of drafting the ITO Charter, it had been proposed that the broader notion of 'directly competitive' be included. *See* New York Report, U.N.Doc. E/PC/T/34/Rev. 1, UN Sales No. 1947.11.3 (1947), at 20, cmt. g (commenting on Art. 25(2)(e)(1) of the ITO Charter).

[194] *See* Art. XI:2(c).

[195] *See Ad* Art. XI:2(c).

[196] This language appears in both Art. 25 of the London Conference's ITO Charter and Art. 19 of the earlier United States draft Charter, which served as the basis for discussions at the 1946 London Conference.

[197] *See* Geneva Report, U.N.Doc. E/PC/T/186, UN Sales No. 1947.11.4, at 20, Art. 20, interpretative note.

[198] *See* U.N.Doc. E/PC/T/A/PV/19 (1947).

[199] *See* U.N.Doc. ICITO/I/8, at 93–94, para 39 (1948).

[200] Ibid.

[201] The same could be true, if only to a lesser degree, of fully-processed imports. But because of the danger of protectionism, *Ad* Art. XI seems to have limited the permission of the quantitative restriction only to the early-stage processed imports.

[202] *See supra* note 195 and accompanying text. But, of course, in a rare case it is possible that two products at issue could be defined as 'like' products despite a difference in processing stages.

[203] With regard to the relationship between the likeness or substitutability concept and the stage of processing, the United States Trade Act of 1974 has an interesting provision of general definition concerning the phase 'directly competitive with' for the purpose of the Act: 'An imported article is "directly competitive with" a domestic article at an earlier or later stage of processing, and a domestic article is "directly competitive with" an imported article at an earlier or later stage of processing, if the importation of the article has an *economic effect on producers of the domestic article comparable* to the effect of importation of articles in the same stage of processing as the domestic article. For purposes of this paragraph, the unprocessed article is at an earlier stage of processing' (emphasis added). *See* sec. 601(5). This Act adopts the 'effect' test.

[204] *See* Chapter II, note 189; this chapter, notes 8 and 96; and accompanying texts.

[205] And probably that is why the drafters used slightly different language here.

[206] Even certain products that are not competing now (thus, not 'directly substituted' products) can be qualified as 'directly substitutable' products provided they have sufficient potentiality of competition in the near future.

[207] *See* Chapter II, note 338 and accompanying text.

[208] With respect to comparison with 'competitive', *see* this chapter, at 3.2.

[209] *See* Art. XI:2.

[210] *See supra* notes 56 and 172, and accompanying text. *Compare with supra* note 64.

[211] *Compare with supra* note 174 and accompanying text.

[212] In actuality, there are many 'easy cases' in which the first-step analysis yields a clear conclusion on likeness (*de facto* completion of case). In tough cases, however, the second-step analysis becomes indispensable and more influential. *See* Chapter II, note 405.

[213] Because the TPS and PSE are suitable standards for 'closely similar' and 'directly substituted' product tests respectively. *See supra* note 72 and accompanying text. The basic scope of 'directly substituted' is no different from that of 'directly competitive or substitutable' because the potential or future competition consideration can be dealt with by the *additional* tools of the PMP or Future Competition Questionnaire. *See* Chapter II, notes 356–362 and accompanying texts.

[214] The switched product is still restricted in access to the market. This result does not change depending on whether the like product test or directly substituted product test is involved. To use the familiar example, suppose that a country proceeds to a price support program for domestic tomatoes and imposes quantitative restrictions on imports. Suppose there is no substantial domestic production of tomato concentrates. The country will usually place quantitative restrictions on *foreign tomatoes as well as tomato concentrates* (*supra* note 184). Domestic tomatoes and foreign tomato concentrates are proven to share demand substitutability slightly higher than the PSE threshold level, while supply substitutability between tomatoes and tomato concentrates is known to be very high. Should the tribunal rely on the high supply substitutability and rule that the two products are not directly substituted products? Because the foreign producer of tomato concentrates subject to the restriction has no way to export tomatoes to the regulated market, a high supply substitutability between tomatoes concentrates and tomatoes has no meaning for them. It does not cure their competitive disadvantage. Absent the mitigation effect, there is no rationale for the supply substitutability analysis.

Suppose there is no substantial domestic production of tomato concentrates in the regulated market. The country will place restrictions only on foreign tomatoes (*supra* note 185). Still, the foreign tomato producers cannot switch production to 'domestic' tomatoes.

Of course, foreign tomato producers can switch to tomato concentrates and export them into the domestic market. But since *the issue is whether domestic and foreign tomatoes are like products*, the supply substitutability concept is concerned with the two products at issue: domestic tomatoes and foreign tomatoes. Do we have to take into consideration here the high supply substitutability between domestic *tomatoes* and foreign *tomato concentrates*? In other words, in addition to 'cross' price substitutability (between domestic and foreign tomatoes), does one have to consider the implications of 'own' price substitutability (e.g., between domestic tomatoes and foreign tomato concentrates here)? The answer will be a cautious 'No'. One might argue that in order to take account of the 'mitigation' effect completely, such own price substitutability should not be totally disregarded. But this argument seems to go too far. Let alone the methodological difficulty in calculating own price substitutability, this argument could be used to justify virtually every discrimination by reason of the existence of substantial own price supply substitutability to the benefit of the discriminated good. After all, most products have at least some close supply substitutes. In fact, is it not true that by adopting the *Industry Average* Substitution Rate (IASR) Standard for supply substitutability analysis, our model has already internalized, to some extent, the *own* price substitutability aspect?

[215] *See infra* note 228.

[216] *See* this chapter, at 2.1.2.

[217] *See infra* note 253.

[218] *See* Zedalis, Chapter II, note 232, at 40.

[219] *See* Gifford and Matsushita, Chapter I, note 32, at 299.

[220] *See* Cass, R.A. and Boltuck, R.D., 'Antidumping and Countervailing-Duty Law: The Mirage of Equitable International Competition,' in Jagdish Bhagwati and Robert Hudec, eds., *Fair Trade and Harmonization*, vol. 2 (MIT Press, 1996) 356.

[221] Ibid.

[222] Differences between 'free trade' and 'fair trade' have been a source of numerous debates. In general, 'fairness' means that equally situated firms are treated equally. According to the fair trade proponents, without offsetting difference in the trading conditions, the free trade would engender more unfairness and distort to the disadvantaged economies. Their position is well represented by the slogan of Malcolm Baldrige who was the US Secretary of Commerce: 'Free, but fair, trade!' For further discussion, *see* Bhagwati and Hudec, *op. cit. supra* note 220; Kaplan, G.B. and Haggerty Kuhbach, S., 'The Interface of Trade/Competition Law & Policy: The Causes of Unfair Trade: Trade Law Enforcers' Perspective', 56 Antitrust L.J. 445 (1987).

[223] Concerning a trend for change of focus of fair trade provisions, *see infra*.

[224] *See supra* note 3 and accompanying text. But, *see also supra* note 7.

[225] The United States furnished the basic negotiating text for the ITO Charter employed during the 1946 London Conference. The language of Art. II of the text (now GATT Art. VI), as examined by the Technical Subcommittee of Committee II at the Conference, referenced not only 'like' but also 'similar' products. Australia proposed that the Subcommittee delete any reference to 'similar' from the provision, presumably because of an awareness of the possibility of disruptive protective action by the importing countries. *See* First Session of the Preparatory Committee of the United Nations Conference on Trade and Employment (London Conference), U.N.Doc. E/PC/T/C.II/48, at 1 (1946); Draft Report of the Technical Subcommittee of Committee II (Nov. 1946), U.N.Doc. E/PC/T/C.II/54, at 12, 13 (1946).

[226] The meaning of 'likeness' was discussed by a group of experts in 1959 (8S/149). The Group agreed that the term 'like product' should be interpreted as 'a product which is identical in physical characteristics subject, however, to such variations...'. The Group pointed out that the meaning of 'like product' as agreed by them 'should not be interpreted either too broadly... or too stringently'. Furthermore, it should be noted that in the French text of para 1 of Art.VI, the words used are '*un produit similaire*'. The group thought that 'this slight discrepancy between the two texts would have no practical effect if the term "like product" were interpreted as suggested'. *See* a Study by the GATT Secretariat, 'The Most-favoured-nation Clause in GATT: The Rules and the Exceptions', *Journal of World Trade Law*, Vol. 4, No. 6 (1970).

[227] 'Upon the request of Mr Corea (Ceylon) for a definition of "for the like products", Mr Morton (Australia) said it meant in this sentence the same product. Mr Tinoco (Costa Rica) requested that the Drafting Committee should note that "similar" was the word used in the Spanish text. This was not the equivalent of "the same".' *See Third Committee Commercial Policy, Summary Record of the Thirtieth Meeting*, UN Conference on Trade and Employment, 3d Comm., 30th mtg., U.N.Doc. E/Conf. 2/C.3/SR. 30, at 5 (1948).

[228] '...a product is to be considered as being introduced into the commerce of an importing country at less than its normal value, if the price of the product exported from one country to another

(a) is less than the comparable price, in the ordinary course of trade, for the *like product* when destined for consumption in the exporting country, or,

(b) in the absence of such domestic price, is less than either

(i) the highest comparable price for the *like product* for export to any third country in the ordinary course of trade, or

(ii) the cost of production of the product in the country of origin plus a reasonable addition for selling cost and profit.' (Art.VI:1 of GATT (emphasis added).)

It should be noted that Art.VI:1 is referred to by Art.VI:2. Thus, the likeness concept in para 1 has a direct effect on the use of valuation purposes in relation to the determination of margin of dumping in para 2.

[229] Bronckers and McNelis, Introduction, note 27, at 76.

[230] Antidumping Agreement, Art. 4:1 provides: 'For the purpose of this Agreement, the term "domestic industry" shall be interpreted as referring to the domestic producers as a whole of the like products or those of them whose collective output of the products constitutes a major proportion of the total domestic production of those products...'

[231] *See* Bronckers and McNelis, Introduction, note 27, at 77.

As to standing criteria, the Antidumping Agreement requires that application of investigation should be sufficiently supported by the domestic industry. *See* Arts 5.2, 5.4 of the Antidumping Agreement. Thus, by defining 'like product' narrowly, the complainants would be able to confine the scope of industry producing the 'like products' only to heavily affected groups, which would make it possible to garner enough support for their action.

This domestic industry (interested parties producing like products) is given notice of the information which the authorities require and ample opportunity to present in writing all evidence which they consider relevant in respect of the investigation in question. *See* Art. 6.11.

Even if the complainants pass the standing threshold, in order to impose antidumping measures, the antidumping authority should determine whether the dumping 'causes or threatens material injury to an established industry in the territory of a contracting party or materially retards the establishment of a domestic industry' (*see* Art.VI.1 of GATT). Since the Antidumping Agreement defines 'domestic industry' as industry whose collective output of the products constitutes a major proportion of the total domestic production of like products (*see* Art. 4.1 of the Antidumping Agreement), a narrow scope of 'like product' would make the task of proving injury much easier.

Aside from these considerations, the determination of the 'like product' is also important for the calculation of dumping. In determining whether products are sold abroad for less than they are sold at home, and are therefore 'dumped', antidumping authorities will try to compare sales abroad to sales of a 'like product' at home. By defining the category of 'like product' too broadly, complainants may water down the calculation of dumping, if they have to take into consideration even such goods as have a very small dumping margin. The same can be said for the *de minimis* threshold, which provides that 'dumped imports shall normally be regarded as negligible if the volume of dumped imports from a particular country is found to account for less than 3 per cent of imports of the like product in the importing Member'. *See* Art. 5.8 of the Antidumping Agreement. It is perhaps easier to avoid falling foul of this provision with a narrower 'like-product' definition.

However, as noted above, the scope of 'like product' will have an impact upon the scope of application of any antidumping measures. Thus, narrowing the 'like product' definition means that eventual antidumping measures will apply to a smaller class of products.

See Bronckers and McNelis, ibid., at 78.

[232] L/5814, adopted on July 18 1985, BISD 32nd Supp., 55, 68, paras 4.5–4.6.

[233] *See* Chapter II, notes 4 and 5, and accompanying texts.

[234] Ibid.

[235] Ibid.

[236] *See supra* note 228 and accompanying paragraph.

[237] Perhaps one of the most significant issues ignored in the Antidumping Agreement text might be the anti-circumvention problem. There has been concern for years, especially in the United States, that antidumping orders were sometimes circumvented by the respondent companies making minor changes in the dumped product, or a change in the country of origin. Although this problem is referred to in the Ministerial Statement accompanying the Uruguay Round, the text of the relevant agreements does not deal with it. In general, it could be noted that the narrower the definition of 'like product' is, the freer the orders become from circumvention concerns: it would be more difficult for the respondent to justify the alleged price difference by putting forward other less similar products, as like products. According to the 'conditional approach' taken in the provisions, such a reference would be possible only in the absence of an identical product. *See* Mastel, G., *American Trade Laws After the Uruguay Round* (M.E. Sharpe Inc., New York, London, 1996) 182.

[238] SCM Agreement, Art. 3.1 (emphasis added).

[239] Annex I of the SCM Agreement, item (l). Moreover, there could be types of export subsidies other than those included in the Annex, because Annex I is an 'illustrative' list of export subsidies.

[240] Protocol Amending the Preamble and Parts II and III of the GATT (1955); Reports Relating to the Review of the Agreement: Other Barriers to Trade, GATT L/334 (3 March 1955), BISD 3d Supp. 222, at 224–27.

[241] 'The contracting parties recognize that the granting by a contracting party of a subsidy on the export of any product may have harmful effects for other contracting parties, both importing and exporting, may cause undue disturbance to their normal commercial interests, and may hinder the achievement of the objectives of this Agreement.' (Art. XVI:2.)

[242] *See* Report of the Joint Drafting Subcommittee of Committees II and IV on Subsidies on Primary Products, U.N.Doc. E/PC/T/C.II/61, at 4–5.

[243] One should be reminded that the existence of price difference (of like products) between the home market and the export market is a common necessary condition for antidumping measures (Art. VI:1) and for the prohibition of certain types of export subsidies (Art. XVI:4).

[244] *See supra* note 228.

[245] *Compare* Art. VI:1 (*supra* note 228) with Art. XVI:4 at 2.1.2 of this chapter.

[246] *See* Zedalis, Chapter II, note 232, at 41–2.

[247] A narrow definition of 'like' would result in more instances in which the two products, put forward as 'like products' by the countervailing state, would be determined as 'not like'. This possibility increases in the absence of the alternative methods of constructed-price or third-market-price formulae in subsidy contexts.

[248] *See* Chapter I, note 4.

[249] In many provisions of the SCM Agreement, the 'like product' concept is used: (1) to determine serious prejudice (6.3, 6.4, 6.5, 6.7), standing/investigation (11.2, 11.4, 12.9, 16.1), and injury (15.1, 15.2, 15.3, 15.6); and (2) in the context of special/differential treatment (27.9, 27.10) and the illustrative list of export subsidies (Annex 1(d), (g), (h)).

[250] Article VI:4 in particular employs the common 'like product' concept for the purpose of exemption from both antidumping and countervailing duty impositions.

[251] *See* Agreement on Agriculture, Art. 9.1. Other export subsidies are provisions requiring export performance condition, payment on export, subsidies to reduce the costs of marketing exports, internal transport and freight charges on export, subsidies contingent on their incorporation in exported products. *See* ibid.

[252] *See* Art. 3.1 of SCM Agreement: 'Except as provided in the Agreement on Agriculture, the following subsidies, within the meaning of Article 1, shall be prohibited: . . .'

[253] Article VI:4 provides: 'No product of the territory of any contracting party imported into the territory of any other contracting party shall be subject to *anti-dumping or countervailing duty* by reason of the exemption of such product from duties or taxes borne by the *like product* when destined for consumption in the country of origin or exportation, or by reason of the refund of such duties or taxes.' *Compare with* Art. VI:1, *supra* note 228.

[254] *See* Zedalis, Chapter II, note 232, at 43.

[255] For example, suppose country X has been producing tomatoes and exporting some of them to country Y. Domestically, X has imposed VAT of 5 per cent and 10 per cent on tomatoes and tomato concentrates respectively. Then, country X earmarks tomatoes for export only and gives '10 per cent' tax exemption or refund to tomato exporters, while arguing that tomatoes and tomato concentrates are like products under Art. VI:4. This 10 per cent refund would enhance the price competitiveness of the exporters to the detriment of Y tomato industry.

[256] *See* Zedalis, Chapter II, note 232, at 42.

[257] 'The exemption of an exported product from duties or taxes borne by the *like product* when destined for domestic consumption, or the remission of such duties or taxes in amounts not in excess of those which have accrued, shall not be deemed to be a *subsidy*' (emphasis added). *See Ad* Art. XVI of GATT 1994. The origin of this provision dates back to the Suggested Charter for ITO (Havana Charter), which emphasized that the concept of export subsidy '. . . shall not be construed to prevent any Member from exempting products from duties or taxes imposed in respect of like products when consumed domestically or from remitting such duties or taxes which have accrued'.

²⁵⁸ Annex I of the SCM Agreement illustrates export subsidies:

'(g)   The exemption or remission, in respect of the production and distribution of exported products, of indirect taxes in excess of those levied in respect of the production and distribution of *like products* when sold for domestic consumption.

(h)   The exemption, remission or deferral of prior-stage cumulative indirect taxes on goods or services used in the production of exported products in excess of the exemption, remission or deferral of like prior-stage cumulative indirect taxes on goods or services used in the production of *like products* when sold for domestic consumption; provided, however, that prior-stage cumulative indirect taxes may be exempted, remitted or deferred on exported products even when not exempted, remitted or deferred on *like products* when sold for domestic consumption, if the prior-stage cumulative indirect taxes are levied on inputs that are consumed in the production of the exported product (making normal allowance for waste). This item shall be interpreted in accordance with the guidelines on consumption of inputs in the production process contained in Annex II . . .' (emphasis added)

²⁵⁹ This narrow interpretation was already reflected in the term 'same goods', used by a Working Party of the GATT in 1960: '[Defining a subsidy to include] . . . The exemption, in respect of exported goods, of charges or taxes, other than charges in connection with importation or indirect taxes levied at one or several stages on the *same goods* if sold for internal consumption; or the payment, in respect of exported goods, of amounts exceeding those effectively levied at one or several stages on these goods in the form of indirect taxes or of charges in connection with importation or in both forms . . .' (GATT, BISD, 9th Supp. 1961, 185.)

The current term, 'like product', in the export subsidy list comes from the Tokyo Round Code on Subsidies and Countervailing Measures, which in turn referred to the Havana Charter language. *See* Tokyo Round Code on Subsidies and Countervailing Measures.

²⁶⁰ SCM Annex I(d) reads: 'The provision by governments or their agencies either directly or indirectly through government-mandated schemes, of imported or domestic products or services for use in the production of exported goods, on terms or conditions more favourable than for provision of *like or directly competitive products or services* for use in the production of goods for domestic consumption, if (in the case of products) such terms or conditions are more favourable than those commercially available on world markets to their exporters' (emphasis added).

²⁶¹ GATT Art. VI:7 reads:

'A system for the stabilization of the domestic price or of the return to domestic producers of a primary commodity, independently of the movements of export prices, which results at times in the sale of the commodity for export at a price lower than the comparable price charged for the *like commodity* to buyers in the domestic market, *shall be presumed* not to result in material injury within the meaning of paragraph 6 *if it is determined by consultation* among the contracting parties substantially interested in the commodity concerned that:

(a)   the system has also resulted in the sale of the commodity for export at a price higher than the comparable price charged for the like commodity to buyers in the domestic market, and

(b)   the system is so operated, either because of the effective regulation of production, or otherwise, as not to stimulate exports unduly or otherwise seriously prejudice the interests of other contracting parties.' (emphasis added)

²⁶² GATT Art. XVI:3 provides: 'Accordingly, contracting parties should seek to avoid the use of subsidies on the export of primary products. If, however, a contracting party grants directly or indirectly any form of subsidy which operates to increase the export of any primary product from its territory, such subsidy shall not be applied in a manner which results

in that contracting party having more than an equitable share of world export trade in that product, account being taken of the shares of the contracting parties in such trade in the product during a previous representative period, and any special factors which may have affected or may be affecting such trade in the product.'

[263] Note 2 to para 3, Section B of *Ad* Art. XVI reads:

'A system for the stabilization of the domestic price or of the return to domestic producers of a primary product independently of the movements of export prices, which results at times in the sale of the product for export at a price lower than the comparable price charged for the like product to buyers in the domestic market, shall be considered not to involve a subsidy on exports within the meaning of paragraph 3 if the Contracting Parties determine that:

(a) the system has also resulted, or is so designed as to result, in the sale of the product for export at a price higher than the comparable price charged for the like product to buyers in the domestic market; and

(b) the system is so operated, or is designed so to operate, either because of the effective regulation of production or otherwise, as not to stimulate exports unduly or otherwise seriously to prejudice the interest of other contracting parties.

Notwithstanding such determination by the Contracting Parties, operations under such a system shall be subject to the provisions of paragraph 3 where they are wholly or partly financed out of government funds in addition to the funds collected from producers in respect of the product concerned.'

[264] Note 2 to Section B of *Ad* Art. XVI states: 'For the purposes of Section B, a "primary product" is understood to be any product of farm, forest or fishery, or any mineral, in its natural form or which has undergone such processing as is customarily required to prepare it for marketing in substantial volume in international trade.'

[265] *Ad* Art. XVI:3, Note 3 states that 'A system for the stabilization of the domestic price ... *shall be considered* not to involve a subsidy on exports ... if the Contracting Parties determine that: ...'.

In comparison, Art. VI:7 states that 'A system for the stabilization of the domestic price ... *shall be presumed* not to result in material injury ... if it is determined by consultation among the contracting parties substantially interested ... that: ...'.

[266] *Compare supra* note 263, last paragraph, *with supra* note 261.

[267] *Compare supra* note 261, with *supra* notes 262 and 263.

[268] *See* Zedalis Chapter II, note 232, at 49.

[269] Ibid. *Webster's Dictionary* defines commodity as an economic good (something used or valued esp. when regarded as an article of commerce), esp. a product of agriculture, mining, or (sometimes as distinguished from services) commodities such as meat, fats, and sugar; and good as something that has economic utility or satisfies an economic want.

[270] *See supra* note 264.

[271] Ibid.; *supra* note 268.

[272] On the condition that certain determinations are made through consultation between substantially interested parties. *See supra* notes 267 and 268, and accompanying texts.

[273] *See* this chapter at 2.1.2; and notes 238 and 239, and accompanying texts.

[274] Except Annex I(d), in which 'like or directly competitive' means 'directly competitive or substitutable'. *See supra* note 260 and accompanying text.

[275] Even though two items having different HS tariff rate are determined as 'like' products in the antidumping/subsidy context, it has no effect whatsoever on the tariff

classification nomenclature. According to Art. II:2 (b) of the GATT, the schedule of tariff concession does not 'prevent any contracting party from imposing... any antidumping or countervailing duty'.

[276] *See supra* notes 233–235 and accompanying texts.

[277] *See* Introduction, note 30 and accompanying text.

[278] This interpretation is confirmed by the negotiating history of this definition. As noted above, this definition of 'like product' is virtually unchanged from that which first appeared in the Kennedy Round Anti-Dumping Code. Thus, the penultimate draft of that Code defined the term 'like product' to mean a product which 'has physical characteristics close to those of the exported product'. T.64/NAB/W/16, dated 3 March 1967. In the revised draft of 28 March 1967, the word 'physical' had been deleted from the text, which was revised to the formulation ('characteristics closely resembling') that exists today. T.64/NAB/W/17.

[279] *Indonesia National Car* Panel Report, para 14.173. It should be noted that in this case the 'identical' product issue did not arise because no party had argued that there was an 'identical' product that should be treated as the 'like product' with the domestic product, the Timor. *See* para 14.172. One could pose an interesting question: if the identical product issue had been raised in this case, would the Panel have accepted the presumption effect of the objective characteristic test?

[280] In actuality, there are many 'easy cases' in which the first-step analysis yields a clear conclusion with regard to likeness. In tough cases, however, the second-step analysis becomes indispensable and more influential.

[281] It is not impossible for the importing country to indicate *other* illegal barriers of the exporting country to support its potential competition argument. One should be reminded, however, that at issue is whether the imposition of an antidumping or countervailing duty or prohibited subsidy designation is appropriate. Thus, that argument goes beyond the subject matter. Sometimes it might amount to a counter-complaint within the meaning of DSU Art. 3.10.

[282] *See supra* note 255.

[283] *See* Antidumping Agreement, Arts 3.1, 3.2, 3.6, 4.1, 5.2, 5.4, 5.8, 6.11; SCM Agreement, Arts 5, 7, 9, 11, 15–19, 21.

[284] Of course, the potentiality can also be invoked in an 'injury determination' context to take account of potential injuries to the *current* like product.

[285] *See supra* notes 244, 245, and 273 and accompanying texts. Similarly, *see infra* note 313 and accompanying text.

[286] *See* Antidumping Agreement, Art. 3, fn 9.

[287] *See* SCM Agreement, Art. 5.

[288] Of course, the future competition factors can help make a determination of 'threat' of injury or 'threat' of prejudice (i.e. injury test). *See supra* note 284.

[289] Enhanced weight can be given either by (1) applying a certain threshold rate of supply substitution lower than the IASR Standard ('weighted' IASR), or (2) increasing the level of 'slightly higher (demand substitutability)' in SITUATION V, despite which level the two products at issue are determined to be 'not like' due to a high mitigation effect.

[290] In addition to a like product test (or definition of domestic industry), injury tests can also include examination of supply substitutability. This issue is beyond the scope of this book.

[291] *See* Jackson, Chapter I, note 54, at 152–3.

[292] Ibid.

[293] Ibid.

[294] Ibid.

[295] *See* Arts 2.1(a), 3.1(a), 5.1(a) of the Customs Valuation Agreement.

[296] *See* Art. VII:2(a), (b).

[297] *See* e.g., Note to Art. 1, para 2, s 3 of the Customs Valuation Agreement.

[298] If a certain good is not transacted in the market but has the potential to be transacted, we can call that good a 'product'. Sometimes we can include within the concept of 'product' certain goods that can hardly be transacted through the market system. Atomic bombs (Uranium 235, Plutonium) and human beings could be products but not merchandise. But this conceptual differentiation has little meaning in a practical sense, as will be explained later.

[299] *See* Art. V:1, 2, 6, 7.

[300] *See* most provisions of the Customs Valuation Agreement.

[301] *See supra* notes 269–271 and accompanying texts.

[302] *See* Art. 3.1(a) of the Customs Valuation Agreement.

[303] Ibid.

[304] *See* Art. 7.2(b) of the Customs Valuation Agreement.

[305] *See* Art. 15.2(e) of the Customs Valuation Agreement.

[306] *See* Art. 3.1(a) of the Customs Valuation Agreement.

[307] The deducted or computed value methods tend to figure out the customs value at the exact value of products almost identical to the imported product. Thus, when the drafters juxtaposed such strict calculation methods as alternatives, it is reasonable to consider that they did not have in mind any broad scope of likeness that would contradict the strict calculation spirit of the provision. The understanding of broad likeness would not only result in less frequent usage of these alternatives, but it would increase the difference between customs value based on the like product method and the calculated value based on the alternative methods.

[308] These requirements equally apply to identical as well as similar goods. *See* Arts 2, 3, and 15 of the Customs Valuation Agreement.

[309] *See supra* notes 56–58 and 64, and accompanying texts. Even in the worst case in which a customs authority determines two merely, substitutable products, which have been previously negotiated and classified as different items subject to different duty rates, as 'like' products for the customs valuation purposes, or in which an authority determines two products, which have been negotiated as the same tariff line subject to the same duty rate, as not 'like' products, these determinations cannot possibly modify the 'duty rates' themselves. Of course, they can 'indirectly' affect the classification system through the manipulation of the valuation process: e.g., different products may *end up paying the same amount* of duty. But this is not the issue of the 'integrity' of the tariff system. Moreover, given the extremely strict definition of likeness (resulting from many additional requirements), it is virtually impossible for these worst situations to occur.

[310] *See* text of Art. 15 of the Customs Valuation Agreement, at 3.1.1.

[311] Ibid.

[312] Ibid.

[313] *See* Customs Valuation Agreement, Arts 5, 6. *See also supra* note 285 and accompanying text.

[314] In medium demand substitutability–high supply substitutability situation (SITUATION V), the two products in question are determined to be 'not' like or directly substitutable despite slightly high demand substitutability. *See* Chapter II, at 3.1.

[315] *See supra* notes 289 and 290, and accompanying texts.

[316] *See supra* notes 302–306 and accompanying texts.

[317] In fact, the supply substitutability analysis does not help in curing any circumvention by the customs authority.

[318] Article XIX:1(a) prescribes: 'If, as a result of unforeseen developments and of the effect of the obligations incurred by a contracting party under this Agreement, including tariff concessions, any product is being imported into the territory of that contracting party in such increased quantities and under such conditions as to cause or threaten serious injury to domestic producers in that territory of *like or directly competitive products*, the contracting party shall be free, in respect of such product, and to the extent and for such time as may be necessary to prevent or remedy such injury, to suspend the obligation in whole or in part or to withdraw or modify the concession.' (emphasis added)

[319] Safeguard Agreement, Art. 2.1 reads: 'A Member may apply a safeguard measure to a product only if that Member has determined, pursuant to the provisions set out below, that such product is being imported into its territory in such increased quantities, absolute or relative to domestic production, and under such conditions as to cause or threaten to *cause serious injury* to the domestic industry that produces *like or directly competitive products.*' (emphasis added)

[320] Agreement on Textiles and Clothing, Art. 6.2 provides: 'Safeguard action may be taken under this Article when, on the basis of a determination by a Member, it is demonstrated that a particular product is being imported into its territory in such increased quantities as to cause serious damage, or actual threat thereof, to the domestic industry producing *like and/or directly competitive products...*' (emphasis added). This Agreement is equipped with a special safeguard provision free from MFN obligations.

[321] *See* GATT Arts XIX:1(b), XIX:2; and Safeguard Agreement, Arts 5, 12.

[322] *See* London Report, U.N.Doc. E/PC/T/33 (1946), Annex 11, 52, 59, Art. 29; U.N.Doc. E/PC/T/C.II/PV.7, at 3 (1946) (statement by United States delegate at London Conference, expressing fear that freer trade might undermine economic health).

[323] *See* London Report, App., at 33, Art. 34 (1946). This parallels the United States Draft Charter, Annex 11, 52, 59, Art. 29.

[324] *See* New York Report, U.N.Doc. E/PC/T/34/Rev. 1, UN Sales No. 1947.11.3 (1947), at 29, Art. 34(1); draft GATT, ibid. at 76, Art. XVIII:1.

[325] *See supra* note 192 and accompanying text.

[326] *See* Zedalis, Chapter II, note 232, at 75.

[327] Such retaliation is prohibited for the first three years if the safeguard measure has been taken as a result of an absolute increase in imports. Article 8.3 of the Safeguard Agreement.

[328] Safeguard Agreement, Art. 2.2. This requirement distinguishes safeguard procedures from antidumping and countervailing procedures. Note that the MFN requirement can be exempted by the Committee on Safeguards in certain situations. *See* Art. 5.2. *See also supra* note 320.

[329] *See and compare with supra* notes 102–104 and accompanying texts.

[330] *See supra* note 188 and accompanying text.

[331] *See supra* notes 205–206.

[332] But, depending on circumstances, it is not impossible to have a different scope. *See* Chapter II, notes 30 and 39, and accompanying texts.

[333] *See supra* note 331 and accompanying text.

[334] Interpreting the phrase 'cause or threaten serious injury to domestic producers of like or directly competitive products', if one tries to inject the future or potential factor not only into the term 'serious injury' but also into the words 'domestic producers' (or 'like or directly competitive products'), the resulting scope of the whole phrase would become too broad, which is clearly contrary to the purpose of the safeguard provision. It should be noted that even the concept of the threat (to the existing like product relationship) is interpreted narrowly. The Agreement on Safeguards provides that the 'threat of serious injury shall be understood to mean serious injury that is clearly imminent' and be 'determined based on facts and not merely on allegation, conjecture or remote possibility'. *See* Art. 4 of the Agreement on Safeguards. The phrase 'any product *is being imported*' in GATT Article XIX:1 further supports the above interpretation.

[335] Different from the context of fair trade provisions in which the importing country can impugn 'unfair trade' by the exporting country (*see* this chapter at 2.1), there is no such target to attack in the safeguard context.

[336] If relevant requirements including 'likeness' are met, the injured state is free to suspend the GATT obligation, or to withdraw or modify the concession to the extent necessary. *See* Art. XIX.

[337] In actuality, there could be many 'easy cases' in which the first-step analysis yields a conclusion with regard to likeness clear enough to complete the process. *See* Chapter II, note 405. In tough cases, however, the second-step analysis becomes indispensable and more influential.

[338] Safeguard policies often sacrifice consumer welfare or efficiency.

[339] *See supra* notes 321 and 327, and accompanying texts.

[340] This 'narrowing down' will result in the inclusion of only heavily injured producers within the concept of domestic industry ('gerrymandering', as stated already). The Safeguard Agreement, Art. 4.1 provides: '. . . in determining injury or threat thereof, a "domestic industry" shall be understood to mean the producers as a whole of the like or directly competitive products operating within the territory of a Member, or those whose collective output of the like or directly competitive products constitutes a major proportion of the total domestic production of those products.'

[341] In addition to the like product test (or definition of domestic industry), supply substitutability can be considered in injury tests. The main purpose and role of considering supply substitutability in such tests is to delineate the appropriate scope of injury, whereas in the case of like product tests supply substitutability complements demand-side analysis to determine likeness in certain marginal cases.

[342] *See supra* note 289.

[343] Customs Valuation Agreement, Arts 1, 2 (including Note), 3 (including Note), 5 (including Note), 7 (including Note), 15.

[344] Antidumping Agreement, Arts 2:1, 2:2, 2:6, 3:1, 3:2, 3:6, 4:1, 5:2, 5:4, 5:8, 6.11.

[345] SCM Agreement, Arts 6.3, 6.4, 6.5, 6.7, 11.2, 11.4, 12.9, 15.1, 15.2, 15.3, 15.6, 16.1, 27.9, 27.10, Annex 1(d), (g), (h).

[346] Agreement on Agriculture, Art. 9.1(b).

[347] TBT Agreement, Arts 2:1, 5:1, 5:2, Annex III:D.

[348] SPS Agreement, Annex C:1.

[349] SCM Agreement, Annex 1(d).

[350] Safeguard Agreement, Arts 2.1 and 4.1.

[351] Agreement on Textiles and Clothing, Art. 6.2.

IV CONCLUSION

[1] *See* Chapter III, note 1; Appendix I, note 1.

[2] *See* Chapter III, note 4 and accompanying text.

[3] *See* Chapter III, notes 5–6 and accompanying texts.

[4] Lafer, C., *The World Trade Organization Dispute Settlement System* (1996 Gilberto Amado Memorial Lecture, United Nations 1996) 11. *See* Palmeter, D. and Mavroidis, P.C. *Dispute Settlement in the World Trade Organization: Practice and Procedure* (Kluwer Law International, 1999) 175.

[5] Remarks by the former World Court President Naendra Singh in Rosenne, S., *The World Court* 5th ed. (Martinus Nijhoff, 1995), 259.

[6] Professor Young wrote that the enhancement of dispute resolution procedure in the Uruguay Round meant the triumph of a more adjudicatory and legalistic approach over a more diplomatic or equitable approach. Young, M.K., 'Dispute Resolution in the Uruguay Round: Lawyers Triumph over Diplomats', *The International Lawyer*, Vol. 29, No. 2 (1995).

[7] *See* Chapter III, notes 113–119 and accompanying texts.

[8] In 1949 the Contracting Parties examined a complaint concerning taxes levied by the government of Brazil on domestic and imported products. One of the products involved was 'beverages containing aromatic or medical substances known as tar, honey or ginger *conhaque*' which were said to be 'quite different from French cognac'. The Brazilian representative gave an assurance that the authorities responsible for administering the taxes 'were able to distinguish between those products and cognac imported from abroad' and would be sent 'careful instructions concerning the distinction to be drawn between these various products'. On the other hand, 'home-produced beverages similar to the cognac produced abroad' were subject to the same tax. *See Brazilian Internal Taxes*, adopted on 30 June 1949 and 13 December 1950, BISD II/182, para 7: GATT Secretariat, 'The Most-favoured-nation Clause in GATT: The Rules and the Exceptions', *Journal of World Trade Law*, Vol. 4, No. 6, p. 803 (1970).

[9] *See* Introduction, note 27.

[10] *See* Chapter II, notes 220–222 and accompanying texts.

[11] *See* Chapter II, notes 200–208, and section 3.

[12] *See* Chapter II, note 383.

[13] *See* Chapter II, notes 122–127, and 344.

[14] *See* Chapter II, note 231.

[15] *See* Chapter II, notes 126 and 127, and accompanying texts.

[16] Justices Stewart and Fortas' dissenting opinion in *Grinnell*. *See* Chapter II, notes 96, 142, and 256.

[17] Ibid.

[18] *See* Chapter II, notes 97 and 98.

[19] *See* Chapter I, notes 59–61 and accompanying texts.

[20] Through a series of cases in which challenging economic analyses were submitted by the parties, the WTO tribunal ended up admitting, in *Chile Alcoholic Beverages*, that a high coefficient of cross-price elasticity would be 'important evidence to demonstrate that products are directly competitive or substitutable, provided that the quality of the statistical analysis is high'. *See* Chapter II, note 115 and accompanying text.

[21] The Chilean Panel held that a low elasticity is 'not necessarily fatal to a claim of direct competitiveness or substitutability'. Ibid.

[22] *See* Chapter I, note 7.

APPENDIX I

[1] Treaty of Amity, Commerce and Navigation between Great Britain and the United States, signed at London, 19 November 1794, in Miller, H., *Treaties and other International Acts of the United States* (US Government Printing Office, 1934) Vol. II, p. 245. With regard to its background, *see* Combs, J.A., *The Jay Treaty: Political Battleground of the Founding Fathers* (University of California Press, 1970) ('The arguments that were ... made against the concessions granted to the United States in the Peace Treaty of 1783 raised issues that were to help push England and the United States to the brink of war in 1794 and set the stage for negotiation of the Jay Treaty': ibid., at 4).

[2] An embryonic version of an MFN clause has been found in a treaty of 8 November 1226 between Emperor Frederick II and the city of Marseilles. However, the history of the MFN clause in commercial treaties seems to have begun around the middle of the 17th century. *See* Hornbeck, S.K., 'The Most-Favoured-Nation Clause', *American Journal of International Law*, Vol. 3 (Nos 2, 3, and 4) (1909) pp. 395–402; Ito, N., *La Clause De La Nation La Plus Favorisée* (Les editions internationals, 1930) 80. In those periods, what provided a background for political reality for the development of the non-discrimination notion seems to have been the bad effects of a country policy that engendered retaliation and other bitterness. *See* Jackson, Introduction, note 2, at 249, 250.

[3] *See*, e.g., Treaty of Amity and Commerce between France and the United States (1778), Miller, *op. cit. supra* note 1, Vol. II, p. 3; Treaty of Amity and Commerce between the Netherlands and the United States (1782), ibid., p. 59; Treaty of Amity and Commerce between Sweden and the United Sates, ibid., p. 123; Treaty of Amity and Commerce between Prussia and the United States (1785), ibid., p. 162. For the history of the MFN principle, *see* McGovern, Introduction, note 22, at 8.3; Laing, E.A., 'Equal Access/Non-Discrimination and Legitimate Discrimination in International Economic Law', 14 Wis.Int'l L.J. 246 (1996).

[4] *See* Chapter II, note 233.

[5] *See Japan SPF Lumber* Panel Report, paras 3.30, 3.54.

[6] GATT Art. I:1 provides that: '... any advantage, favour, privilege or immunity granted by any contracting party *to any product originating in or destined for any other country* shall be accorded immediately and unconditionally to the *like product originating in or destined for the territories of all other contracting parties.*' (emphasis added)

[7] *See Spain Unroasted Coffee* Panel Report, paras 4.9 and 4.10; and *see Japan SPF Lumber*, paras 5.9 ('originating in different contracting parties') and 5.10 ('different extraneous sources'). But no reference to country of origin discrimination in *Australia Sulphate*, *see* Chapter II, note 228.

[8] According to the Economic Committee of the League of Nations, which considered a 'multilateral tariff-reduction treaty' during the late 1920s, the MFN clause 'implies the right to demand and the obligation to concede all reductions of duties and taxes and all privileges of every kind accorded to the most-favoured *nation*, no matter whether such reductions and

privileges are granted autonomously or in virtue of conventions with third parties.' *See* LN Docs. C.138.M.53.1929.II, p. 5 (emphasis added). This conclusion becomes clearer when attention is paid to the more 'nation-oriented' text of the draft articles of MFN clauses prepared by the International Law Commission. In its 1978 annual report, the Commission defined MFN treatment as 'treatment accorded by the granting State to *the beneficiary State, or to persons or things in a determined relationship with that State*, not less favorable than treatment extended by the granting State to a third State or to persons or things in the same relationship with that third State.' *See Report of the International Law Commission on the Work of Its Thirtieth Session* (1978) 2 Y.B. Intl L. Comm'n 5, UN Doc. A/33/192 (1978), reprinted in 17 Int'l Legal Materials 1518 (1978).

More tersely, the Restatement (Third) Foreign Relations Law of the United States defined MFN treatment as 'an obligation to treat that *state, its nationals or goods*, no less favorably than any other state, its nationals or goods'. *See Restatement (Third) Foreign Relations Law of the United States* §801(1) (1987). (emphasis added)

[9] *See*, e.g., Treaty of Amity, Commerce and Navigation between Sweden and Norway and the United States (1816), Miller, *supra* note 1, Vol. II, p. 601.

[10] *See*, e.g., Treaty of Amity and Commerce between Prussia and the United States (1799), ibid., p. 433.

[11] *See*, e.g., Convention of Navigation and Commerce between France and the United States (1822), Miller, *op. cit.*, Vol. III, p. 77; Treaty of Peace, Amity, Commerce and Navigation between the Central American Federation and the United States (1825), ibid., p. 209; Convention of Friendship, Commerce and Navigation between the Hanseatic Republics and the United States, ibid., pp. 387, 447; Treaty of Navigation and Commerce between Russia and the United States (1832), ibid., p. 732; Treaty of Peace, Friendship, Navigation and Commerce between Ecuador and the United States (1839), von Martens, G.F., *Nouveau Receuil des Traites*, Vol. V, p. 3; Treaty of Commerce and Navigation between Portugal and the United States (1840), Miller, *op. cit.*, Vol. IV, p. 295.

[12] *See* e.g., Convention of Friendship, Commerce and Navigation between Denmark and the United States (1826), Miller, *op. cit.*, Vol. III, p. 239; Treaty of Peace, Friendship, Commerce and Navigation between Brazil and the United States (1828).

[13] *See*, e.g., Treaty of Amity, Commerce and Navigation between Great Britain and Mexico (1826), *British and Foreign State Papers*, Vol. XIV, p. 614; Treaty of Commerce and Navigation between Hanover and the United States (1840), Miller, *op. cit.*, Vol. IV, p. 256.

[14] *See*, e.g., Treaty of Commerce and Navigation between Sweden–Norway and the United States (1827), Miller, *op. cit.*, Vol. III, p. 283.

[15] *See*, e.g., Treaty of Commerce and Navigation between Sardinia and the United States (1838), Miller, *op. cit.*, Vol. IV, p. 145.

[16] *See*, e.g., Treaty of Commerce and Customs between Hesse-Darmstadt and Prussia (1828), von Martens, *Nouveau Recueil des Traites*, Vol. VII, p. 550; Treaty of Friendship, Commerce and Navigation between Chile and Mexico (1831), von Martens, *op. cit.*, Vol. XIII, p. 1.

[17] *See*, e.g., Treaty of Commerce and Navigation between Austria and the United States (1829), Miller, *op. cit.*, Vol. III, p. 507; Treaty of Commerce and Navigation between Sardinia and the United States (1838), Miller, *op. cit.*, Vol. IV, p. 145.

[18] *See*, e.g., Treaty of Amity, Commerce and Navigation between Mexico and the United States (1831), Miller, *op. cit.*, Vol. III, p. 599.

[19] *See,* e.g., Treaty of Navigation and Commerce between Russia and the United States (1832), ibid., p. 732.

[20] *See,* e.g., Treaty of Friendship, Commerce and Navigation between Chile and Peru (1835), *British and Foreign State Papers,* Vol. XXIII, p. 742.

[21] *See,* e.g., ibid.

[22] *See,* e.g., Treaty of Commerce and Navigation between Greece and the United States (1837), Miller, *op. cit.,* Vol. IV, p. 107.

[23] *See,* e.g., ibid.

[24] *See,* e.g., Treaty of Commerce and Navigation between the Netherlands and the United States (1839), Miller, *op. cit.,* Vol. IV, p. 171.

[25] *See,* e.g., Treaty of Peace, Friendship, Commerce, and Navigation, May 13, 1858, US–Bolivia, Art. 6, T.S. No. 32; Treaty of Peace, Amity, Commerce, and Navigation, May 22, 1882, US–Korea, Art. XIV, T.S. No. 61; Treaty of Amity, Commerce, and Navigation, April 3, 1783, US–Sweden, Art. 2, T.S. No. 346; Treaty of Amity, Commerce, and Navigation, Oct 1, 1885, US–Two Sicilies, Art. 15, T.S. No. 365. *See also* Staff of House Comm. on Ways and Means, 104th Cong., 1st Sess., *Overview and Compilation of US Trade Statutes* (Comm. Print, 1995) 191.

[26] *See,* e.g., Treaty of Friendship, Commerce, and Consular Rights, Dec. 8, 1923, US–Germany, Art. VII, T.S. No. 725; Treaty of Friendship, Commerce, and Consular Rights, June 24, 1925, US–Hungary, Art. VII, T.S. No. 748; Treaty of Friendship, Commerce, and Consular Rights, June 19, 1928, US–Austria, Art. VII, T.S. No. 838.

[27] *See* Treaty of Friendship, Commerce, and Consular Rights, Dec. 8, 1923, US–Germany, Art. VII, T.S. No. 725; Treaty of Friendship, Commerce, and Consular Rights, June 19, 1928, US–Austria, Art. VII, T.S. No. 838.

[28] Bhala and Kennedy, Chapter I, note 22, at 70–71.

[29] Treaty of Friendship, Commerce, and Consular Rights, June 19, 1928, US–Austria, Art. V, T.S. No. 838 (emphasis added).

[30] *See* Bhala and Kennedy, Introduction, note 22, at 71. One author carried out an examination of 510 bilateral agreements entered into between 1931 and 1939 and found MFN clauses in 227 treaties. *See* Snyder, R.C., *The Most-Favoured-Nation Clause: An Analysis with Particular Reference to Recent Treaty Practice and Tariffs* (King's Crown Press, 1948) 133.

[31] *See* Analytical Index, Second Revision, p. 2. London Report p. 9.

[32] *See* (1) LN Docs. C.138.M.53.1929.II, pp. 9–11 ('... (among comparable terms of "like", "similar" and "identical") the word "like" is far preferable to the others, the expression "identical" being the least desirable of the three since the condition of identity may in practice involve a too restricted application of the clause, and is too difficult to determine ... we may hope that the difficulties inherent in this question will be diminished with the introduction of the uniform Customs nomenclature ... the following stipulations are clearly incompatible with the clause: (a) Provisions which restrict Customs privileges to products of a particular country or district simply because they originate in the country or district, thus ruling, a priori, that no other country can produce products like to those which it is sought to favour; (b) Provisions which make similarity depend on entirely external characteristics or conditions which, by the very nature of things, only the products of given countries can possess or fulfill ...'; (2) C.641.M.260. 1930.II, p. 3 ('The object of the enquiry into the question of *similar products,* or products of the same kind, should be to indicate, by consideration of the tariff provisions in the various commercial treaties, cases of discrimination based on the essential characteristics of commodities, and on the other hand, cases in

which the discrimination is based on purely unessential characteristics and may therefore be regarded as having been imposed with a view to restricting artificially the operation of the most-favoured-nation clause'); (3) C.180.M.68.1931. II.B, p. 3 (endorsing the view already expressed by the Committee in 1929); and (4) C.427.M. 177.1931.II.B, pp. 2–3 (*see infra* note 33).

[33] *See* Fauchald, Introduction, note 11, at 123–25; LN Doc. C.427.M.177.1931.II.B, p. 2 ('As regards the interpretation of the expression "*like products*" ... A *contractual tariff discrimination*—i.e., introduced into a Customs tariff by means of a treaty—can be justified only if and to the extent that the product entitled to the Customs facility possesses *intrinsic* qualities clearly distinguishing it from any other similar product. This was a somewhat general rule ... A dispute might always arise as to the existence or absence of the intrinsic characteristics differentiating goods; but, as these characteristics naturally vary from one product to another, any endeavour to find a more precise formula ... appears to be Utopian; and only expert examinations in each particular case could be decisive ...').

[34] *See* Fauchald, ibid.; League of Nations, *The Monetary and Economic Conference: An Account of the Preparatory Work for the Conference and an Outline of the Previous Activities of the Economic and Financial Organization of the League of Nations* (Information Section, Secretariat of the League of Nations, 1933) 75–76.

[35] *See* UN Docs. E/PC/T/C.II/W.14, pp. 7–8 and E/PC/T/C.II/W.28, p. 4. *See also* Introduction, note 14 and accompanying text.

[36] According to a study by the GATT Secretariat, the League of Nations definition of 'like products' was products 'practically identical with another product'. *See* GATT Secretariat, 'The Most-favoured-nation Clause in GATT: The Rules and the Exceptions', *Journal of World Trade Law*, Vol. 4, No. 6, p. 802 (1970). *See also* Chapter III, note 1. Regrettably, the details on this definition and its background are not known.

APPENDIX III

[1] *See* Chapter, II, at 3.2.4.

[2] It is interesting to be witness to the existence of certain parallels between trade law and competition law. The notion of a 'pre-measure price' (discussed above) can be compared to that of 'competitive price' in an antitrust context. In competition law, since the current price of a product concerned might well be a monopoly price rather than a competitive price that exists in the absence of such a monopoly, any substitutability test based on the current price might show a 'symptom' of the monopoly power rather than test for the existence of the monopoly itself. Thus, in antitrust law, the hypothetical price change should be given based on the 'competitive price' level (such as average cost or marginal cost), not on the current price level. In other words, this notion of competitive price can be rephrased as 'pre-monopoly price' in comparison with the concept of 'pre-measure price' in trade law.

[3] *See* Chapter III, note 72 and accompanying text.

Index